☆☆☆☆☆☆☆☆☆☆☆☆☆☆☆☆

**"WE, THE PEOPL**[...] **S0-ATF-225**
**STATES, IN ORDE**[...] **MORE PERFECT UNION, ESTABLISH**
**JUSTICE, INSURE DOMESTIC TRAN-**
**QUILITY, PROVIDE FOR THE COM-**
**MON DEFENSE, PROMOTE THE GEN-**
**ERAL WELFARE, AND SECURE THE**
**BLESSINGS OF LIBERTY TO OUR-**
**SELVES AND OUR POSTERITY . . ."**

☆☆☆☆☆☆☆☆☆☆☆☆☆☆☆☆

These words, and the Constitution to which they
are a preamble, emerged from a complex drama
of men, ideas and political realities acted out in
Philadelphia in 1787. What happened in that
momentous summer today shapes our life as a
nation, and profoundly affects the entire world.
With the vision of a master historian—both
recreating the past and placing it within the
framework of contemporary relevance—Clinton
Rossiter unforgettably depicts "The Great Happening" that was

### THE GRAND CONVENTION

"This is sure-footed history, concise in argumentation, rich in narrative, and composed for both the
layman and the scholar." *Saturday Review*

*About the author:* Clinton Rossiter, one of America's most distinguished historians, is Senior Professor of American Institutions at Cornell. He is the
author of many articles in leading periodicals and
professional journals, and twelve books, among them
*The American Presidency* and *Seedtime of the Republic.* His honors include the Bancroft Award, the
Woodrow Wilson Foundation Award, and the prize
of the Institute of Early American History and
Culture.

# Other MENTOR Books of
## Special Interest

# 1787
# The Grand Convention

by CLINTON ROSSITER

A MENTOR BOOK

Published by
THE NEW AMERICAN LIBRARY

*To* ANN ROSSITER BERRY

*with a younger brother's love and devotion*

Library of Congress Catalog Card Number: 66–11211

This is an authorized reprint of a hardcover edition published by The Macmillan Company.

MENTOR TRADEMARK REG. U.S. PAT. OFF. AND FOREIGN COUNTRIES
REGISTERED TRADEMARK——MARCA REGISTRADA
HECHO EN CHICAGO, U.S.A.

*MENTOR BOOKS are published by*
*The New American Library, Inc.,*
*1301 Avenue of the Americas, New York, New York 10019*

FIRST PRINTING, SEPTEMBER, 1968

PRINTED IN THE UNITED STATES OF AMERICA

# CONTENTS

# IV   CONSEQUENCES

# ILLUSTRATIONS

(between pages 192 & 193)

THE PRESIDENT OF THE CONVENTION    GEORGE WASHINGTON  Painting by Charles Willson Peale (courtesy of the Pennsylvania Academy of the Fine Arts)

THE LEADING SPIRIT OF THE CONVENTION    JAMES MADISON  Painting by Charles Willson Peale (courtesy of the Thomas Gilcrease Institute, Tulsa, Oklahoma)

TWO PRINCIPAL ARCHITECTS OF THE CONSTITUTION
JAMES WILSON  Painting by Philip Wharton, after a miniature attributed to James Peale (courtesy of the Independence National Historical Park Collection)    GOUVERNEUR MORRIS  After a drawing by Quenedey made in Paris in 1789 or 1790

FOUR FRAMERS WHO MADE THEIR PRESENCE FELT
BENJAMIN FRANKLIN  Mezzotint by Charles Willson Peale (courtesy of the American Philosophical Society)    RUFUS KING  Painting by John Trumbull (courtesy of the Yale University Art Gallery)    NATHANIEL GORHAM  Painting by James Sharples, Sr. (courtesy of the New York Public Library Picture Collection) HUGH WILLIAMSON  Engraved from a painting by John Trumbull

THE "NABOBS" OF SOUTH CAROLINA    CHARLES COTESWORTH PINCKNEY  Painting by Albert Rosenthal, after an unknown artist (courtesy of the Independence National Historical Park Collection)    CHARLES PINCKNEY  Painting attributed to Gilbert Stuart (courtesy the American Scenic and Historic Preservation Society)    JOHN RUTLEDGE  Painting by John Trumbull (courtesy of the Yale University Art Gallery)    PIERCE BUTLER  Engraving by Albert Rosenthal (courtesy of the MS Division of the New York Public Library, Emmet Coll. #1209)

THE "HALF-WAY MEN" OF CONNECTICUT    ROGER SHERMAN  Painting by Thomas Hicks, after Ralph Earl (courtesy of the Independence National Historical Park Collection)    OLIVER ELLSWORTH  Painting by Albert Rosenthal, after James Sharples, Sr. (courtesy of the Independence National Historical Park Collection)    WILLIAM SAMUEL JOHNSON  Painting by Albert Rosenthal, after Gilbert Stuart (courtesy of the Independence National Historical Park Collection)

BIG MEN FROM SMALL STATES    JOHN DICKINSON  Painting by Charles Willson Peale (courtesy of the Independence National Historical Park Collection)    WILLIAM LIVINGSTON  Engraving by Albert Rosenthal (courtesy of the MS Division of the

New York Public Library, Emmet Coll. #4779) WILLIAM PAT-ERSON Engraving by Albert Rosenthal GEORGE READ Paint-ing by Thomas Sully, after Robert Edge Pine (courtesy of the Inde-pendence National Historical Park Collection)

DISAPPOINTMENTS IN THE CONVENTION, GREAT MEN OUTSIDE IT ALEXANDER HAMILTON Engravings by E. Prud-homme from the original miniature by Archibald Robertson ROBERT MORRIS Painting by Charles Willson Peale (courtesy of the Independence National Historical Park Collection)

THE EMINENT FRAMERS WHO REFUSED TO SIGN THE CONSTITUTION EDMUND RANDOLPH Painting by Flavius J. Fisher (courtesy of the Virginia State Library) GEORGE MASON Painting by H. Walsh, after the original by Gilbert Stuart (courtesy of the Independence National Historical Park Collection) EL-BRIDGE GERRY Engraving by Albert Rosenthal

AN ENTRY FROM MADISON'S NOTES: THE CLIMACTIC EXCHANGE OF JULY 16, 1787 (courtesy of the Library of Con-gress)

THE PRESIDENT'S CHAIR Photograph (courtesy of Independ-ence National Historical Park Collection)

THE CONSTITUTION IS PRESENTED TO THE PEOPLE The front page of the *Pennsylvania Packet,* September 19, 1787 (cour-tesy of the New York Historical Society, New York City)

# 1787

## THE GRAND CONVENTION

# 1 THE PRIMACY OF 1787

*The deliberate union of so great and various a people
in such a place is, without all partiality or prejudice,
if not the greatest exertion of human understanding,
the greatest single effort of national deliberation that
the world has ever seen.*

JOHN ADAMS, December 25, 1787[1]

1787 was, beyond all but the faintest shadow of doubt, the
most fateful year in the history of the United States. Those
who seek the meaning of this history—anxious citizens, puz-
zled friends, peevish critics, malevolent foes—would do well
to start digging in the months just before and after the eleventh anniversary of American independence, for in those
months was shaped the destiny of a continent.

To admit almost no doubt of the primacy of 1787 is certain to raise cries of protest. A story sprinkled with such lus-
trous symbols as 1492, 1607, 1620, 1776, 1803, 1812, 1846,
1861, 1896, 1917, 1933, 1941, and 1945 is not easily brought
to focus in a solitary date. Yet 1787 is the year of the supreme event in the life of the American people: the Convention that sat in Philadelphia from May 25 to September 17
and hammered out the Constitution of the United States, the
shrewd, resilient, enduring charter of government under
which the first and only continental republic has risen from
impotence and obscurity to power and glory. The Convention
was, as some writers might want to put it, a Great Happening.
There has been no greater happening in American history; there have not been many greater, certainly of a political nature, in the history of the world. If the future of the
world rests largely on the way in which the United States
wields its power and responds to the challenge of glory, the
year in which the people of the United States chose to be one
nation—rather than a confederacy or a league or a parcel of
independent sovereignties—ought to be recognized as one of
the handful of dates that all men everywhere are commanded
to remember.

Only three other years in our history—1776, 1861, and
1941—offer a challenge to the primacy of 1787, and each of
them takes on so much added meaning from the Great Hap-

11

pening in Philadelphia that it seems to be an orbiting planet rather than the central sun in the heaven of notable dates. For if 1776 was the Year of Disruption, 1861 the Year of Forestalled Disruption, and 1941 the Year of Enforced Maturity, 1787 was the year that brought the first of these great happenings to fruition and made the other two possible. The decisions arrived at so painfully and prudently during those sixteen and a half weeks in Philadelphia shaped the enduring character of the disruption brought off by Washington, Franklin, Jefferson, the Adamses, and their colleagues; they guaranteed historical legitimacy to Abraham Lincoln's determination not to permit a second disruption; and they touched off a course of political, economic, and social development that summoned the America of Franklin D. Roosevelt to accept a principal responsibility for the peace and good order of the world. The decisions, moreover, were the kind that force men to be intelligent as well as brave, imaginative as well as tough, creative as well as dutiful. It is this quality of what the imaginative editors of the time saluted as "the Grand Convention"—high and successful political creativity —that seals the case for the primacy of 1787. That year was, as no other in our history has been (and as no other is ever likely to be), the year of political creation. If it is admirable for a people to seek independence, fight for survival, or commit itself to the care and feeding of many countries, it is uncommon for a people to resolve to be a nation unlike any other that has ever existed and, in the course of a single season, to lay an almost complete political foundation for its unique form of nationhood. That, in essence, was the achievement of the men of 1787, and from that achievement all else has followed.

So commanding a milestone in the history of a great nation has inspired a vast amount of writing. The Convention of 1787 is *history*, an event that took place at a known point in time and helped mightily to redirect the course of all subsequent events. It is also *History:* an event about whose nature, meaning, origins, purposes, staging, techniques, cast of characters, and consequences men have been speculating in print ever since it was first recognized as history (as early, it would appear, as 1789), and about which they will continue to speculate until the end of the Republic—and perhaps, if History is still being written after that calamity, until the end of recorded time. Like the Revolution and the Civil War, the Convention is a subject that will never be exhausted.

Nor, like those other memorable events, should it ever be exhausted. Even if all historians were to agree—the most unlikely of occurrences—on the "truth" of each of the thousands of episodes, decisions, incidents, and accidents that add up to the Great Happening of 1787, they would still be left with the larger question of the meaning of the happening for the men of their own generation. And since each generation of Americans has its own problems and aspirations, its "rendezvous with destiny" unlike that of any other generation, the scholars of each must be prepared to think about the Grand Convention as if it had never been thought about at all. It is in the nature of a memorable event that it must be restudied and retold by each generation; it is the fate of historians that, as they cannot in good conscience accept any past interpretation of the event as final, they must not expect their interpretation to be accepted as any more final.

Still, if they cannot bind the future, they can try to convince the present; and this latest in the long line of books that have sought to describe and explain the whole event in one volume has been written in that spirit. It is the work of one who has himself been convinced of the primacy of 1787, and thus would like to do some convincing of his own, yet who realizes that there is a limit in time beyond which his own voice will not be heard except as the not unpleasing croak of the antiquarian. Short of that limit, however, one can hope for an audience that will listen not merely respectfully but attentively, and that will respond if it is tempted with enthusiasm and imagination, as it could not respond to a teller of the same tale out of another generation. This, in any case, is what has persuaded me to rise up out of the swamp of doubt: the pleasant recognition of the fact that the story is worth telling all over again—not alone because many important things about the Convention and its cast of characters have never been told correctly (and some important things have never been told at all), but because men of the 1960's are bound to think about the Convention in ways that might have seemed irrelevant or even frivolous as recently as 1940 or even 1950. The event-as-history cannot be relived by us or imitated by any other people; the event-as-History needs once more to be aired.

Three aspects of the Convention of 1787 should have a special appeal to this generation of Americans. Each of these major themes, whether stated separately or joined with the others in an immense orchestration, will be sounded again and again in this book.

The first is the view of the Convention as a case-study in the political process of constitutional democracy. Americans of this generation are much concerned about the state of their famous form of government. Once upon a time we thought that constitutional democracy, by the simple force of good example, was destined to spread its benevolent sway over all the earth, and we went about our business under the comforting assumption that we, with some useful assistance from our British ancestors and cousins, were the bearers of final political truth. Today this assumption comforts us no longer, and every thinking American is sharply aware that many nations, some new and some old, have neither time nor use for the system of political decision that emphasizes discussion and compromise, open choice and institutionalized dissent, fragmentation of power and balance of interests, constitutional limits and personal rights. Constitutional democracy is hated in some parts of the world, derided in others, and branded as irrelevant in still others. Even in its ancestral homes severe doubts exist about its capacity for identifying social problems, generating policies for solving these problems, and moving courageously to transform policy into effective action.

In such a time of doubt Americans may well turn back for inspiration and instruction to their own past and go rummaging through it for periods and events in which the process of democracy worked effectively to achieve the purposes of the people. Such a period was the golden age of American politics between 1765 and 1801; such an event was the Convention of 1787, the creative zenith of the age. Whatever else it was—and it has been many things to many men—the Convention was a notable exercise in the arts of democratic (or, to be precise, pre-democratic) politics. Just how much "democracy" was present in the deliberations and decisions before, during, and after Philadelphia is not an easy question to answer: I shall be touching upon it off and on throughout this book. It should be enough at this point to assert that the Convention—if not as thoroughly democratic in origin, composition, procedure, and accountability as such a body would have to be today (or would have had to be as few as five years after the event)—was popular and responsible enough to be acclaimed as a superlative example of goal-setting and decision-making for a proud, ambitious people through the processes of frank, reasoned discussion and alert, disciplined bargaining. If the political process of the liberal West has any successes to its credit, none can be much more memorable than the intense session of give-and-take at Philadelphia in the summer of 1787.

When we say that the Convention was a superlative example of the workings of a famous political process, we are also saying that the men of the Convention were superlative politicians—in the best sense of that word. It often seems that historians of the period have been commissioned to paint the Framers of the Constitution in any guise other than the one in which they appear most naturally. We know them well as everything from selfless instruments of Divine Intent to selfish agents of Economic Interest. We hardly know them at all as what they were first and foremost: skillful operators of the political machinery of constitutional democracy, men whose chief lesson for Americans of this generation has to do with the capacities and limits of this form of government. As such men—as members of an elite adjusting the tensions of principle and interest within its own membership, and at the same time interacting with the publics to which it was ultimately accountable—they will be portrayed in this book.[2]

The second large aspect of the Convention that invites the attention of our generation of Americans is the results rather than the methods of this archetype of decision-making. The one result of 1787 that has proved most consequential to all men living today was the resolve, which was gradually brought to life in a hundred or more touch-and-go decisions, to become a self-conscious fledgling nation and to set a political course toward becoming a self-sustaining mighty one. We live in an era of nation-building, a stage of history in which nationalism has been recalled by men of good will from the exile of thirty years ago and begged to serve (without arrogance, of course) as the chief spur to the development of the "underdeveloped" or "disadvantaged" or "emerging" peoples of the world. Although the nationalism of what President Sukarno derides as the Old Established Forces—the United States, Britain, France, Germany, Japan, and perhaps even the Soviet Union—is still suspect in many enlightened circles in these countries, the nationalism of what he hails as the New Emerging Forces—Indonesia, India, Cuba, Ghana, Burma, and perhaps even Tunisia—is recognized as a necessary spur to progress. The promotion of nation-building is pursued relentlessly in the seats of power throughout the West; the study of nation-building is all the rage in the groves of contemplation.

Because the United States of the 1790's was the first of the New Emerging Forces, and because the first of the New Emerging Forces became the United States of the 1960's, the nation-building acts of Washington, Franklin, Hamilton, John Adams, Marshall, Jefferson, Madison, and their successors ought to command far more scholarly and popular interest (if not political imitation) than they have hitherto received, and the largest amount of this interest ought to be focused on the Convention at Philadelphia. Although the full story of how "our fathers brought forth upon this continent a new nation" is one that begins well before 1787 and ends well after, that year was the moment of decision as well as of creation. Although much had been done already to produce the raw materials of nationhood (as witness the raising of a continental army in 1775 and the creation of a national domain in 1784), and much remained to be done to form a nation out of these materials (as witness the tensions of 1798, 1814, and 1832 and the agonies of 1861–1865), the hard bargaining at Philadelphia laid the firm foundation of the American Republic. As a self-conscious act of successful nation-making, the signing of the Constitution on September 17, 1787, stands out starkly in the annals of mankind. The United States of Washington and Jefferson may not be a useful model for the new nations of the twentieth century to imitate—so different indeed from the world today was the world in which we grew to manhood—yet it is an experience from which at least a few hard lessons can still be drawn, and which, in any case, invites attention in its own right as a unique course of events. By far the most remarkable event in the course that ran from, let us say, 1765 to 1815 was the Convention of 1787 in Philadelphia.

The third aspect grows immediately out of the first two: it is the fascinating question, unanswerable yet always demanding to be answered, whether men are the makers or wards of history. Here again we may point to an intense concern of the present age, whose splendid promises and ghastly problems have set us all to wondering whether we may hope to control our destiny, and here again we may find in 1787 an encouraging if not entirely comforting case-study. At several stages I shall attempt to measure the extent to which the Framers were masters or wards, principally by calling attention to those of their notable decisions which were truly decisions (because of the existence of genuine alternative choices), those which were not decisions at all (because the Convention was forbidden by circumstances to decide otherwise than it did), and those which turned out within a few years to be decisions that no one had intended (because even the most masterful statesmen may think they are doing one thing and in fact be doing another). Here I will say only that the Convention made enough decisions of the first description to permit us to look upon the delegates as men who made some history for themselves, their descendants, and all the world, and that the one problem about which they were most at liberty to choose among competing alternatives was whether and how to build a nation. The range of choices, as we shall learn in Chapter 4, ran from the edge of disintegration to the edge of total consolidation, and in making their choice for a union both continental and federal the Framers took history by the collar and gave it a rousing shake. Statesmen who dared to seize control of their own destiny, the heroes of Philadelphia deserve study as well as applause.

I call these men heroes in deliberate defiance of the ban placed upon this word by most serious-minded historians. By *hero* I mean a leader of men who engages with clear eye and stout heart in an uncertain enterprise for some purpose larger than the gratification of his own ambition or the rewarding of his own friends, and whose deeds work a benevolent influence on the lives of countless other men. I would contend that an experiment in nationhood as vast and successful as the American Republic could not have been brought through at least a half-dozen of its trials except by men of heroic stature, and that few trials could have demanded more extraordinary talent, virtue, hope, and tenacity than this year of political creation. If not every one of the fifty-five men who gathered in Philadelphia was a hero—then or before or after—the Grand Convention itself was both uncertain enough in prospect and benevolent enough in result to be classed as a heroic event. If not every one of its leading figures was as clear of eye as Madison, as stout in heart as Washington, or as selfless of purpose as Franklin—then or before or after—at least a dozen other delegates rose, in the long struggle to build the political and emotional foundations of nationhood, to join these three giants on the high plateau of heroism. Since men, even at their most heroic, are always men and never gods (nor even demigods), it disturbs me only a little to record that every leader of the Convention, not even excepting Washington, had already had or was later to have brushes with poor judgment, self-indulgence, and one or more of the seven deadly sins.

To assert that some men on some occasions are able to shape the destiny of their society is not at all to deny that even the freest agents of history are, in the end, just that: agents. They are men who are shaped even as they shape, who are given directions by a past they are powerless to alter, who work their apparent miracles within the limits of time and place. Such men manage to turn the flow of history into some new channel only by putting themselves in the middle of the old channel. They are distinguished from other would-be makers of history not by any power to leap over the limits of circumstance—for no man, not even Napoleon or Lenin, has had that godlike power—but by their understanding of what things can and cannot be achieved within those limits.

The men of 1787 were, in short, both dutiful wards of the past and creative makers of the future, and that is why they should have a special appeal to the troubled men of this generation. They were heroes who stayed within the limits of the political, social, economic, and cultural circumstances of their time, heroes who seemed to know instinctively just how far to push their luck in choosing among the alternatives that were to be found within these limits. They were especially alert to the possibilities, and thus also to the restraints, of their position on the continuum of time, and they made, as we shall see, virtually no decision that did not run with the grain of American development. This, in any case, is their claim to greatness as agents of history: on one hand, they knew that 1787 would never have been possible except for 1776 (and 1777, 1778, 1781, and 1783); on the other, they knew that 1776 had not foreclosed 1787, that the agenda for this year left a number of choices open to those who were willing to make them. 1787, to vary the metaphor, was the natural child of 1776, but 1776 was the father of at least three or four possible 1787's. The Framers shaped history as no other group of Americans has ever done exactly because they forced a choice that did not have to be made—certainly not then, perhaps not ever. The Constitution was a possible, but not at all a probable, in the circumstances of the peace that came at last to America with the Treaty of Paris of 1783. While all the happenings in America (and many elsewhere) between 1607 and 1783 prepared the way for Philadelphia, and while Philadelphia prepared the way for all the happenings in America (and many elsewhere) ever since, no one can say that this Great Happening had to unfold in just the way it did.

1787 was, then, a year for political heroes, for men who could distinguish the possible from the impossible and then convert the boldest of possibilities into the most solid of realities. As the one man among the missing who had the best title to be in Philadelphia wrote in December of that year, the Convention was, "if not the greatest exertion of human understanding, the greatest single effort of national deliberation that the world has ever seen." Even after more than 175 years, this judgment of John Adams covers all other deliberate efforts at nation-building. The Framers made a gamble with the destiny of the American people so hazardous and yet so calculated, so contingent and yet so prudent, that they command the highest homage granted to makers of history: an endless retelling of the manner of their ascent to glory.

# I

## Setting

## 2 THE UNITED STATES IN 1787

*This people . . . is the hope of the human race.*
TURGOT TO RICHARD PRICE, March 22, 1778[1]

*We are the most perfect society now existing in the world.*
HECTOR ST. JOHN DE CRÈVECOEUR, 1782[2]

THE UNITED STATES in 1787 was a good country in which to live, work, and aspire—if not for men with the tastes of English dukes, the appetites of French tax collectors, or the memories of Italian bishops, certainly for men with a modest desire to be free, prosperous, and respectable. "Europe with all its pomp," the French-American Crèvecoeur wrote, "is not to be compared to this continent, for men of middle station, or laborers" [3]—so long, he would have been the first to admit, as their skins were white.

In the opinion of half the philosophers of Europe and all citizens of the United States itself, there was no better country on the face of the earth. It had extent, resources, and opportunities unbounded; it harbored a "numerous, brave, and hardy people"; it had dreams of glory that summoned this people to be up and doing. It had problems, too, as would any country still licking the wounds of a quarter-century of disruption, invasion, and civil war, but the problems were unfelt by many Americans and unseen by many others, and were by no means thought to be insoluble by those who could both feel and see.

The largest problem of all was the momentous question whether America was a country like England and France or a "country" like Germany and Italy, whether the Union formed under the pressures of Boston, Valley Forge, and Saratoga was to be the groundwork of a true nation or a polite title for a league of petty sovereignties. The hardheaded men in the courts of Europe were fairly certain that the American experiment in nationhood, complicated as it was by simultaneous experiments in independence, republicanism, and expansion, would never succeed. Although some hardheaded men in the assemblies, law offices, and countinghouses of America were disposed to agree, others were hopeful that, given a forceful political and emotional shove, the United States would move into the fullness of nationhood. It was just such a group of men, with a few unhappy exceptions, who came together in Philadelphia in May of 1787 to "revise" the confederate, congressional form of common government under which the United States had muddled through the first years of its existence—informally but in the main successfully from 1774 to 1781, formally but ever more ineffectively under the Articles of Confederation ratified at last on March 1 of that year. In order to understand the intentions and assess the performance of the men of Philadelphia, we must first look at the society out of which they came. The conditions and prospects of this society gave direction, and at the same time set limits, to their gropings for a political solution to their overriding problems.

The very size of the United States was enough to set alarmists to shivering, dreamers to dreaming, and realists to gambling. From the Atlantic to the Mississippi, from the Great Lakes to just short of the Gulf of Mexico stretched a land as vast as France, Italy, Spain, Germany, Britain, and Ireland combined, a land that, give a few parcels of forest to Spanish greed in the far south and take a few from British obstinacy in the far north, counted some 890,000 square miles. No man knew, except in a casual way, that rich stores of coal, iron, copper, and other minerals waited below the surface for the pick and shovel of industry; every man knew that the surface itself was a profligate treasure-house of the one thing for which all men of that age hungered: deep, well-watered, fertile soil, which commanded toil beyond our imagining yet often paid off in rewards beyond theirs.

Less than one-half of this expanse of land had come under effective control of the new Republic, whether the control was designed by state authorities or Congress, whether it was exercised by officers of a government, agents of a land company, or impatient pursuers of their own happiness. Most Americans lived where their colonial fathers had lived—between the Appalachians and the sea—and even in this territory, larger than all France, they seemed hardly to have begun the task of subduing the wilderness. Except in the eastern parts of the Middle States and the southern part of New England, the forest, not the clearing, was the dominant feature of the landscape. "Compared with such a country as France," a tart-voiced stranger noted in 1796, the United States "may justly be denominated one vast forest." [4]

Travel through this forest, or even through the most settled parts of the country, was not lightly to be undertaken. Roads were bad, bridges few, ferries leaky, rivers whimsical, stagecoaches cranky, and inns ill-kept. Yet a determined man—a peddler bound from Boston to Richmond, a settler bound from Pittsfield to Pittsburgh, a delegate bound from Charleston to Philadelphia—could always make his way even in the worst season. What is intriguing about transportation in early America is not so much its primitive state as the startling mobility of a "determined man" like Washington the surveyor, warrior, and statesman.

No one knew—although several inquiring minds had tried to guess (almost always too modestly)—how many persons the United States could count as citizens and chattels. The census of 1790, a handsome exercise in demography for so new and inexperienced a nation, turned up a population of 3,929,214, of whom 681,834 were Negro slaves.[5] (Most of the thousands of Indians lived uncounted and unloved beyond the advancing frontier.) Since Spain had a population of around ten million, the German states twenty million, France twenty-five million, and the British Isles fifteen million (Ireland alone counting five million), the Americans were not yet a people of more than trifling consequence in a world that took its orders from London, Paris, Madrid, and Rome. Most Americans lived on the land, many in towns and settlements but just as many in isolation. Only twenty-four places had more than 2,500 inhabitants, only five cities had more than 10,000: Philadelphia (45,000), New York (33,000), Boston (18,000), Charleston (16,000), and Baltimore (13,500). However proud the leading men of these busy ports might be of their shops, libraries, and paved squares, enough of them had been to industrious Amsterdam (200,000), arrogant Paris (600,000), or teeming London (950,000) to realize that theirs was the pride of provincials. Some of them, it might be added, had looked hard enough behind the glitter of Paris and London to wish a kinder fate than mere tumescence for New York and Philadelphia.

The most attractive and exciting city in the new Republic was Philadelphia, which, thanks to the imaginative energy of Benjamin Franklin and several dozen exponents of one or another aspect of his many-sided genius, was a center of commerce, finance, politics, science, art, architecture, learning, philanthropy, and good living. The wharves of Philadelphia were piled high with everything for which American housewives might yearn, from the cutlery of Sheffield to the teas of Canton; the presses of Philadelphia groaned without rest to produce ten newspapers for the edification of its citizens, especially those interested in disasters, funerals, furniture sales, or political name-calling; the academies, streetlamps, fire companies, mansions, museums, and prisons of Philadelphia were models for civic-minded men all over America. "The cleanliness, evenness, and length of the streets," an admiring visitor from South America wrote, "their illumination at nighttime, and the vigilance of the guards, posted at each corner to maintain security and good order, make Philadelphia one of the most pleasant and well-ordered cities in the world." [6] A city in which Franklin lived out his last days, Robert Morris stirred a hundred financial pots, Benjamin Rush dispensed medical lore to eager youths, Charles Willson Peale painted portraits and collected old bones, and David Rittenhouse divided his time between inventing telescopes and surveying disputed boundaries was a place in which to think big thoughts about the American future. When the same visitor complained that "the men are almost always immersed in their business affairs and in political intrigue," little did he realize that this bustling city was setting a pattern for Americans for generations to come. [7]

For most citizens of the new Republic the pleasures and opportunities of civilized Philadelphia, Salem, and Savannah, even of half-civilized Pittsburgh and Boonesboro, were unreachable, unpurchasable, and almost unimaginable. Although life for the American down on the farm was more rewarding than it had been for him or for his ancestors in the Old World, it was certainly no easier. Most men, women, and children of that simple age spent most of their waking hours in the backbreaking toil of plow and hoe; and for those who pushed beyond the settled regions of New England, the valleys of the Middle States, and the coastal plains of the South, the hours of rest and recreation brought contact with only a scatter of neighbors. Cut off from the centers of commerce and culture, forced to rely on his own wits for survival in a hard game with a half-smiling, half-fierce nature, farming largely and often wholly for subsistence, the pioneering yeoman developed a self-respecting dependence on those around him and a headstrong independence of those remote from him—qualities that boded well for democracy yet ill for nationhood. There were, as we shall see, many lines dividing the

Americans of 1787 into groups or classes, but none so sharp as that between the involved and the isolated, the necessarily concerned and the fortuitously indifferent, the men who lived in cities and along lines of communication and therefore were in society and the men who lived by themselves and therefore were not. It took an extra measure of effort to dwell in the backwoods and stay in touch with the issues of civilization. For many Americans the gains to be expected were not worth the effort to be expended. Isolation, of a kind and to a degree we cannot imagine, was the dominating fact in the lives of perhaps a half-million Americans.

One thing was certain about the people of the United States: they were growing in numbers every year, and it was not just audacious patriotism that moved learned men to foretell a day when this newest nation in the world would also be the largest. The growth of population in this period was largely natural, and was a monument to the unexampled fertility of American mothers. Although the Republic was already being celebrated as "the Asylum of the Oppressed," and although boatloads of Germans, Irish, Scots, and others who had been oppressed (or simply bored) in the Old World docked from time to time in New York and Philadelphia, migration from Europe to America was light all through the troubled years from 1775 to 1815. For every new citizen gained by immigration in this period, twelve new citizens were born in America.[8]

The Union of 1787, like the Union of today, was made up of a number of demographic, social, and political components. Nature and the responses of men to it were chiefly responsible for the five large sections into which the entire country was loosely but visibly divided.

Three of these were settled areas, although thousands of square miles in each were still wilderness: New England, a region of small farms, busy docks, far-ranging fisheries, democratic manners, proud memories, and ingrained habits of self-reliance and frugality; the Middle States, a region boasting the best-balanced economy, most diverse origins and faiths, and largest cities in America; and the South, then as now a nation within a nation pursuing its own version of the American way of life. The line between any two of these historic sections was no sharper than that, let us say, between England and Scotland. Sizable parts of New York—for example, the area east of Albany as well as most of Long Island —were culturally if not politically related to New England, while Maryland faced with open eyes in two directions. According to the census of 1790 the population of the settled

areas was: New England, just over 1,000,000; the Middle
States (including Maryland), more than 1,300,000; the South,
just over 1,500,000.

Two other sections were only beginning to open up to permanent settlement: the wilderness north of the Ohio, which
promised to be an extension of New England and the Middle
States, and the wilderness south of the Ohio, much of which
was already marked out for an economy and society based on
chattel slavery. The census takers of 1790 found in the old
Northwest only about 5,000 forerunners of the swarm to
come, in the old Southwest something over 100,000. The first
three sections were therefore the ones that counted politically
in 1787; the pioneer areas, especially the country between the
Ohio and the Great Lakes, were shadows gradually taking on
substance in the minds of leading men, captivating some and
disturbing others. Although the thirteen states that had fought
the Revolution were still in command of the political situation—to the extent that it was subject to command at all—no
decisions could be taken that ignored the three new states
that were at the gates (Vermont, Kentucky, and Tennessee)
and the eight or ten others that were no farther down the
road than the eye of Thomas Jefferson of Virginia or Rev.
Manasseh Cutler of the Ohio Company could see. The decisions of 1787 were taken by men who represented the communities long ago marked out, in casual style but with
enduring consequences, by gentleman adventurers and their
patrons in London.

Yet these men, many of whom had their own plans for the
West, could see for themselves that the country was on the
move. Not immigration from abroad but migration within
the land was the dynamic of American demography in the
1780's. By boat, wagon, horse, and foot the men of the old
states were moving on in an ever-rising flood. "A rage for
emigrating to the western country prevails," the Secretary of
Foreign Affairs wrote in wonder to an American in Paris in
1785, "and thousands have already fixed their habitations in
that wilderness. . . . The seeds of a great people are daily
planting beyond the mountains." [9] Kentucky, still a part of
Virginia, counted almost 75,000 persons in 1790 where 150
woodsmen had roamed in 1776; Maine, still a part of Massachusetts, had grown almost overnight to one-fourth the size
of its parent; New Yorkers, long confined to the southwest
part of colony and state, now pushed in startling numbers up
the Mohawk; and as many as 100,000 people gave up
scratching for a living in New England in the years just after
the Revolution and set off for greener, less rock-strewn
fields.[10] The "course of empire," as never before in Ameri-

can history, pressed relentlessly westward even as the Convention was sitting.

However jumbled the social order might be on the banks of the Cumberland and Muskingum, it had long since shaken down into a pattern of classes and distinctions on the banks of the Merrimac, Hudson, Delaware, Potomac, and Santee. Each of the thirteen states, even intensely republican Connecticut, had a more visible class structure than that of modern America. The Old World tradition of social stratification, which had been challenged but not demolished in the Revolution, and an ever more versatile economy, which offered large profits to the adventurous and well-being to the industrious, provided solid underpinning for a social system less rigid than that of England yet clear-cut enough to work a decisive influence on culture, education, religion, and above all politics. From the bottom of society to the top was a short step; from top to bottom was not much longer a slide. Top and bottom nevertheless existed, and none knew better than the sturdy farmers, shopkeepers, and independent artisans in between—the "middling sort," as they were still known in parts of post-Revolutionary America—of the enviable prestige of the rich merchants, large landholders, and successful lawyers who made up the "better sort," or of the latent power of the laborers, servants, and hardscrabble farmers who crowded the ranks of the "meaner sort." While men from Europe were constantly exclaiming about the absence both of "great lords who possess everything" and of "a herd of people who have nothing," and reporting the sight of large areas in New Jersey and Connecticut in which no person was "ill clothed, hungry, sick, or idle," Americans were not so sure that "a pleasing uniformity of decent competence" was the mark of their society.[11]

These visitors from the old, privilege-ridden countries of Europe who found no peers and few peasants in their journeys from Savannah to Portsmouth were also constantly exclaiming about the "spirit of republicanism" and bewailing or applauding (depending on the prejudices they had brought with them) the general lack of deference in American manners. Yet anyone who had dined with a Rutledge in Charleston, ridden out with a Blair in Virginia, exchanged bows with a Mifflin in Philadelphia, or heard the opinions of a Schuyler in New York would have agreed with the French chargé d'affaires that although there were "no nobles in America," there were "gentlemen" who enjoyed a kind of "pre-eminence" because of "their wealth, their talents, their education, their families, or the offices they hold."[12] Some enjoyed a good deal more pre-eminence than others because they had helped to launch, guide, fight, and finance the Revolution. The Tory gentry who had fled from the wrath of rebellious America left room at the top in places like Boston and Philadelphia which patriots—some well-born, others self-made, and still others so "upwardly mobile" as to invite envy rather than respect—were quick to fill and determined to defend.

Although all thirteen states had some kind of property-owning or taxpaying qualification for political participation, most Americans who cared could meet these qualifications with something to spare—which means that most Americans had the vote, even though many were too preoccupied or isolated to use it. Then as now poverty was more a psychological than a legal bar to entrance into the political arena, and the bar was too formidable for the "meaner sort" to assault. As a result, the Republic for which the Constitution of 1787 was written had two classes that counted politically: the "rich and well-born" and the "body of sober and steady people." [13] Men divided politically, as they still do in America, on the basis of personal allegiances and sectional jealousies as well as along class lines. Although organized political parties had not yet sprung to life, except perhaps in the struggle of Constitutionalists and Republicans in Pennsylvania, semipermanent factions flourished in every state, and the most powerful of these factions depended on gentlemen for leadership and yeomen for votes. The line between the thinly populated top and the numerous middle in American society was therefore kept healthily fuzzy; the line betwen the middle and the bottom was more clearly seen, and was perhaps more politically meaningful. Despite the efforts of some historians to cram almost all Americans of the new Republic into one big, happy middle class, at least three per cent of the people had risen upward to form an American-style aristocracy; perhaps 20 per cent were mired in a swamp of much poverty and little hope, and thus were victims of a depressing political apathy.

Below the bottom of the class system of the new Republic, in legal status if not always in economic condition, was that vast group of "strangers in the land," the Negro slaves, who were an important component of the American economy, a presence if not a power in American politics, and a challenge to the American conscience. That the challenge had never been taken up, that only a handful of Negroes had been set free (and only a handful of white men accepted such Negroes as even second-class citizens) in a country proclaiming the natural rights and equality of "all men," has been attributed to many causes. Four of these bear particular mention because they are so often and easily overlooked: inertia, by which I mean that slavery flourished in the new Republic primarily because it had flourished in the old empire, and that to legislate it out of existence in any state south of Pennsylvania would have called for an economic, political, and cultural revolution far greater than that of 1776; apprehension, by which I mean the suspicions voiced by even the most decent men that American society could not absorb so numerous and culturally alien a people without changing its own ways for the worse; lack of imagination, by which I mean both the ability of ordinary Americans to look right through the Negroes around them and the inability of leading ones to devise even small-scale schemes to give emancipated slaves the substance as well as the appearance of freedom; and ideology, by which I mean the rising American commitment to the principle of equality. If whites in the new Republic were to think of blacks as men at all, they were bound by the articles of their republican faith to think of them as equals, which was an impossible thought for all but a handful of eccentrics to entertain about persons who did not seem to be even potentially Americans. An America less dedicated to the principles of liberty and equality might, like the more status-conscious and caste-bound societies of Latin America, have had less trouble taking the first step toward emancipation of slaves and their incorporation as citizens of a free society. Since the first step seemed to command every other step to the end, few Americans could bring themselves to take it. Negroes were Africans, and that was that. The fact that they had not come to America of their own will and could never leave it was one with which few white men were willing to grapple courageously.

Whatever the causes of this unhappy situation, the facts are clear: at the time of the Convention there were perhaps 650,000 Negro slaves in the United States; well over nine-tenths of them lived in the five southernmost states, and in those states they made up more than one-third of the total population; in one northern state (Massachusetts) emancipation had taken place, in four (New Hampshire, Connecticut, Rhode Island, and Pennsylvania) it had begun, in two it was being pushed (New York and New Jersey), and in all except Negro-hungry Georgia the slave trade had been halted or at least heavily discouraged by law. Although men of good will in many parts of America professed to be sure in their hearts that slavery was on the way to extinction, their minds held no timetable for this vast revolution.

The American economy, although it lagged well behind that of England on the road to industrialization, was one about which farsighted men had every right to be "bullish."

It displayed, as it had from the first planting, an essentially agrarian character: perhaps eight in ten Americans dug for their living in the dirt; one in ten worked in a closely allied extractive industry such as fishing or lumbering; one in ten had a place, whether as merchant, lawyer, sailor, clerk, or cartman, in the scheme of commerce. Small wonder that the possession of land—what Crèvecoeur saluted as the "precious soil," the "riches of the freeholder"—was still the widest door to well-being, profit, independence, status, and political power.[14]

Although much of American farming was for subsistence or barter, much was for shipment to people in other lands. The prosperity of many families in the United States depended on the export of produce—wheat, corn, tobacco, rice, and indigo, as well as meat, fish, furs, naval stores, hides, lumber, whale oil, potash, and horses—to the West Indies and Europe. The American economy was a trading economy, and few parts of the Atlantic world could do for long without its products. American commerce, in turn, depended on the soil for its articles of trade. Although farmed in a generally primitive and wasteful way, this soil was able to produce a large enough surplus to permit America to be a factor in the world economy.

No part of America, on the other hand, was willing to do for long without the manufactured goods of Europe, which the new Republic was not yet ready to produce for itself in more than trifling quantities. Here and there in the rural landscape were tiny shops for converting wood, iron ore, skins, sugar, fibers, and wheat into finished articles, but most of what we would call manufacturing was carried on in households, and most members of these households did their share of digging in off hours. The fact that only three of the fifty-five delegates to the Philadelphia Convention had invested in manufacturing enterprises is evidence enough that the sway of agriculture went as yet unchallenged.[15]

Although not yet officially dedicated to the glories and hazards of free enterprise, America was a country of free-enterprisers. Private ownership of the land and all other means of production was virtually universal; the profit motive sent men up over the mountains in search of new lands or down to the sea in ships; the use of credit and the wage system were fixed parts of the pattern of commerce. Mercantilism was dying, and feudalism had never had more than a marginal existence. Commercial capitalism was already preparing the way for America's surge to industrial might.

If the state of manufacturing was primitive, the state of learning was a cause for self-congratulation, a fashion in which many articulate Americans were not slow to indulge. Although reliable statistics do not exist, a long look through official records, deeds, petitions, letters, diaries, and other documents of the period leaves an impression of a remarkably literate people. This high state of literacy had not been easily won. Primary schools and academies were few and crude, and almost non-existent in rural areas; the family was therefore counted on, as we would never count on it today, to shoulder most of the burden for teaching young Americans to read, write, and cipher, as well as to understand their duties to God and their fellow men. The strongly knit family system, to its eternal credit, responded with an effectiveness that surprised many European observers. The new Republic was full of men who had never seen the inside of a schoolhouse and yet were extremely well educated for the responsibilities of their stations in life.

The fifteen-odd colleges (one can never be certain in egalitarian America whether a "college" is really a college, a self-inflated academy, or simply a board of trustees) were the special pride of the new Republic. Nine of them—Harvard, William and Mary, Yale, Princeton, Pennsylvania, Columbia, Brown, Rutgers, and Dartmouth—had been founded before 1776, and were now well established despite some economic, ideological, and political troubles stemming from the Revolution and its aftermath. At least six others—among them Dickinson, Hampden-Sydney, St. John's (Annapolis), Franklin and Marshall, the College of Charleston, and Washington College—were added in the 1780's; and even as the Convention sat, the first state universities were struggling to be born. It is easy to smile at the crabbed, often dogmatic methods of instruction that prevailed in these colleges, yet if we judge them by their fruits, they appear to have been rich fields of learning, reason, and the love of liberty. The overall performance of the college graduates in the Convention of 1787 speaks forcefully for the proposition that Latin, rhetoric, philosophy, and mathematics can be a healthy fare for political heroes.

Equally deserving of notice as servants in the cause of republican liberty and learning were the newspapers of America, of which there were a full eighty (most of them weeklies) scattered from Portland to Savannah, and from Bennington in Vermont to Lexington in Kentucky, at the time of the Convention. The eagerness with which editors published the full text of the proposed constitution and the amount of precious space they then made available to both the proponents and opponents of ratification reveal the useful role of the press in the politics of the young Republic. Then as now the dutiful citizen had to wade through pages of advertising in order to find the news; then as now he could be fairly certain that the news he read was uncensored and, so far as it ever can be, unperjured.

Although the secular culture of the new nation was still in a thinly productive state—with Noah Webster, David Rittenhouse, Francis Hopkinson, Philip Freneau, Charles Willson Peale, Jedidiah Morse, David Ramsay, Joel Barlow, Thomas Jefferson, and John Trumbull the "hopeful proofs of genius" [16]—its religion was moving into new ways of believing and behaving. The Old World pattern of state-church relations had been hurried toward its doom by the Revolution, the most splendid milestone being Virginia's (that is to say Jefferson's) Statute of Religious Liberty of 1786; the New World pattern of multiplicity, democracy, private judgment, mutual respect, and widespread indifference was well on its way to maturity. Although America was still largely a nation of believers in 1787, many of the believers—and almost all of them in high political station—were thoroughly tolerant of the beliefs of others. Neither upper-class ritualism nor lower-class enthusiasm had much appeal for the solid citizens of the United States, and men who still claimed to enjoy a monopoly of religious truth were no longer in a position to impose their dogmas on dissenting neighbors. As the perceptive Crèvecoeur wrote for the instruction of the Old World:

> Persecution, religious pride, the love of contradiction, are the food of what the world commonly calls religion. These motives have ceased here; zeal in Europe is confined; here it evaporates in the great distance it has to travel; there it is a grain of powder inclosed, here it burns away in the open air, and consumes without effect.[17]

Live-and-let-live, worship-and-let-worship was the essence of religion in this land of vast distances and a hundred religions, of which the most important in terms of politics was the vaguely Christian rationalism that governed the tolerant minds of men like Jefferson, Franklin, Hamilton, and Washington. (The last and least skeptical of these rationalists loaded his First Inaugural Address with appeals to the "Great Author," "Almighty Being," "invisible hand," and "benign parent of the human race," but apparently could not bring himself to speak the word "God.")[18] Although it was still far more comfortable for Americans to be Congregationalists, Presbyterians, Episcopalians, Methodists, Quakers, Lutherans, or Baptists than to be Catholics, the ever milder climate encouraged the feared and harried "Papists" to come out in the open, especially in Baltimore and Philadelphia. Even in old-fashioned parts of Connecticut and Massachusetts, the new orthodoxy of America was a many-voiced unorthodoxy.

One of the strongest forces in American society in 1787 was the fresh memory of the Revolution. For some men the tortuous course of events from 1765 to 1783 had been primarily a war against imperialism, for others a savagely fought civil war, for still others an upheaval that had sent them careening upward or downward in the social order. For all it had been an experience that had given new directions to their lives. Although these directions had been anticipated in the development of colonial America, the winning of independence had made them fixed conditions of the American way of life, conditions that would-be givers of a new fundamental law to the people would ignore at their peril.

The first of these was independence itself, which encouraged Americans to turn their backs on the old world of "corruption and decay," to pursue a self-reliant foreign policy, to dream of a continental "empire" from which every last Briton and Spaniard had been driven, and to consider themselves, like the children of Israel, a "peculiar treasure" singled out for a destiny higher than their own well-being. The second was republicanism, which was both a system of political, religious, and social institutions that had been cleansed of any taint of hereditary privilege and a spirit of self-respect that forbade the tugging of forelocks to even the grandest merchant in Boston or planter in Prince George County. And the third was dynamism, a wholesale quickening of ambition and aspiration, which stirred Americans of every class and calling to reach out for prosperity as persons and for glory as citizens. The pace of American life had picked up sharply during the Revolution; progress had become a favorite topic of preachers, poets, and politicians.

Yet another solid legacy of the Revolution was the existence of thirteen near-sovereign states, every one of which, with the possible exceptions of Delaware and New Jersey, had a vision of the American future in which it was a proud, permanent, respected, and largely self-contained unit. The British colonies in North America had developed over the generations as separate entities; the course of events from resistance in 1765 to victory in 1783 first turned these colonies into states and then stiffened them in the sense of their own importance. Each state, even doubting Delaware and New Jersey, was or wanted to be a self-directing republic, a discrete social and economic community, and an object of loyalty to its inhabitants. Whether any state, even lordly Virginia or ambitious New York, was a rising nation was a question that few Americans were able to answer with a convincing "yes," and it was exactly this widespread assumption—that the states, however indestructible, were nothing more than states—which opened the way to the building of the American nation.

This assumption was both effect and cause of another legacy of the Revolution, itself the consequence of generations of unplanned yet hardy growth: the fact of incipient nationhood hinted at by the Stamp Act Congress, affirmed in the Declaration of Independence, nourished by the blood shed at Bunker Hill and Cowpens, reaffirmed in the Articles of Confederation, and felt in the bones by almost every alert, active, literate man in the new Republic. Most of the ingredients of American nationalism were in the pot by 1787: common language, common origin and outlook, common legal and political institutions, common culture, common enemies, and common memories of a successful drive toward independence. There lacked, indeed, only that condition of political unity and sense of emotional unity which would follow on the creation of a central government with dignity and authority.

Here, then, were both the problem and the opportunity of the forward-looking leaders of the 1780's: that while many of their fellow countrymen everywhere in America feared *the fact of a national government,* few men anywhere opposed *the idea of a nation.* While men like George Clinton, Patrick Henry, and Richard Henry Lee were ready to be Americans, they were not ready to submit to the commands of an American government, which could not, they were convinced, extend its sway over half a continent without destroying the states and turning away from republican principles. It was up to men like Washington, Madison, and James Wilson to persuade those who thought like Clinton, Henry, and Lee that such a government, if prudently constructed out of the soundest materials, would respect and indeed confirm the existence and legitimate interests of the states and would be a support rather than a menace to American republicanism. Although handicapped in many ways in the battles of rhetoric and political maneuver with the fearful republicans, the nationalists had one advantage that, in the long run and therefore in the end, would prove decisive: they knew, as did many of their opponents, that the prescriptive course of nation-building in America had run beyond the capacity of the Articles of Confederation to serve national needs. By 1787, as we shall learn in the next chapter, the constitutional lag had become too exaggerated for men like Washington and Madison to bear patiently.

Whether possibly or probably or actually a nation, the United States of 1787, like the United States of every year of its existence, was a society trying to have the best of the two worlds of unity and diversity. Common forces and principles worked powerfully to hold it together; a jumbled array of antagonisms tended just as powerfully to pull it apart. Although the Framers of the Constitution would never even have assembled at Philadelphia if the elements of a "more perfect Union" had not existed in abundance, they were well aware of the countervailing elements of disruption in the society they had come to rescue from the defects of its virtues.

To James Madison, in particular, as the keenest student then living of the causes and consequences of "faction," the cross-cutting tensions of American society were a source of wonder and worry. Everywhere one looked the lines of suspicion were drawn: between states and nation, and between one state and its neighbors; between New England and the Middle States, between North and South, and between one part of the South and the other; between over-represented seaboard, under-represented piedmont, and unrepresented frontier; between city, village, and countryside; between mercant, farmer, and artisan, and between the successful and less successful in each calling; between rich, substantial, struggling, and poor; between the holders of various kinds and amounts of property, and between all those who held property and all those who did not; between better sort, middling sort, and meaner sort, between all white men and all Negroes, and between free Negroes and slaves; between one kind of Protestant and another, and between all Protestants and the rest; between zealous Revolutionists, reluctant Revolutionists, indifferents, and former loyalists; between, I repeat, the involved and the isolated; and, wherever Madison and his friends were finally able to force the issue, between those who wanted a new government and those who preferred to drift indefinitely with the old one. How to prevent these lines of suspicion from hardening into lines of battle, how to convince all these private interests of the necessary existence of a public interest, how to reinforce politically all the elements in the emerging American consensus—these were the principal tasks of statesmanship ordained by the twin facts of unity and diversity in the new Republic.

The United States in 1787 was a society in which the means for accomplishing these tasks were abundant if not prodigal. Let us go back, by way of conclusion, to the three "large aspects" of the Philadelphia Convention that were singled out in the introductory chapter, and let us take careful note that each of these aspects has meaning for us today exactly because it reflects a major reality of 1787. The Convention is a classic case-study in the political process of constitutional democracy because the Republic abounded in public skills, because it was full of capable men who had had years of experience in issue-posing, information-gathering, interest-adjusting, and decision-making. It is a classic case-study in nation-making because the Republic had already moved so far toward nationhood in its institutions and emotions. And it is a classic case-study in the attempt of men to take control of their own destiny because the emerging nation was, or at least appeared to be, the product of a conscious effort to lay a hand on history.

If we will put these three realities together and view them as one massive fact, the fact was the existence throughout the new Republic of an extraordinary political elite, most members of which, having already made their share of history, had a mind to make a little more before going to rest. The fifty-five men who got to Philadelphia and the hundreds who were ready to support them throughout the thirteen states were, in a more than symbolic sense, the United States in 1787.

# 3 ILLS AND REMEDIES

*No morn ever dawned more favorable than ours did;
and no day was ever more clouded than the present!
Wisdom and good examples are necessary at this
time to rescue the political machine from the impending storm.*

WASHINGTON TO MADISON, November 5, 1786[1]

THE MOOD of the United States in 1787 was a bittersweet blend of hope and apprehension. Many leading men, as they went about the daily round of private and public business, felt the sharp tug of both these contradictory sentiments on their hearts and minds.

Hope was aroused by the memory of the recent past and by contemplation of the distant future. The success of the Revolution—above all the stupendous fact that mighty Britain had been forced to disgorge its treasured colonies—had set even skeptical men to wondering about "the hand of God in American affairs"; and to live imaginatively in that bountiful, unbounded land was to agree with President Stiles of Yale that "glory and honor" were the likely destiny of the United States.[2] On the other hand, the situation of the moment, one of muddle in private enterprise and drift in public affairs, was a cause of mounting apprehension. Although the long-range possibilities of the Republic were excellent, the short-range probabilities were unsettling; and more and more Americans were coming to realize that the road to the "long range," for nations if not for men, leads over a series of "short ranges," any one of which, if not assaulted with courage and traversed with success, may turn out to be the end of the line. Although few men in 1787 really thought that the Republic was at the end of the line, many were disturbed enough to contemplate the possibility of some forceful action on a continental scale.

The forceful action of 1787, the extraordinary gathering in Philadelphia, is itself the most convincing evidence of the unsettled state of affairs in the new Republic. Most members of the Convention had more pressing or inviting things to do than to spend a sticky and contentious summer in Philadelphia; most came to Philadelphia with a feeling of reluctance

35

or even displeasure; most agreed in spirit with George Mason's remark—although his price did seem boastfully high—that he "would not, upon pecuniary motives, serve in this convention for a thousand pounds per day." [3] Two such gatherings had already taken place in their generation—the Stamp Act Congress in New York in 1765, the Continental Congress in Philadelphia in 1774—and only a powerful sense of misgiving could have forced a third in the face of the localism of many leading politicians, the apathy of most ordinary men, and the inertia built into this as into most political systems. Men like John Dickinson and John Rutledge were moved to disrupt their lives, as they had been moved in 1765 and 1774, not by personal ambition or the hope of gain for state or section, but by a recognition that once again the time had come for a "national deliberation." If the extraordinary gathering of 1787 was harder to bring off than those of 1765 and 1774, that was because it is always harder for a people to take counsel and create than to rebel and destroy. Since the troubles of the 1780's were disturbing enough to force men of standing throughout the Republic to commit their reputations to a hazardous undertaking, we ought to look briefly at the ills of which they complained and the remedies they proposed. We ought also to acknowledge the existence of men who either did not see the ills or, seeing them, feared them less than they feared the obvious remedy.

The first complaint of the troubled men of 1787 has a familiar ring: although the economy of the country was basically sound, it was depressed enough in many ports and rural areas to justify sober talk of "stagnation" and "dislocation." Eight years of whimsical war had shut off many of the old channels of trade, dealt a severe blow to such enterprises as fishing and shipbuilding, disrupted the structure of prices and wages, and destroyed an untold amount of productive property. Four years of restless peace had first been marked by an extravagant importation of British and European goods, then had been marred by a rolling series of failures of firms unable either to sell or pay for these goods. Whereas inflation had been the curse of the whole economy during the war, deflation was the bane of critical parts of it in the aftermath. "In every point of view," Madison wrote of Virginia in 1785, "the trade of this country is in a deplorable condition. A comparison of current prices here with those in the Northern States . . . will show that the loss direct on our produce, and indirect on our imports, is not less than fifty per cent." [4]

In some sections of the country, to be sure, the post-war cycle of boom and bust had leveled off on a high plateau of prosperity, and many merchants and farmers were enjoying profits they had never known before. They were enjoying their profits, however, because of lucky circumstances that might not last—and at the expense of other merchants and farmers who might grow weary of being left out in the cold. The health of the American economy in 1787 was too spotty to please men who thought of the Republic, whether sentimentally or cold-bloodedly, as an interdependent array of sections and interests.

Their second complaint, which tied in with the first, was directed toward the state of private and public finance. Whatever gains might be made in productivity, whatever new markets might be opened up, however many banks might be founded by enterprising men, deep uneasiness was bound to prevail all through a country in which hard money was scarce and growing scarcer, paper money was a threat and growing more threatening, private debts were an invitation to political meddling, and public debts, contracted with the best of wills for the highest of purposes, were a burden that would not be lightened in a hundred years under existing modes of taxation. The critical problem was the alarming dearth of specie with which to pay for everything from taxes levied on the land to goods imported and still wanted from abroad. The drain of specie kept the back country in a state of political and social tension, while the balance of trade seemed to tip so drastically against the United States that even the most solid merchants wondered how long their credit would hold up in London and Amsterdam. At the same time, the absence of a uniform currency in the thirteen states made every dealing across a state line a small exercise in financial wizardry.

Paper money, which was issued in varying amounts and guises during the 1780's in seven states (Rhode Island, New York, New Jersey, Pennsylvania, the Carolinas, and Georgia) and was a subject of bitter controversy in three others (New Hampshire, Massachusetts, and Maryland), was the tie that joined financial dislocation to social discontent. What John Jay derided as "the doctrine of the political transubstantiation of paper into gold and silver" had a powerful appeal to men with crushing debts and unpopular taxes to pay, and with no coin in which to pay them.[5] Although there were exceptions to the rule, as in devastated but hopeful (and therefore slave-hungry) South Carolina, most battles over paper money were fought between men of status and property and men well below them on the economic and social scale. Some of these battles were extremely nasty; a Marxist historian, if he looked hard and narrowly enough at states like Pennsylvania,

New Hampshire, Maryland, and Rhode Island, could find many signs of "class struggle" in the new Republic.

The non-Marxist historian, although he may acclaim the republican consensus that kept these battles from getting entirely out of hand, is bound to admit that such incidents as the descent of an armed mob on the New Hampshire legislature in Exeter in September, 1786, and the famous "rebellion" symbolized (if not exactly led) by Captain Daniel Shays in Massachusetts were full of the animosity of distressed men toward their "betters." Beneath the veneer of deference there had always been malice and envy in the attitude of the "lower orders" toward the gentry in America, and the pressures of the 1780's brought such feelings frothing to the surface. They also set some sober members of the gentry to complaining aloud about the "heats and excesses of a mad democracy." The class structure in America has rarely been more visible, nor more visibly scarred by mistrust, than in the paper-money turmoils of the 1780's. The restoration of many loyalists to high standing in the community was another spur to social resentment. Yet another was the founding of the Society of the Cincinnati by some of Washington's officers, and even the repeal of the principle of hereditary membership in 1784 did not allay the fears of dedicated republicans (many of them in high places and themselves eligible for membership) that the Cincinnati were the forerunners of an American peerage.

For men who looked beyond the boundaries of the Republic, its weak position in the squabbling family of nations was a greater cause for worry than was a sluggish commerce or a deranged currency or even an agitated society. Of all the impulses that drove men like Washington and Hamilton to Philadelphia in 1787, none was stronger than the uncomplicated, patriotic sense of shame at the contempt in which the United States seemed to be held—from Britain at one end of the scale of power to the Barbary states at the other. As Hamilton wrote to the editor of the *New-York Packet* as early as July 4, 1782:

> There is something . . . diminutive and contemptible in the prospect of a number of petty states, with the appearance only of union, jarring, jealous and perverse, without any determined direction, fluctuating and unhappy at home, weak and insignificant by their dissensions in the eyes of other nations.[6]

Although the British were the chief offenders against American interests and sensibilities—because of their discriminations against trade, their retention of seven northwest posts in defiance of the terms of the Treaty of Paris, and their refusal to send an envoy to a Republic that might or might not turn out to be a sovereign nation—France and Spain, each in its own arrogant way, pursued policies based on the cheerful suspicion that the United States would probably not survive. Few Americans, oddly enough, feared a military attack by one or more of the great powers; the immediate threat of war was not one of the impulses that drove men to Philadelphia in 1787. What concerned the Framers was not force but intrigue. They were quite certain that America could not be conquered in the foreseeable future; they were quite worried that parts of it could be bought. Enough Spanish gold flowed maliciously through the specie-starved future states of Kentucky and Tennessee to give substance to this worry. Men in this area had their own reasons to be distressed about the direction of American diplomacy, for only an angry surge of southern and western opinion in 1786 had prevented the Secretary of Foreign Affairs in the Confederation, John Jay, from bargaining away American rights to navigate the lower Mississippi for thirty years to come.

By 1787 men like Washington and Madison had come to see the commercial, financial, social, and diplomatic disorders of the new Republic as primarily political in character. The trouble with almost every state was that it was governed weakly or erratically; the trouble with the United States was that it was governed hardly at all. Since they also saw these disorders as primarily national in scope, as afflictions that no state could hope to cure on its own, the most unbearable ill was a palsied common government.

Except for Rhode Island and Connecticut, for each of which the transition from self-governing colony to statehood was a simple affair, the states had adopted new constitutions between 1776 and 1784. Most of these constitutions were commendable experiments in republicanism, and several were admirable, but none was a guarantee—no constitution ever is —against impetuosity, error, or indecision. By the middle of the 1780's the unrest in every state had impelled all but the steadiest men in power to act impetuously, all but the luckiest to make mistakes, all but the bravest to turn their backs on hard problems that clamored for attention. Despite official protestations of enduring devotion to the doctrine of the separation of powers, the governments of most states were in the hands of self-willed legislatures. Despite the energetic efforts of the gentry and its political allies, the control of most legislatures fell at one time or another into the hands of a small-farmer class that was chiefly interested in paying off old scores and new debts as speedily as possible.

The record of the more headstrong or simply shortsighted state legislatures was a major source of the discontent that finally welled up into resolute action. In compiling a list in early 1787 of some eleven "vices of the political system of the United States," Madison laid a full seven, with the hearty concurrence of every friend to whom he showed the list, at the doors of the legislatures.[7] Whether the laws of the derelict states were guilty of "mutability" or "multiplicity" or "injustice" was then, as it is today, a point of some controversy, but no man could gainsay, although he might explain away, Madison's indictment of these states for "failure . . . to comply with the constitutional requisitions" of Congress, for "encroachments" on the "authority" of the United States, for "violations" of some of the key articles of the Treaty of Paris, and for "trespasses . . . on the rights of each other" in the form of commercial discriminations. The states had played fast and loose with the liberty and property of many of their citizens; they had failed in their elementary duty to support the common government of the United States; the "pride of independence," as even the forgiving Jefferson wrote in 1783, had taken "deep and dangerous hold on the hearts" of too many of their politicians.[8] Although few members of the Convention would have gone so far as General Knox and pronounced the state governments to be "sources of pollution," [9] none whose views or interests transcended state boundaries could manage more than a wry smile over the antics of turbulent Rhode Island or parochial New York in this unsettled period.

They could not even manage a smirk over what James Madison, a loyal and industrious member of Congress, described tartly as "the existing embarrassments and mortal diseases of the Confederacy." [10] The government under the Articles of Confederation was on its last legs in 1786 and 1787. When the Articles had been anticipated in 1774, mulled over in 1776, proposed in 1777, and finally ratified in 1781, a confederate, congressional form of government was clearly what most Americans wanted to handle their common affairs. It had to be confederate because they were in no mood to give a faraway, central regime in the United States what they were busy denying to a faraway, central regime in Britain, and because small states like Delaware and Rhode Island believed honestly that they were, in ways that mattered, equal partners of large states like Pennsylvania and Virginia. It had to be congressional because they were in no mood to give an independent executive in the United States what they were busy denying to an independent executive in Britain. In the light of the embryonic state of American nationalism, the fear of political power that pervaded Revolutionary thinking, and the lack of experience in lawmaking and administration on a continental scale, the Articles of Confederation—in effect, a codification of the methods and experiences of the first three years of the Continental Congress—seem to have been just about as viable a form of common government as could have been offered to the American people in the second year of independence. Only a few persons were moved to think uncomfortable thoughts at the sight of a charter that gave an equal vote to each of the thirteen states, required nine votes to do anything significant in the areas of war, diplomacy, and finance (this was in fact a concession to the larger states), and required the approval of the legislatures of every state to any "alteration" in its wording. The "authors" of the Confederation, Edmund Randolph stated in behalf of the whole Convention of 1787, had "done all that patriots could do, in the then infancy of the science of constitutions and of confederacies." [11]

By the second year of peace, however, government under the Articles had lost most of its viability, and arrangements that had made sense in 1777 were beginning to look more and more like "mortal diseases." As a result, some men had begun to wonder out loud whether a government without power to tax, to regulate trade, and to pass laws that individuals were bound to obey was a government at all. A charter of "perpetual" Union that gave equal votes to Delaware and Virginia was headed from the beginning toward trouble; a charter that relied for the replenishment of the "common treasury" on a system of requisitioning funds from the legislatures of Delaware, Virginia, and their eleven sisters—each of which retained its "sovereignty, freedom and independence" and thus could defy any requisition—was headed toward atrophy or even oblivion. Although commanded by the Articles to look at the "common defense," "security," and "mutual and general welfare" of the United States, Congress lacked the power, both in fact and theory, to raise the funds necessary for the discharge of these high duties. The delegates in Congress were reluctant to vote substantial requisitions; the states were delinquent in meeting the most modest ones. And one state legislature—whether that of Rhode Island, New York, or Virginia—could always be counted on to block unanimous approval of any proposal to give Congress even a conditional power to levy tariffs. By 1785 the government of the United States was a wheedling beggar. It could not raise enough money at home or abroad to meet the modest expenses of peace; it could not even raise enough to pay interest on the debts it had contracted during the war. A convincing measure of its financial plight is the fact that the total income of this government in 1786 was less than one-third of the charges for annual interest on the national debt.[12] So cautious a delegate as William Paterson of New Jersey could speak in the Convention of 1787 of the "deranged state of our finances," and so flatly anti-nationalist a delegate as Luther Martin of Maryland had to admit that Congress had been "weak, contemptibly weak." [13]

The weakness of the confederate features of the Articles of Confederation was compounded by the arrangement under which the total authority of the government was centered in one institution: "the Delegates of the United States in Congress assembled." The first constitution of the United States —if constitution it was—set up a one-chambered assembly as the organ of governing and made no provision whatever for a permanent, independent executive or judiciary. The pressure of events, indeed the simple demands of effective government, gave rise in time to at least rudimentary executive and judicial branches. Having lumbered along ever since the extralegal days of 1774 with a system of calling upon any agency within reach to execute its decisions (including committees of its own members, state conventions or councils, the commander in chief, and other citizens with or without official status), Congress underwent a limited constitutional revolution in 1781 that put single officers in charge of each of the three areas of principal concern: diplomacy, war, and finance.* While Congress itself flitted from one abode to another, and often simply vegetated because the necessary quorum of two delegates from each of seven states was not on hand, men like Benjamin Lincoln (Secretary of War, 1781–1783), Henry Knox (Secretary of War, 1785–1789), Robert R. Livingston (Secretary for Foreign Affairs, 1781–1783), John Jay (Secretary for Foreign Affairs, 1784–1789), and above all Robert Morris (the first and last Superintendent of Finance, 1781–1784) labored to give the United States the appearance of a government of permanence and promise. The three-man Court of Appeals in Cases of Capture, which operated under the authority of Congress between 1780 and 1786, did its restricted but useful judicial tasks in a manner reasonably worthy of the only plausible

---

* In 1784, as the result of a sharp political and theoretical struggle, Congress beat a retreat in the area of finance to a three-man board of treasury.

candidate for the title of "direct ancestor" to the Supreme Court of the United States.

It is conceivable that a stable, effective pattern of government for the Union could have emerged prescriptively out of the Confederation Congress, and that scholars today might be arguing among themselves whether Superintendent Morris, Secretary Jay, or General Washington was "really the first prime minister of the United States." But the Articles betrayed a fatal flaw, and the flaw was in the foundation, not the superstructure. The first constitution of the United States went from crisis to crisis and finally into a long slide toward death, not because it defied the commonly accepted American principle of the separation of powers by giving total authority to a single organ, but because it made the exercise of the limited authority it granted almost exclusively dependent on the good will of each of thirteen states, not one of which had any overpowering reason, even in the worst days of 1777 and 1778, to trust any or all of the other states. "So long as any individual state has power to defeat the measures of the other twelve," a politically minded grammarian named Noah Webster wrote in 1785, "our pretended union is but a name, and our confederation, a cobweb." [14] The states failed Congress—by refusing to honor resolutions, to fill requisitions, to approve new powers, and often even to maintain a delegation at that seat of government—far more grievously than Congress failed the states. The troubles of the Republic's confederate form of government were starkly revealed in the weeks between November 26, 1783, and January 14, 1784, when the Treaty of Paris, almost a "steal" for the United States, lay unratified before a Congress that could not muster the nine state delegations necessary for approval.

The record of the Confederation government was not wholly bad, and the years between 1774 and 1789 should be judged as a period of useful (if also nearly fatal) experiment rather than of inglorious folly. The first government of the United States fought a successful war, made a viable peace, laid the foundations for a new order of diplomacy, established enough credit at home and abroad to pay its most pressing expenses, conducted a kind of political and social academy for the continental elite, created a functioning bureaucracy, and above all maintained itself as a symbol of American unity even in the most parochial times after 1783. In one paramount instance, the creation of a national domain out of the unsettled lands north of the Ohio between 1780 and 1784 and the provision for its eventual incorporation as full-fledged states in the Northwest Ordinance of 1787, Congress went beyond mere symbolism to strike a blow for

American unity. The struggle between the states with no western lands (New Hampshire, Rhode Island, New Jersey, Pennsylvania, Delaware, and Maryland) and those with claims extending westward to the Mississippi, or even so far as "the South Sea" (Connecticut, Massachusetts, New York, Virginia, North Carolina, South Carolina, and Georgia) had been another source of political and social contention during the first years. Only the promises of the latter to surrender these claims—which New York and Virginia did with telling effect in 1780–1781—had persuaded restricted, recalcitrant Maryland to accede finally to the Articles of Confederation. The existence of a Congress legally able to accept title to these lands and politically willing to organize them was an immense blessing to the Republic and a strong cement for the Union. If Congress had done nothing else in its fitful career, the Resolution of 1780 and the Ordinances of 1784, 1785, and 1787—the last of these enacted in New York even as the Convention sat in Philadelphia and planned the demise of the Articles—would be monument enough to this first government of the United States. The United States was the first country in history to provide for orderly expansion into new territory on the basis of republican principles. With few alterations the program of 1784–1787 was to carry the nation westward to "the South Sea."

Yet, when every plus has been recorded, when every concession to the friends of the Articles has been made, the hard truth remains that Congress was not a viable government for a self-respecting, self-directing, expanding, and maturing nation, which was the kind of nation most leading men wanted America to be. Congress could make treaties with powers great and small but could not persuade the state legislatures to honor them; it could authorize foreign trade but could neither regulate nor tax it; it could call for money but not collect it, borrow money but not repay it, print money but not support it. Above all, it could resolve and recommend but could not command and coerce. As Hamilton was later to write in *The Federalist*, it was crippled permanently by that one "great and radical vice": the "principle of LEGISLATION for STATES or GOVERNMENTS, in their CORPORATE or COLLECTIVE CAPACITIES, and as contra-distinguished from the INDIVIDUALS of whom they consist." If this principle was not true of "all the powers delegated to the Union," it "pervaded" those—especially the responsibility to raise money for common purposes—"on which the efficacy of the rest" depended.[15]

In its very best days the Confederation government was a "firm league of friendship" and perhaps something more, in its very worst a sign of the common experiences and hopes of the American states; but never, on any of its five thousand or more days, was it the government of a nation except in a hortatory or symbolic way. Although it has been plausibly argued that the decision of the nationalists to strengthen or even replace the charter of the Confederation was the most painful blow ever dealt to Congress, it can be just as plausibly argued that most of its wounds were self-inflicted. Congress was already falling when the Framers gave it their famous push.

Whether all these commercial, financial, social, and political troubles added up to a major crisis in the life of the nation depended very much on where one lived, what work one did, how far one saw, and especially what one understood by the word "nation." For many Americans the 1780's were a time of good luck and growing prosperity, and they refused to worry about paper money in Rhode Island, glutted docks in New York City, humiliation in London and Madrid, or Indian raids in Georgia. For many others the only real troubles were personal, and thus best solved by pulling up stakes, or local, and thus best solved by voting new faces into the state legislature. And for still others, who could see almost as far as James Madison or Alexander Hamilton and who cherished the idea of nationhood almost as fondly, the obvious remedy was still more to be feared than the obvious troubles.

This obvious remedy was, of course, some kind of extraordinary meeting like that of 1765 or 1774 which would fortify the authority of Congress and make it less dependent on the pleasure of the states or, failing that, would recommend a new government in its place. Such a meeting had been talked about off and on ever since 1780, when Hamilton (in camp with Washington) had written a detailed letter to James Duane (in Philadelphia with Congress) cataloguing "the defects of our present system," indicting Congress for "diffidence" in using its "discretionary powers" and "want of method and energy in the administration," and proposing "immediately a convention of all the states" with "plenipotentiary authority to conclude finally" upon a common government worthy of a nation.[16] Other men had already begun to talk and write this way, although in vaguer terms, and by 1785 it was generally understood that the one meaningful alternative to a policy of hopeless drift was a gamble on a "convention of all the states"—a legal convention if Congress would support it fully, an extralegal one if Congress would merely tolerate it.

The possibility that Congress might heal itself could no

longer be considered seriously. Even if the delegates could
agree on a list of new powers, they could hardly expect that
all thirteen legislatures would then register approval—not, for
example, when so respectable a servant of Congress as Samuel Osgood of Massachusetts could express a fear "that if
permanent funds are given to Congress, the aristocratical influence, which predominates in more than a major part of
the United States, will finally establish an arbitrary
government." [17] Future Federalists like Madison, Hamilton,
James Wilson, and Charles Pinckney were compiling and
even bringing in lists as late as 1786;[18] future anti-Federalists
like William Grayson, Joseph Jones, James Monroe, George
Clinton, and Patrick Henry were admitting that Congress
could not go on forever without the addition of new powers
and the invigoration of old ones. Yet with the sight of an ill-
attended, low-spirited, penniless Congress always before their
eyes, it was hard for either description of men to believe that
the Articles of Confederation contained the means of their
own salvation. By 1786 the only questions left for consideration were whether the Union brought to life by the pressures
of 1774–1781 would wither away with a whimper or break
apart with a bang, and whether enough men would be persuaded of the reality of the crisis in time to do more than
speak a prayer over the remains.

In the end, obstinate events made it possible for purposeful
nationalists like Madison and Hamilton to override the fears
of less purposeful nationalists like Osgood and Monroe, to ignore the warnings of committed states-righters like Clinton
and Henry, to break through the apathy of inward-looking
men in every state, and to bring off the small miracle of sum-
moning a convention in Philadelphia. Although much credit
should be given to the nation-minded men of the 1780's, even
more decisive was the cumulative effect of the fiascos over
the proposed imposts of 1781 and 1783, the continuing pressures of British contempt and Spanish greed, and the derelic-
tions and depredations of the state legislatures. These events
led to the famous preliminary meeting at Annapolis in September, 1786,* and beyond Annapolis to Philadelphia.

The Annapolis Convention was a quite extralegal gathering
of twelve "commissioners" from five states (Virginia, Pennsylvania, Delaware, New Jersey, and New York) who declined to be put off from a historic task by the hostile or
careless attitude of the other eight states. Convoked at the

---

* A sort of preliminary to the preliminary took place at Mt. Vernon
in the spring of 1785 when commissioners from Maryland and Virginia met to discuss problems of their common treasure, the Potomac.

call of the Virginia Assembly to "take into consideration the trade of the states," to explore the possibility of a "uniform system in their commercial regulations," and to report "an act relative to this great object" to the states and to Congress,[19] it snatched a clever victory from the jaws of a contemptible defeat by adopting a report that called on the legislatures of these five states, and thus indirectly on the other states, to appoint delegates "to meet at Philadelphia on the second Monday in May next,"

> to take into consideration the situation of the United States, to devise such further provisions as shall appear to them necessary to render the constitution of the federal government adequate to the exigencies of the Union; and to report such an act for that purpose to the United States in Congress assembled as, when agreed to by them and afterwards confirmed by the legislature of every state, will effectually provide for the same.[20]

Annapolis was, so it appears from the austere record, a joint victory for Hamilton and Madison. Hamilton, acting his favorite part of the audacious man of destiny, persuaded Egbert Benson, John Dickinson, George Read, Edmund Randolph, and his other colleagues to go beyond their restricted mandates and to strike for a full constitutional solution to all the ills of the Republic, and then wrote out the report of September 14. Madison, acting his favorite part of the creative politician, had brought about this meeting in the first place by pulling the political wires in Virginia; and, once he saw to his delight the way things were going, he was able (with the aid of Randolph) to persuade Hamilton to couch this proposal in words that would ring strongly but not offensively from Portsmouth to Augusta. Otto, the French chargé d'affaires, was certain that the men of Annapolis "had no hope, nor even desire, to see the success of this assembly," and had planned all along for a successful failure.[21] This, however, is to give too much credit to Hamilton and Madison, students but not disciples of Machiavelli. They may have hoped that Annapolis would lead to Philadelphia, but not by quite so devious a route.

Any passable road to Philadelphia would almost certainly have to lead through New York. The necessary step was taken there February 21, 1787, when Congress, spurred into unaccustomed activity by yet another series of events, called for a convention to meet in Philadelphia "on the second Monday in May next," for the sole and express purpose of revising the Articles of Confederation and reporting to Congress and the several legislatures such alterations and provisions therein as shall when agreed to in Congress and confirmed by the states render the federal constitution adequate to the exigencies of government and the preservation of the Union.[22]

Several of these events were the work of purposeful men: for example, the action of seven states (Virginia, New Jersey, New Hampshire, Pennsylvania, North Carolina, Delaware, and Georgia) in "jumping the gun" on Congress and naming delegations to Philadelphia even before it had passed this resolution. Several others were largely fortuitous: for example, the attendance of a quorum in Congress, and the presence of Madison, who was never entirely healthy at this time, in the Virginia delegation. And one was so completely fortuitous, and in addition so frightening, that it provided all the push that was still needed to get the right men to Philadelphia in the right frame of mind.

This was, of course, the celebrated Shays Rebellion, one of the few events in American history that was as important in fact as it has become in legend. The rebellion—perhaps too strong a word, but Captain Shays and his men are stuck with it forever—was an uprising in the fall of 1786 of hard-pressed rural debtors in western Massachusetts. Before they were finally routed by the loyal militia under General Lincoln early in 1787, some two thousand of the most desperate or merely adventurous of them managed to raise the largest fuss of its kind since the affair at Alamance in 1771. They called impromptu conventions to demand changes in the state constitution, resisted payment of taxes and fees, used force to prevent county courts from sitting, and finally rose in arms to march hither and yon in search of justice, which proved elusive, and excitement, which became too much for almost everybody when an assault was launched on the arsenal at Springfield.

Although the Shaysites were not Jacobins, and although they collapsed quickly when force was mustered and applied, the news from Massachusetts spread alarm throughout the Union, for every state felt the unsettling effects of the persistent drain of specie and had its share of debt-ridden farmers who might take it into their heads to appeal from the courts to the streets and camps. Even Washington, who did not frighten easily, was worried about the "combustibles in every state" waiting for a spark and a breeze to set them afire. "I feel . . . infinitely more than I can express . . . for the disorders which have arisen," he added. "Good God! Who besides a tory could have foreseen, or a Briton have predicted them!"[23] Of all the incidents that persuaded Washington to leave home once again and put his reputation in hazard, none had quite the impact of the news that an officer in the late Continental Army had brought the celebrated state of Massachusetts to the brink of civil war. Whatever "the cause of all these commotions"—"licentiousness," "British influence," or "real grievances" admitting of "redress"—the time had come to "look to our national character" and to find a national solution.[24]

If Washington was "mortified beyond expression,"[25] other men were now sufficiently concerned, even in doubting New York and reluctant Maryland, to act on the suggestion of Congress and name delegates to the Convention. By early May only obstinate Rhode Island, a state from which no good news for the Union had ever been heard, had failed to respond to the calls from Annapolis and New York, and most of those fifty-five men who were to win (if not necessarily deserve) the accolade of "Framers" were on their way to Philadelphia. They came with a will because they felt and saw the troubles of the United States as the troubles of a nation and because, as one of them was later to put the matter in behalf of all, a "NATION without a NATIONAL GOVERNMENT" was "an awful spectacle." While many of their old comrades were worried lest a third "national deliberation" betray the legacy of 1776, they were quite clear in their own minds that the Revolution commanded rather than forbade the gathering at Philadelphia. "The American war is over," an unknown but knowing citizen of New Jersey wrote late in 1786, "but this is far from being the case with the American Revolution. . . . It remains yet to establish and perfect our new forms of government."[26]

Whether the United States in 1787 was in truth on the edge of dissolution is a question that will be argued among historians until the United States is no more. That a majority of the continental elite believed this to be the truth is the most solid, incontrovertible fact in the records of that year. A feeling in the bones that the United States was intended to be a full-fledged nation, a recognition that such a nation must have a national government, a loss of confidence in the capacity of Congress to heal itself and become such a government, a fear that the vast potential of the American people might never be realized, and above all a desire to bring the Revolution at last to completion—these were the principal political sentiments that carried Washington, Madison, Hamilton, and the rest down the dusty road to Philadelphia.

# 4 MATERIALS AND CHOICES

> *They kept the same ground as the Revolution had taken, and which was seen in all the state governments. They took their principles from that set of political economists and philosophers now generally denominated in the English language Whigs, and consecrated them as a Constitution for the government of the country.* ABRAHAM BALDWIN on his fellow Framers in the House of Representatives, January 11, 1799[1]

> *The Declaration of Independence and the Constitution of the United States are parts of one consistent whole, founded upon one and the same theory of government.*
> JOHN QUINCY ADAMS, April 30, 1839[2]

MUCH HAS BEEN MADE in the twentieth century—much must be made—of economic interest, social status, and political ambition in explaining the Convention of 1787. Yet no explanation can have validity that does not also acknowledge the Framers as men of ideas, and give to ideas a leading place among the influences that shaped their behavior and decisions. If none of the Framers was a doctrinaire, almost all were men of doctrine, and doctrine scored a smashing victory in 1787 as it had in 1776. We must therefore sift through the intellectual baggage they carried with them to Philadelphia, for from the materials in this baggage they shaped their proposals for a new constitution of the United States.

Three points should be made as a preliminary to this survey of the ideas of the Framers, points perhaps most clearly made with the aid of the words "continuity," "consensus," and "constraint." By *continuity* I mean to say that the principles of 1787 were a projection of the principles of 1776, which in turn were the product of a hundred years of unbroken intellectual development, which in its turn was a consequence of two thousand years of theory and at least four hundred years of practice; by *consensus*, that these ideas were a kind of unforced but nevertheless ascendant "party line" to which the Framers subscribed in common with all but a handful of thinking men in America, from headstrong frontiersmen at one end of the spectrum of political sophistication to grave merchants at the other; and by *constraint*, that the shared principles of 1776 and 1787 set just as unbreachable limits on the range of possibilities at Philadelphia as did the dictates of time, place, and politics we have reviewed in Chapters 2 and 3.

Although a few of the Framers may have fancied themselves intellectual free agents "with full power . . . to form and establish the wisest and happiest government that human wisdom can contrive," [3] most were fully aware of these dictates of principle. Their awareness was not merely full; it was dutiful and contented. They, like all the men they represented or hoped to persuade, were happy prisoners of a political tradition that was the new Republic's most cherished worldly possession—and that for many citizens of the Republic had, in addition, an otherworldly source and sanction. They had no hope—what is more, they had no intention—of ignoring the commands of this tradition. Whatever sort of charter they were to come up with in Philadelphia, they expected to defend it as a faithful reflection of the ideas of the Revolution, which all of them agreed had been stated most forcefully in the Declaration of Independence, and a creative synthesis of the best previous efforts to convert these ideas into institutions, which most of them agreed had taken place in Massachusetts, Virginia, and New York.

The largest part of the intellectual baggage of the Framers, whether of stars like Madison, Mason, and Wilson or of bit-players like Richard Dobbs Spaight, Jared Ingersoll, and William Pierce, was a tempered version of the oldest and most famous of liberty-oriented political philosophies: the school of natural law and natural rights. Americans, remembering their origins and honoring their teachers, generally used the word "Whig" to identify this cluster of political and constitutional ideas. Emerging from the mists as far back as the Stoic masters of Cicero, rising again and again in the Dark and Middle Ages from the ashes of cynicism and despair, finding its most persuasive exposition in the English language in John Locke's second treatise *Of Civil Government* (1690), this philosophy had become the dominant political faith of the American colonies in the second quarter of the eighteenth century. A thousand pulpits thundered with its benevolent principles; a hundred editors filled their pages with its famous slogans; the men of thirteen assemblies spent the better part of each legislative year cannonading at each other and at the agents of the Crown with appeals to the law of nature and the rights of man. At every stage of the Revolution—protest in 1765, resistance in 1774, rebellion in 1775, the strike for indepen-

dence in 1776, and the initiation of new governments between 1776 and 1780—the assumptions of natural law and
natural rights continued to govern the minds of men. In
George Mason's Declaration of Rights for Virginia, in John
Adams's Constitution for Massachusetts, and above all in
Thomas Jefferson's Declaration of Independence for the Republic, the principles of Whiggery flowered into a consensus
of ideas that compelled the allegiance of every politically
minded American, and compelled it principally because they
expressed so majestically the best political experiences of both
the colonial period and the Revolution. The political ideas of
the Framers met the test of theory, for they seemed clear, ordered, and altogether self-evident to reasonable men; they
had also met the test of practice, for they seemed to have
"worked," and worked surprisingly well, in teaching Americans how to govern themselves, in helping them to dissolve
the old connection with the mother country, and in solving at
least some of the stupefying problems of life as a "separate
and equal" nation among the nations of the earth.

The key ideas in the consensus of political thought in the
new Republic were essentially these:[4]

The political and social world is governed by laws as certain and universal as those which govern the physical world.
Whether direct commands of God, necessities of nature, or
simply hard lessons of history, these laws have established a
moral order that men ignore or violate at their peril.

The chief means through which men come to understand
these laws are the mutually enriching techniques of reason
and experience.

The law of nature (the generic title covering all these
laws) is a set of moral standards governing private conduct, a
system of abstract justice to which the laws of men should
conform, a line of demarcation around the permissible sphere
of political authority, and the grand source of natural rights.

The law of nature is essentially a call to reasoned, moral
action on the part of men as individuals and government as
their servant. To men and nations that obey this law come
happiness and prosperity; to men and nations that defy it
come sadness and adversity.

The nature of man, which is an expression of the law of
nature, is a durable mixture of ennobling excellencies and degrading imperfections. Man's "good" qualities, which need all
the support they can get from education, religion, and government, are sociability, reasonableness, generosity, and the
love of liberty; his "bad" qualities, which flourish quite unaided, are selfishness, passion, greed, and corruptibility.

Many things can corrupt a man, but none more drastically than the taste and touch of political power.

The nature of man is such as to make free government possible but far from inevitable.

The natural state of man is one of freedom and equality. Men may be endowed in grossly different degrees in talents, intelligence, and virtue, but to this extent at least they are fully equal: no man has any natural right of dominion over any other; every man is free in the sight of God and in the plan of nature.

The rights of man flow from the law of nature itself, and as such are natural, unalienable, and essential to meaningful existence.

The greatest of these rights are: the right to life, which carries with it the power of self-preservation; the right to liberty, to act as one pleases without external restraint; the right to property, to use and dispose of the fruits of honest industry; the right to happiness, or at least to pursue it on equal terms with other men; and the right to a free conscience, to reach out for God without the permission or even help of any other man.

In the good society these natural rights are recognized and protected by law, and thus take on the character of civil and constitutional rights.

The origin of government—that is to say, legitimate government—is a compact or contract among equal men, who pledge allegiance and obedience in return for protection of their natural rights and peace in harvesting the fruits of their labors. Sovereignty rests, if it rests anywhere at all, in the body of the whole people.

The basis of government is therefore the consent of the governed. The most valid obligation to obey the law is self-obligation.

The essence of government is trust. Those who are chosen to govern must remember that they act, whether by the terms of the contract or of the law of nature itself, as servants and never as masters of the governed.

The purpose of government is to protect men in the enjoyment of their natural rights, secure their persons and property against violence, remove obstructions to their pursuit of happiness, help them to live virtuous and useful lives, adjust the complexity of their social relations, and in general fill those limited but essential collective needs that they cannot fill as individuals or in families.

The nature of government, like the nature of man, is a mixture of good and bad—"good" because it has been ordained by the law of nature to serve some of the most basic needs of men, "bad" because it can always get out of hand and turn arbitrary, corrupt, wicked, and oppressive.

The great task of political science is to devise a form of government that will not get out of hand, but will serve as a protecting and civilizing agency for the men who have consented to obey it.

The best form that has ever been devised or even imagined is republican government, which is to say popular, representative, responsible, and non-hereditary.

Even the most stable and benevolent of such governments, however, must be kept under constant surveillance, since the corrupting effects of political power can be controlled but never banished.

Against any government the people retain the right of resistance as a last refuge. This right is to be exercised only under overriding compulsion, when the terms of the contract have been so grossly flouted as to dissolve all pledges of obedience. The people have a solemn duty to be peaceful and law-abiding as long as possible, to temper their methods to the nature and degree of oppression, and to aim steadily at the formation of a new contract.

Finally, it takes more than a perfect plan of government to preserve that state of ordered liberty which is the mark of the good society. Something else is needed, some quality of mind and heart diffused among the people to strengthen the urge to peaceful obedience and among their governors to keep them from sliding into corruption. In a republic that "something else" is, quite simply, public and private morality. Free government rests at bottom on the moral basis of decent, brave, honest, liberty-loving, industrious, patriotic men. Such men are the raw materials of free government, and there must be enough of them in every society to overcome the obstinate forces of dishonor, unreason, sloth, and cruelty.

To this consensus of political thought was attached a consensus of constitutional thought, whose key ideas were calculated to produce the best of all possible republican governments:

Government must be plain, simple, and intelligible. The common sense of a reasonably educated man should be able to comprehend its structure and functioning.

Government must be limited—in purpose, reach, methods, and duration.

Government must be kept as near to the people as possible through frequent elections and provisions for rotation-in-office.

Government must be constitutional, an empire of laws and

not of men in which the discretion of all those in power is reduced to the lowest level consistent with effective operation of the political machinery, and in which the majority, in order to have its way in matters both great and small, must prove itself persistent, undoubted, knowledgeable, and sober.

Constitutionalism calls for a written constitution, a known law superior to the acts or decrees of any officer or organ of government.

It also calls for inclusion in the constitution of a specific declaration of natural and civil rights.

The best of all possible constitutions will have three claims to obedience and even veneration: it will be the command of the people, an original contract based on their sovereign will; it will be the handiwork of the wisest men in the community; and it will be an earthly rendering, imperfect but well-intentioned, of the enduring principles of the law of nature.

The one agency essential to republican government is a representative legislature. Its basic function is to act as an instrument of consent through which the people tax and restrict themselves.

The fact of legislative primacy does not mean, however, that all authority should be lodged in the representative assembly. In those governments that are stable as well as republican the total sum of permissible power is divided among three branches: a legislature, preferably bicameral; an executive, preferably single; and a judiciary, necessarily independent.

These branches, in turn, are held in position by a system of checks and balances. Although divided government is something of a retreat from the ideal of simplicity, this form, which encourages rule by the sober majority, is most likely to strike the right balance between the urges of liberty and the needs of authority.

Finally, government in a republic is properly the concern of all those who have an enduring attachment to the community. The right to vote, as well as to hold office, should be limited to men who have a tangible "stake in society"—because only such men can make competent and uncorrupted judgments and because only they have the right to consent to laws that regulate the use of property.

Within the American consensus there were, to be sure, sharp differences of emphasis, especially over the application of these constitutional abstractions to concrete problems of governing free men. In the course of the Revolution seventeen constitutions were written in the eleven states and one quasi-state (Vermont) that needed new rules—a remarkable achievement for a people beset by disorder, violence, and uncertainty about the future. Even more remarkable, most of these constitutions worked better than the ill-wishers (and many well-wishers) of American independence had expected in 1776, and a few—notably the Virginia Constitution of 1776, the New York Constitution of 1777, and the Massachusetts Constitution of 1779–1780—worked as well as any political systems in the world. Massachusetts (which New Hampshire then imitated) offered a startling preview of things to come in the history of American constitutionalism, for this most democratic and self-confident of states took the lead in bringing the body of citizens fully into the process of constitution-making: first, by creating a special instrument, the constitutional convention, to write a charter for the commonwealth; and second, by providing for popular ratification of the charter in the town meetings.

At the time of writing and later under the pressures of use, most of the state constitutions gave rise to lively disputes. These were, for the most part, political rather than theoretical in inspiration, for men in those days, like men in these, shaped their constitutional interpretations to their social, economic, and emotional ends. In the struggle for power in states like Maryland, Pennsylvania, and Massachusetts, conservatives and radicals (if we may use those dangerous descriptions for want of any that are more precise) agreed on such fundamentals in the American consensus as republicanism, declarations of rights, a strong legislature, the separation of powers, and some sort of property-owning or tax-paying qualification for political participation. Although their differences were those of men who spoke the same political and constitutional language, they were as real, let us say, as those of Webster and Calhoun, Lincoln and Jefferson Davis, or Franklin D. Roosevelt and George Sutherland.

In the first place, conservatives were more interested in divided and balanced government, radicals in the clear supremacy of the legislature. All said they favored an executive separate from the legislature, but they fell out over the questions of number, tenure, independence, qualifications, powers, and method of election. Radicals found comfort in the almost powerless office of governor in North Carolina and the many-headed executive council of Pennsylvania; conservatives found cheer in the rather stronger and more independent executives of New York and Massachusetts. Radicals were irritated by John Adams's prescription for an independent judiciary: appointment by governor and council, salaries "ascertained and established by law," and tenure for life. Conservatives considered this prescription a pillar of orderly government—which was, of course, a government in which men like themselves had the last word.

A second difference had to do with the precious doctrine of popular sovereignty, which conservatives preferred, for obvious reasons, to serve up garnished with "ifs" and "buts" and radicals were inclined, for obvious reasons, to accept at face value. A consistent radical thinker, not an easy man to find, favored suffrage for all men who paid taxes or bore arms, no property-owning qualifications for officeholding, elections of all officers, and short terms. A consistent conservative, a somewhat easier man to find, preferred a more restricted suffrage, high property-owning qualifications for officeholding, appointment of most officers, and longer terms.

Finally, the whole emphasis of conservatives was on government more complicated, delaying, and "high-toned" than the fairly simple scheme fixed in the minds of eager democrats. An instructive piece of evidence is the healthy difference of opinion between patriots like Franklin who rejoiced in the one-chamber legislatures of Pennsylvania and Vermont and patriots like John Adams who paled at the thought of a government without a senate. No upper house was more of a comfort to the gentry than the indirectly elected senate of Maryland.

The struggles for political power in the new states gave rise to a lusty literary debate over the pattern and purpose of government, yet never did the debaters lose touch with each other. While the distance was immense between conservative and radical in South Carolina or Pennsylvania, or between Carter Braxton's high-toned *Address to the Convention . . . of Virginia* (1776) and the anonymous New Hampshire egalitarian tract *The People the Best Governors,*[5] it was somehow the distance between men who stood at opposite edges of an unbroken plateau. Both the skeptical conservative at one edge and the sanguine radical at the other could look back at the great mass of American patriots in between, all of whom shared the same political ideas, perhaps four in five of whom shared the same constitutional ideas. In the exact center of this plateau, a consensus in himself, stood John Adams of Massachusetts. His pamphlet *Thoughts on Government,* published in Boston and Philadelphia in 1776 (a year of dissolution but also of creation),[6] was perhaps the most lucid statement of the American Whig philosophy of ordered liberty out of which the best of the new constitutions arose, and his constitution for Massachusetts, which he wrote in 1779, was the best of the best.[7] The message of both the pamphlet and the constitution about the polity was simply this: the great ends of the community, the protection of the liberty and property and the advancement of the welfare of the men who have consented to its rule, are most likely to be achieved under a government that is popular, republican, representative, divided, balanced, limited, responsible, and constitutional, and that is saturated in the spirit of public and private morality. John Adams, in his turn, had read this message in the whole history of the endless struggle for constitutional government, as well as in the evolution of "Whig principles" from Cicero to St. Thomas Aquinas to Richard Hooker to Locke to the preachers of New England.

By 1787 those men who demanded less mutability in the states and more authority at the center had refined the principles of American Whiggery into a philosophy almost perfectly designed for their purposes. These purposes, be it remembered, had shifted since 1776—from dissolution to consolidation, from destruction to creation, from rebellion against alien tyranny to domestication of native chaos—and their thoughts had shifted, too, in temper and emphasis if not in basic content. "Ordered liberty" had always been their grand goal for America, and they could hardly be blamed for concentrating their second thoughts on the search for order. Although they stood fast in devotion to every last teaching of the tradition of natural law and natural rights, they began to make room in their minds for assumptions and suspicions that almost no American had entertained in the first heady days of the Revolution. Although they continued to pledge their faith to such real or honorary Whigs as Locke, Sidney, Coke, Harrington, Cicero, Burlamaqui, Vattel, Montesquieu, and Pufendorf, not to forget that Tory instructor in Whig principles of law, Sir William Blackstone, they became slightly less uneasy in the presence of such hardheaded teachers of the facts of political life as Hobbes, Hume, and Machiavelli.

A vivid case in point is the redirection of American thinking about the nature of man. The legacy of Anglo-American Whiggery had always been ambiguous in this crucial matter. When a colonial thinker like Jonathan Mayhew sang a hymn to the goodness, rationality, and innate decency of men, he usually added a few cautionary lines about their weakness in the face of temptation and their fondness for power; and even so dedicated a man of the Revolution as Samuel Adams could often sound more like a spiritual descendant of John Calvin (which, of course, he was) than an intellectual descendant of John Locke (which he also was). By the middle of the 1780's the dark side of this legacy was much in evidence, and even warmhearted Whigs like Thomas

Jefferson (who was accused of many things in his life but never of Calvinism) were shaking their heads over the headstrong behavior of men who were supposed to know better but apparently never would. Other leading Americans, of whom John Adams, James Madison, and Alexander Hamilton were the most prominent, were in the meantime moving beyond both Locke and Calvin to seek new lessons about human behavior in their experience, and were finding that these lessons had already been confirmed in Adam Smith's *Theory of Moral Sentiments* and David Hume's *Treatise of Human Nature*. Although these tough-minded Americans continued to attach much importance to the everlasting tension in the nature of man between frail virtue and well-armed vice, they had also become interested in the political implications of such morally neutral "drives" as the need for security, the hope of gain, and the love of fame. Most of the Framers went into the Convention more tempered and sophisticated political psychologists than they had been in 1776.

The sobering effects of time and frustration gave rise to still other refinements in the American consensus as it was understood by Hamilton, Madison, and Adams. These men thought more clearly than Americans had ever thought before about the inevitable division of society into two or three classes. They paused more often in celebrating the rights of men to speculate about their "interests," and also to notice how self-interested individuals cluster together in "factions" as they struggle for gain, esteem, power, and security. And therefore, as the community-minded men they were, they revived and proclaimed the idea, one of the oldest in political philosophy, of "the public good." We cannot begin to understand the mind of a man like Washington unless we recognize his consuming belief in the existence of a common, enduring interest of the whole community that encompassed and yet rose above all private interests, that held out the hand of peace, order, and welfare to all men of all classes, and that provided the grand context of liberty, stability, and progress within which each man could pursue his own version of happiness. To the purposes of government that had always been acknowledged in the Whig tradition there now were added the hard tasks of controlling the play of factions, of regulating the "various and interfering interests" of men,[8] and of checking those "impulses" of individuals and groups that were clearly "unfriendly to the public good." [9]

The laissez-faire principles of Adam Smith were no part of the American consensus in 1787. The men who wrote the Constitution would have looked upon the "rugged individualism" of William Graham Sumner and his disciples as a silly ideology. Although they believed in the rights of man, and especially in the right of private property, they expected government to nourish these rights as well as to protect them. Although they might look askance at a central government that regulated private enterprise in the public interest, they expected the states and localities to be as active in the economic sphere as the public good might require. They were full of respect for the integrity of the individual, but they were also alert to the needs and services of the community.

This strategic withdrawal from exuberance to sobriety in the political thought of the 1780's was matched by a hardening of the lines against simple-minded radicalism in constitutional thought. The two great "evils of our republican system" identified by that model Whig George Mason on the floor of the Convention—"the danger of the majority oppressing the minority, and the mischievous influence of demagogues" [10]— were much on the minds of leading men in this period; and both seemed to them to flourish most luxuriantly in states whose constitutions had failed to provide guards against the known tendency of every legislature to draw all other offices and powers into its unappeasable "vortex." As Thomas Jefferson wrote in 1781 of his own Virginia, in words quoted with telling effect in 1787 and 1788:

> All the powers of government, legislative, executive, and judiciary, result in the legislative body. The concentrating these in the same hands is precisely the definition of despotic government. It will be no alleviation that these powers will be exercised by a plurality of hands, and not by a single one. 173 despots would surely be as oppressive as one. . . . As little will it avail us that they are chosen by ourselves. An *elective despotism* was not the government we fought for; but one which should not only be founded on free principles, but in which the powers of government should be so divided among several bodies of magistracy, as that no one could transcend their legal limits, without being effectually checked and restrained by the others. [11]

And as John Adams had written in 1776 in a letter to Richard Henry Lee:

> A legislative, an executive, and a judicial power comprehend the whole of what is meant and understood by government. It is by balancing each of these powers against the other two, that the efforts in human nature toward tyranny can alone be checked and restrained, and any degree of freedom preserved in the constitution. [12]

Fear of legislative tyranny, concern that the majority govern soberly and according to law, faith in the techniques of checking power with power—these were the major elements in the consensus of constitutional thought that enveloped the minds of the Framers. Whatever else they were thinking about "the science of politics" as they journeyed toward Philadelphia, they knew with Madison or suspected with Mason (the suspicion troubled Mason greatly) that the United States would never be governed well until it, too, like the most successful of the thirteen states, had a constitution of divided, checked, and balanced powers. The great philosophy of antiquity, the notable Whigs of England, the "celebrated Montesquieu" and the "judicious Locke" (as they read him), the institutional legacy of the colonial period, their own experience as legislators, judges, and administrators—all joined to persuade them that only such a constitution could secure the blessings of the treasure they held in common: "liberty, charming liberty." Once they had made the decision to have a national government, there was no other kind of constitution they could recommend in republican good faith to the American people. The very fact that the Articles of Confederation had failed to provide for the distribution and balancing of power was proof to many of them that Congress was not and never could be the government of a nation.

First, however, they would have to make that decision, and both the fear of centralized power and the jealousies among the states promised that it would be hard to make. Tradition and experience guided the Framers firmly to their choice of a *form* of government for the United States, but not to their choice of a *basis*. All thinking Americans agreed about the mixed nature of man, the primacy of ordered liberty, and the limited reach of government, and thus warmed (with varying degrees of enthusiasm) to the idea of checks and balances, but they did not agree—as Madison learned every time he talked to Patrick Henry—about the nature of the Union that had been declared "perpetual" in the Articles of Confederation. The range of choices was very large in 1787: one could advocate anything from a consolidation of the states to a dissolution of the Union without losing one's standing as a true Whig and a reasonable man. To be more specific, the Framers were faced with three conscious choices that might have some chance of success; and in the all too likely event of no success, at least two other courses seemed within the realm of possibility.

The first of the conscious choices was to preserve the confederate basis of government as outlined in the Articles, but to move the balance between incipient nation and self-willed states two or three degrees across the spectrum toward centralization by giving Congress real if limited powers to tax and to regulate trade, and by making the use of these powers somewhat less dependent on the voluntary cooperation of each state. This is essentially the solution that the fearful republicans—those who stayed home like George Clinton and those who came to Philadelphia like John Lansing—felt that Congress had intended to authorize in its resolution of February 21, 1787. The second was to abandon this basis and to strike boldly for a national system under which the states would be guaranteed existence but would no longer enjoy either the fact or attributes of sovereignty. This is essentially the solution to which Hamilton had come as early as 1781, and toward which Madison was moving in the early months of 1787 as he tried out his ideas in a series of letters to Washington, Jefferson, Edmund Pendleton, and Edmund Randolph.[13] The third, which no one had clearly in mind, yet which was to be the solution of the Convention, was some sort of cross between confederacy and consolidation that would produce a system never before tried, one that would, however, prove acceptable, workable, and enduring.

If this convention (and others that might subsequently be called) were to fail, if it were to make proposals for "revising" the Articles that were unacceptable or fall into a deadlock and make no proposals at all, the most likely outcome, some wise men predicted, would be a dissolution of the Republic into its three natural and historic parts. Each part would then have to make its own choice in its own time whether to be a loose confederacy or a strong union or something in between, and also whether to link up for defense with one or both of the other parts. As Madison wrote to Pendleton a few days after the resolution of February 21 about the possibility of a monarchy as a bitter end to all the troubles of the Republic:

> The bulk of the people will probably prefer the lesser evil of a partition of the Union into three more practicable and energetic governments. The latter idea I find after long confinement to individual speculations and private circles, is beginning to show itself in the newspapers.[14]

The trouble with this possibility, which fortunately never had to be faced, was that the jealousy and inertia that made it so difficult to form a "more perfect Union" in 1787 would have still been present in 1790 or 1800 to make it almost as difficult to form three more perfect unions in New England,

the Middle States, and the South. It is hard to imagine South
Carolina knuckling under to Virginia or Rhode Island to
Massachusetts, hard to guess in which direction Maryland or
New York would finally have decided to move, not at all ri-
diculous to conceive of New York City trying to have the
best of all possible worlds as a "free city" like Bremen or
Lübeck. It is very easy to imagine a condition of continuing
instability within each of these clusters of states and, thanks to
the rise of new states in the West, of growing hostility between the Middle States and the cluster on either side—all of
which may help to explain the sense of urgency that pro-
pelled nation-minded men to Philadelphia in 1787.

The next most likely outcome was for the Confederation
government to stumble along indefinitely, rousing itself to
common action if the British attempted to grab some of the
unsettled lands (or perhaps sent punitive raids against American seaports), but in general moving, as many a confederacy
has moved in history, from one mess to the next with just
enough energy to stay half-alive. Although it was fashionable
among the Framers and their supporters to say that Congress
was "at an end" and was headed for "anarchy and confusion"
unless a "remedy" were "soon applied," [15] there is much reason to believe that the Confederation could have spent several decades withering away.

Two other possibilities seem to have been so remote, at
least in retrospect, as never to have been possibilities at all.
One was total consolidation: the bringing of the whole of
America under one central government (and that government
under some kind of monarch), the breaking-up of the large
states into small and subordinate administrative units, and the
erasing of most state boundaries from the pattern of politics
and, over the long run, from the minds of men. Despite some
talk in the Convention about throwing all the states into
"hotchpotch," [16] no one could really imagine the extended
Republic, or even the original states, under one government
like that of France. And despite General Knox's impassioned
advice to Rufus King about how to deal with the state
governments—"Smite them in the name of God and the
people" [17]—no plan that did more than restrain them politely
was worth laying before the people. To repeat a point made
in Chapter 2, the states were indestructible, considerably
more indestructible than the Union. Moreover, even if they
could have been destroyed as political entities by conquest
and the passage of time, the regions of America—two, three,
five, or even more, depending upon the fancy of the observer
—would have remained behind as facts of demography.

The other impossible possibility was total fission, the disintegration of the Union into not three but thirteen (and perhaps even more) sovereignties; and in this instance, too, men who dabbled in the thought were prisoners of an illusion. To repeat another point from Chapter 2, the states were always states and never anything more. A few like Virginia and New York might have made a good try at going it alone, but sooner or later their exposed situation, the jealousies or needs of neighbors, and the memory of the Union that had fought the Revolution would have forced them into close association with other states. If New England could form "a firm and perpetual league of friendship and amity," "mutual advice and succor," and "mutual safety and welfare" in 1643,[18] New England could hardly have done less, if forced back on its own devices, 150 years later.

In the incipient nation of 1787 the choices of the basis for a new government were clearly more numerous than the choices of the form. Whatever government the Framers might propose to the people, it would certainly have to be republican and almost certainly have to be divided, checked, and balanced—not because Montesquieu or John Adams had taught them to celebrate the beauties of such government but because this was the pattern toward which America had been moving from the beginning. But whether this government would be confederate, national, or something in between was a question left open for the clash of wills to resolve. Having inherited the sticky problem of imperial organization from the British in 1776, the Americans were now being offered one more chance to find the solution that had been eluding them ever since. They found that solution, as John Quincy Adams was to exult years later, by forming "their social compact upon principles never before attempted on earth." [19]

Yet even here, in the tricky process of putting together a new kind of federal system, the Framers worked with inherited materials to produce a result that was a continuity rather than a break with the past. They demonstrated their ingenuity as founders of a commonwealth chiefly by making the shrewdest possible selection of familiar techniques and institutions, and by making it with suitably mixed feelings of reverence for the past and concern for the future. Animated by an enduring devotion to the self-evident truths of the Declaration, sobered by the lessons of a decade of self-government under the pressures of social disorder, the Framers now summoned the twin guides of all good Whigs, reason and experience, to lead them to the policy of ordered liberty. Like the English masters of the school of natural law and natural rights, they denied the inevitability of conflict between these two ways of knowing and deciding. When they appealed to reason (of which these practical men also had more than their share), they meant tested reason—reason applied within the limits of history, facts, and human nature. When they appealed to experience (of which these practical men also had more than their share), they meant digested experience—experience appraised with the aid of critical intelligence. For the statesmen-philosophers of 1787, experience was the proof of reason and reason the interpreter of experience, and together they were the highest source of political wisdom.

# II

## Men

## 5  THE MEN OF THE NORTH

*He had himself, he said, prejudices against the
eastern states before he came here, but would acknowledge that he had found them as liberal and
candid as any men whatever.*
GENERAL CHARLES COTESWORTH PINCKNEY
to the Convention, as reported by Madison,
August 29, 1787[1]

ON THE "second Monday in May next"—May 14, 1787—a
dozen to fifteen men walked into the State House in Philadelphia to begin the great work of "rendering the federal constitution adequate to the exigencies of government and the
preservation of the Union." Since the delegations of only two
states—Pennsylvania and Virginia—were present in force,
nothing could be done this day except to agree informally to
check in each morning until five more delegations were on
hand. Not until Friday, May 25, was a quorum of seven
states present, and not until the following Tuesday did the
"main business" of the Convention get under way.[2]

While this two-week delay is said to have soured the temper of some of "the punctual members" who did not "like to
idle away their time," [3] most of them were quietly confident
that the Convention, although it might have an uncertain
ending, would have a certain beginning. They knew from experience that meetings of this kind never started on schedule,
and knew also that several parts of the country had been hit

hard by bad weather. They could see with their own eyes that
General Washington had come to do his duty. The news that
he had been welcomed by the citizens of Philadelphia with
shouts, salutes, and bells was a summons to the tardy to come
and do theirs. And they could read in Mr. Dunlap's *Pennsylvania Packet,* delivered daily to the best boardinghouses, the
names of other gentlemen like themselves who were reported
to be on the way to Philadelphia.

Let us put ourselves in the place of one of "the punctual
members" and scan the list of delegates to what was already
being called, even before a quorum could be counted or a
vote taken, "this august body."[4] The only hindsight we shall
exercise is the knowledge of exactly which men were finally
to appear in Philadelphia. Otherwise we see the delegates as
they were seen in early May of 1787, when the enduring reputations of most were still in the making, when the victories
and tragedies of later years could not even be imagined. We
see them as men, as discrete individuals who had already
demonstrated, each in his own way, the importance of will
and nerve in history; and we see them as delegates, as instructed members of one or another of twelve separate teams
that represented one or another of twelve "sovereign, free
and independent" states. The organizing category of the
Convention, as it was of Congress and had always been of
American continental politics, was the state, the dubious
pygmy like Delaware along with the illustrious giant like Virginia. One who studies the Philadelphia Convention must
never forget, no matter how impressed he may be by the performance of individuals or by the special quality of the whole
body, that this was first and foremost a gathering of states.
Each delegation was elected by the legislature of its state;
each cast one vote as a state; each reported back to a state
that held in its own stubborn keeping the power to approve
or spurn the handiwork of the Convention.

We begin this survey in the North, and we do it out of
habit, not pride or prejudice. In most listings of the delegates
in the eighty newspapers of America—and, most important,
in all votes in the Convention itself—New Hampshire came
first and Georgia last, with Massachusetts, Connecticut, New
York, New Jersey, Pennsylvania, Delaware, Maryland, Virginia, North Carolina, and South Carolina in between and in
that order. This is exactly the course along which the gaze of
our punctual member would have traveled, even if his name
were Pinckney or Mason, and in the next three chapters we
will show deference to the custom of the age.

New Hampshire (141,727 and 158 slaves),* an admirable but hardly distinguished state, elected an admirable but hardly distinguished delegation of four men, two of whom— John Pickering of Portsmouth and Benjamin West of Charlestown—never left home. As a matter of significant fact, the two Framers from New Hampshire, John Langdon of Portsmouth and Nicholas Gilman of Exeter, did not get to Philadelphia themselves until July 23, and then only because Langdon had been anxious, irritated, and patriotic enough to pay the expenses of the delegation out of his own pocket. He and Gilman, along with Pierce Long and John Sparhawk of Portsmouth, had been elected delegates as far back as January 17, but neither then nor in a second election on June 27 did the legislature sweeten its commission with a little hard coin or even a letter of credit. New Hampshire was a poor state, but not all that poor; times were hard, but not all that hard; and it seems clear that inertia, isolation, suspicion, and apathy, which were obstacles to the hopes of nationalists in almost every state, came close to a demoralizing victory in this instance.

In the end, New Hampshire showed up and was counted because the two most prominent men in the state, each the head of his own political faction, agreed that the central government was in need of an overhaul. One was General John Sullivan, who had come to this conclusion as far back as 1780. A strong nationalist who had won continental fame in his fierce expedition against the Six Nations in 1779, Sullivan was now in his second term as president of the state, and would almost certainly have journeyed to Philadelphia except for this responsibility. The other was Langdon, who had come to this conclusion only after a long bout of mild anti-nationalism. Langdon had defeated Sullivan for the presidency in 1785, then lost to him in both 1786 and 1787. By June of this last year the one big thing that united these two powerful men was clearly more important than the many small things that divided them.

So far as one can tell, Langdon became a nationalist and went to Philadelphia to vote the right way for two reasons: he was the leading merchant of a famous port that depended for its livelihood on trade with ports all over the world, many of which were still not open to ships of the new Republic; and he had agreed to be the agent in Portsmouth for that engine of union, the Bank of North America, and that outrider of

---

* The population figures for each state are taken from the first census of 1790. Estimates voiced or assumed in the Convention were generally on the short side, especially in the cases of New York and North Carolina.

nationalism, Robert Morris. John Langdon was a man whom Morris could like and trust. Born in Portsmouth in 1741 of prosperous farming stock (the youngest of nine sons), he had gone down to the sea in ships, learned every aspect of the merchant's trade, and become a pillar of his community while still a young man.

The Revolution was the making of Langdon in more ways than one. As perpetrator of an attack on the British fort in Portsmouth in 1774, mobilizer of General Stark's expedition against Burgoyne, commander of a detachment of troops in the Rhode Island campaign, and agent for continental prizes in New Hampshire, he was a dedicated and effective patriot; and as member of the New Hampshire senate, speaker of its house, delegate to all its constitutional conventions, and delegate to Congress, he was an equally dedicated and effective politician. First of all, however, he was a model of that famous breed, the New England merchant. His pluck and luck in the war made him rich from privateering and blockade-running, even richer in the 1780's from sending ships to the French West Indies full of lumber and livestock and welcoming them home to Portsmouth full of sugar and rum. He was, it has been estimated, the third largest holder of public securities among all the Framers. Affable, handsome, a good liver and a gracious entertainer, Langdon was a man of whom New Hampshire could be proud. While he reciprocated this feeling of pride in full measure he was not blind to the fact that the future of his doughty state was bound up closely with the cause of union.

In experience, wealth, power, and stature, Nicholas Gilman was bound to suffer by comparison with Langdon. Indeed, it is hard to understand why he rather than any one of a dozen other more experienced men like Josiah Bartlett and Samuel Livermore should have been set upon this road to glory, and certainly his older brother John Taylor Gilman, who was then serving as state treasurer, would have cut a more useful figure in Philadelphia. Perhaps it was because he was friendly to Sullivan, and had given him welcome support during the paper-money riots of 1786; perhaps it was simply because he was willing to go, which was true, after all, of almost no one else in New Hampshire. In any case, he was a Gilman, and that meant a great deal in New Hampshire if not in Philadelphia. He was born in Exeter in 1755, worked from a young age in his father's general store, served faithfully as a staff officer during the Revolution, and at the end of the war—which he saw for himself at Yorktown—returned dutifully to his place behind the counter. When the store was sold in 1785, Gilman, now a man of means, went into politics and sat both in the New Hampshire senate and in Congress, of which he was a member (of the largely absent variety) in 1786 and 1787. Those who knew Gilman expected little of him except a voting record of which General Sullivan would approve.

The most remarkable feature of the delegation from proud Massachusetts (378,787) was the absence of most of her justly famous sons. John Adams was in London plying a dogged diplomacy for a feckless Congress and had to be represented in Philadelphia by the newly published first volume of his ponderous *Defense of the Constitutions of the United States of America*. Samuel Adams was in Boston growing old and had to be represented by his lively friend Elbridge Gerry. James Bowdoin had just paid for his own liveliness in suppressing the Shays Rebellion by losing the governorship to John Hancock, and Hancock was busy settling back into the routine of a job he had held five times before and loved dearly. William Cushing was chief justice, Nathan Dane was in Congress, and Henry Knox—whose views were quite unpopular—was in New York serving as Secretary of War. The elder Samuel Dexter was too old and the younger too young, as were a half-dozen other recent graduates of Harvard who were to make names for themselves in later years. Benjamin Lincoln, John Lowell, Theophilus Parsons, Fisher Ames, Theodore Sedgwick—each of these capable men, for one reason or another, was also passed over by the Massachusetts legislature. One of the world's two most productive nurseries of able politicians and lawyers, Massachusetts was the only state in the Union that could have squandered its resources so carelessly and still produced a respectable delegation.

Of the five men elected March 10 to represent Massachusetts, one—Judge Francis Dana of Cambridge—failed to honor his commission, probably because of ill health and the press of judicial business. Of the active delegation the senior member was Nathaniel Gorham of Charlestown, who was so full of good health as to appear "rather lusty" to William Pierce of Georgia.* The news of the election of this distinguished figure, who had just finished serving a term as President of Congress, must have comforted those nationalists like Madison and Hamilton who had been wondering whether the strife-torn state of Massachusetts would do its duty to the Union.

* Pierce's famous "sketches" of the Framers, as well as the thumbnail portraits of eminent Americans sent home in 1788 by Otto, the French chargé d'affaires, are not always trustworthy.[5] I have used them only when I could find independent confirmation of the judgments they expressed in letters and observations of the period.

Gorham, who celebrated his forty-ninth birthday on the road to Philadelphia, was the son of a packet-boat operator in Charlestown. Educated skimpily and then apprenticed at the age of fifteen as a mechanic in New London, he had become both a modestly successful merchant and a moderately useful politician by 1775, in which year most of his property was destroyed by British troops. Nothing daunted, Gorham, like John Langdon to the north, turned to privateering and other such activities, and he emerged from the war with enough money to live well and invest poorly. He emerged also with a wealth of experience as a public servant, which he had gained in a series of deliberative bodies ranging from the town meeting of his native Charlestown to the Congress of the United States. Having served in the old provincial legislature, the provincial congresses of 1774–1775, both houses of the legislature (including three years as speaker of the lower house), the convention of 1779–1780, the board of war, and the Middlesex court of common pleas, Gorham could feel that no mistake had been made in choosing him to speak in Philadelphia for Governor Bowdoin's brand of nationalism.

Another follower of Bowdoin, and thus also a man with decided leanings toward nationalism, was Caleb Strong of Northampton. Strong was the only delegate from Massachusetts who lived more than two miles from salt water, a fact that demonstrates what the nationalists thought of the back country and the back country of nationalism. The son of a tanner in Northampton, he had graduated from Harvard in 1764, and then, having survived a siege of smallpox that left him nearly blind, had read law with the great patriot of western Massachusetts, Joseph Hawley—rather, his father and sister had read Hawley's copy of Coke aloud to him. Admitted to the bar in 1772, he settled down to a comfortable practice, at the same time lending his talents to the public as selectman of Northampton, attorney for Hampshire County, member of first the lower and then the upper house of the state legislature, and delegate to the convention of 1779–1780, where he, along with Gorham, was a member of the drafting committee. He was not, however, an overly ambitious man, for he declined election to Congress in 1780 and appointment to the state bench in 1783. In manner, dress, and tastes, Strong was an old-fashioned son of New England—simple, sober, kind, and devout. He was a pillar of his church, and also a hard fighter for American independence. It was always a much debated question in Northampton whether Caleb Strong was more zealous as the leading light of the Hampshire Bible Society than he had been as a member of the town's committee of safety.

Few delegates to the Convention had more prestige throughout America than the third man of Massachusetts, the spare and dapper Elbridge Gerry of Marblehead, and none could have seemed more unclear in purpose and unpredictable in behavior as he jogged his way to Philadelphia. Gerry had background, for he was the son of a prominent merchant who had made a small fortune shipping dried cod and other delicacies to the West Indies. He had wealth, for he had inherited this fortune and increased it many times over. He had learning, for he had graduated from Harvard in 1762 and then had continued to read widely in the literature of Whiggery. Most of all, he had political experience at both the state and national levels, which gave him, in the revealing words of William Pierce, "a great degree of confidence." [6] As a follower of Samuel Adams in the heady days of agitation and resistance, he had served Massachusetts without stint as legislator, administrator, supplier, and mobilizer. His patriotism carried him to Congress in 1776, where he signed both the Declaration of Independence and the Articles of Confederation, took a leading part in debates and in committee work, and made himself an expert in the crucial areas of finance and fisheries.

Yet always Gerry was a man with a chip on his shoulder —and one who was tugged in too many directions to permit even his closest friends to guess what he might do in the situation of 1787. While he had built up a reputation as a tried-and-true republican who abhorred standing armies and wanted to have the Cincinnati abolished, he had also been heard to say unkind things about the political wisdom of ordinary men. While he was known to be a suspicious anti-nationalist, even in his happiest days in Congress, a number of pressures seemed to be driving him into the arms of his friend James Madison: he was by far the largest holder of continental securities in the Convention, and was also a major investor in western lands; the economy of his beloved Marblehead had suffered grievously because of British restrictions on trade with the West Indies; and, perhaps the largest worry of the moment on an always worried mind, he had been shaken by the news from western Massachusetts. If anyone deserved credit for driving Elbridge Gerry to Philadelphia, it was Daniel Shays and his riotous ways.

The last member of the delegation, Rufus King of Newburyport, was not much more predictable than Gerry. As recently as September, 1785, he and Gerry, then serving together in Congress, had responded to a resolution of the Massachusetts legislature recommending a convention for "revising and altering the Confederation" by sending home a letter that spoke of the dangers of "prematurity" and raised the specter of a "baleful aristocracy" determined to destroy republican institutions.[7] Yet King was still young, barely thirty-two on the day the Convention opened, and he was on the move to bigger and better things—financially, socially, and politically. Born in Scarborough, Maine, in 1755 of a farming and storekeeping family, he had spent the years of the Revolution studying at Harvard, soldiering on a part-time basis in Rhode Island, and reading law with the redoubtable Theophilus Parsons in Newburyport, where he began a rewarding but unexciting practice in 1780.

In 1784 King was elected to Congress, and, once having seen New York, he was never the same man again. He worked hard and intelligently as a member of important committees, helped to shape the Ordinances of 1785 and 1787, won a reputation as an orator of dash and conviction, and made friends with such other young men on the rise as Madison, Hamilton, and James Monroe. The most useful thing this handsome man did during his years in Congress, however, was to marry a young lady (and an only daughter) whose station in life was well above his own, and whose father was both rich and eminent. The young lady was Elizabeth Alsop, the father John Alsop—merchant, member of the first Continental Congress, president of the chamber of commerce in New York—and the pull of these two was so strong that by 1787, although even his closest friends probably did not know it, King was preparing to move to New York. He, too, had been troubled enough by the insurrection in Massachusetts to suppress serious doubts about the "legality" of the proposed convention; and, as he wrote to Gerry in February while both Congress and Massachusetts were trying to make up their minds, he was now ready to "coincide with this project." "Events are hurrying to a crisis," he warned in words that he must have heard a hundred times from Madison. "Prudent and sagacious men should be ready to seize the most favorable circumstances to establish a more permanent and vigorous government." [8] If Rufus King, a hitherto antinationalist follower of John Hancock, could think that, James Madison had reason to believe that the Convention might succeed after all.

While New Hampshire sent a half-willing delegation and Massachusetts an uncertain one, Rhode Island (67,877 and 948 slaves) sent no delegation at all. This small, proud, deeply divided, fiercely independent state had long been a thorn in the side of the Union because of its disdain and occasional defiance of Congress, as well as a scandal to its neighbors because of its riotous (and rather ingenious) excursions into the maze of paper money. To tell the truth, Rhode Island did not deserve more than one-tenth of the mud thrown in its direction, and at least some of its legendary cussedness was the natural posture of a community that had been taking abuse ever since Roger Williams paddled his canoe from Seekonk over to Providence.

For some months in early 1787 it seemed that Rhode Island, despite its truculent attitude toward the nationalist movement, might send a delegation to Philadelphia, if only to make trouble for the other delegations. Then, however, the two houses of the legislature fell into a deadlock over the decision, and by the time the Convention was fully under way, the other states were counting Rhode Island out. On May 28 the Convention took semiofficial notice of the missing state when it listened thoughtfully to a letter of good wishes from a number of leading merchants in Providence and Newport. Such men as John Brown, Nicholas Brown, Jabez Bowen, and Welcome Arnold—who had been rallied by the redoubtable General James Varnum—let it be known publicly that they deplored their state's failure to send delegates, hoped the "commercial interest" would not be made to suffer for the sins of the wicked, and looked forward to receiving recommendations of the Convention designed "to strengthen the Union, promote commerce, increase the power, and establish the credit of the United States." [9] A few weeks later Varnum himself wrote to Washington begging him not to forget that Rhode Island, too, had its share of solid merchants, professional gentlemen, and "respectable farmers and mechanics" who were working relentlessly to regain power from the "licentious" and to bring an end to "anarchy and confusion." [10] As for Washington and his fellow nationalists, they were probably just as glad that this capricious state would go unrepresented. Although they would have been happy to welcome Varnum and a couple of Browns, they knew that they were far more likely to get such turbulent spirits as David Howell and Jonathan Hazard. The *Massachusetts Centinel* summed up the feelings of most nationalists when it reported (and also, as was its wont, editorialized):

Twelve states will be represented in the grand federal convention, now sitting in Philadelphia.—*Rhode Island* is the delinquent state—but . . . this is a circumstance far *more joyous than grievous;* for her delinquency will not be permitted to defeat the salutary object of this body, and her deputation, if, as is supposeable, they should have been *birds of feather* with the majority of her present administration, must have been the cause of much mortification to the illustrious characters who now compose that assembly, and must have reflected discredit on its proceedings.[11]

And that, it was hoped, took care of Rhode Island.

Connecticut (235,182 and 2,764 slaves), a state that had never been accused of rushing headlong into the unknown, did not choose a delegation until May 10; but when the names of its three representatives were published in Philadelphia May 17, it must have been obvious to all that "the land of steady habits" meant business. Dr. William Samuel Johnson of Stratford, Mayor Roger Sherman of New Haven, and Judge Oliver Ellsworth of Windsor and Hartford were as prominent, experienced, and shrewd a team as the state could have mustered. Although a good many notables had been left behind to "mind the store"—among them Governor Samuel Huntington, General Jedediah Huntington, Judge Richard Law, Matthew Griswold, William Williams, and a sprinkling of Wadsworths, Davenports, Trumbulls, and Wolcotts—Connecticut had plainly decided to put its best foot forward.

Johnson was the nearest thing to an aristocrat in mind and manner that Connecticut had managed to produce in its 150 years. As the son of a learned and pious Anglican clergyman who became the first president of King's College (Columbia), he got a headstart toward learning that carried him through both Yale (B.A., 1744) and Harvard (M.A., 1747) to a solid reputation as one of the leading "classics" of the colonies. Although his father intended him for the ministry, and although he dabbled in theology all his life, Johnson made his choice as a young man for the bar of Connecticut, of which, when he concentrated his attention on wealthy clients, he was recognized as one of the most distinguished members. More often than not, however, he let the clients go to other lawyers. Independently wealthy, thanks to a substantial inheritance and a handsome marriage, he was more interested in making a life than a living, and the life, much of which was spent in a gracious house on the great road between Boston and New York, was one of culture and comfort.

An unadventurous man with strong friendships among the more conservative and loyal circles of Connecticut society, Johnson was nevertheless so disturbed by British policy in 1765 that he accepted a place in Connecticut's delegation to the Stamp Act Congress. During the next four years he was the colony's agent in England, where he won the friendship of Franklin, a D.C.L. from Oxford, and the praise of *the* Dr. Johnson. Returning home in 1771, he found himself unable to keep pace with the progress of patriotic sentiment. Fearful of the consequences, he declined an appointment to the first Continental Congress. The coming of war drove him into a sort of semi-retirement, a no man's land between patriotism and loyalism from which he was several times lured to perform small services for his community—and once, in 1779, rudely pried loose to take a forced oath of fidelity to the patriotic cause. Having lost a good deal of his property, he then became more active as a lawyer than he had been in many years.

Despite this record of equivocation, Johnson could never quite be branded a Tory, and the men who knew him best showed what they thought of him in 1784 by sending him, despite his independence of all factional politics, to Congress in the Connecticut delegation. There, especially after Congress had moved to New York, he continued to make friends easily with his sweet and gentle manner, and there he succumbed to a temptation that comes sooner or later to most learned men of his caliber: on May 21, 1787, as he was on his way to the Convention, the trustees of Columbia announced his appointment as president of the college.

It must have been hard for some southern gentlemen in the Convention to believe that two men as different as William Samuel Johnson and Roger Sherman came from the same state; yet, as those who had traveled in New England could testify, Sherman was a more typical product of the area and its culture than was the urbane lawyer-scholar of Stratford. If any one man among the Framers represented the virtues and limitations of the Yankee way of life, it was this pious, canny, honest, ungainly, slightly comical jack-of-all-trades from New Haven. Born in Massachusetts in 1721 of a farming family of humble station, Sherman trudged with tools in hand to New Milford, Connecticut, in 1743, and there made his own way up in the world by trying his hand at everything from farming and cobbling to surveying and storekeeping. A publisher of almanacs, a self-taught lawyer, and a citizen who thought nothing of holding four or five public offices at the same time, Sherman was a man of considerable standing by the time he finally settled in New Haven in 1761. He served Yale so well as treasurer and, in effect, proprietor of the campus book store that he was awarded an honorary M.A. in 1768, the colony so well that it sent him along with Joseph Trumbull, Silas Deane, and others as a delegate to the first Continental Congress, and then kept sending him back year after year. He served with Jefferson, John Adams, Franklin, and R. R. Livingston on the drafting committee of the Declaration of Independence, which he signed with prayerful fervor; he served with John Dickinson, R. R. Livingston, Edward Rutledge, Samuel Adams, Stephen Hopkins, and others on the drafting committee of the Articles of Confederation, which were his idea of a proper government for America. His devotion to public business, his patriotic investment in state and continental securities, and his solicitude for a large and importunate brood of children brought him to the edge of insolvency in the 1780's, yet he managed somehow to stay afloat.

As a mild anti-nationalist, Sherman provided balance against the other two men, both mild nationalists, in the Connecticut delegation. Indeed, he was a source of some concern to those who hoped for a clean break with the feckless Confederation. One of the strongest of Connecticut nationalists, Jeremiah Wadsworth of Hartford, wrote to Rufus King, June 3, 1787:

> I am satisfied with the appointment—except Sherman, who, I am told, is disposed to patch up the old scheme of government. This was not my opinion of him, when we chose him: he is cunning as the Devil, and if you attack him, you ought to know him well; he is not easily managed, but if he suspects you are trying to take him in, you may as well catch an eel by the tail.[12]

The syntax of Wadsworth's letter may have been muddy, but the message was clear: Roger Sherman was a man to watch. William Pierce was only one of the southern delegates who watched him in wonder, pronouncing him "grotesque and laughable, indeed the oddest shaped character I ever remember to have met with," then adding quickly: "Yet he deserves infinite praise—no man has a better heart or clearer head." [13]

Although the third man from Connecticut, Oliver Ellsworth, had less gravity and learning than Johnson and less experience and common sense than Sherman, he was expected to make a steady member of this notable team. Ellsworth, the son of a respected family of Windsor, had graduated from the College of New Jersey (Princeton) in 1776, having gone there with his father's approval after two unhappy years at Yale. Then, after a hard bout with theology and schoolteaching in New Britain, he had turned to the law, and had begun to practice in 1771. The law was not at first kind to Ellsworth, who was reduced at one point to chopping wood in order to supplement a meager income. A marriage to a Wolcott, a move of his office to Hartford, and a strenuous application to business soon brought him a reputation as one of the "mighties" of the Connecticut bar.

Throughout the Revolution Ellsworth served his state faithfully as both legislator and administrator, and in the course of six years as a delegate to Congress he worked hand-in-hand with men like Madison and Hamilton to keep the Union, which he cherished more fondly than most citizens of self-contained Connecticut, from withering away. His real loves, however, were business and the bench. Even in his most active days as lawyer and officeholder, his hand was in a variety of ventures, most of them small and only modestly rewarding. By 1785 Ellsworth had done well enough in business and in his law practice to accept an appointment to the superior court of Connecticut. Service on the council of his state and on the Court of Appeals of Congress had prepared him well for judicial life, and he was widely respected for the fairness and logic of his opinions. A tall, neat, commanding figure, Ellsworth had two eccentric habits that his friends had never quite learned to live with: he talked to himself constantly and with relish, and he was, according to reliable witnesses, the largest single consumer of snuff in the United States.

New York (318,796 and 21,324 slaves) harbored perhaps the most distinguished group of dedicated nationalists in the Union in 1787. General Philip Schuyler, Secretary John Jay, Alexander Hamilton, James Duane, R. R. Livingston, Philip Livingston, Egbert Benson, John Sloss Hobart, and William Duer were men of standing whose fondest hopes for the Republic—and for their fortunes in it—were caught up in the movement for a stronger national government. The only trouble was that their influence within the state was no match for their standing outside it. Political power in New York throughout the 1780's lay with a dominant faction mustered around the doughty person of Governor George Clinton; and for a dozen reasons—ranging from an enduring anger with a Congress that would not support New York's claim to Vermont to a growing confidence that this state had the best chance of any to "go it alone" (and go it handsomely at the expense of its neighbors)—the Clintonians had turned stoutly anti-nationalist. No one would have been surprised if New York, like Rhode Island, had decided to ignore the Convention. In the end, Clinton was just enough unsure of his own mind to let a delegation be named February 28, but its composition was an announcement to the other states that New York would not be a party to any radical change in the Articles of Confederation. Three men made up the strangest of

all delegations to Philadelphia: two confirmed anti-nationalists whom Clinton could trust not to be led astray, Robert
Yates and John Lansing, jr., of Albany, and the most zealous
of nationalists, Alexander Hamilton of New York, whom
General Schuyler, a solicitous father-in-law, managed to
squeeze onto the list as part of a complicated political bargain.

Since 1777, when he had given up a rewarding practice in
Albany in exchange for security and dignity, Yates had been
a judge of the supreme court of New York. Born in 1738
into an old and well-connected upstate family, he had been
given a solid classical education in New York City and then
had read law in the office of the famous William Livingston.
He had taken a useful part in the work of the state's committee of safety during the Revolution, and had also been a
member of the committee of thirteen which, under the leadership of John Jay, had drafted the New York Constitution
of 1777. In general, however, Yates was not a man of much
distinction, and it is hard to say why Clinton chose him,
rather than a more colorful figure like General John Lamb or
a more solid one like Melancton Smith, to carry New York's
defiant colors at the Convention. As for Clinton himself, he
was doubtless glad to plead the pressure of official responsibility, and thus to avoid any unpleasantness in Philadelphia
—for example a baleful look from his old friend General
Washington or a passage-at-arms with his new enemy Colonel
Hamilton.

Lansing was a more understandable choice, for, although
he was only thirty-three at the time of the Convention, he
had already become speaker of the assembly and mayor of
Albany. A wealthy man who owned forty thousand acres of
land in Schoharie County, he had connections throughout the
New York aristocracy. He had studied law with Yates and
James Duane, acted as military secretary to General Schuyler
in 1776–1777, and served with Egbert Benson in New York's
delegation to Congress in 1784–1785. Lansing was, according
to those who knew him best, a kind, pleasant, and handsome
man whose hospitable estate in Lansingburgh was a magnet
for gentlemen of good taste and good cheer regardless of
their politics. Most of all, he was known with Yates as a man
on whom George Clinton could depend for vigilant obstinacy
in behalf of New York's policy of independent anti-nationalism.

If Yates and Lansing had not been trustworthy at any distance from Albany and under any sort of pressure, Governor
Clinton would never have agreed to let Alexander Hamilton
go to Philadelphia, especially since Hamilton had done everything in his power—and was still doing it in mid-April—to

get two more nationalists like Jay and Duane added to the delegation. Hamilton was, of course, one of the prodigies of America, a man of style, skill, ambition, and energy who had risen in just thirty-two years from obscure and star-crossed origins in the West Indies to a continental reputation in the new Republic. A student at Columbia at the outbreak of resistance to England and a patriot already known for his dazzling pamphleteering in the American cause, Hamilton marched off to war without his degree at the head of a company of artillery. Taken onto Washington's staff in 1778, he served the commander in chief faithfully until February, 1781, when, his itch for military glory having gone too long unscratched, he brought about an uncivil break with his patron. Yet somehow he persuaded Washington to give him the command for which he longed, and he was there, a child of destiny, to storm the last redoubt at Yorktown. Having also crossed the Delaware and frozen at Valley Forge, he had reason to think—although he never boasted of the fact—that he had known the glories and agonies of the fighting Revolution as had few other men of his years.

After Yorktown Hamilton turned to the study of law, and by 1787, thanks to a brilliant mind and a network of useful connections (of which the most useful and also tender was that with his wife, the former Elizabeth Schuyler), he was an acknowledged leader of the most talent-laden bar in the United States. Almost from the beginning of his post-war career, however, he had been more interested in public service than in private affluence, and an active year in Congress (1782–1783) persuaded him, not that he needed much persuading, that he could be as successful in politics as he was fast becoming in the law.

From first to last, from his prophetic letter to Duane in September, 1780, to his election to the New York delegation in February, 1787, Hamilton was an uncompromising nationalist, and everyone knew that he was coming to Philadelphia to throw all his talent and charm into the cause of a permissive charter for a sovereign nation. His pamphleteering as The Continentalist in 1781–1782, his labors for Robert Morris as receiver of continental taxes in New York, his devoted service in Congress, his soaring argument for the supremacy of the Union in *Rutgers* v. *Waddington* (1784), his clever stroke at Annapolis, and above all his refusal to permit New York to ignore the summons that he had himself written —all these actions proved a fierce and unusually disinterested commitment to the American nation. Few men, indeed, could have been more likely than Hamilton to find glory in Philadelphia in 1787. Yet there was something ominous to his many friends in the fact that he was condemned to be a minority of one in the most openly anti-nationalist of delegations.

Taken all in all, the twelve men of New England and New York were a sight neither to gladden nor dampen the spirits of nationalists in other states. Although John Adams and John Jay would be missed, and although New York promised trouble immediately and Rhode Island in the future, Madison and Washington could take satisfaction in the knowledge that such figures as Langdon, Gorham, Johnson, Ellsworth, and Hamilton had been elected to join with them on the fateful occasion now about to unfold.

# 6 THE MEN OF THE MIDDLE STATES

*Our harvests are plenty, our produce fetches a high price in hard money, and there is in every part of our country incontestible marks of public felicity. We discover, indeed, some errors in our general and particular constitutions; which it is no wonder they should have, the time in which they were formed being considered. But these we shall mend.*

FRANKLIN tO EDWARD BANCROFT,
November 26, 1786[1]

THE STATES nearest to the scene of the Convention sent larger delegations than those from distant, thrifty, and somewhat suspicious New England. New Jersey, for example, with a population considerably smaller than that of Connecticut (172,716 and 11,423 slaves), named five delegates who got to Philadelphia (William Livingston, David Brearly, William Paterson, William Churchill Houston, and Jonathan Dayton) and two others who did not (Abraham Clark and John Neilson). No state had more to gain than New Jersey—described in a familiar metaphor as "a keg tapped at both ends"—from a strengthened central government. The fact that it was the first to name its delegation, acting a full three months before the Congressional resolution of February 21, shows the eagerness of all factions and sections of this peculiarly disadvantaged state. The delegation could have been the most distinguished from any of the small states if President Witherspoon of Princeton, a signer of the Declaration of Independence, and Elias Boudinot, New Jersey's only President of Congress, had not taken themselves out of public life after the Revolution. Nevertheless, it was a group of "commissioners" of which the state could be proud.

The leader of the delegation was the leader of the state, the celebrated William Livingston of Elizabeth, who had served continuously as governor ever since 1776, and whose relentless activities in the Revolution had led a Tory newspaper in New York to salute him derisively, and of course to the delight of his larger following, as "Don Quixote of the Jerseys." (He was also known as "Old Flint," because of his rugged concern for political and religious liberty, and "the Whipping Post," because of his astonishing thinness.) Born in Albany in 1723 into one of America's great families, Livingston was educated at home, among the Mohawks (with whom he lived a year as a youth), at Yale (B.A., 1741), and in the law office of the famous James Alexander in New York City, where he was admitted to the bar in 1748. Successful lawyer, hell-raising politician, eloquent pamphleteer, tart-voiced controversialist, and better-than-average poet, Livingston was probably the most complete Whig in the American colonies, and the royal governors and Anglican ministers of New York must often have wondered how any one man could combine such democratic urges with such an aristocratic bearing.

Wearying of it all in 1772, Livingston retired to lead the life of a gentleman farmer on an estate in New Jersey, which he named Liberty Hall. The coming of the Revolution swept him back into active politics. A delegate to the first and second Continental Congresses, he left Philadelphia just before the adoption of the Declaration of Independence to take command of the New Jersey militia. He was not, however, cut out to be a soldier, and he was happy to move soon thereafter into the newly created governorship. Although as a younger son he had inherited virtually none of his family's wealth, and although he lost a good deal of property to the fortunes of war and the misfortunes of post-war politics, Livingston had all the substance for which he could have wished. He had, moreover, a kind of prestige that few men in America could match. Secretary Jay was not the least bit envious of his young friend Colonel Hamilton's happy connection with General Schuyler, for he had exactly the same connection with Governor Livingston. Much was expected in Philadelphia from the witty, learned, experienced symbol of New Jersey's commitment to nationhood.

To show that it, like Connecticut, took the Convention seriously, New Jersey sent its chief justice, David Brearly of Allentown and Trenton, along with its chief executive. "A man of good, rather than of brilliant parts," [2] Brearly was a pleasant combination of Whig and Mason. Not quite forty-two at the opening of the Convention, he could look back on a quiet life as a rural practitioner of law and three heady years as a lieutenant colonel of militia, a commission he resigned in 1779 to accept appointment to the supreme court of New Jersey. Although his education was largely informal, he apparently made enough of an impression on President Witherspoon to be awarded Princeton's honorary M.A. in 1781. He was modestly prepared to lend a useful hand in the Convention, having served as a delegate to the provincial congress that drafted New Jersey's Constitution of 1776, and having spoken the opinion in *Holmes* v. *Walton* (1780), an early if somewhat fuzzy precedent for the power of judicial review. Like few other members of the Convention, Brearly seems to have lived entirely on his salary, which means that he must have lived very simply.

William Paterson, who was the same age as Brearly, was born in County Antrim, Ireland. Brought to America in the second year of his life by a father who traveled widely in tinware, Paterson was raised in the pleasant town of Princeton, from whose pleasant college he won a B.A. in 1763 and an M.A. in 1766. Admitted to the bar in 1768 after reading law with Richard Stockton, he settled into a practice in Hunterdon County, then returned to Princeton in a few years to supplement his meager earnings by keeping a store with his brother. Paterson, like Brearly, served in all the right places in the Revolution: provincial congress, council of safety, militia, and the upper house of the legislature. In 1779 he was chosen as attorney general of New Jersey; in 1780 he was too busy in this post to accept election to Congress; in 1783 he resigned to devote all his time to the private practice of law in New Brunswick, where he also indulged his developed tastes for poetry and the classics. Paterson's public mind, so far as anyone could interpret it, was a blend of the not incongruous views of the moderate nationalist and the dogged small-stater. He had made something of a gamble on the future of the United States by purchasing a confiscated loyalist estate for a ridiculously small sum of hard cash in 1779. Since the Treaty of Paris provided for the return of such estates to their former owners, the creation of a national government that could enforce this provision would seem at first glance to have been a step for Paterson to oppose.

William Churchill Houston, a native of North Carolina, was another product of the College of New Jersey. Winning his B.A. in 1768 after a strenuous siege of self-help, he remained in Princeton as schoolmaster and college tutor, and in a few years became a professor of mathematics and natural philosophy. The academic life, however, was not for Houston, or perhaps not for his wife, who was a granddaughter of Princeton's first president. Even as he taught his students and performed worthy services in the Revolution (including one year in the militia and three as delegate to Congress), he began to study law in a determined manner. Before he could decide whether to go fully into private practice, he was offered the rewarding position of clerk of the New Jersey supreme court. He was still holding this position in 1786 when he went with Abraham Clark and James Schureman to the Annapolis Convention. A confirmed nationalist, he also served as New Jersey's receiver of continental taxes in 1782–1785. He was, unfortunately, in bad health in 1787, dying, as he probably suspected, of tuberculosis.

The last member of the New Jersey delegation, Jonathan Dayton of New Brunswick, was added to the list June 5, 1787, when it became clear that his patron, Abraham Clark, preferred to stay in New York with Congress, and that his father, the estimable General Elias Dayton, was quite ready to defer to the young man. And young he was, at twenty-six the youngest delegate to the Convention. He had, it must be said to his credit, lived his few years with intensity. In 1776, at the ripe age of sixteen, he graduated from Princeton and went off to war. Promoted to captain at nineteen, he saw service everywhere (including the inside of a British prison), and at Yorktown came into the orbit of the Marquis de Lafayette, an experience he never forgot. After the war he plunged into the law, to which he seems to have devoted his odd Tuesdays; politics, which he played hard in the New Jersey legislature; and speculation, in which he showed the kind of daring that either makes men obscenely rich or sends them to perdition. His ambition having far outrun his capacity for reflection, Dayton was something of an unknown political quantity when he arrived in Philadelphia to take counsel with his elders.

Pennsylvania celebrated its choice as host state by naming the largest delegation, one whose all-around distinction was matched only by that of Virginia. The politics of this bustling state (430,636 and 3,737 slaves) was unique in the 1780's, for two well-organized parties were pitted against each other: the Constitutionalists, a loudly democratic, anti-nationalist coalition of farmers and tradesmen committed to defending the radical state constitution of 1776; and the Anti-Constitutionalists or Republicans, a more high-toned, nationalist group of merchants, lawyers, and their allies committed to destroying it root and branch. Taking advantage of their recently won command of the legislature, as well as of the disposition of their opponents to have nothing to do with the Convention, the Republicans elected a seven-man delegation almost entirely to their liking on December 30, 1786, and then, in a gesture that joined grace with shrewd politics, added Benjamin Franklin to it just before opening day.

A living legend at eighty-one, Dr. Franklin was, in his capacity as President of Pennsylvania, the nominal head of the delegation. This "citizen of Boston who dwelt for a little while in Philadelphia" was famous throughout the Atlantic

World for his achievements as scientist, inventor, printer, publisher, moralist, businessman, administrator, politician, public servant, civic organizer, patron of learning, diplomat, and democrat; and, even though he was feeble and often wracked with pain as he neared the end of his splendid pilgrimage, men everywhere in America must have felt both pride and comfort at the news of his election to the Convention.

Franklin had served a notable apprenticeship—if that is the correct word for sixty years of devotion to the public weal—for the role of senior member among the Framers. He had been a uniquely American official long before half the others were born—"I am Deputy Postmaster-General of North America," he announced to the British House of Commons by way of self-identification in 1766—and his Albany Plan of 1754 was a major source of the American idea of a common destiny. Although he was abroad in the service of his colony and then his nation almost steadily between 1757 and 1785, he did get back in 1775–1776 to attend the second Continental Congress, make some pioneering proposals for "perpetual union," help to draft and then sign the Declaration of Independence, and preside over the gathering that wrote, quite to his satisfaction, the controversial Pennsylvania Constitution of 1776. An independent in politics who was generally identified with the Constitutionalists, Franklin was in fact a nationalist who surpassed even the bedazzled Colonel Hamilton in his vision of an America united and strong. He had always disliked the Articles of Confederation, whether for failing to apportion representation according to population or for hampering his maneuvers on the heights of diplomacy; he had never understood how men of sense could take such overweening pride in being Pennsylvanians or Virginians or New Yorkers. A nationalist democrat, and therefore almost the only one of his kind, Franklin was sure to be a valuable intellectual as well as sentimental addition to the Convention—if he could stand the strain.

Next in line in seniority, and also in prestige, was Robert Morris, known to friends and foes alike (and he had a full share of each) as "the Financier" or "the Great Man." In him was centered an aggregate of economic and political power such as no other man had enjoyed in American history. Born in Liverpool in 1734 and only sketchily educated, he had migrated to America with his father, a tobacco merchant, in 1747. Apprenticed in the famous countinghouse of Charles Willing in Philadelphia, he became a partner—thanks to his own brilliance and a timely inheritance—at the confident age of twenty. By 1775, when he threw in his lot with the patriot cause by accepting appointment to Congress, he was the most successful merchant in Philadelphia.

While continuing to tend to his own affairs, Morris poured his talents as financier and mobilizer into the war effort, especially in the critical days of late 1776 and early 1777 when he stayed behind in Philadelphia to act for a Congress on the run. Although he had voted against independence as a premature move, he signed the Declaration with an apparently clear conscience in August, 1776, and he was also a signer of the Articles of Confederation. Having declined the presidency of Congress and then retired from that body according to Pennsylvania law in 1778, he remained active in state politics, so active indeed that the Republicans were usually known simply as "the Morris party."

In the crisis of the Republic's finances, which came to a boil early in 1781, he was named to the controversial post of Superintendent of Finance. Picking his way like a magician through the swamps of depreciated currency, unpaid debts, and unanswered requisitions, he managed somehow to keep the enterprise from sinking without a trace, and the manner in which he financed the Yorktown campaign brought him the undying devotion of General Washington. After the war, having survived several investigations that would have broken a lesser man, Morris spread his wings and really began to fly. As if founding the Bank of North America and sending ships to China were not enough, in 1784 Morris negotiated a monopolistic three-year contract to supply twenty thousand hogsheads of tobacco annually to the French Farmers-General, and then a few years later began a plunge in land speculation that was eventually to ruin him. At the time of the Convention, however, he was the most successful entrepreneur in the burgeoning American economy. Brilliant, energetic, and commanding of presence, a gracious host and a man whose word was his bond, Morris was known far and wide as an unabashed nationalist. He and Dr. Franklin had come by far different roads to the same approving view of the glories of American union.

George Clymer was a native Philadelphian who had been orphaned in 1740 at the age of one, and had been raised in the family of his uncle William Coleman, a prosperous merchant and close friend of Franklin. He married a daughter of Reese Meredith, another prosperous merchant and a close friend of Washington, and was doing splendidly in the firm of Meredith and Clymer when the Revolution called. An ardent and early advocate of independence, he was a captain of militia, a member of the state's council of safety, a hard-working delegate to Congress in 1776–1778 (where he was a strong supporter of the movement to grant broader powers to the commander in chief), a commissioner of prisoners, one of two continental treasurers, and a signer of the Declaration of Independence who was honored for his patriotism by having his house ransacked by British troops. After putting his affairs in order on his return to Philadelphia, and indulging in his lifelong fondness for art and music, he went again for three years to Congress, where he associated closely with the more impatient nationalists. He was the fourth largest holder of public securities among the Framers, and thus in head as well as heart was an advocate of a more respectable central government. Not at all a forceful man, he was considered rather diffident in using his undoubted talents.

Thomas Fitzsimons, another merchant of substance and standing in Philadelphia, was born in County Wicklow, Ireland, in 1741 and migrated to America sometime around 1760. He, too, found the daughter of a prosperous merchant irresistible, and worked with her brother, George Meade, to build up a rewarding trade with the West Indies. A warm patriot in the Revolution, he served on both the committee of correspondence and the council of safety, raised and commanded a company of militia in the campaigns of 1776–1777, and helped to procure supplies for the army. In 1782–1783 he was a delegate to Congress (where he served with Madison and Hamilton on a crucial committee attempting to deal with Rhode Island); in 1783 he was a member of Pennsylvania's ill-starred Council of Censors (which was set up under the Constitution of 1776 to review the operations of the government every seven years); and in 1786 he was elected to the state legislature as an independent Republican. A founder of the Bank of North America, he had a finger in many economic pies, including the early trade with China. What distinguished Fitzsimons from many another successful merchant in Philadelphia was his devout Roman Catholicism; he was one of the two men of this long-feared faith to appear in the Convention.

James Wilson, at forty-four the next most senior member of the Pennsylvania delegation, was regarded on all sides as a very special person. A native of Scotland and a product of the university at St. Andrews, he had come to America in 1765 as an ambitious man of twenty-three. While acting as tutor in Latin at the College of Philadelphia (for which service he received the honorary M.A. of this future University of Pennsylvania), he studied law with the celebrated John Dickinson. After a spell in Reading, he then settled down to a large practice in Carlisle among the litigious people of western Pennsylvania.

The coming of the Revolution opened new doors to Wilson's talents. Having won wide notice with a pamphlet entitled *Considerations on the Nature and Extent of the Legislative Authority of the British Parliament* (1774), which was a brilliant statement of the radical view of the American colonies as freely consenting dominions of the British empire, Wilson was elected as a delegate to the second Continental Congress. Although he had all the qualms of the nervous lawyer and precise theorist, he voted for independence and signed the Declaration. Despite a first-class performance in Congress, Wilson had to leave in 1777 because of his bitter opposition to the Pennsylvania Constitution of 1776, which this student of Locke and Montesquieu considered a dangerously simple-minded affair.

A move to Philadelphia in 1778 turned Wilson from a shrewd country lawyer into a somewhat greedy man of affairs. He plunged so heavily into the steaming politics of the city that on one occasion his home was assaulted by a radical mob, and he made himself so useful as a legal advisor to Robert Morris that he was admitted into the innermost circle of the Great Man's friends. While continuing his service to the nation, especially as a nation-minded member of Congress in 1782–1783 and 1785–1787, he managed to do a little work on the side for the French government. Most of his energies in this period, however, seem to have been expended in an earnest effort to be a second Morris. He invested broadly and, to tell the sorry truth, not very wisely in bank shares, shipping, land, and manufactures. At the very moment when the Convention was assembling, he was overextended in an unsound scheme for mills and forges at the falls of the Delaware and was teetering on the edge of bankruptcy.

Despite private worries that must have weighed heavily upon his mind, Wilson kept a steady interest in public matters and steered a steady course toward a new national government. No man had a higher reputation for legal and political learning in 1787, and he was expected to play a major role in the Convention. William Pierce expressed the opinion of all his colleagues when he wrote of this stout, ruddy, stiff-mannered, somewhat artful Scot (known both derisively and fondly as "James the Caledonian"):

> Mr. Wilson ranks among the foremost in legal and political knowledge. He has joined to a fine genius all that can set him off and show him to advantage. He is well acquainted with man, and understands all the passions that influence him. Government seems to have been his peculiar study, all the political institutions of

the world he knows in detail, and can trace the causes and effects of every revolution from the earliest stages of the Grecian commonwealth down to the present time. No man is more clear, copious, and comprehensive than Mr. Wilson, yet he is no great orator. He draws the attention not by the charm of his eloquence, but by the force of his reasoning.[3]

Thomas Mifflin was the only member of the Pennsylvania delegation who did not live in Philadelphia, but since he lived grandly just five miles out of the city his election was no balm to the farmers of western Pennsylvania. In fact, few men of the time could have been farther removed from the habits and interests of the average American. Mifflin was born in Philadelphia in 1744 of an old and wealthy Quaker family. After graduating from the College of Philadelphia in 1760 and spending a year in Europe, he entered upon an immensely profitable career as merchant. One of the youngest and most eager delegates to the first Continental Congress, he accepted a commission as major—and was read, for his sin, out of meeting. Although his principal wartime service was as quartermaster general of Washington's army, he saw his share of action at Long Island, Trenton, and Princeton. Rising eventually to the rank of major general, he was deeply involved as a Gates man in the Conway Cabal and thus had no claim upon the friendship of Washington. At the same time, and like many another patriot, Mifflin carried on with his business activities, which became so complicated (and so mixed up with his dealings for the army) that in 1782 he found it necessary to publish a detailed record of his wartime accounts and current holdings.[4] By that year he seems to have had enough of money-making, and he turned his attention from business back to politics. He was sent as a delegate to Congress in 1782, and a year later was chosen to succeed Richard Henry Lee as President. At the time of the Convention this commanding figure was speaker of the Pennsylvania legislature, among other reasons because he was a man of continental reputation, a lavish entertainer, and an adept at walking an independent path between the two warring parties.

Jared Ingersoll also had to break with his past in the course of the Revolution. Born in New Haven in 1749 and graduated from Yale in 1766, he followed his father to Philadelphia in 1771 when this eminent lawyer and public servant was named a judge of one of the new courts of vice-admiralty. After reading law in that city, he went to England in 1773 for three years at the Middle Temple, then spent the first years of the Revolution in travel and further study in Europe. The call of America finally proved stronger than Ingersoll's respect for the loyalism of his father, and he returned to Philadelphia in 1778 to practice law. No one seems to have held either his long absence or his father's politics against him, for he was elected to Congress in 1780. He made a good marriage financially and socially to a daughter of Charles Pettit, but the maverick political views of his wealthy father-in-law, an anti-nationalist Constitutionalist who was not on speaking terms with Robert Morris, did nothing to help him in a city dominated by nationalist Anti-Constitutionalists.* Himself a mild sort of nationalist with little respect for the Articles of Confederation, Ingersoll was doubtless added to the list of delegates as a man who would provide balance without becoming obstreperous.

The youngest of the Pennsylvanians was a temporarily transplanted New Yorker. Gouverneur Morris, fourth son of the lord of the manor of Morrisania (in what is today the Bronx), had moved to Philadelphia in 1779 after a sharp clash with Governor Clinton over the question of what to do about Vermont. He had been well educated—at home, in a Huguenot school in New Rochelle (where he acquired excellent if provincial French), at Columbia (B.A., 1768), and in the law office of William Livingston's great Whig friend, William Smith—and was always able, when he put his mind to it, to make plenty of money at the bar.

A somewhat reluctant patriot, because of his cold-eyed anticipation that one consequence of rebellion would be widespread popular disorder, Morris nevertheless served brilliantly in the American cause, even though this meant a break with most of his family. His mother rejoiced to see British troops take New York, and his half-brother was a major general in the British army, as well as the second husband of the Duchess of Gordon. In the provincial congress of 1775, the council of safety, the peripatetic New York convention (where he was John Jay's chief lieutenant in writing the Constitution of 1777), the first New York assembly, and the Congress of the United States (where his skills as drafter of resolutions and instructions were honed and polished in the course of three years of service), he showed himself a man of decided views. The most decided of these were skepticism of the wisdom of the people, admiration for constitutional government, respect

---

* It must be borne in mind that these labels express attitudes toward the radical Pennsylvania Constitution of 1776. Most gentlemen who supported the movement for a national convention and then accepted its result were extremely unhappy with the constitution of their state—and thus, quite openly, *anti*-constitutionalists."

for strong executive power, hostility to slavery, and dedication to the Union. Like Franklin and Hamilton he had been a nationalist even before the rise of the nation, a fact that helped him to take a larger view than most of his impatient comrades in the 1780's. While others fumed over the harassment of American trade, Morris wrote at least half-seriously to Jay in 1784: "Do not ask the British to take off their foolish restrictions. Let them alone, and they will be obliged to do it of themselves. While the present regulation exists, it does us more political good than it can possibly do commercial mischief." [5] And so it did, as Morris foretold.

Both Washington and Robert Morris considered themselves patrons of this talented young man. He had defended the commander in chief eloquently in Congress and had come out to Valley Forge to see things for himself; he had assisted the Great Man shrewdly in the effort to rescue the Confederation from financial chaos. Although not as rich as he could have been at this time, Gouverneur Morris lived and entertained in style at his bachelor's quarters in Philadelphia, and dazzled the ladies with his "lively intellect." [6] Magnificent of bearing despite the loss of a leg in a traffic accident in 1780, he was an aristocrat to the core. If his morals were too relaxed,[7] his wit too sportive, his temper too sophisticated, and his manner too cynical for some solemn people, he was nevertheless widely regarded as one of the brightest young men in a country full of bright young men. "He winds through all the mazes of rhetoric," William Pierce reported in awe, "and throws around him such a glare that he charms, captivates, and leads away the senses of all who hear him." Then, as if he had said too much, Pierce added: "But with all these powers he is fickle and inconstant,—never pursuing one train of thinking,—nor ever regular." [8] Would Gouverneur Morris settle down in the Convention and be a beaver, or would he flit about like a butterfly—this is a question that must have occurred to his friends Washington, Robert Morris, Wilson, and Hamilton when they learned that he would be a participant in the great event.

From the smallest state (50,209 and 8,887 slaves) came a full delegation of five, all ready to strike a blow for nationalism so long as it did not lead to the "enslavement" of Delaware by the large states. Caught in a squeeze, perhaps more stimulating than suffocating, between Pennsylvania and Maryland, Delaware had ten times the pro-Union sentiment of Rhode Island, and proved it by responding more faithfully than most other states to the requests of Congress for money and power.

The leader of this delegation, John Dickinson, was a man of continental reputation—and also of continental views, which he had exhibited bravely as early as 1776 as principal draftsman of the first (and rather too centralizing) version of the Articles of Confederation. In 1787, at the age of fifty-five, he was living in comfortable semi-retirement on an estate near Dover and paying occasional visits to a fine town house in Wilmington, and he had to care deeply about the cause of union to be persuaded to set forth for Philadelphia. But he had set forth twice before on just such a mission—to the Stamp Act Congress in 1765 and the first Continental Congress in 1774—and to many of his fellow delegates his arrival must have given a sense of the continuity of American history.

Born in Maryland in 1732 into a respected family, he had moved as a child to Dover in 1740; and although he was to achieve fame and wealth as a lawyer in Philadelphia, he never cut his ties with Delaware. He was tutored at home, went off to London and its famed Middle Temple to study law, and returned in 1757 to begin practice in Philadelphia. Dickinson did the other Framers who married well one better: he found his heiress, a Norris of Philadelphia, but at his insistence she gave away much of her inheritance to a relative. He prospered greatly as attorney for some of the city's leading families and countinghouses, and also took the natural road into politics for men of his class and connections. Active in the Pennsylvania legislature in the early 1760's (where he and Franklin clashed head-on as leaders of opposing factions), he was an obvious choice to go to the Stamp Act Congress in New York in 1765, in which he played a vital part as debater and drafter.

In 1767–1768 Dickinson won his greatest fame, which stayed with him the rest of his life, for his *Letters from a Farmer in Pennsylvania*. The *Letters*, which appeared in all but three or four American newspapers and won him a Princeton LL.D., were quoted as secular scripture by American patriots for their attempt to draw a fine line—so characteristic of all Dickinson's work—between the proper power of Parliament to tax the colonies in regulating trade and the improper power to tax them in search of revenue. Although he was thereafter one of the most helpful members of the first and second Continental Congresses, especially as drafter of many of the important resolutions and appeals of 1775–1776, he was too much the legalistic, perhaps even pettifogging conservative to sign the Declaration of Independence. In the course of the war he did a small amount of soldiering, put in two years as delegate to Congress from Delaware

(1776–1777, 1779–1780), served as president of both Delaware (1781–1782) and Pennsylvania (1782–1785), and took an active part in Pennsylvania politics as a committed Anti-Constitutionalist. In 1785, weary of the pace in bustling Philadelphia, he fled to his books and fields in Dover. He had already achieved, although he may not have realized it, a special kind of immortality by serving as principal benefactor to the new college in Carlisle.

Second only to Dickinson in prestige and experience was George Read of New Castle. One of six sons of a substantial family in Maryland, he had read law in Philadelphia before settling permanently in New Castle, where he lived decently on the proceeds of a modest practice, a small farm, and a succession of ill-paying public offices. Before the outbreak of the Revolution he was attorney general of Delaware as well as a member of the assembly. As a firm Whig he was sent to the first and second Continental Congresses, where he, like his friend Robert Morris, voted against independence and then signed the Declaration. In the course of the war he served Delaware in at least three vital roles; president of the convention of 1776, leading member of the legislature, and, when President John McKinly had the misfortune to be captured by the British, acting president in 1777–1778. His natural leanings toward nationalism were reinforced by a stint as judge of the Court of Appeals under Congress and as commissioner for settling the boundary between New York and Massachusetts. By 1786 he was as ready as any man in the state to take a gamble on a new national government, and as a commissioner to Annapolis he signed the report of September 11, 1786, with considerable relish. A small-state man with big-nation ideas, this fifty-three-year-old friend of General Washington was a welcome addition in Philadelphia to the forces of nationalism.

The rest of the delegation from Delaware was less distinguished. They may have been big men in their world, but their world was a small one. Richard Bassett of Dover, who was born in Maryland in 1745, was the adopted son of a well-to-do lawyer-planter, his own father, a tavern-keeper, having deserted his mother when he was an infant. Bassett, like Dickinson and Read, read law in Philadelphia and began to practice in Dover around 1770. Having inherited a sizable amount of productive land in Maryland, he never had to work too hard for a living, and he was able to indulge in the unusual hobby of holding Methodist camp meetings on his estate. He was indeed, as befitted a man who had been converted by the formidable Bishop Asbury, the one genuine enthusiast among all the rationalists, traditionalists, and amateur theologians in the Convention. During the Revolution, about which he was lukewarm, he captained a troop of lighthorse militia, served on the state's council of safety, and was a member of the convention of 1776. In the 1780's he sat off and on in both houses of the legislature, and became well enough known as a firm nationalist to join his state's delegation to the Annapolis Convention.

Gunning Bedford, jr., was attorney general of Delaware. Born in Philadelphia in 1747, he went through Princeton as a classmate of James Madison, studied law in the office of the redoubtable Joseph Reed, and, after some undistinguished service in the Revolution, settled down to a modest practice, first in Dover and then in Wilmington. Except for three halfhearted years as a delegate to Congress (1783–1786), he, like Bassett, confined his political activities within the limits of his tiny state. Although he was elected to the Annapolis Convention, he failed to attend. If Pierce's judgment can be trusted, he was about three times as large as James Madison —"bold and nervous" as a speaker, "commanding and striking" in manner, "warm and impetuous in temper," and "very corpulent." [9]

The least known representative from Delaware, and thus perhaps the most obscure of the Framers, was Jacob Broom of Wilmington. The son of a blacksmith who had turned to farming and had prospered, the thirty-five-year-old Broom was the only native of the state in the delegation. A modestly successful farmer himself, he also dabbled in surveying, toolmaking, and other small enterprises. He apparently had one moment of glory in the Revolution, when he drew some maps for General Washington; otherwise he labored at a host of small local tasks. He had another moment in 1783, when as a burgess of Wilmington he wrote an address of welcome to Washington. Since the hero was bombarded with bombast wherever he went, especially on his happy return from the wars, it is doubtful that he even remembered Broom's face when they bowed to each other in the State House on May 21. Broom was not entirely without experience, for he had served several terms in the Delaware legislature. He, like Bedford, was a delegate to Annapolis who chose not to attend.

Maryland (216,692 and 103,036 slaves) was not at all as anxious as Delaware to see a reforming convention meet and flourish, and its warring factions had trouble finding men who would go to Philadelphia and keep an eye on the proceedings. Charles Carroll of Carrollton, Robert Hanson Harrison, Thomas Sim Lee, Thomas Stone, and Gabriel Duvall were elected but declined to serve, most of them for quite acceptable reasons such as ill health (Harrison), wife's ill health (Stone), and unwillingness to leave a state in which political tension was distressingly high (Carroll). Thomas Johnson, William Paca, George Gale, John Henry, and the egregious Samuel Chase declined even to be considered. In the end, Maryland managed to put together a slate on May 26, but it was not one especially worthy of a state that took itself very seriously.

The senior member was a sixty-four-year-old planter and public servant, Daniel of St. Thomas Jenifer, whose estate Stepney in Charles County was a center of Maryland politics and society. An affable bachelor—"always in good humor" [10] —the wealthy Jenifer was a respected product of the old aristocracy. He had a friendship with Washington, with whom he had often exchanged visits, that extended over several decades. In his early years he had performed a wide range of public services—as agent and receiver general for the last two lords proprietors, justice of the peace, commissioner for settling the Pennsylvania-Delaware boundary, member of the governor's council—and some of the anti-proprietary leaders were surprised to find him on their side at the outbreak of resistance to England. This conservative patriot was first president of both the Maryland council of safety and the senate, that cleverly designed bulwark of the leading families; and he went on from these posts to four years (1778–1782) as a delegate to Congress, where he proved himself an excellent committee man and a moderate nationalist. In 1782 he took on the important and rewarding office of financial agent for the state (and intendant of its revenues). This position, combined with leadership of one of the four major factions, made Jenifer a figure of considerable power in the state.

Daniel Carroll was likewise an offshoot of the Maryland aristocracy, a wealthy tobacco planter of Prince George County whose estate, worked by more than fifty slaves, made up a good portion of what is today the District of Columbia. Born in 1730, he was sent by his piously Catholic family, which endured its share of discrimination in this period, to be educated by Jesuits at St. Omer in Flanders. He then took the grand tour before returning home to fulfill his duties as a Carroll, one of which apparently was to preserve the faith by marrying a Carroll. He was much too quiet and conservative a man to plunge headlong into the patriot cause, and not until early 1781, when he arrived in Congress (and announced that his obstinate state was at last ready to sign the Articles of Confederation), did Carroll make any sort of splash in public. Shortly thereafter he succeeded Jenifer as presiding officer of the upper house in Maryland. A leading member of the faction headed by his second cousin Charles Carroll of Carrollton, he was one of the most nation-minded men in the state. He was, in addition, a man with the future on his mind, as he proved by serving as one of the original promoters of the trail-blazing (rather, canal-digging) Potomac Company.

James McHenry, who was thirty-three or thirty-four at the time of the Convention, was from a somewhat different background. A native of County Antrim in Ireland, he set off for America in 1771, to be followed shortly by his merchant father who set up an importing business in Baltimore. Having already been educated in the classics in Dublin, McHenry spent one year at Newark Academy in Delaware, then went on to two years of medical studies with the eminent Benjamin Rush in Philadelphia. As becomes an Irishman, McHenry was zealously anti-English, and he rushed to Cambridge at the outbreak of hostilities to volunteer his services. He saw a good deal of action as a surgeon with the army. Captured at Ft. Washington in the debacle of 1776, he was eventually exchanged, whereupon he rejoined his comrades in time to freeze at Valley Forge. Apparently tired of his long career as a physician, he became a secretary to Washington (and thus an intimate of Hamilton), and later took a position on Lafayette's staff. In 1782 the death of his father, who had prospered in America, left him more money than he knew what to do with, and he thereafter lived the life of an independent gentleman. He went into politics as a member of the Maryland senate in 1781 (where he was equally independent), and was an active delegate to Congress in 1783–1786. Although he was a decent, sociable, and well-meaning person, McHenry was out of his depth with men like Madison, King, and Hamilton. Pierce expressed the opinion of most who knew McHenry when he wrote that "he was a very respectable young gentleman" of, alas, "specious talents." [11]

The fourth member of the Maryland contingent was an even younger man, John Francis Mercer of Anne Arundel County, who was barely twenty-nine on the day the Convention got down to business—without John Francis Mercer. The son of a well-connected Virginia planting family, he graduated from the College of William and Mary in 1775, and thereupon went soldiering with a vengeance. Service as an officer in the Third Virginia Regiment brought an honorable wound at Brandywine, after which Mercer did a stint as aide to General Charles Lee. When Lee was court-martialed for his shilly-shallying at Monmouth, Mercer loyally resigned his own commission. In 1780, after a year's study of law in Williamsburg under Thomas Jefferson, he returned to the wars as a lieutenant colonel and behaved with conspicuous gallantry in the Yorktown campaign. After the war he left his plantation in the keeping of an overseer and began to practice law in Williamsburg. Almost immediately he was elected to both the Virginia legislature and Congress. Although he hardly needed the money, he married the daughter of a rich Maryland family in 1785 and moved his base of operations to her estate, Cedar Park. Mercer was hand-in-glove with the powerful Samuel Chase, the well-born leader of Maryland's paper-money faction, and thus could be counted upon to adopt a strongly anti-nationalist point of view.

The last of the Maryland delegation, Attorney General Luther Martin of Annapolis, was a misfit of splendid proportions, one of the most fascinating characters among the Framers. Born sometime around 1748 on a small farm in New Jersey, he managed to make his way to Princeton, from which he graduated with honors in 1766. After teaching school for several years in Maryland, he began to practice law, in which he did extremely well. Although he was a notable drinker, he could sober up when he had to; and although he was shockingly careless in handling his money, he could earn it with ease. A strong patriot who served in a number of useful capacities in the first years of the Revolution, he was so faithful a servant of Samuel Chase that he was rewarded with the attorney generalship in 1778, a post in which he amused himself by prosecuting loyalists with an almost savage vigor. As a delegate to Congress in 1784–1785 he had impressed his colleagues equally with his alcoholic content, which gave him a permanently red face, and his devotion to the sovereignty of Maryland, which gave him the reputation of a committed anti-nationalist. The hearts of Carroll and Jenifer did not rejoice when they learned that this ornery, brilliant, in some ways spectacular man was to go with them to Philadelphia.

Except for always unpredictable Maryland, the Middle States seemed ready for a stiff dose of constitutional medicine in 1787. If a prescription could somehow be found that mixed more power for the central government with continued protection for the interests of the small states, the delegates from New Jersey and Delaware, and at worst two of those from Maryland, seemed ready to join the avowed nationalists from Pennsylvania to come to the rescue of the paralyzed Union.

# 7 THE MEN OF THE SOUTH

> *There is, however, a circumstance attending these
> colonies, which ... makes the spirit of liberty still
> more high and haughty than in those to the north-
> ward. It is, that in Virginia and the Carolinas they
> have a vast multitude of slaves. Where this is the
> case in any part of the world, those who are free,
> are by far the most proud and jealous of their free-
> dom. Freedom is to them not only an enjoyment,
> but a kind of rank and privilege. . . . Such will be
> all masters of slaves, who are not slaves themselves.
> In such a people, the haughtiness of domination
> combines with the spirit of freedom, fortifies it, and
> renders it invincible.*
>
> EDMUND BURKE in the House of Commons,
> March 22, 1775[1]

IN AND YET not entirely of the United States in those days as
in these, the South was an area of proud memories, dazzling
prospects, and large problems, the largest of which it was
managing to ignore. Nothing could be done to save the
Union without the South, not a great deal more, according to
some hardheaded men, with it. When seen from a distance,
from Boston or Hartford or Trenton, it appeared (with most
of Maryland thrown in) as a social, economic, and cultural
unity; when seen from within, from Richmond or Charleston
or Augusta, it appeared as a battleground of other-minded
classes, sections, and sects. Perhaps even more firmly than in
the northern and middle states, political leadership still rested
in the hands of a self-conscious gentry, and it was men of this
description, harried at every step by some of their best
friends, who led the move toward a stronger central government.

The monarch of the South, no matter what certain people
in Charleston may have thought, was mighty Virginia
(454,983 and 292,627 slaves) whose size, location, and reputation led men to conclude that as it went, so would go the
Union. A state full of yeomen who had no thoughts to spare
for the world outside, and also at least half-full of gentlemen
who thought about it a lot but still did not like it or trust it,

Virginia, fortunately for the causes of union, had a healthy sprinkling of nationalists in high places. These men, gingered by the maneuvers of James Madison and comforted by the support of George Washington, led the procession of the states through Mt. Vernon, Annapolis, and New York to Philadelphia. "We all look up to Virginia for examples," John Adams had written to Patrick Henry many years before; [2] and nationalists everywhere were encouraged by the actions of Virginia (if not of Patrick Henry) in sparking the Annapolis Convention, taking a quick lead in naming a delegation (authorized October 16 and elected December 4, 1786), and above all in choosing and persuading some of its best men to go to Philadelphia. Readers of the *New-York Journal* or the *Columbia Herald* of Charleston or the *American Herald* of Boston could tell that something big was in the wind when they saw the list of delegates from Virginia.

First of all, there at the head, printed in large type so that no one would miss it, was the name of "his Excellency Gen. GEORGE WASHINGTON." [3] The greatest man in America—and, in the opinion of most Americans, the greatest in the world —Washington enjoyed a personal prestige in 1787 that has never been matched in all our history. He had won this prestige the hard way through more than eight years of command of the armies of the Revolution; and, whatever some doubters might find to question in this or that aspect of his generalship, all agreed that his perseverance in the face of British arms and American irresolution had been the key to victory for the rebellious colonies.

At the time of his election to the Virginia delegation, Washington was at home in Mt. Vernon living the life he loved—and had ached for in Cambridge, Valley Forge, Morristown, and Newburgh—the life of the industrious planter, unafraid investor, avid foxhunter, useful citizen, and courteous host, with just enough of a finger in the affairs of the Republic to remind men that he was still interested in the things he had always wanted for America: peace, order, progress, justice, honor, and union. Although he was now the very model of the peace-loving country squire, he could look back across his fifty-five years to experiences that had tested him as they had tested few other men of his time. He had not, after all, sprung from the earth in 1775, as John Adams was later to write in bitter jest, at the touch of "Dr. Franklin's electrical rod." [4] He had served an exacting apprenticeship for glory in his youth, rising as early as 1755 to the command of all Virginia forces and serving bravely and intelligently in the struggle with France for control of the frontier. He knew what it was to survey a tract in the wilderness, ford an icy stream, break a horse, outwit Indians, manage slaves, rotate crops, dance an intricate pattern, speak the law in Alexandria, and play politics in Williamsburg—and to build an awesome character by learning to control a rib-busting temper. Fortunate in marriage, courtly in manner, impeccable in taste, skilled in management, trustworthy in all things, he was just the man to be sent with Patrick Henry, Richard Henry Lee, Peyton Randolph, and Richard Bland to the first Continental Congress, just the man to be sent by the second to take command of the armed rabble besieging Boston. Not quite a Fabius, for he was in fact a fighting general whenever he could be, he was a complete Cincinnatus: no man since the fabled Roman headed home for the farm more joyfully than did Washington at the end of the longest of American wars.

A Virginia nationalist who loved both state and nation dearly, and who had a large emotional and financial stake in the westward "course of empire," Washington had never hidden his disgust over the weakness of the central government that was supposed to be supporting him; and men remembered that his solution had always been, not a monarchy or a military dictatorship even in the worst times, but, in the words of a toast he had offered in Philadelphia in 1783, "competent powers to Congress for general purposes." There was, then, a twofold reason for getting General Washington to Philadelphia: he was a hero whose presence would raise hopes and quiet fears everywhere; he was a nationalist whose influence would be on the side of purposeful reform. Although he had a dozen personal and professional reasons for not accepting election, Washington finally gave in, unconditionally if not exactly gracefully, to the pleas of Madison and the other young nationalists and set out for Philadelphia on May 9. Being Washington, he set out to do a whole job. He meant to stay to the end, and he hoped that the end would be a new government for the Republic. "My wish," he wrote to Madison a few weeks before leaving Mt. Vernon, "is that the Convention may adopt no temporizing expedient, but probe the defects of the Constitution to the bottom, and provide radical cures, whether they are agreed to or not." [5]

The second of four senior delegates from Virginia was, in his own way, almost as impressive a figure as Washington. George Mason, squire of Gunston Hall in Fairfax County, was as influential and respected as a man can be in public affairs and still lay honest claim to the title of "private gentleman." Born in 1725 and educated by tutors in the homes of his wealthy father and even wealthier uncle, the noted lawyer John Mercer, Mason married a rich heiress from Maryland

and settled down to the life of the planter-aristocrat. Wheat and tobacco were the crops he grew, land the thing in which he put his money. Although he did his duties faithfully to his parish and county, he was not easily persuaded to stand for the House of Burgesses in 1759, and before the year was up he was fleeing from its "babblers." He did not reappear in politics at the state level until 1775, when, as admired author of the Fairfax Resolves in 1774, he was named first to the committee of safety and then to the Virginia convention. In that famous gathering he came into his own as a learned draftsman, having much to do with the Virginia Constitution of 1776 and almost everything to do with the Declaration of Rights. It is, surely, one of the supreme ironies of our history that the man who wrote this first and most eloquent of bills of rights, in the first article of which he proclaimed the natural freedom and equality of "all men," should have been the owner of some three hundred slaves.

Mason retired from the Virginia legislature as soon as he could in good conscience, refused even to be considered for election to Congress, and spent most of the next ten years at Gunston Hall, which he seems to have managed personally without the aid of a steward—an unusual procedure for a Virginia gentleman. Even in this private capacity he had much public influence, for Jefferson, Madison, Monroe, and Edmund Randolph formed a circle of the politics of intellect that had him at the center. In 1785 Mason was lured back to public life, when he attended the conference on the navigation of the Potomac at the home of his old friend General Washington. A year later he was elected to the Virginia legislature, where he adopted, as became George Mason of Gunston Hall, a totally independent line. He was chosen to go to Annapolis, but refused the honor; he was chosen to go to Philadelphia, and accepted—doubtless to the astonishment of all who knew him. Just what persuaded this admirable but prickly man, a fanatic for privacy and a detester of the unfamiliar, to make the longest journey of his life at sixty-two will never be known; one suspects that he considered some such meeting the last hope for the preservation of property-owning republicanism in the United States. And so, swallowing his fears and suppressing his crotchets, this most Virginian of Virginians set out for Philadelphia, where soon he was making clear that he "would not, upon pecuniary motives, serve in this convention for a thousand pounds per day." [6]

The third worthy member of this team was George Wythe of Williamsburg, chancellor of Virginia and professor of law in the College of William and Mary. Born into a respectable planting family in 1726 and educated at the grammar school attached to William and Mary (and, for perhaps one year, at the college itself), Wythe studied law with Stephen Dewey and was admitted to the bar in 1746. Having used up most of a substantial inheritance, he began to practice law in earnest when he was about thirty. At the same time, he served in a number of public offices, most prominently as representative of three different constituencies (1754–1755, 1758–1768) and clerk (1768–1775) in the House of Burgesses. Caught up like most Virginians of his class in the tide af Revolution, he went off as delegate to the second Continental Congress, where he supported Richard Henry Lee's motion for independence and put his name to the Declaration. His most valuable services to Virginia, however, were performed at home in Williamsburg. As judge of the court of chancery and member (with Jefferson, Mason, Henry, and Edmund Pendleton) of the committee to revise and codify the laws of the state, he won a firm reputation, which Pierce duly recorded, as "one of the most learned legal characters of the present age." [7] Whether as draftsman, codifier, guardian, or teacher of the law (the first professor of the law in the United States), Wythe was a man of profound influence. In the case of *Commonwealth* v. *Caton* (1782), he, like Judge Brearly in New Jersey, had found himself suddenly engaging in judicial review of legislation.

John Blair, who was exactly the age of Washington, was a colleague of Wythe in the court of chancery. A son of one of the best families of Virginia, he received a good education at William and Mary, which his uncle had founded, and went off to read law at the Middle Temple. He returned to Virginia about 1755 and began a rewarding practice in Williamsburg. Entering public life at the time of the Stamp Act crisis, he sat as representative of the college in the House of Burgesses (1766–1770), then took on the pleasant job of clerk of the governor's council (1770–1775). After serving as a quiet but respected member of the convention of 1776, he went by way of the new privy council and the general court to the court of chancery, where he joined with Wythe in the decision in *Commonwealth* v. *Caton*. A mild nationalist and a man quite out of politics, Blair added broad learning, professional distinction, and an eminent name to the Virginia delegation.

The three other men who went with Washington, Mason, Wythe, and Blair were from the next generation of the Virginia elite. The first was Edmund Randolph, a striking and accomplished member of another celebrated Virginia family. Not yet thirty-four in the spring of 1787, Randolph was Governor of Virginia and head of his own political faction. He had graduated from William and Mary in 1771, studied law with his prominent father, and begun to practice in Williamsburg. When his father fled in 1775 with the last royal governor, the son moved closer to his patriot uncle, the eminent Peyton Randolph. The death of his uncle cut short a stint on Washington's staff, and he returned to Virginia to sit as the youngest member of the convention of 1776, where he served with Mason, Madison, Henry, and others on the drafting committee. For the next ten years, until his elevation to the governorship to succeed Patrick Henry, he was attorney general of Virginia, and in addition served three years (1779–1782) as a delegate to Congress, in which he was a leader in the fight for the impost of 1781. Despite the glamor of his name, he was not one of the rich men of Virginia, and he once asked Madison somewhat shamefacedly if it was an "unpardonable sin" to "reprehend" his departed father "for not handing down a fortune" to him.[8] He held some fourteen thousand dollars in Virginia securities, which were worth roughly twenty-five cents on the dollar in 1787.

Randolph's nationalism was evident but far from fervent. Although he was interested in strengthening the central government, especially in giving it additional powers to settle squabbles between the states and to defend the United States against invasion, he was too alert to the shadings of Virginia politics to strike quite as firm and exposed a posture as that of his friend James Madison. Still, he cared enough to attend the Annapolis Convention, and was now ready, despite the political dangers in being away from Virginia too long, to take a decisive step in Philadelphia.

The one delegate from Virginia whose selection is difficult to explain, unless it be that the other delegates (especially the ailing Mason) did not trust Philadelphia medicine, was Dr. James McClurg of Richmond. He was, to be sure, a man of character, achievement, and reputation, but in a state full to the brim with experienced political figures he was a conspicuous rarity: a gentleman with no experience in politics at all. The son of a well-to-do physician who lived near Hampton, McClurg became as learned a "natural philosopher" as William Samuel Johnson was a "classic." After graduating from William and Mary with the highest honors in 1762 at the age of sixteen, he went on to win an M.D. from the University of Edinburgh in 1770. In the course of several more years of study in London and Paris, he produced pioneering scientific papers on such subjects as the properties of heat and the uses of bile. Upon his return to America he became physician general and director of hospitals for the Virginia forces and a professor of medicine at William and Mary. Sometime around 1783 he settled in Richmond, where he went about his daily business in the bracing knowledge that he was the most admired physician in the state. Although he had never held political office, he must have impressed men with his ability. Madison thought him a suitable man to succeed R. R. Livingston as Secretary of Foreign Affairs in December, 1783; and when Patrick Henry finally made clear that he was not going to Philadelphia, Governor Randolph, perhaps at Madison's suggestion, appointed McClurg in his stead on May 2. A city dweller uninterested in land and, perhaps on principle, unencumbered with slaves, Dr. McClurg was second only to Elbridge Gerry among the Framers in his holdings of state and continental securities.

To the seventh man in this admirable delegation the gathering in Philadelphia held out the ambiguous promise of a face-to-face encounter with destiny. James Madison was born in Port Conway in 1751, the son of a respectable, middle-class farming family of Orange County. From his early childhood he was marked out for a life of the mind; and, after an excellent schooling, he went off to Princeton to receive a B.A. in 1771 and spend another year studying Hebrew and ethics with President Witherspoon. On his return to Virginia he fell, according to his own testimony, into a state of severe melancholy, from which he was rescued by the passing of time and the coming of the Revolution. Madison responded with a will to the state's call for help: he chaired his county's committee of safety, sat in the convention of 1776 (where he was conspicuous for his advocacy of freedom of conscience), and served in both houses of the Virginia legislature.

Election to Congress followed in 1780. Although he took his seat as one of the youngest members, his learning, common sense, and attention to business soon brought him to prominence. If all the delegates to Congress from all the states had taken their work as seriously as did Madison, we might still be living under the Articles of Confederation. Whether as debater, committeeman, draftsman, note-taker, advocate of the impost, writer of instructions for Jay, negotiator of the terms of Virginia's cession of the Northwest, or parent (perhaps not proud, but certainly useful) of the formula of counting five slaves as three persons in determining state contributions, Madison was probably the most effective member of Congress during this harrowing period. He was, moreover, the stoutest of Virginia nationalists, and he struck up friendships with like-minded delegates that were to prove immensely helpful in his campaign for a stronger national government.

With a full mind and empty pockets—Virginia failed repeatedly to pay the salaries of its delegates—he went home in December, 1783, to a winter of study of law, and was elected almost at once to the lower house. There, as we know, he helped to bring off the Annapolis Convention, and there he acted in the spirit of his absent friend Jefferson by pushing for separation of church and state, favoring the creation of a new state in Kentucky, and proposing a system of public education. In February, 1787, he returned to Congress, then located in New York, to fight for the right of free navigation of the Mississippi and to encourage his friends in other states to make their own plans for the "second Monday in May next."

In a series of letters to Jefferson, Washington, and Randolph, Madison laid out his ideas for constitutional reform and, in the process, sharpened the thinking of these friends. Although not every piece of the puzzle was in place on the day he left New York for Philadelphia, he was prepared to put forward these propositions: a change "in the principle of representation" to give more weight to the large states; arming of the new government (which he described as "national") with "positive and complete authority in all cases which require uniformity, such as the regulation of trade"; provision for a national "negative *in all cases whatsoever* on the legislative acts of the states"; creation of a national judiciary with "supremacy" over the courts of the states in all general matters, a bicameral legislature, a council of revision, and an executive (about which, he confessed, he had "scarcely ventured" to think in detail); a guarantee of "tranquility" within each state; an express declaration of the "right of coercion" against delinquent or fractious states; and, in order "to give a new system its proper validity and energy," a ratification of the new charter "obtained from the people, and not merely from the ordinary authority of the legislatures." As to the central question of drawing a line between nation and states, he wrote to Washington suggestively (and plainly not for publication):

> Conceiving that an individual independence of the states is utterly irreconcilable with their aggregate sovereignty, and that a consolidation of the whole into one simple republic would be as inexpedient as it is unattainable, I have sought for middle ground, which may at once support a due supremacy of the national authority, and not exclude the local authorities whenever they can be subordinately useful.[9]

While other men were just as determined nationalists as Madison, he was well out front in early 1787 in outlining the details of a "new system." A slightly built bachelor of simple tastes (except for a craving for books) who lived on small handouts from his father and friends, Madison must have struck his acquaintances as a single-minded political monk in these months of study and maneuver just before the Convention.

Although the absent Virginians made up almost as splendid a galaxy of talents as these seven delegates, the leading American state had once again set a high example for lesser states to match as best they could. Thomas Jefferson, who was in Paris, would certainly be missed, as would also be the aging Edmund Pendleton, but otherwise the delegation was a sign of Virginia's concern. Of the three men who could have been on it if they had wished—Richard Henry Lee, Thomas Nelson, and Patrick Henry—only Lee, who seems to have misjudged the importance of the impending meeting, would have added an active, creative, reasonably flexible mind to the group. Indeed, there must have been a few sighs of relief when Henry, who had turned almost as provincial as George Clinton, declined the honor. We, who have the gift of hindsight, may be pardoned a sigh of regret that two up-and-coming lawyer-politicians named James Monroe and John Marshall were not tapped for service.

Some of Virginia's often insufferable pride may have arisen from contemplation of its neighbor to the south, the badly favored, poorly governed state of North Carolina. Although it was considered to be a larger state (293,179 and 100,572 slaves) than Connecticut or New Jersey or South Carolina, it had failed to produce much in the way of political talent; and its delegation, although distinguished in terms of the state itself, was not one of which a great deal was expected. If Willie Jones, the improbable Etonian who led the radical, anti-nationalist faction, had been willing to serve, or if Governor Richard Caswell, a respected moderate, had been able, the delegation would have been more distinguished—and more divided—than it was. James Iredell, who seems to have been simply too poor at the time, and Samuel Johnston, who was too truculently anti-populist, were other men who could have added weight. Taken all in all, however, North Carolina did rather better than might have been expected of a community so far out of the stream of American national development.

The senior member of the North Carolina delegation, the politically independent Hugh Williamson of Edenton, had no reason to feel out of place in any gathering in America. Born in Pennsylvania in 1735 to an Irish father who was a clothier

and an Irish mother who had once been captured by Black-
beard the pirate, he graduated from the first class of the College of Philadelphia, studied theology in Connecticut (and
was licensed to preach), and took up a professorship of
mathematics in Philadelphia. A man whose mind was almost
as lively as Franklin's (Otto found him "excessively
bizarre"),[10] he then turned his attention to medicine, studied
in Edinburgh, and won an M.D. at Utrecht. After four years
of practice in Philadelphia and three of travel in Europe (in
the course of which he produced essays on comets, electric
eels, and American rights), he settled in Edenton and tried
his hand at trading with the West Indies. In the latter part of
the war he served as surgeon general for the North Carolina
forces, and in 1782 made his belated entrance into politics by
taking a seat in the state legislature.

Elected to Congress in 1782, Williamson proved himself
one of its most conspicuous members, attending faithfully
and also joining with Thomas Jefferson as one of two southerners to vote for a ban on slavery in the Ordinance of 1784.
He made a determined effort to get to the Annapolis Convention in 1786, and is said to have arrived just a few hours too
late to sign the report of September 14. A strong nationalist
out of both principle and interest—he was, for example, an
investor in western lands who expected his holdings to increase in value under the protection of an "efficient federal
government"[11]—this affable man of parts must have been a
welcome sight to James Madison. To Benjamin Franklin he
was a reminder of hard-fought battles of long ago: Williamson, while waiting for a ship in Boston in 1773, had been an
interested observer of the world's most talked-about tea party,
and he had been the first to bring the news to the beleaguered
Franklin in London. He had then been brought before the
Privy Council, perhaps through Franklin's influence, to en-
lighten it on the state of American manners.

A second native of the Middle States who had settled in
North Carolina was Alexander Martin of Stokes County, the
active head of a political faction of small farmers—although
he himself owned a plantation worked by more than forty
slaves. After graduating from Princeton in 1756, Martin made
his way south by stages and established himself as a lawyer,
farmer, and local politician. Conservative enough to be given
a roughing-up by the Regulators, he nevertheless went along
with the other gentlemen of his acquaintance and served as a
legislator in the opening stages of the Revolution. He marched
off to war in 1775 as a lieutenant colonel in the Second North
Carolina Regiment; he came home as a civilian in 1777, having resigned his commission after acquittal of the charge of

cowardice in the battle of Germantown. Whatever may have been thought of Martin in Pennsylvania, he was trusted and admired in North Carolina, where he now served four years in the senate, two on the board of war, and three as governor, declining, however, to go north once again as a delegate to Congress. A man whose hobbies included poetry and Anglophobia, Martin was not celebrated for his nationalism, and he and Williamson were expected to cancel one another out in Philadelphia.

Another Princetonian was William R. Davie, a well-to-do young lawyer of Halifax. He was born in England in 1756 and brought to America by his father in 1763, where he was reared by his uncle, a prominent Presbyterian minister. While studying with President Witherspoon in 1776, he did some part-time soldiering around New York in defiance of a warning by the Princeton faculty, which thereupon voted to expel him (for willful disobedience, not partisan zeal) and was foiled only by the sympathetic intervention of Witherspoon. In the later stages of the war he served audaciously—he was three times wounded—as a major and then colonel of cavalry, especially at Camden where, by again disobeying orders, he helped to save the American forces from total disaster. He also put in a difficult year as commissary general under General Greene for the Carolina campaign. Returning to the bar, to which he had been admitted in 1780, Davie soon built up a handsome practice. He did not enter politics until 1784, when he was elected to the lower house from Halifax, but an ambitious nature and a commanding manner carried him swiftly to the top of the loose alliance of factions opposed to the radicalism and anti-nationalism of Willie Jones, whose niece he had married in 1783. A moderate nationalist who had close ties with former Governor Samuel Johnston, Davie is said to have been largely responsible for persuading the delegation from North Carolina to make the long journey to Philadelphia.

The fourth member of this delegation, William Blount of Pitt County, was noted approvingly by William Pierce as "a character strongly marked for integrity and honor." [12] Unlike Williamson, Martin, and Davie, he was a native Carolinian who had been born into a substantial planting family in 1749 and put to work at a young age. In the Revolution he served as a paymaster for the North Carolina forces, but spent most of his large stock of energy in improving the fortunes of the Blounts. As the war came to an end, he went boldly into politics. He was a leading figure in the North Carolina legislature, and was serving his second term in Congress when he was chosen to go to Philadelphia. The most important fact about William Blount in 1787 was his growing interest in the Tennessee lands. More than any other man in the Convention, he was someone who might speak for the settlers who had gone west as well as the speculators who had encouraged them to go.

At twenty-nine Richard Dobbs Spaight was one of the youngest and most handsomely situated men in the Convention. He was born in 1758 in New Bern of wealthy parents, and was sent at an early age to Ireland, his father's home, to be educated properly. After some years there, and perhaps also at the University of Glasgow, he returned to North Carolina in 1778. Almost immediately he was elected to the lower house, defeating none other than William Blount. From this time on he was one of the most active politicians in the state, although he did take time off to serve with the militia in the battle of Camden. Leaving his estate to the care of overseers, he went off in 1783 to two terms in Congress. Something of a straddler on the critical issues, Spaight was thought to lean toward a more orderly government in North Carolina and a more powerful one in the United States. Like a number of other men in the Convention, he was waiting for a lead from a stronger will.

The ruling gentlemen of South Carolina (141,979 and 107,094 slaves) yielded not an inch to the Virginians in pride of ancestry and confidence in the future. Accustomed as they were to the deference of their own constituents and to the envy of gentlemen in other states, they had always acted in the councils of the United States as if South Carolina were about three times as large as it was. The economic, political, and social life of the state centered on gay and handsome Charleston, which had made a remarkable recovery from the ravages of war; and it is indicative of the way in which both business and politics were carried on in South Carolina that all four members of the delegation to Philadelphia were planter-lawyer aristocrats who maintained one or more residences in both Charleston and the countryside. To the men of the North they were known as "nabobs" and "bashaws," and nabobs and bashaws they most certainly were.

At the head of this delegation was a hero of the Republic, John Rutledge, whom Pierce gladly accorded "distinguished rank among the American worthies" and Otto pronounced "the proudest and most imperious man in the United States." [13] Like John Dickinson a veteran of both the Stamp Act Congress and the first Continental Congress, he was a happy addition to the list of delegates to this third great "national deliberation." At the time of his birth in 1739 the Rutledges were not yet one of the grand families of the colony, but by 1776 his successes in the worlds of planting, law, and politics had made him a first citizen of South Carolina. Everything he did in the course of the Revolution added luster to his name.

Educated privately by the most celebrated tutor of Charleston, Rutledge was sent to England for legal training at the Middle Temple and was admitted to the English bar in 1760. Upon his return to Charleston, he began a practice so successful that fifteen years later he owned five plantations. He was a leading figure in the politics of the colony, the prototype of the American aristocrat who sparred ceaselessly with the royal governor from a front seat in the assembly; and, as an activist in the council of safety and a principal author of the Constitution of 1776, he was a natural choice for first president of the state. Although temporarily dislodged from office after the writing of a new constitution (which he disliked) in 1778, he was soon back in action with a vengeance. When the focus of war shifted violently southward, he became the virtual dictator of South Carolina. No one could have been more persevering in support of American arms, and Rutledge was rewarded for his remarkable services to the patriot cause by having his entire estate confiscated by the British. After the war he seems to have lost some of his energy, for he made only modest efforts to recoup his fortune and contented himself with an appointment in 1784 as presiding judge of the supreme court. He did spend one year (1782–1783) as a delegate to Congress, and there showed himself to be a firm nationalist.

General Charles Cotesworth Pinckney was a fit companion for Rutledge on the pilgrimage to Philadelphia. He was born in 1746 in Charleston, and was taken at a young age to London by his eminent father, who had agreed to serve as the colony's agent. Pinckney's formal education was perhaps the best given to any Framer: Westminster, Oxford (Christ Church), and the Middle Temple. He had even been a faithful auditor of Blackstone's lectures in the law. After one final year of study and travel on the Continent, he returned to Charleston in 1770 to practice law, manage his estates, and do the public duties expected of a Pinckney. He, too, was a warm patriot, and divided his time throughout the war between civil and military affairs. A member of South Carolina's council of safety and provincial congress, he had a hand in the Constitution of 1776, and never through all the vicissitudes of the war years was his name missing from the roster of the state legislature. His reputation was chiefly based, however, on his deeds as a soldier—in the defense of South Carolina in 1776, in the battles of Germantown and Brandywine (as an aide to Washington), and in hard fighting all over the South in the last stages of the war. Captured at Charleston in the surrender of 1780, he, too, had his property confiscated. By 1786, thanks to hard work, indulgent laws, and one fine crop of rice, he was well on the way to financial recovery. A genial, intelligent, and imposing man, he was not afraid to be pointed out as a committed member of the Cincinnati (which, in any case, drew less hostile fire in the South), and he shared the views of his old commander at Mt. Vernon about the need for stiff measures to restrain the urges of arrant democracy and to strengthen the bonds of union.

Charles Pinckney, second cousin of General Pinckney, was only twenty-nine when he set out for Philadelphia, but he was already well known to many of his fellow Framers-to-be. While Rutledge was a legend, Pinckney was a living presence in the high councils of the Republic. Deprived by the coming of war of his rightful place as student of the Middle Temple, he had read law in Charleston and had begun to practice in 1779. In the same year he was elected to the state legislature. He, too, was captured while serving as an officer in the defense of Charleston, and he, too, was a victim of British reprisals. In 1784 his fortunes as lawyer and planter were sufficiently mended to permit him to go off to New York as a delegate to Congress, and for the next three years, despite his youth and inexperience, he was one of the most active men in continental affairs, attracting particular attention for his opposition to the Jay-Gardoqui treaty. More than that, he was a relentless advocate of steps to strengthen the central government, whether by amending the Articles of Confederation to grant additional powers to Congress or by convoking a "grand convention" to draft an entirely new charter. His attempts to strengthen Congress reached their peak in the summer of 1786 when a committee under his chairmanship proposed seven specific additions to the Articles of Confederation in order to render the "federal government adequate to the ends for which it was instituted." [14] Pinckney came to Philadelphia with some rough plans for a new constitution. Handsome, vain, eager, and slightly rakish, he also seems to have come with a fixed determination to be known as the youngest man in the Convention (as he had been in Congress), for he led Pierce and others to understand that he had acquired all his "promising talents" and "polite learning" in just twenty-four years. [15]

The last member of this platoon of nabobs was a latecomer to Charleston, but as the second son of a baronet and the husband of a Middleton (a distinction he shared with General Pinckney) he did not worry his head about problems of precedence. Pierce Butler was born in County Carlow, Ireland, in 1744. His father was a worthy representative of a celebrated Anglo-Irish family, and was even then sitting in the House of Commons. After getting a good education, including a working knowledge of law, Butler was commissioned in the army and came to America—a most unusual migration—when his regiment was sent to tempestuous Boston. Having found his heiress, perhaps while she was summering in Newport, he resigned his commission in 1773 and moved to Charleston, there to pursue the life of an active gentleman. He was elected to the state legislature in 1778, and was still serving in it (as a somewhat cantankerous advocate of up-country causes) at the time of the Convention. He was named adjutant general of the state's forces in 1779, and found himself, like other men of his rank and views, dispossessed of his property. Despite strenuous exertions—he even journeyed to Amsterdam to negotiate a sizable loan at an endurable rate of interest—he was still in financial trouble in 1787. Nevertheless, as a man of conscience and a committed nationalist, Butler accepted appointment in March of that year to the South Carolina delegations to both Congress and the Convention.

South Carolina in 1787 had plenty of other nabobs in reserve. The eminent Henry Laurens, whose daughter was being courted confidently by Charles Pinckney, declined election because of age and ill health. Rutledge's younger brother Edward and C. C. Pinckney's younger brother Thomas stayed home lest the delegation consist of nothing but Rutledges and Pinckneys. Aedanus Burke was too anti-nationalist on the radical side, Rawlin Lowndes too anti-nationalist in a reactionary sort of way. Ralph Izard had, as almost always in his life, what he thought were bigger fish to fry, and Christopher Gadsden, the Sam Adams of Charleston in the days of resistance, was nursing his memories in semi-retirement. Still, the team of Rutledge, Pinckney, Pinckney, and Butler was considered to be a first-class representation of the nation-minded aristocrats of South Carolina. That this nation-mindedness arose primarily out of a concern for their state's place in the sun (and for their place in the state) was only mildly disturbing to nationalists like Madison and Hamilton, who were less interested in the motives of the South Carolinians than in their clear intention to strengthen the Union.

Georgia (53,284 and 29,264 slaves), the most remote, thinly populated, and poorly developed of the thirteen states, managed to insure representation in Philadelphia by the expedient of including its delegates to Congress in the slate elected on February 10. When George Walton and Nathaniel Pendleton refused to make the long journey to the north, this meant that Abraham Baldwin, William Few, William Houstoun, and William Pierce would have to do double duty in New York and Philadelphia. All were expected to take a moderately nationalist line. Although Georgians had the usual fears of faraway centralized power, the menace of the Creek Indians did not permit them to smile indulgently over the weakness of Congress. And although they were few in numbers, they looked forward to a day when their state would rival Virginia in numbers, Pennsylvania in riches, and Massachusetts in fame. The men of Georgia wanted protection as they grew to greatness, and they had a notion where it might be found.

Baldwin was a youthful Connecticut Yankee who had arrived in Georgia only in 1784. Since there were many such newcomers in this growing state, especially in the piedmont area west of Augusta, he was a more representative man than many native Georgians would have been. The son of a learned blacksmith of North Guilford, he graduated from Yale in 1772 and then, after further study, was licensed to preach in 1775. While putting in four years as tutor in theology at Yale and another four as chaplain in the army, he managed to read enough law to be admitted to the Fairfield County bar in 1783. He was apparently respected as a theologian, for he declined a professorship in divinity at Yale in 1781. In late 1783, with feet itching for a new stage, he took off for faraway Augusta and the practice of law; in 1785 he was elected to Congress by some of his fellow immigrants, and also took a seat in the Georgia lower house. In the legislature he was noted for his hard work in drafting statutes for a state system of education, in Congress for his exertions in behalf of both Georgia and the Union. A learned, good-humored, serene bachelor, Baldwin lived austerely on a small practice of the law and the uncertain pay of a public servant. He also had a tiny investment in continental securities and stock in the Bank of New York. He was, it was agreed by all, the ablest man in the Georgia delegation.

Few was a man of even more humble origins. Born on a farm near Baltimore in 1748, he moved at the age of ten with his unsuccessful father to North Carolina, where he worked as a farm laborer and a bricklayer. When his family came to grief—and one of his brothers went to the gallows

—in the Regulator agitation of 1771, Few moved on to the upcountry of Georgia. After several years of farming, reading history (supposedly in quiet moments between bouts with the plow), and disposing of his father's confused affairs in North Carolina, Few settled down for good in Georgia and went at once into politics. His new neighbors must have thought well of this self-taught man, for they elected him to the Georgia convention of 1776 and, shortly thereafter, to the legislature. In addition, he served the state as a member of its executive council, surveyor general, commissioner in dealing with the ever-present Indians, trustee of the nascent University of Georgia, and militia officer of the savage guerrilla warfare against the British. Although he was a man of extremely modest means, and thus should have been working his farm at home, he went north as a delegate to Congress in 1780–1782 and again in the fall of 1786. In the interval between these two periods of service he seems to have studied enough law to begin a modest practice. A dignified man, although one of the least aristocratic in the Convention, he impressed his colleague Pierce as a person of "strong natural genius." [16]

Very little was known about the third member of this delegation, William Houstoun of Savannah, except that he was an aristocrat from the coast rather than a yeoman from the piedmont. A member of a loyalist family that had served the Crown in colonial days, he made his own choice for the patriot cause while reading law at the Inner Temple in London, and returned to America to serve in a number of local offices. Like the imposing South Carolinians, he was a lawyer and planter, and although his purchase of confiscated estates (at least one of which belonged to a departed relative) made him just one more land-poor gentleman, he lived unconcernedly with his debts. In 1784 he was elected to Congress, and was still serving with reasonable faithfulness when he was authorized to join the other Georgians in Philadelphia. Although Pierce credited Houstoun with a "sweet temper" and "honorable principles," he had to admit that "nature" had done more for the "corporeal than mental powers" of his friend.[17]

As to Pierce himself, perhaps we should hear what he said at the end of his famous "sketches":

> My own character I shall not attempt to draw, but leave those who may choose to speculate on it, to consider it in any light that their fancy or imagination may depict. I am conscious of having discharged my duty as a soldier through the course of the late revolution with

honor and propriety; and my services in Congress and the Convention were bestowed with the best intention towards the interest of Georgia, and towards the general welfare of the Confederacy. I possess ambition, and it was that, and the flattering opinion which some of my friends had of me, that gave me a seat in the wisest council in the world, and furnished me with an opportunity of giving these short sketches of the characters who composed it.[18]

One wishes that Pierce had been less modest, for not much more is known about him than about Houstoun. He was born of humble circumstances in either Georgia or Virginia sometime around 1740, and appeared in Savannah, a modestly educated and capable man, sometime in 1776. For his services as aide to General Sullivan in 1779 and to General Greene at the battle of Eutaw Springs (where he showed exceptional bravery), a grateful Congress presented him with a sword. Upon his return to Savannah he went into the import-export business and for a while, thanks to his wife's dowry, did fairly well. A fluctuation in the European rice market brought him to the edge of disaster in 1786, so that it was a debt-ridden Pierce who was sitting in Congress, perhaps trying to pick up a little business on the side, when he was commissioned to appear in Philadelphia. During a short period of service in the Georgia legislature Pierce had voted for paper money. Since it was an issue of £50,000 for financing war against the Indians, and since he was a high officer in the local chapter of the Cincinnati, Pierce was obviously no more an agrarian radical than the nabobs immediately to the north who, in the special circumstances of post-war South Carolina, had also found it necessary to vote for paper money and debtor relief.

The delegation from Georgia was probably the least distinguished in the Convention. What Madison and his friends expected of this delegation, in any case, was not ideas but votes, and they expected these votes to come in handy in the sparring with the doubtful delegations from New York and Maryland.

# 8  THE MEN OF PHILADELPHIA

> *If all the delegates named for this Convention at Philadelphia are present, we will never have seen, even in Europe, an assembly more respectable for the talents, knowledge, disinterestedness, and patriotism of those who compose it.*
>
> OTTO, French chargé d'affaires, to the COMTE DE MONTMORIN, April 10, 1787[1]

WHEN Thomas Jefferson, serving apprehensively as minister in Paris, first saw the list of delegates to the Convention, he exclaimed in writing to his friend John Adams, serving uncomfortably as minister in London: "It really is an assembly of demigods." [2]

Jefferson was not alone in this view (although no one else expressed it so fulsomely), for it was widely held outside the Convention and demurely suspected within. The *Daily Advertiser* in New York described the gathering as "the collective wisdom of the Continent"; the *Pennsylvania Herald* found it "a wonderful display of wisdom, eloquence, and patriotism"; and the *New-York Journal*, which followed many other newspapers in identifying it as "the Grand Convention," thought that "AUGUST" was the only word that could convey the quality of these men.[3] Franklin told a friend that it was truly *"une assemblée des notables"*: Madison remarked that it was "the best contribution of talents the states could make for the occasion"; and even crusty George Mason had to admit to his son that "America has certainly, upon this occasion, drawn forth her first characters." [4] The high opinion of the French chargé d'affaires was confirmed by Crèvecoeur, who informed the Duc de La Rochefoucauld that the Convention was "composed of the most enlightened men of the continent." [5]

We, of course, have the unfair advantage of hindsight; and, knowing that an enduring success was to be the fruit of the Convention's labors, we wonder at the rightness of these judgments and applaud them loudly. We recognize that Jefferson was exaggerating for effect (or simply expressing delight that Virginia had chosen so well), yet we too can detect a quality of the heroic in this gathering, even when its members are seen as they were in May of 1787. There were also, as we know, several touches of foxiness, pretension, and self-interest, but that is only to say that the most admirable half-gods are half-human.

The fact is, as we have learned in the last three chapters, that these fifty-five men were completely human, and the question is therefore not whether they displayed virtues and abilities we would expect to find only among the most favored of Zeus's illegitimate children, but whether they were, as Madison wrote, "the best contribution of talents"—and also the most representative—the infant Republic could have made at this time, in this place, and for this purpose of writing a new constitution. Let us attempt to answer that question by constructing a broad profile of the Grand Convention, in which we take account of every meaningful feature in its make-up from geography to age by way of wealth and experience, and also by taking a second look at the leading men who stayed home by choice or chance.

*Geography.* A knowledgeable scholar of the Convention has identified fifty-five "major geographical areas" in 1787 in the twelve states that sent delegations.[6] Since fully two-thirds of these areas were home bases to men who got to Philadelphia, since every important center of commerce and politics sent at least one resident to the gathering, and since many delegates were alert to the problems of sections in other parts of their states, we may conclude that the Convention, except for one notable weakness, was a reasonably accurate projection of the American pattern of settled living in 1787. The weakness was the dearth of men who lived in the back country, a weakness especially manifest in the composition of the delegations from Massachusetts, Pennsylvania, Virginia, and the Carolinas. The chief explanations are that the political talent of the nation was heavily concentrated in the older areas near the ocean and along the great rivers, that people in the under-represented sections were inward-turning in preoccupation, and that their leaders were therefore so anti-nationalist in temper as to look with suspicion on the designs of Madison and Hamilton. Since they could not imagine a national government in which they had their fair share of influence, nor even could feel the need for such a government, most men of the West who thought about the matter all wanted nothing to do with a gathering like the one planned for Philadelphia. It was clear at the outset of the Convention that the western counties of states like Massachusetts and

Pennsylvania would be no more directly represented than all the truculent counties of Rhode Island,[7] and more than one hardheaded nationalist must have breathed a sigh of relief. If the Convention was to be a success as a nation-building enterprise, nation-minded men would have to be in the overwhelming majority, and few such men, whether sound or shortsighted or merely silly of motive, were to be found in the back country.

The membership of the Convention also showed a high state of geographic mobility, which had been a characteristic of most American society from the beginning. Eight Framers were born outside the United States (all, to be sure, under the British flag), and sixteen others were not natives of the states they were representing. At least eighteen had spent a year or more of their lives as grown men working or studying abroad. New Hampshire, Massachusetts, and Virginia sent "pure" delegations consisting entirely of native sons; North Carolina, Delaware, Georgia, and Pennsylvania sent "impure" ones. Pennsylvania, in particular, was a lesson in cosmopolitanism, joining a Scot, an Englishman, an Irishman, a Bostonian, a Connecticut Yankee, and a comedian from the Bronx with two birthright Philadelphians in a delegation considerably more "American" than that of Virginia.

*Politics.* Many a faction in states like Massachusetts and North Carolina rose and fell with the fortunes of a very few men (in some cases, of only one man), and thus a process of splintering and merging was constantly under way in the pattern of American politics. Nevertheless, it is possible to identify roughly thirty stable factions (including the two Pennsylvania "parties") in state politics in 1787, of which all but a half-dozen were represented in the Convention. For the most part, the leaders of factions stayed home and let themselves be represented by men more skilled in constitution-making or more national in reputation and outlook—or, as in the special case of the Clintonians, by men who could be counted on to understand their duty and to do it. In Langdon, Robert Morris, Read, Jenifer, and Alexander Martin the Convention had its fair share of political bosses; in Johnson, Livingston, Brearly, Franklin, Washington, Blair, and Williamson it had a useful leaven of independents. Although the legal disfranchisement of the desperately poor, the effective disfranchisement of the totally isolated, and the malapportionment of most state legislatures in favor of the older areas all worked to make the Convention less perfectly representative than it might have been, the largest factor in determining its make-up was, quite simply, free choice: those who were there wanted to be there; and, with the few glaring exceptions of which we have learned, they wanted to be there to give a boost to the nation. If a dozen men like Patrick Henry and Willie Jones had been delegates to the Convention, it would have been much more perfectly representative of the active citizenry of 1787. It would also, one is bound to point out, have been crippled as a nation-building instrument. Henry and Jones, in any case, had no right to complain on this score, for each had been elected officially, and only then had chosen not to serve.

*Reputation.* What must have struck knowledgeable men most forcefully about the lists in the newspapers was the large number of names with which they were familiar. The combined reputations of the delegates were a surety that any proposals of the Convention would be listened to with the greatest respect. The Republic had two men of world-wide fame, and both were on the list. It had perhaps ten who were well-known within the bounds of the old empire, and at least five of that description (Johnson, Livingston, Robert Morris, Dickinson, and Rutledge) were on it, too. Gorham, Gerry, Sherman, Ellsworth, Hamilton, Mifflin, Wilson, Madison, Wythe, Williamson, Charles Pinckney, and the untraveled Mason had won themselves—as best one could in those days of poor communications—continental reputations; Langdon, Read, Randolph, Alexander Martin, Jenifer, and C. C. Pinckney were major figures in their states; and almost every other delegate was someone whose standing was unchallenged in his part of the country. Of all the fifty-five Framers-to-be, only Jacob Broom of Delaware seemed totally out of place in a gathering of the "first characters" of the land. Nicholas Gilman of the Exeter Gilmans at least had his name to give him courage.

*Family.* The "annals of the poor," as Thomas Gray sang and Abraham Lincoln once reminded his constituents, are "short and simple." If the records were as full as we would like them to be, we might discover that a few Framers—for example, Sherman, Houston, Luther Martin, and Few—began life in the next-to-the-bottom layer of white society. For the most part, however, they came from respectable if not always substantial families, and from their earliest days they were well launched toward the careers of public service in which they were to win undying fame. Although the annals of the rich in early America are often just as hard to find and then to interpret, we may say with some confidence that sixteen or more of the Framers were born aristocrats—Johnson, Livingston, Ingersoll, Gouverneur Morris, Mifflin, Carroll, Jenifer, Mercer, Blair, Mason, Randolph, Washington, Butler, the Pinckneys, Rutledge, and perhaps Yates, Lansing, and Houstoun—and that fully half this number were sons of un-challenged "first families." The one man of questionable origins, Colonel Hamilton, had answered the leading question to the satisfaction of all but a few malicious persons by marrying into a first family. Indeed, if there is one talent the Framers seem to have had in common, it was an admirable agility at marrying their way up the social and economic ladder. This was as true, after all, of General Washington as it was of his ambitious young friend from New York.

*Wealth.* It is not easy to place each of the Framers precisely in one of the categories with which we like to separate the rich from the not-so-rich and the modestly fixed from the poor. The finances of the period were chaotic; debts were as prominent a feature of the early republican way of life as they had been of the late colonial; and many of the delegates, like many of their spiritual descendants today in business, law, and politics, worked hard at looking richer or poorer than they really were. Still, it would seem that the Framers divided roughly as follows:

Rich: Langdon, Gerry, Lansing, Mifflin, Robert Morris (although his debts were vast), Carroll, Jenifer, Mercer, Mason, and Washington (although he could never put his hands on enough hard cash).

Trying to be rich (or having once been): Gorham, Dayton, Fitzsimons, Wilson, the four South Carolinians, and Houstoun.

Well-to-do: Johnson, Livingston, Franklin, Clymer, Dickinson, Gouverneur Morris, McHenry, Randolph, McClurg, Spaight, and Alexander Martin.

Comfortable: Gilman, Strong, King, Ellsworth, Hamilton, Yates, Houston, Ingersoll, Read, Bassett, Bedford, Wythe, Blair, Davie, Williamson, and Blount.

Of modest means: Paterson, Brearly, Broom, Luther Martin, Madison, and Baldwin.

Of very modest means: Sherman, Few, and Pierce.

Although the Framers invested their money (whether owned or merely borrowed) in all manner of enterprises, the most common categories were land and slaves. Ten had invested in city real estate, twelve held western lands for speculative purposes, and twenty got all or most of their income from land that was being cultivated. A full sixteen—many of them, of course, the same men—owned what we might call productive slaves. The known holders of such slaves among the delegates were Carroll, Jenifer, Mercer, Mason, Washington, Randolph, Blair, Spaight, Blount, Davie, Alexander Martin, the four South Carolinians, and Houstoun; Luther Martin, Few, Madison, Wythe, and even men like Livingston, Fitzsimons, Read, Dickinson, and Johnson had a few slaves around the house and in the garden. At least eight delegates had put sizable amounts of money in bank securities or loans, and at least six had ships at sea; but only three—Ellsworth, Johnson, and the imprudent Wilson—had looked to the far future by investing in manufactures. Although the records are imperfect and often confusing, we may say with some confidence that perhaps two dozen Framers held securities of state and nation.[7]

*Calling.* The eighteenth century was an age of enviable versatility, and few of the delegates can be pinned down in one vocation. This list, nevertheless, should give a fair notion of the way in which each man was making his living in 1787.

Planters or large-scale farmers: Lansing, Carroll, Jenifer, Mercer, Mason, Washington, Butler, Charles Pinckney, C. C. Pinckney, Spaight, Davie, Blount, and Houstoun. Several of these men were also practicing lawyers or officeholders.

Lawyers: King, Strong, Ellsworth, Hamilton, Dayton, Paterson, Gouverneur Morris, Wilson, Ingersoll, Read, Dickinson (retired), Bassett, and Alexander Martin, at least half of whom were engaged in other income-producing activities.

Merchants: Langdon, Gerry, Gorham, Clymer, Fitzsimons, Robert Morris, Mifflin (retired), and Pierce.

State officeholders: Gilman, Yates, Livingston, Houston, Brearly, Bedford, Luther Martin, Blair, Wythe, Randolph, Rutledge, and Baldwin. Several of these men, too, could almost as easily be placed under other headings, and several had income from investments.

Small farmers: Broom and Few, the second of whom also dabbled in law and surveying.

Physicians: McClurg and Williamson.

Non-practicing physician living on an inheritance: McHenry.

Retired printer and diplomat: Franklin.

Retired lawyer and independent gentleman about to become an educator: Johnson.

Jack-of-all-trades: Sherman.

Impossible to classify: Madison.

Most of the Framers, as can be plainly seen, were leading members of four of the principal vocations in republican America.

*Experience.* Every man among the Framers, even the politically inexperienced McClurg, had been on the public payroll at some time in his life. It was, of course, almost im-

possible for a person of even modest ability to escape public
service in those simpler days, yet in this matter, as in so
many others, the Framers were an elite of the American elite.
No gathering of the leaders of a newly independent nation at
any time in history has had more cumulative political experience than the Convention of 1787.

In the first place, they had shared the toughening experience of fighting and directing the fateful Revolution they now
hoped to bring to fruition. Although it was more than twenty
years since the beginning of resistance and ten since the beginning of war, the men of the Revolution were still in the
saddle all over America, and the Convention was a gathering
of just such men. Those historians who have portrayed Philadelphia as a furtive meeting of an old generation that had
stood aloof with a new generation that had never suffered
have done the Framers a gratuitous injustice. With the single
exception of Dr. Johnson, a decent man tormented by the
pull of opposing loyalties, they could all have passed any fair
test of patriotism set up by Samuel Adams and Christopher
Gadsden. Although some had been more eager than others—
some revolutionists always are—the Framers made up an assembly of men who had very positively committed their
"lives," their "fortunes," and their "sacred honor" to the
American cause, even if this meant breaking with their own
families. Three had been in the Stamp Act Congress, seven in
the first Continental Congress. Eight—Gerry, Sherman, Robert Morris, Wilson, Clymer, Franklin, Read, Wythe—had
signed the Declaration of Independence, and five others—
Langdon, Livingston, Mifflin, Rutledge, Washington—were
cheated of this distinction because they had gone off to fight
the British. At least thirty had done some kind of military
duty, and half that number—notably Hamilton, Dayton,
Mifflin, McHenry, Mercer, Alexander Martin, Davie, Pierce,
and "the immortal Washington"—were hardened veterans.
Even the most hardened would gladly have welcomed civil-
ians like Langdon, Livingston, Read, Rutledge, and Franklin
into the inner circle of Revolutionary heroism.

Perhaps an even more remarkable statistic is that forty-two
of the Framers had already served at one time or another in
the Congress of the United States, and thus had been given a
chance, which most had exploited intelligently and in good
faith, to find out for themselves what it meant to pursue national ends through confederate means. Among those who
had used their time in Congress especially well were Langdon, Gerry, Gorham (President, 1786–1787), King, Sherman,
Johnson, Ellsworth, Hamilton, Clymer, the Morrises, Mifflin
(President, 1783–1784), Wilson, Dickinson, Read, Bedford,

Carroll, Jenifer, McHenry, Madison, Wythe, Randolph, Williamson, Spaight, Charles Pinckney, Rutledge, and Baldwin. Together these men formed a pool of deliberative, legislative, investigative, and administrative experience that would have been a credit to the mightiest nation then existing.

All but two or three Framers had also served as public officials of colony or state. Indeed, at the moment the Convention met, more than forty were lending thir energies to keeping the state governments from foundering: Franklin, Livingston, and Randolph as chief executives; Houston, Bedford, Jenifer, and Luther Martin as administrators; Gorham, Ellsworth, Sherman, Yates, Brearly, Blair, Wythe, Rutledge, and several others as judges; and thirty (of whom seven were or just had been speakers) as legislators. Perhaps twenty had helped to write the constitutions of their states, and a half-dozen had been put to work as codifiers of laws. Even the most suspicious anti-nationalists could not deny that the members of the Convention were in close touch with local and regional problems. The difference between the Framers and many equally powerful and wealthy men who stayed at home is that the former wanted to face the future as citizens of a well-founded nation, while the latter felt it more important to preserve the states inviolate in "sovereignty, freedom and independence."

*Education.* The Convention was just as rich in learning as in property and experience. In an age when few men went to college, even from the most lofty families, the Framers were conspicuous for the number of their degrees, whether earned or honorary. For the instruction and perhaps comfort of the alumni of several venerable institutions, let us sum up the undergraduate record of the Framers, taking note that in this list of names there was only one "dropout" who never returned, Alexander Hamilton, who had a good reason to drop out and even better reasons not to return:

College of New Jersey (Princeton): Bedford, Davie, Dayton, Ellsworth, Houston, Madison, both Martins, Paterson.

Yale: Baldwin, Ingersoll, Johnson, Livingston.

William and Mary: Blair, McClurg, Mercer, Randolph.

Harvard: Gerry, King, Strong.

King's (Columbia): Gouverneur Morris, Hamilton.

College of Philadelphia (University of Pennsylvania): Mifflin, Williamson.

Oxford: C. C. Pinckney.

St. Andrews: Wilson.

If we add to this list the names of those (like Dickinson and Rutledge) who studied law at one of the Inns of Court in London, attach to names already on the list (like Johnson, Paterson, McClurg, and Williamson) the degrees they won for graduate work at home and abroad, take note of the professorships or tutorships of Baldwin, Houston, Williamson, Wilson, McClurg, and Wythe, and count up the honorary degrees that had already come to such as Franklin (LL.D., Edinburgh, 1759) and Washington (LL.D., Harvard, 1776—an interesting year to get an honorary degree from Harvard), we arrive at a sum of college experience that was perhaps the most astonishing feature of the Convention. At the same time, we should not let our astonishment blind us to the fact that there were roads other than college to learning in those days. The self-taught Franklin, the privately educated Mason, and the Jesuit-trained Carroll were not at all uncomfortable in the presence of all those bachelors of arts from the Ivy League.

Another interesting point about the intellectual preparation of the Framers is the large number who were trained in the law. Although no more than a dozen were active members of the bar in 1787, almost three dozen had spent time in one of the "law schools" of that simpler age (that is, in the office of an established attorney); and Coke and Blackstone vied with Locke and Montesquieu for the allegiance of learned members of the Convention. If the Constitution has become, in one of its many roles, a "lawyer's document," that is perhaps because so many lawyers had a hand in writing it.

*Religion.* Whatever else it might turn out to be, the Convention would not be a "Barebone's Parliament." Although it had its share of strenuous Christians like Strong and Bassett, ex-preachers like Baldwin and Williamson, and theologians like Johnson and Ellsworth, the gathering at Philadelphia was largely made up of men in whom the old fires were under control or had even flickered out. Most were nominally members of one of the traditional churches in their part of the country—the New Englanders Congregationalists and Presbyterians, the Southerners Episcopalians, and the men of the Middle States everything from backsliding Quakers to stubborn Catholics—and most were men who could take their religion or leave it alone. Although no one in this sober gathering would have dreamed of invoking the Goddess of Reason, neither would anyone have dared to proclaim that his opinions had the support of the God of Abraham and Paul. The Convention of 1787 was highly rationalist and even secular in spirit.

*Age.* The Framers were well distributed on the spectrum of maturity. Perhaps a dozen had "come of age" in the colonial period, and thus had gone into the crisis of 1765 as men of experience and purpose: Carroll, Dickinson, Jenifer, Johnson, Livingston, Mason, Robert Morris, Read, Sherman, Washington, Wythe, and of course Franklin, who had lived five lives before Jonathan Dayton was born. Perhaps a half-dozen were still coming of age when the Convention met: Bedford, Broom, Davie, Dayton, Mercer, and Spaight. The rest were, quite simply, men of the Revolution whose normal rate of growth had speeded up dramatically in one of the steamiest hothouses of political talent the world has ever known. The average age of the entire Convention was just over forty-three; that of the two dozen or more delegates of whom most was expected was just over forty-six.

In 1788, during the struggle over ratification, Melancton Smith of New York got tired of hearing that he ought to approve the Constitution simply because of the extraordinary "character and ability" of its authors. "The favorers of this system," he wrote, were "not very prudent in bringing this forward."

> It provokes to an investigation of characters, which is an invidious task. I do not wish to detract from their merits, but I will venture to affirm that twenty assemblies of equal number might be collected, equally respectable both in point of ability, integrity, and patriotism.[8]

Although Smith was guilty of exaggeration—and, being a sensible man, must have known he was—he was no more guilty than those who had begun to talk in May, 1787, as if fate had chosen the fifty-five most eminent men of the new nation to assemble in Philadelphia. In fact, if we go carefully through the list of political leaders in the twelve participating states, we can construct at least one additional assembly "equally respectable," not only in "ability, integrity, and patriotism," but also in prestige. Had all the men we cherish as Framers been dead, dying, abroad, or otherwise occupied, and had all the other well-wishers of a stronger national government been available for duty, the roster of the Convention might have read like this:

New Hampshire: General Sullivan and any one of Josiah Bartlett, Samuel Livermore, and John Taylor Gilman.

Massachusetts: John Adams, James Bowdoin, Theophilus Parsons, and, for window-dressing, John Hancock or Samuel Adams, with Theodore Sedgwick, John Lowell, Fisher Ames, William Cushing, and a dozen other stalwarts in reserve.

Connecticut: any three of Governor Huntington, General

Huntington, Jeremiah Wadsworth, William Williams, and Oliver Wolcott, sr.

New York: as anti-nationalists, John Lamb and Melancton Smith; as the single nationalist permitted to go, any one of a half-dozen "first characters" like General Schuyler, John Jay, James Duane, and R. R. Livingston.

New Jersey: General Dayton, Rev. Witherspoon, Elias Boudinot, and the two delinquents Clark and Neilson.

Pennsylvania: Thomas McKean, General Arthur St. Clair, William Bingham, Dr. Benjamin Rush, Tench Coxe, Timothy Pickering, F. A. Muhlenberg, and any one of a dozen merchants no less respectable than Clymer or Fitzsimons.

Delaware: John Vining, President Thomas Collins, Nathaniel Mitchell, Colonel Gunning Bedford (a cousin of the Framer), and, borrowed for the occasion if Pennsylvania could not use him, Thomas McKean.

Maryland: the five who declined, with Thomas Johnson, William Paca, and William Pinkney as possible substitutes, and with Samuel Chase coming himself instead of sending Luther Martin to do his work.

Virginia: Thomas Jefferson, Richard Henry Lee, Henry Lee, Edmund Pendleton, Colonel Edward Carrington, Cyrus Griffin, and John Marshall, with a dozen hardly less admirable men in reserve—but Patrick Henry still in his Cave of Adullam.

North Carolina: Governor Caswell, James Iredell, Samuel Johnston, William Hooper, and, for a touch of color, John Sevier—but Willie Jones, too, a conspicuous truant.

South Carolina: Thomas Pinckney, Edward Rutledge, William L. Smith, and David Ramsay, with Henry Laurens and Ralph Izard still permitted to go free.

Georgia: The two delinquents, Walton and Pendleton, plus any two of James Gunn, Lachlan McIntosh, and James Jackson.

This exercise is, to a large extent, a matter of opinion, yet one must conclude that Massachusetts, New York, New Jersey, Maryland, North Carolina, and Georgia could, with a little more pluck and luck, have sent stronger delegations; that New Hampshire and South Carolina could have done just as well; that Pennsylvania and Virginia could have done almost as well; and that only Connecticut (without Johnson and Sherman) and Delaware (without Dickinson and Read) would have put a weaker foot forward. Washington and Franklin were, to be sure, irreplaceable as giants of the Revolution and symbols of nationhood, and a keen observer in early 1787—we are still looking at these men from that perspective—might have guessed that Madison was a combination of learning, experience, purpose, and imagination that not even Adams or Jefferson could have equalled. With these exceptions, however, the Republic had in reserve at least one team, and perhaps two, that would have been no less eminent and capable than the team actually chosen.

I make this point not to slight the Framers, but to acclaim the fledgling nation that produced them. The Framers were a phenomenon, yet so was the nation. It could keep some of its best men at work in London, Paris, Boston, Hartford, New York, and Charleston, permit others to sulk or stew or rusticate, and draw hardly at all on one entire description of leaders (the suspicious anti-nationalists)—and still it could provide an elite for an extended act of political creation that has rarely been matched for "talents, knowledge, disinterestedness, and patriotism." One feels a tug of admiration for a young country that could spawn such a gathering despite all the vicissitudes, impediments, and strokes of bad luck that kept many "first characters" from journeying to Philadelphia. One also feels a twinge of sorrow that fate could not have reserved places for Thomas Jefferson and John Adams, and perhaps also for John Marshall. Since fate was gracious in producing a live Franklin and a dutiful Washington, perhaps we ought to leave well enough alone.

That "well enough," after all, was a political elite both willing and able to act with creative boldness in behalf of an entire nation. It was, as we have just seen, both talented and tested; it was also, as it had proved in the maneuvers of 1786 and early 1787, both troubled enough to act and confident enough to gamble. And it was, as a political elite in a rising nation should be, legitimate, unalienated, self-perceiving, and purposeful.

The legitimacy of the Grand Convention is attested by the fact that its self-appointed strategists had gone through open channels to reach their immediate end of convoking a reform-minded meeting. Congress had authorized some such meeting in its grudging but straightforward resolution of February 21, 1787, and the twelve legislatures, each of which had been recently elected, had chosen delegates in the approved manner of choosing delegates to Congress. Several of the state legislatures, to be sure, were overloaded with seats from the more settled areas; several were based on a franchise from which less fortunate members of the community were excluded by law, custom, or circumstance. They were, nevertheless, by far the most democratic legislatures then existing in the world, and the delegates were not indulging in hypocrisy when they talked of themselves as "representatives of the people of the United States." As they assembled in Philadelphia they had the comforting feeling of legitimacy that comes to extraordinary bodies which are both legal and popular. If they were not an exact miniature of the pattern of American politics in 1787—for if they were, where were the Shaysites?—that was in large part because a natural process of selection (and self-selection) had excluded the Clintons, Henrys, and Joneses from a course of events to which they would have been unhappy witnesses—and to which, indeed, they might have presented an insurmountable barrier. They and all their anti-nationalist followers would have their day, in any case, when the Convention reported back to Congress and sought approval for its handiwork.

Unlike the founding fathers of many new nations of the twentieth century, the Framers felt no sense of alienation from the mass of people for whom they had come together to write a new charter. Although perhaps one-third of them had studied, worked, or traveled abroad, they were all, whether men of the old breed like Franklin and Sherman or of the new like Dayton and Davie, thoroughly American in mind, spirit, style, taste, and even prejudice. Leaders whose commitment to the Revolution and dedication to republican principles had been tested and found solid, they could identify themselves closely with their neighbors and constituents. If they were richer, better educated, and more influential than a random sample of even the upper one-third of American society, what such gathering in the history of western democracy has not been? Although the Convention was roughly representative in geography and politics, it was propitiously unrepresentative—or perhaps the word should be "uncommon"—in most other qualities.

The Framers knew that they were special men; and, with the exception of Broom and two or three others, they exhibited a pervasive, developed *esprit de corps* from the beginning. An auspicious feature of the Convention, about which there was approving comment at the time, was the happy reunion of old friends and comrades, men who had been out together in all sorts of weather and were still not afraid of storms. Washington could look around the room and see a half-dozen men who had voted him into command far back in 1775, a dozen who had been with him at Trenton, Monmouth, or Yorktown (one of whom, Thomas Mifflin, he was still trying to forgive), and another dozen who had won his friendship by supporting him in Congress or fishing with him in the Potomac. The signers of the Declaration were a special band of brothers, as were young men like Pierce and Dayton who had gone on the Sullivan expedition and young men like

Hamilton and McHenry who had endured Valley Forge. Dickinson, Rutledge, and Johnson had worked together closely in the Stamp Act Congress, and the last of these had made a score of friends in Congress after 1784 with his keen mind and sweet temper. Yates had studied law with Livingston, Livingston had been a patron of Hamilton, Hamilton had brightened the life of Madison, Madison had swapped books with Williamson, Williamson had done experiments with Franklin, Franklin had been amused by Sherman, Sherman had sold books to Baldwin, Baldwin had talked of the ancients with Johnson, Johnson was an old friend of the Morrises of Morrisania, and Gouverneur Morris had worked closely with Yates in New York's dark days of 1776–1777. Bedford and Madison were classmates from Princeton; so, too, were Ellsworth and Luther Martin. Robert Morris knew at least ten men intimately from the early days in Congress; ten others had been his associates in schemes for bolstering the credit of the United States or improving the fortunes of Robert Morris. Above all, the leading Framers knew each other well through service in Congress, for more than thirty of them had shared the frustrations of the years since Yorktown and learned in the hardest way of the need for a stronger union. They were, indeed, a continental elite, the nearest thing to an "establishment" that could have existed in those days of poor communications, limited horizons, and divided loyalties.

In the end, what made the Framers an elite of elites was their ability to broaden their horizons and to concentrate their loyalties. With those glaring exceptions we have mentioned—Lansing, Yates, Luther Martin, and Mercer—the delegates came to Philadelphia because they were nationalists, and came therefore with the purpose of strengthening the common government. Some, like Sherman and Paterson, were moderates, and expected to go at the problem by working out several additions to the Articles of Confederation. Some, like King and Jenifer, were already moving toward stronger views, and were probably of two minds about the Articles. Most, however, had passed the bounds of patience, and were ready—given any sort of lead—to scrap the Articles and begin anew. One man in particular, as we know, was ready to give that lead. Although his ideas of a constitution for a nation were still unformed on many crucial points, Madison had concluded—as had most of his friends and colleagues—that a government of divided powers legislating directly for individuals must now be created to replace the confederate, congressional form that had failed the Republic.

The mandate actually given to Madison and the others was less detailed and purposeful than the one he carried in his mind as the gift of destiny, and it might be useful to set down the exact words with which the delegates were sent on their way. There were two principal versions of the task set before the Framers. One was the broad formula worked out by Hamilton, Randolph, and Madison in the Annapolis report of September 14, 1786, which expressed the hope (and legally it was no more than a hope) that provisions would be "devised" to "render the constitution of the federal government adequate to the exigencies of the Union." [9] The other was the narrower formula of the Congressional resolution of February 21, 1787, which expressed the wish (and legally it was more than a wish) that the delegates convene for "the sole and express purpose of revising the Articles of Confederation." [10]

For the record, here is a summary of the authorizations of the twelve delegations,[11] in which are listed for each state the date of election, the mandate to the delegates, and the quorum required for full participation in the business of the Convention:

Virginia: October 16 (authorization) and December 4 (election), 1786; the Annapolis formula; three.

New Jersey: November 23, 1786; the Annapolis formula; three.

Pennsylvania: December 30, 1786; the Annapolis formula; four.

North Carolina: January 6, 1787; "for the purpose of revising the federal constitution"; three.

New Hampshire: January 17 (repeated June 27), 1787; "to remedy the defects of our federal Union"; two.

Delaware: February 3, 1787; the Annapolis formula; three.

Georgia: February 10, 1787; the Annapolis formula; two.

New York: February 28, 1787; the Congressional formula; no number mentioned.

South Carolina: March 8, 1787; the Annapolis formula; two.

Massachusetts: March 10, 1787; the Congressional formula; three.

Connecticut: May 10, 1787; the Annapolis formula; one.

Maryland: May 26, 1787; the Annapolis formula; no number mentioned.

In addition, the resolution of Congress and all authorizations of the states save those of New Jersey and North Carolina made clear that the proposals of the Convention would not go into effect until "agreed to in Congress and confirmed by the states."

Although there were other admonitions sprinkled through the resolutions of the state legislatures—Connecticut, for example, warned its delegates to report only such provisions as would be "agreeable to the general principles of republican government." [12]—only one restriction of a binding nature was included: the Delaware legislature told its delegates to stand fast on the clause in the Articles of Confederation which gave each state one vote.[13] It did this largely at the prompting of George Read, a determined nationalist who was, however, unwilling to see Delaware reduced to a "cypher," and who felt that such a restriction would "relieve" him and his colleagues "from disagreeable argumentation." [14]

Why, in the end, did these fifty-five men gather in Philadelphia for the third and, as it turned out, last extraordinary "national deliberation" of the American people? What ambitions drove them? What fears disturbed them? What hopes summoned them?

These are questions, needless to say, that will never be answered conclusively. The public and private records are distressingly sketchy; and even if each Framer had been interviewed discreetly and in depth by a panel of social scientists as he arrived in Philadelphia (a thought both intriguing and horrifying), how sure could we be that he understood his own motives, how sure that he had expressed them fully and fairly? Historians of different persuasions, moreover, mean very different things when they talk about motives and purposes, and even the most complete, certain, and neutral mass of evidence lies virtually helpless before the maker of definitions.

None of these considerations excuses the student of the Convention from making his own answers as honestly as he can, and I have tried to make mine with candor in the course of this narrative. To repeat and embellish the conclusions reached at the end of Chapter 3, it seems to me that all but a handful of Framers were engaged in a quest for nationhood, that they saw this quest as both a fulfillment of the Revolution and a promise of future glory, and that they recognized the creation of an effective, republican national government as the next step in the quest. If they had been pressed to elaborate upon some of the happy results they expected from such a step, they would have answered with varying degrees of fervor: an end to disorder, a forestalling of despotism, protection for personal liberty, security for private property, honor for the Republic. If pressed hard, most would have acknowledged that they were certainly not there to sell out the interests of their states and sections, to transfer the reins of authority to another class of men, or to lay the groundwork for a social revolution. And if asked to talk in terms of personal ambition, most would have suggested, like the eighteenth-century gentlemen they were, that to talk in such terms in this situation was quite misleading. Service to the public was a "given" in the lives of men of their description, they would have insisted, and one did not total up all the pluses and minuses of personal aspiration before one set out to perform this kind of service.

Even the most apparently selfless Framers could, of course, have been fooling themselves, and fooling us in the process. Some must have expected a successful convention to be a gateway to bigger and better things for themselves and their friends as well as for the country. It may be that Hamilton was driven to Philadelphia primarily by a love of fame, Langdon by a hope of profit, King by a thirst for power, and Dayton by an uncomplicated vanity. Nevertheless, when all the evidence has been examined thoughtfully in the context of 1787, one must conclude that both the revealed and concealed purposes of most Framers—including the first three of the four just mentioned—were largely public in character, and that to explain their actions exclusively in terms of private ambitions and interests is an affront to historical truth. In the moral and intellectual climate of early republican America, devotion to the public good and concern for the national reputation were forces with lives of their own; and these forces, as perceived and personified by such men as Washington, Franklin, Madison, Gerry, Sherman, Livingston, and Baldwin, were the underlying causes of this momentous event.

# III

## Event

# 9 THE CONVENTION, MAY 14–JUNE 20: THE NATIONALIST ASSAULT

> *The true question is whether we shall adhere to the federal plan, or introduce the national plan. The insufficiency of the former has been fully displayed by the trial already made. . . . A national government alone, properly constituted, will answer the purpose; and he begged it to be considered that the present is the last moment for establishing one. After this select experiment, the people will yield to despair.*
>
> EDMUND RANDOLPH to the Convention,
> as reported by Madison, June 16, 1787\*

SUNDAY, MAY 13, 1787, was a day to be remembered by the small boys and old soldiers of Philadelphia. Shortly after dinner General Washington, the greatest man in the world, arrived in his coach at Mrs. Mary House's celebrated boardinghouse at Fifth and Market amidst the thunder of artillery, the pealing of bells, and the flash of the sabers of the City Light Horse. To the delight of the crowd that had assembled to greet him (although to the distress of Mrs. House, who had

---

\* At this stage of the great debate over the nature of the American Union, the word "federal" had not yet been appropriated by those who were to come to be known as "Federalists," and it was almost exactly synonymous with "confederate." 1

been scouring her best rooms), he was immediately led a short distance up Market Street by former Superintendent Morris, the richest man in the world, and settled comfortably in one of the grand mansions of the city. No sooner was his baggage unloaded than he was off again down Market to pay a call of courtesy and sentiment on the wisest man in the world, President Franklin of Pennsylvania.[2] By the time the small boys had gone to their beds and the old soldiers to their firesides, no one in the city would have been so crabby or dreary as to deny that another exciting chapter in the history of the young Republic was about to be written.

James Madison, who had never been crabby and had given up being dreary, must have gone to bed himself in a mood of quiet exultation. The first of the out-of-state delegates to arrive in Philadelphia, he had already been at Mrs. House's for ten days working hard among his books, notes, and papers; and the show of public confidence in his friend and fellow Virginian—whose hand he probably managed to grasp in the press of the crowd—confirmed his hunch that America was ready for the next step to glory. Mrs. House, for her part, was comforted by the knowledge that plenty of gentlemen were eager to move into the rooms reserved for Washington. Four other conventions—Baptists, Presbyterians, Cincinnati, and abolitionists—were also meeting in America's first city.

After the excitement of Sunday afternoon on Market Street, Monday morning at the State House was something of a letdown. Pennsylvania had a quorum on the floor because most of its representatives lived within shouting distance of Sixth and Chestnut, Virginia because Madison had goaded his colleagues to be punctual; but otherwise, for reasons mentioned at the beginning of Chapter 5, the attendance was no better than on a listless day in Congress. Not until Friday, May 25, when the states of New York, New Jersey, Pennsylvania, Delaware, Virginia, North Carolina, and South Carolina all mustered a quorum, did the Convention come legally into being.

While these eleven days were a source of irritation to some "punctual delegates" and of boredom to others—Mrs. Morris carried off General Washington at one point to hear a reading by a lady "reduced in circumstances," a "performance" which he recorded gallantly as "tolerable" [3]—Madison put them to such effective use that one would think he had planned the delay. A gathering of this character needs something to work with—a draft, a plan, a set of proposals or resolutions—and he now took it upon himself to provide what no other delegate or delegation seemed ready to provide, certainly in any detail. Since Virginia had led the way to the

Convention, and was expected to take the lead in it, Madison had little trouble persuading his fellow Virginians to sit through a series of daily conferences "in order," as Mason put it, "to form a proper correspondence of sentiments." * The sentiments were those that Madison had been communicating to his closest friends in the winter and early spring of the year. Although he had good tactical reasons for not posing as the driving force in this caucus in May, 1787—and even better political reasons for disclaiming the role in later years—there is little doubt that the fruit of its labor, the celebrated Virginia Plan presented by Governor Randolph on May 29, was largely a product of Madison's creative genius. Of all the services he rendered to the Constitution, this "consultation among the deputies" of Virginia,[5] which he brought together and then pushed delicately toward the end he had in mind, was the most consequential. Elaborated, tightened, amended, and refined under three months of unceasing pressure—much of which Madison resented at the time—the Virginia Plan became the Constitution of the United States.

The twenty-nine gentlemen present on May 25 made short and successful work of the business of a rainy day.[6] Credentials were read, a committee of three (Wythe, Hamilton, and the younger Pinckney) was appointed "to prepare standing rules and orders," and Major William Jackson of Philadelphia, who had lobbied energetically for the post, was chosen secretary after a brief struggle by the friends of Franklin's grandson, William Temple Franklin. The most significant action, however, was the very first. "By the instruction and in behalf of the deputation of Pennsylvania," Robert Morris nominated Washington, who disliked lobbying and had neither need nor desire to do it, "for president of the Convention." "Expressing his confidence that the choice would be unanimous," John Rutledge seconded the motion, whereupon the choice was made unanimously. Morris and Rutledge then led Washington to the chair,

> from which in a very emphatic manner he thanked the Convention for the honor they had conferred on him, reminded them of the novelty of the scene of business in which he was to act, lamented his want of better qualifications, and claimed the indulgence of the house toward the involuntary errors which his inexperience might occasion.

* As for Mason himself, he confessed on May 27 to be already "heartily tired of the etiquette and nonsense so fashionable in this city." [4]

"The nomination," Madison noted, "came with particular grace from Pennsylvania, as Dr. Franklin alone could have been thought of as a competitor." Franklin himself, he added, "was to have made the nomination of General Washington, but the state of the weather and of his health confined him to his house." With all respect to the venerable Franklin, he was not the man for this critical post, while Washington seems almost to have been designed in heaven and then trained on earth to fill it with distinction.

One other choice was made on May 25, perhaps the most fortunate of its kind in American history. Nominated, as it were, by himself and elected by the indulgence of his fellow delegates, Madison embarked on a labor of love and duty as the unofficial secretary of the Convention. Suspecting that Jackson would confine himself to keeping a simple record of motions and votes, and knowing that posterity would be grateful for "an exact account of what might pass in the Convention," he made his decision reluctantly but firmly. "In pursuance of the task I had assumed," he wrote as an old man,

> I chose a seat in front of the presiding member, with the other members on my right and left hand. In this favorable position for hearing all that passed, I noted . . . what was read from the chair or spoken by the members; and losing not a moment unnecessarily between the adjournment and reassembling of the Convention, I was enabled to write out my daily notes during the session or within a few finishing days after its close. . . .
> In the labor and correctness of this I was not a little aided by practice, and by a familiarity with the style and the train of observation and reasoning which characterized the principal speakers. It happened also that I was not absent a single day, nor more than a casual fraction of an hour in any day, so that I could not have lost a single speech, unless a very short one.[7]

The labor to which Madison committed himself was stupefying; its fruit is a narrative so unique as to render it a major treasure of the Republic. While other delegates—notably Yates, Lansing, King, McHenry, Paterson, Hamilton, and Pierce—kept notes at one time or another, Madison is the principal source of our knowledge of the debates in the Convention. Although he very humanly nodded at several stages in the proceedings, although he began to reel under his burden in late August, and although he tinkered with the manuscript off and on throughout the rest of his life, Madison seems to have been a faithful and honest reporter. As one learns in comparing his notes with those of the other self-appointed but only part-time scribes, the record he left us is remarkably full, impartial, and accurate. Although we can never be entirely sure that what Madison wrote down was "history as it actually happened," we can have more confidence in his celebrated *Notes* than in almost any other unofficial document of the early years of the Republic. The queasiness one feels in relying on the word of a single man—an involved and badgered man—for knowing what took place in the most historic of American assemblies is, in the end, overcome by the relief one feels in realizing that, if he had not made this sacrifice of time and comfort, we would be lost in a sea of ignorance about the Great Happening. Madison may have lacked a sense of humor, he may have been too pedestrian in describing some of the fireworks, and he may not have been able to spell the names of many of his colleagues —who appear in the record as Patterson, Dickenson, Reed (and Reid), Gorhum (and Ghorum), Elseworth, Carrol, Ingersol, Pinkney, Broome, Sharman, Rutlidge, and even Franklyn*—but they can thank him for a good part of the immortality that has been their lot down through the years, and we may join approvingly in their vote of thanks.

Unfortunately, neither the painstaking Madison nor the bumbling Jackson left us an exact list of the delegates present at each session. Nevertheless, by adding to the *Notes* and to the secretary's journal information gathered from letters, diaries, and newspaper accounts, we have a fairly reliable record of attendance. Since the narrative that follows will be roughly chronological, it might be worthwhile at the outset to set down this record.[8]

Of the fifty-five men who got to Philadelphia, some twenty-nine were "full-timers." They were there by May 29, the first full day of business (or at the worst, as in the cases of Johnson and Jenifer, were only three or four days tardy); they were there, so far as we know, for almost every session; they were there on September 17, the day of the signing:

Gorham, King, and Gerry from Massachusetts.

Johnson and Sherman from Connecticut.

Brearly from New Jersey.

All the Pennsylvanians except Gouverneur Morris (although it is probable that others stayed away now and then to do business or nurse ailments).

All the men of Delaware except Dickinson.

Jenifer from Maryland.

* Many of these men, to be sure, thought his name was Maddison, and continued to think so to the end of their lives.

Madison, Washington, Mason, Blair, and Randolph from Virginia.

Spaight and Williamson from North Carolina.

The four "nabobs" from South Carolina.

Ten others were full-timers except for a few missed weeks:

Strong, who went home around August 20 because of illness in his family.

Ellsworth, who left August 23 because of the press of judicial duties (and because of confidence in his colleagues from Connecticut).

Livingston, whose duties as governor of the state next door kept him away until June 5 and took him away July 3–19, as well as an odd day here and there.

Dayton, who was not appointed until June 5 and did not arrive until June 21 (he, too, may have gone home occasionally to stir his numerous pots).

Gouverneur Morris, who was unaccountably absent during the last three weeks in June.

Dickinson, who missed several days in July and left wearily September 14, having asked Read to sign his name to the engrossed Constitution.

Luther Martin, who arrived in a cloud of suspicion June 9, was absent on state business August 7–12, and took off in a cloud of disgust September 4.

Alexander Martin, who set out for home in late August.

Davie, who left August 13, apparently out of boredom.[9]

Baldwin, who struggled in from Georgia June 11, then worked faithfully to the end.

Twelve missed long and critical portions of the Convention:

Langdon and Gilman, who did not take their seats until July 23.

Yates and Lansing, who withdrew July 10 to fly home to the arms of Governor Clinton.

Hamilton, who left June 29 out of frustration over the pigheadedness of his fellow delegates from New York, put in an unexplained appearance August 13, and returned around September 6 to be in on the closing ceremonies.

Paterson, who, having scored a memorable victory, left sometime around July 23 and returned only at the end to sign his name.

Carroll, whose announced reluctance to spend a summer in Philadelphia was not overcome until July 9.[10]

McHenry, who was present May 28–31, went to Baltimore the next day upon learning that his brother was "dangerously sick,"[11] and did not get back until August 6.

McClurg, who fled for Virginia out of a feeling of useless-
ness late in July.

Blount, who was present June 20–July 1, spent July in
Congress, and returned to stay August 7.

Few, who was present May 19–July 1, went off with
Blount to New York, and returned with him in August.

Houstoun, who sat June 1–July 23, then left when he had
been assured of Few's return.

Finally, four missed so much of the Convention that they
may almost be classed with the absentees like Dana, Clark,
and Walton:

Houston, who went home after a week to die a slow and
painful death.

Wythe, who left June 4 to be with his dying wife.

Mercer, who was both a frivolous and highly critical delegate, and therefore could spare only August 6–17 (on which
days, to be sure, he made his presence loudly known).

Pierce, who scribbled his sketches and then, in a vain effort
to save himself from bankruptcy, went to New York (and
thus to his seat in Congress) at the end of June.

When the Convention reassembled Monday morning, May
28, nine more delegates were in their seats. The sight of
three of them—Gorham, Strong, and Ellsworth—brought
particular comfort to Rufus King, who had hitherto been
"mortified" as the only man from New England among all
the Pennsylvanians, Virginians, and Carolinians.[12] "The deliberations of this day" and of half the next were "employed,"
according to Madison, in working out a set of rules on the
basis of Chancellor Wythe's report for his committee.[13] For
the most part, the rules were those of Congress, with whose
operations many delegates were thoroughly familiar. Four arrangements were especially important in fixing the style and
procedures of the Convention.

First, the voting was to be, as it had always been in Congress, strictly by states, with each state, no matter what its
size and pretensions, having one vote. The Pennsylvanians,
led by the two Morrises, had made it known informally in
the first few days that they were tired of continental gatherings in which the smallest state had exactly the same voting
power as the largest, but the Virginians, "conceiving" that an
"attempt" to do away with equality "might beget fatal alter-
cations," were able to "discountenance and stifle the project"
at birth. They hoped that the small states, if not bullied right
at the start, would come, "in the course of the deliberations,
to give up their equality for the sake of an effective
government."[14] Although Madison and his associates were

determined to do away forever with the confederate principle of one-state, one-vote, they recognized that they would have to accomplish this small miracle in a meeting organized precisely on that principle. Not wishing the meeting to end the day after it had begun, they gave in graciously and, as events were to prove, prudently to the small states.

Second, a decorum befitting a gathering of gentlemen was to be self-consciously maintained. Members were politely forbidden to whisper, read, or pass notes while one of their colleagues was speaking; they could be "called to order by any other member, as well as by the president"; and the president himself was provided with special safeguards for his power and dignity. "When the house shall adjourn," one rule stated sententiously, "every member shall stand in his place, until the president pass him." One would like very much to have seen this sight.

If the proceedings were to be decorous, they were not, however, to be frozen. The members voted down a proposed rule authorizing "any member to call for the yeas and nays and have them entered on the minutes," and provided, at the suggestion of Spaight of North Carolina, for orderly reconsideration of any decision already "determined by a majority." Thus they made it possible to feel their way toward solutions they could not immediately anticipate, by changing their minds as often and easily as men can in the presence of friends and rivals.

Finally, the Convention voted, on the prompting of Pierce Butler, to guard "against licentious publications of their proceedings." In search of privacy, which they knew they would need in abundance, the members voted:

> That no copy be taken of any entry on the journal during the sitting of the house without leave of the house.
> That members only be permitted to inspect the journal.
> That nothing spoken in the house be printed, or otherwise published or communicated without leave.[15]

Although few delegates may have grasped the logic of their action clearly on May 28–29, the adoption of the so-called secrecy rule was the most critical decision of a procedural nature the Convention was ever to make. At the time George Mason found this a "necessary precaution to prevent misrepresentations or mistakes," and in later years Madison insisted that "no Constitution would ever have been adopted by the convention if the debates had been public." [16] It is hard to disagree with these opinions. The secrecy rule stirred the imaginations and loosened the tongues of delegates on the floor, permitted them to take advanced positions and then to withdraw gracefully under fire, guarded them against both careless and willful misinterpretations of their gropings for constitutional solutions and political compromises, permitted one consensus after another to form out of a wealth of half-formed opinions and half-baked prejudices, encouraged them to express honest doubts about such sacred cows as the sovereignty of the states and the glories of the militia, and spared bravos like Randolph and Charles Pinckney the temptation of playing to any gallery save that of posterity, one that usually brings out the best in such men.

The remarkable thing about this rule is not that it was so readily adopted, but that it was so rigidly observed by the delegates and so uncomplainingly accepted by the press and public. Although there were a few minor breaches of discipline in private letters, the delegates generally were scrupulous in keeping even their best friends in the dark about the progress of their work.[17] So careful was Washington, for example, that he decided to record nothing in his diary, and so careful was Madison in writing to a cherished cousin, the president of William and Mary, that the latter replied in exasperation: "If you cannot tell us what you are doing, you might at least give us some information of what you are not doing."[18] The North Carolina delegates reported confidentially on a number of occasions to Governor Caswell, but only once, in a letter from the never fully disciplined Blount, did he get more than a scrap of solid information.[19] And although the newspapers informed their readers that the Convention had elected to carry on in "the greatest secrecy," no one seems to have thought it proper until the end of the summer to say openly, as Jefferson wrote privately to Adams, that the "precedent" of "tying up the tongues" of the delegates was "abominable."[20] In an age when "the right to know" was far more restrained in application than it is today*—and than it was to be only a few years after the event—Madison reported accurately when he wrote to Jefferson that, although "the public mind" was "very impatient" to hear the proposals of the Convention, almost no "discontent" was "expressed at the concealment" of the process designed to grind out these proposals.[22] It is a fact of huge consequence that the spirit and customs of the age encouraged the men of 1787 to produce "an open covenant, secretly arrived at." Indeed, it may be argued plausibly that only by being

---

* So too, apparently, was the right to inform, suggest, and direct. Few letters and no petitions were addressed to the Convention by private individuals, religious and social groups, or state and local officials. The isolation of the Framers was splendid and almost complete.[21]

somewhat less than fully democratic in two crucial respects —the process of selection that left the anti-nationalists at home, and the decision for secrecy that left them quite in the dark—was the Convention able to write a charter on which a stable democracy could arise and flourish.

After the rules had been adopted and an ungracious proposal by Charles Pinckney to "superintend the minutes" rejected, the Convention moved at last to the "main business." Rising from his seat at a nod from General Washington, Governor Randolph of Virginia embarked on a "long and elaborate speech" in behalf of his colleagues. In it he described the character of the common government all patriots were seeking, enumerated the defects of the Articles of Confederation, discoursed upon the troubles—"rebellion" in Massachusetts, the "havoc of paper money," "violated treaties," "commercial discord"—that had brought them all to Philadelphia, and then suggested a "remedy" based on "the republican principle." That remedy, of course, was the Virginia Plan, which was set before the Convention this May 29 in the form of fifteen resolutions.

The first resolution proposed rather timidly that the Articles be "corrected and enlarged" to "accomplish the objects proposed by their institution," but the other fourteen suggested a government so different from the Confederation in form, scope, and basis that no one could have been fooled—except perhaps the unsuspecting Randolph himself. His review of certain "articles of union" designed to preserve "peace, harmony, happiness, and liberty" was—as Madison intended—a call for a new constitution of the United States. The most important features of the plan (numbered in Randolph's order) were these:

2. A scheme of representation based on contributions or population (specially, "the number of free inhabitants").

3. A bicameral legislature.

4. Election of the first branch by the people.

5. Election of the second branch by the first "out of a proper number of persons nominated" by the state legislatures.

6. Authority in the national legislature to pass laws "in all cases to which the separate states are incompetent, or in which the harmony of the United States may be interrupted by the exercise of individual legislation"; to "negative" state laws "contravening . . . the articles of union"; and to use force against recalcitrant states.

7. An executive (the number was left unspecified) to be elected by the legislature, protected in compensation, ineligi-

ble for reelection, and possessed of a "general authority" to execute the laws.

8. A council of revision, consisting of the executive and "a convenient number" of judges, with a qualified veto on acts of the legislature (the margin necessary to override was left unspecified).

9. A judiciary "to consist of one or more supreme tribunals, and of inferior tribunals" (to be chosen by the legislature), whose jurisdiction would be national in scope.

10. Admission of new states on something less than a unanimous vote in the legislature.

11. A guarantee of the republican institutions and the territory of each state.

12. Provision for the "continuance of Congress . . . until a given day after the reform of the articles of union" (which was, in truth, a polite sentence of death).

13. Provision for amendment of the new constitution without the assent of the legislature.

14. A requirement that all state officers be "bound by oath to support" the new constitution.

15. Ratification of the Convention's proposals ("after the approbation of Congress") by state conventions "expressly chosen by the people."

It should be plain that Madison was proposing—through the instrument of Randolph and with the blessing of Washington—the demolition of the Articles of Confederation and the erection in its place of a strong national government on a popular foundation. There was nothing that could be called "confederate," and not much that could be called "federal," about the Virginia Plan, nor were there nearly enough "checks and balances" to have satisfied John Adams. So sharp a break was Virginia asking the other states to make with the American past that one wonders why at least one stunned delegate—Yates or Lansing or Ellsworth or Dickinson—did not rise up and cry havoc at the top of his lungs. Instead, the delegates ended this session by resolving to go "into a committee of the whole house" on the next day in order to "consider the state of the American Union." To this committee were referred "the propositions moved by Mr. Randolph," which became its agenda, and a "draught of a federal government" prepared by Charles Pinckney,* which was ignored. It was thought, quite correctly, that as a com-

---

* Although extravagant claims have occasionally been made for the significance of the so-called Pinckney Plan, historians now agree that it was at best merely a source of familiar phrases for the members of the committee of detail.[23]

mittee of the whole the Convention could deal more freely, informally, and flexibly with the Virginia Plan.

From May 30 through June 13 the Convention wrestled manfully, if at first somewhat shyly, with the resolutions submitted by Randolph. Every morning General Washington called the gathering to order, surrendered the chair to Nathaniel Gorham (who had been chosen to preside in committee because of his experience in Congress, and also as a gesture to New England), listened attentively to old friends and new as they jousted with one another, and then, at the end of the day, reassumed his place of command in order to hear from Gorham that "further progress" had been made "in the matter to them referred."

That progress was made, and that the delegates grew less shy as the days went by, must be credited largely to the political genius and emotional commitment of James Madison. By preparing a plan for discussion that was neither too elaborate nor too vague, and that was an open challenge to the principles of the Articles of Confederation, he seized an initiative in behalf of the reform-minded nationalists that was never relinquished from the first day to the last. Moving boldly, if also prudently, into the area of doubt about the scope of their mandate in which even such men as Butler, C. C. Pinckney, and Gerry found themselves mired at the outset, Madison and his friends set the terms for all discussion and decision-making. Those terms were, as we have already seen, essentially two: first, to strike for a new constitution, and not simply to patch up the Articles; and second, to make the constitution of a government more compound in form and less confederate in basis than the one dying of attrition in New York. The critical decision of the first weeks of the Convention was to proceed on these terms, and it would hardly have been made so quickly (and, as it proved, finally) if Madison had not taken it upon himself to be drafter and manager for the forces of reform.

All doubts about the true intent of the Virginia Plan were resolved on the morning of May 30 when Randolph moved the adoption of his first resolution, was told by Gouverneur Morris (who needed no prompting from Madison) that it was inconsistent with the other resolutions, and then asked bravely that it be put aside "in order to consider the three following":

1. that a union of the states merely federal will not accomplish the objects proposed by the Articles of Confederation, namely common defense, security of liberty, and general welfare.

2. that no treaty or treaties among the whole or part of
the states, as individual sovereignties, would be sufficient.

3. that a *national* government ought to be established
consisting of a *supreme* legislative, executive, and
judiciary.[24]

Since the third resolution covered the first two, the delegates agreed to focus their attention upon it. After some nim-
ble work by Gouverneur Morris and Mason in explaining the
words "national" and "supreme," it passed by a vote of 6
(Massachusetts, Pennsylvania, Delaware, Virginia, North
Carolina, South Carolina) to 1 (Connecticut), with the vote
of New York split between Hamilton and Yates. Had this
vote been taken a few days later, with all states at full
strength, it would have been closer, yet once taken it was
never reversed. On the threshold of the proceedings, when
many a delegate had barely caught his breath, the Convention decided, in effect, to scrap the Articles and to form a
new government that would, in the words of Morris and
Mason, have a *"compulsive* operation" directly "on individuals."

In the course of the next two weeks the Virginians, whom
Madison led more and more openly, and the Pennsylvanians,
for whom Wilson emerged as chief spokesman, drove ahead
almost too blithely. It was one thing for them to press their
vigorous brand of nationalism upon men who still did not
know their own minds—since the number of immovable
anti-nationalists was never very large—quite another to con-
fuse, knowingly or unknowingly, the case for a national
government with the case for "just" representation of the
large states. By refusing to acknowledge that men from small
states like New Jersey and Delaware could be, in their own
way, as anxious as they to write a new charter for a new nation, Madison, Wilson, and their associates nearly threw away
the advantage they had gained on May 30.

Although other divisions emerged in the debates and votes
of May 30–June 13, the deepest disagreement was between
those who insisted, some of them sheepishly, that representation in both houses of the proposed legislature should be
based on population and those who insisted, most of them
doggedly, that this principle, if admissible at all, should apply
only to the lower house. The decisive votes in this matter were
taken June 11: 7–3–1 (Massachusetts, Connecticut, Pennsylvania, Virginia, the Carolinas, and Georgia, aye; New York,
New Jersey, and Delaware, no; Maryland divided) in favor
of representation in the lower house "in proportion to the

whole number of white and other free citizens" and three-fifths of the slaves;* and 6–5 (Massachusetts, Pennsylvania, Virginia, the Carolinas, and small but ambitious Georgia, aye; Connecticut, New York, New Jersey, Delaware, and Maryland, no) in favor of representation in the upper house "according to the rule established" for the lower.[26] Since Paterson, Sherman, and several of the nationalists from Delaware had warned the men of the large states that they "would never confederate" on this plan,[27] yet stayed on without further protest to vote on other resolutions, they were clearly hopeful that the second part of this vote on representation could (because it must) be reversed. The momentum gained by the large-state men in the first days was beginning to slow down; and despite bold words from Wilson about the unwillingness of Pennsylvania and "some other states" to "confederate on any other" terms,[28] everyone knew that a partial retreat, however grudging, would have to be made from the far-out, almost militant nationalism of the Virginia Plan.

When the committee of the whole rose at the end of the day on Wednesday, June 13, it reported a set of nineteen resolutions that were both a confirmation and an elaboration of that plan. The council of revision had found no favor (to Madison's distress), and the authority to use force against recalcitrant states had been dropped (at his suggestion); otherwise the resolutions were a projection of all the hopes he had entertained for a government "truly national." Among the details added in the process of give-and-take were:

A three-year term for the lower house and a seven-year term for the upper.

Payment for members of both houses "out of the national treasury" (a solid blow for nationalism).

Election of members of the upper house by the state legislatures.

A single executive with a seven-year term (still to be chosen by the legislature and still ineligible for reelection), who could be removed "on impeachment and conviction of malpractices or neglect of duty."

---

* This was the first of several essential compromises on the question of slavery between North and South. Many years later Rufus King described it as the "greatest concession" that was made "to secure the adoption of the Constitution," a hindsightful judgment with which I find it impossible to agree.[25] The three-fifths rule was a legacy from the Congress of 1783, and most northern delegates must have realized even before they arrived in Philadelphia that it would be the minimum price of southern acceptance of any new constitution.

A power of veto in the executive, which could be overridden only by a two-thirds majority in both houses.

A "supreme tribunal," the judges of which were to be chosen by the upper house.

Except on the issues of representation, the term of office of the executive, and the oath of state officials to support the new constitution, the thirty-odd critical votes that produced the report of the committee of the whole had been carried by margins ranging from 7–3 or 7–4 to unanimity—including a unanimous vote of June 5 to seek approval for any new constitution in state conventions "expressly chosen by the people." The Convention had come a long way in a short time, and the consensus for a national government was now almost complete. So, too, was the consensus for a large injection of the principle of popular sovereignty. Spurred by the eloquence of Mason, Wilson, and Madison, the Convention had ridden roughshod over the fears of Gerry, Sherman, and Butler and had voted as early as May 31 for election of the first house "by the people." [29] Although some of the impetus for this decision derived from a mistrust of the state legislatures (which had already betrayed itself in the plan for ratification in special conventions), some also was an honest expression of faith in the intelligence of the American people.

The question who should control this national, half-popular government had not really been answered, however, and in an effort to reopen it—and perhaps some other questions as well—Paterson of New Jersey seized the initiative on June 14:

> It was the wish of several deputations, [he announced] particularly that of New Jersey, that further time might be allowed them to contemplate the plan reported from the committee of the whole, and to digest one purely federal, and contradistinguished from the reported plan. He said they hoped to have such a one ready tomorrow to be laid before the Convention: And the Convention adjourned that leisure might be given for the purpose.[30]

On June 15 Paterson "laid before the Convention" a set of nine resolutions which he hoped would be "substituted" for those already voted in the committee of the whole.[31] The New Jersey Plan, as it soon came to be known, was a composite production in which Paterson, Brearly, Sherman, Lansing, Luther Martin, and several others had a hand, and it showed the strains of its multiple paternity. In form a series of amendments to the Articles of Confederation, it proposed that Congress be granted new powers to raise money through import duties and a stamp tax, to regulate commerce, and to compel delinquent states to honor requisitions; that both a plural executive (to be elected by Congress) and a supreme court (to be appointed by the executive) be added to the machinery of the Confederation; and that the executive be authorized to "call forth the power of the confederated states" to enforce the laws and treaties of the United States in the face of state opposition. To prove that they wished the common government well, Paterson and his associates placed these astonishing words in their sixth resolution:

> Resolved, that all acts of the United States in Congress made by virtue and in pursuance of the powers hereby and by the Articles of Confederation vested in them, and all treaties made and ratified under the authority of the United States, shall be the supreme law of the respective states as far forth as those acts or treaties shall relate to the said states or their citizens, and that the judiciary of the several states shall be bound thereby in their decisions, anything in the respective laws of the individual states to the contrary notwithstanding.

Astonishing words, indeed, in a "purely federal" plan, especially since they appear to have been drafted by Luther Martin.

The trouble with the New Jersey Plan was that it was too little, too late, too feeble, and too self-contradicting. Handed over along with the Virginia Plan to the reconstituted committee of the whole, it never had a chance to be adopted as the agenda of the Convention. The delegates who brought it forward were united only in their opposition to large-state nationalism. While the recalcitrant New Yorkers, the cautious sons of Connecticut, and the bibulous legman for Samuel Chase were still clinging (some for dear life, some only loosely) to the Articles of Confederation, the nationalists of New Jersey and Delaware were simply doing what they could to convince Madison and Wilson that they would retreat no farther on the issue of representation. "You see the consequences of pushing things too far," Dickinson said in stern reproach to Madison when chided, it would seem, for having made common cause with the anti-nationalists:

> Some of the members from the small states wish for two branches in the general legislature, and are friends to a good national government; but we would sooner submit to a foreign power than . . . be deprived of an equality of suffrage in both branches of the legislature, and thereby be thrown under the domination of the large states.[32]

One would think that Madison and Wilson could have read that message correctly, yet they still refused, at least for the record, to concede an inch to the small-state nationalists, and so a choice had to be made between the two plans as they stood.

The choice was made finally on Tuesday afternoon, June 19, and the count was 7 (Massachusetts, Connecticut, Pennsylvania, Virginia, North Carolina, South Carolina, Georgia) for the Virginia Plan and 3 (New York, New Jersey, Delaware) for the New Jersey Plan, with the vote of Maryland divided between Jenifer and Martin. The surprising switch of Connecticut can only be explained if we assume that private assurances had been given that a compromise would somehow be worked out on the issue of representation. The assurances, however, were still not good enough for New Jersey and Delaware, both of which voted "no" when they wanted to vote "aye."

The three days of debate that led to the decision of June 19 were memorable, and were, in fact, destined to be long remembered. Lansing and Paterson led off on Saturday, June 16 for the anti-nationalist, small-state coalition. Each man put stress on two points: "the want of power in the Convention to discuss and propose" any plan not grounded squarely on "the Confederacy in being"; and the "improbability that the states would adopt and ratify a scheme" that they had "never authorized" the delegates to consider.[33] Wilson and Randolph met these arguments head-on the same day. The former asserted that, while the Convention was "authorized to *conclude nothing*," it was "at liberty to *propose anything*," the latter suggested that this was one of those "seasons of a peculiar nature where the ordinary cautions must be dispensed with." Both men denied that "public sentiment" forbade the Convention to scrap the Articles of Confederation. Every bit as telling as these lectures in politics, morality, and opinion, however, was a short observation of the younger Pinckney that if the Convention were simply to "give New Jersey an equal vote," she would "dismiss her scruples, and concur in the national system."

Between the forceful exchanges of Saturday and the decision of Tuesday came one of the most puzzling incidents of the summer. On June 18 the two opposing forces pulled back for a rest while Colonel Hamilton of New York, who had been uncommonly silent for three weeks, spent some four to five hours expounding his tough-minded political principles and presenting a plan of government based upon them.[34] The plan was a heady blend of "continentalism" and "high tone" that must have startled Sherman and Paterson and discomfited Madison and Wilson. Its continentalism, that is to say, its urge to consolidate the political authority of the American people in one government and to reduce the states to a subordinate position, was plain in provisions for a two-chambered legislature with "power to pass *all laws whatsoever*" and an executive in each state who, having been appointed by the national government, would have a veto "upon the laws about to be passed." Its high tone, that is to say, its determination to place this authority in the hands of the gentry and to put restraints on "the amazing violence and turbulence of the democratic spirit," was plain in provisions for a "governor" elected for life by "electors chosen by electors chosen by the people," a senate also chosen indirectly and for life, and an absolute power of veto in the executive.

Whatever Hamilton's motives for presenting so unacceptable a plan, and whatever the reasons of his colleagues for giving him a whole day in which to show off his prodigious talents, the session of June 18 was an unreal interlude in a real struggle for power, and his speech provoked almost no response, favorable or unfavorable. One would like to imagine that Madison and Wilson had decided to let Paterson, Sherman, and the others hear the views of a 200 per cent nationalist, and thus to make the Virginia Plan appear as a reasonable middleground between two extreme positions,* but this is, in truth, to imagine a supremely clever bit of strategy for which the evidence is entirely spectral. In any case, Alexander Hamilton had had his day, one that mixed bravery and futility in equal measure, and the Convention could now get back to business.

On June 19 Madison finished off the good work of Wilson and Randolph with perhaps his finest speech of the summer,[35] the vote to bury the New Jersey Plan was cast, and the Convention turned dutifully to a clause-by-clause consideration of the resolutions reported by the committee of the whole—in other words, to a complete review of every step it had just taken. This first stage of the proceedings came to an end the next day when Randolph and his friends, in a conciliatory mood, agreed to drop the offending word "national" from the first resolution,[36] and Lansing, Martin, Sherman, and their friends, in a crabbed mood, failed in one last attempt to preserve Congress as the core of the new government.[37] The next stage had already been anticipated by Madison, who now agreed with Dickinson and Pinckney that

---

* To Hamilton the Virginia Plan looked (or tasted) like *"pork still, with a little change of the sauce."* Yates recorded this satirical thrust; Madison, who was not in a joking mood, let it pass.

if the "affair of representation . . . could be adjusted," all other difficulties "would be surmountable," and by Hamilton, who denied that the small states had anything to fear from large ones as remote from each other on the map and divided from each other in "interests" as Virginia, Pennsylvania, and Massachusetts. Except for the delegation of which Hamilton himself was an uncomfortable member, the Convention was now ready to search its imagination and its conscience for a solution to its chief problem.

The Convention had moved a remarkable distance in these first weeks, and, in moving at a pace neither too fast for Connecticut nor too slow for Virginia, it had taken on a style that was to mark its proceedings to the end.

In the first place, most members had shown a commendable seriousness of purpose. The regime they had adopted was not a light one—five hours a day, six days a week, with all lobbying, correspondence, preparation of drafts and speeches, and committee work taking place before or after hours—nor was it rendered easier by the growing realization that a full "summer's campaign" was in store for them.[38] Yet, as they had not easily been brought together, so they would not easily be dispersed. A sense of mission—for all Americans then living, for generations of Americans unborn, indeed "for the whole human race"—lay heavily upon the delegates. So also did a sense of crisis, and Lansing, for once, spoke the minds of all when he pointed out that "any act whatever of so respectable a body must have a great effect, and if it does not succeed, will be a source of great dissensions." [39] Franklin had already made this point privately in a letter to Jefferson, reminding his young friend that, "if it does not do good," such a meeting with such a mandate "must do harm," [40] and the newspapers of America, which had little else to tell their readers about "the Grand Convention," could at least print letters and dispatches expressing the most extravagant hopes for a constitutional cure for all the ills of the young nation.[41]

Second, most delegates had found that, although one large thing divided them, many other things, both large and small, united them. The ease with which the secrecy rule was adopted and the circumspection with which it was honored, the refusal of the small-staters to bolt after the decisions of June 19–20 had gone against them, and the absence of petulance from even the sharpest confrontations—these were surface manifestations of a deep-seated consensus of principle and purpose. All the delegates were patriots, Whigs, republicans, and men with Lockean views of property; all but two or three were nationalists who recognized the need for a new departure.

They were, moreover, self-respecting gentlemen, and, under the watchful eye of the grand gentleman at their head, they behaved for the most part in a manner that encouraged frankness, dampened suspicion, soothed hurt feelings, and made compromise a virtue rather than a sign of weakness. The Convention, for all its innate dignity and regard for form, operated as a large committee rather than a small assembly, and it was able to move with a minimum of posing and pouting toward a goal only dimly perceived in the opening days. If it did rather more meandering along the road than seems to have been necessary in retrospect, that is because the situation was not quite so simple as Madison and Wilson wanted their colleagues to believe, and because an organic unity rather than a mechanistic consolidation had somehow to be worked out to the satisfaction of small states and large. The search for such unity might easily have gone astray in a gathering any more numerous, divided, and faction-minded than this committee of largely like-minded gentlemen. In a gathering any more exposed, the search would have led to disaster. The more one reads over this record of give-and-take, the more certain it seems that the saving feature of the Convention was the "mask of secrecy" put on by the delegates and respected by their constituents.

Behind that mask, to be sure, the reputation of each man, like the fate of the nation, was at stake, and by late June most delegates had begun to play the roles for which they have been known ever since: Washington as a silent but commanding witness to duty; Franklin as "a spectacle of transcendent benevolence," [42] and also, perhaps too often, as a purveyor of irrelevant information; Madison as faithful scribe, and Madison and Wilson together as forceful co-managers of the nationalist caucus; Randolph, Mason, Gerry, the two Pinckneys, King, and Butler as spokesmen for this caucus; Paterson, Sherman, Brearly, Ellsworth, Bedford, and Dickinson as the men who "kept it honest"; Rutledge, Williamson, and Read as modest seekers for a consensus; Yates and Lansing as the only two men who simply would not go along on the search, at least not under Madison's guidance; Luther Martin as a late arrival who might yet outstrip the New Yorkers as a trouble-maker; Hamilton as a strangely silent and eccentric witness to an event he had labored so diligently to bring about; and Gorham as a fair-minded presiding officer over those first gropings.

On the floor and off it, over tea at Robert Morris's, Madeira at Mrs. House's, and brandy at the Indian Queen—Philadelphia's best appointed inn and the unofficial headquarters of the Convention—the delegates moved toward a consensus on the structure and basis of the new government that could be recommended alike to the citizens of Massachusetts and Connecticut, of New Jersey and Pennsylvania, of Delaware and Virginia. Madison and his friends had a majority for their solution, but in this gathering, it was now quite plain, a simple majority would not be enough. Somehow a "sense of the meeting" would have to be fashioned; and since the large-state nationalists seemed unwilling to retreat from their advanced position, other men would have to fashion it for them. Compromise was now not merely a useful technique of the Convention, but the key to its survival as a nation-building instrument of the American elite.

# 10 THE CONVENTION, JUNE 21–AUGUST 5: COMPROMISE AND CREATIVITY

*The proportional representation in the first branch was conformable to the national principle and would secure the large states against the small. An equality of voices [in the second branch] was conformable to the federal principle and was necessary to secure the small states against the large. He trusted that on this middle ground a compromise would take place. He did not see that it could on any other. And if no compromise should take place, our meeting would not only be in vain but worse than in vain. . . . Let a strong executive, a judiciary and a legislative power be created; but let not too much be attempted, by which all may be lost. He was not in general a halfway man, yet he preferred doing half the good we could, rather than do nothing at all.*

OLIVER ELLSWORTH to the Convention
as reported by Madison, June 20, 1787[1]

THE FIVE WEEKS that followed the shaky victory for nationalism on June 19–20 were the most perilous in the life of the Convention. Two major tasks—one primarily political, the other constitutional—had to be accomplished to the satisfaction, or at least not to the mortification, of all delegates genuinely concerned to create a new government. The first was to make that adjustment in the "affair of representation" of which Madison had spoken June 19 (but toward which he was contributing nothing), the second to reconsider the resolutions of the committee of the whole and to prepare them for a drafting committee.

The quest for a formula of representation acceptable to both James Madison and William Paterson was, as Hamilton said bluntly on June 29,[2] "a contest for power, not for liberty" that drove a sharp wedge between otherwise likeminded men. The working-out of directions for trusted draftsmen was an exercise in constitution-making that brought these men back together. As politicians, representatives of insistent interests, they were divided almost too fiercely within their sanctuary; as statesmen, agents for the "permanent and aggregate good" of the nation, they were united almost too fraternally against all the men outside who feared a new departure. Although we may feel distress that they had to give so much energy and emotion, in the tart words of Gouverneur Morris, to the business of "trucking and bargaining" for their "particular states," [3] we must remember that no true exercise in constitution-making can be entirely rational and non-political, and that their own most passionate struggle for power opened up the crooked but passable road to American federalism.

From Thursday, June 21, through Tuesday, June 26, the delegates behaved, as best they could under trying circumstances, like thinking constitutionalists rather than testy politicians.[4] Debates on important theoretical and political issues proceeded at a high level of courtesy and intelligence: Johnson, Wilson, and Madison on the nature of federalism; General Pinckney, Hamilton, Mason, Rutledge, Wilson, and King on the proper foundation of a lower house; Randolph, Dickinson, Ellsworth, Wilson, Madison, Hamilton, Sherman, and Mason on the nature of representation; Madison, Rutledge, Mason, King, Wilson, Sherman, and Gerry on the causes and cures of corruption in legislatures; both Pinckneys, Gorham, Wilson, Ellsworth, Williamson, Mason, Read, Madison, Sherman, Hamilton, and Gerry on the uses, structure, and tenure of an upper house. Out of these debates came a number of significant decisions (or confirmations of previous decisions): to have a bicameral legislature; to have a lower house elected by the people and an upper house elected by the state legislatures; to have a two-year term for members of the first house; and to have a six-year term for members of the second, with "one-third to go out biennially." On several of these issues some of the more sour or frightened small-state men behaved like politicians rather than constitutionalists, and voted against arrangements of which they had already approved—and, once the "affair of representation" had been adjusted to their liking, would approve again. All the while beneath the surface of polite reason the delegates could feel this affair thrashing to be let loose, and at last they realized that they could hold it down no longer. The first thing in the morning of June 27, on the motion of the respected Rutledge, the resolutions of the committee of the whole "which involved the most fundamental points, the rules of suffrage in the two branches," were let loose in the arena.[5]

Before the delegates could lay a hand on the beast, three side shows, each an acute embarrassment to the president, had to be endured. First, for reasons known only to himself, Luther Martin seized the floor on June 27, argued "at great length and with great eagerness" for a drastically states-rights view of the Union, accused Virginia, Massachusetts, and Pennsylvania of seeking "complete mastery" over the other ten states, tried the patience of his audience with long passages from Locke and the other great Whigs (who did, however, make more sense than Martin), let them go home to dinner only when he was "too much exhausted . . . to finish his remarks, " and did not finally give up until more than half-way through the next day.[6] As Ellsworth was to write publicly to Martin in the struggle over ratification, this speech "held during two days . . . might have continued two months, but for these marks of fatigue and disgust you saw strongly expressed on whichever side of the house you turned your mortified eyes." [7] Even Martin's ally Yates was disturbed by this erratic performance.

Next, for reasons known only to God, Benjamin Franklin proposed in a touching speech that the delegates, who could hardly deny that they were lost in the woods, "implore the assistance of Heaven" by opening each session with prayers led by "one or more of the clergy of this city." Roger Sherman of Connecticut, a somewhat more orthodox Puritan than Franklin, seconded the motion fervently. After Hamilton had worried about the effect on public opinion, which would take it as a sign of "embarrassments and dissensions within the Convention," and Williamson had wondered where the money would come from to pay their godly guides,[8] this proposal was allowed to die an ignoble death. Children of reason in their public lives, the Framers were sure that the path to the resolution of their sticky problem was for them to find unaided. As Gouverneur Morris said in another context a few days later, they were "not to expect any particular interference of Heaven" in their favor.[9]

Finally, for reasons known to every delegate on the floor, David Brearly of New Jersey, a man in search of allies, moved on June 30 that General Washington write a letter to General Sullivan beseeching him to jog the laggards from New Hampshire. After Rutledge had questioned the propriety and Wilson the wisdom of any such call, the motion was voted down by a large margin, and New Hampshire was left to find its own penurious way to Philadelphia.[10]

Now that the sideshows were over, the main show, the fiercest struggle for power of the entire summer, could begin in earnest. For fourteen working days—as well as three Sundays, two days of adjournment for the celebration of the eleventh "anniversary of independence," and night after night of soul-searching—the struggle went on. Huffing and puffing, wheedling and threatening, taking two steps forward and one back (and sometimes one forward and two back), the delegates moved, not like a proud company but a grumbling rabble, toward the only solution they could carry home to their constituents. In order to get at least a half-focused picture of one of the muddiest processes of decision-making in American history, let us take careful note of the point of departure and the destination.

The point of departure was two resolutions (numbers 7–8) of June 11 in the report of the committee of the whole, which provided (7) for representation in the first branch of the legislature "in proportion to the whole number" of "free citizens" and three-fifths of the slaves, and (8) for representation in the second "according to the rule established" for the first.[11]

The destination was four resolutions (numbers 8–11) of July 16, which provided for representation according to population in the first branch (with one slave still counting as three-fifths of a person) * and an equal vote for each state in the second, and which dressed up this hard bargain with provisions for a census every ten years for the purpose of redistributing seats, for an exclusive power in the first branch to originate money bills (which were not to be "altered or amended by the second branch"), and for proportioning representation "according to direct taxation"—and vice versa.[12] This was the Great Compromise—sometimes known, not quite correctly, as the Connecticut Compromise—and without it there would have been no Constitution of 1787 for the United States. There would have been another constitution, perhaps, at another time and for some of the United States, but not this one for all of them.

The principal stages in this journey from an unequivocal

* The distribution of seats before the first census was to be: New Hampshire 3, Massachusetts 8, Rhode Island 1, Connecticut 5, New York 6, New Jersey 4, Pennsylvania 8, Delaware 1, Maryland 6, Virginia 10, North Carolina 5, South Carolina 5, Georgia 3. These numbers were worked out by two committees, whose members made population (at which they could only guess) the principal criterion, but also gave some weight to wealth and apparent rate of growth. The delegates from the large states serving on these committees were kept honest by the sight of the delegates from the small states, as well as by the suspicion, which turned out to be sound, that representation and taxation would somehow go together. This distribution found its way without change into the Constitution.

decision of the majority, which was unacceptable to the minority, to a muddy compromise of the "half-way men," which was endurable for all, were these:

June 29: a vote of 6 (Massachusetts, Pennsylvania, Virginia, North Carolina, South Carolina, Georgia) to 4 (Connecticut, New York, New Jersey, Delaware), with unpredictable Maryland divided, not to go back to the Confederation system of equal voting for states in the first house, and a similar vote to adopt resolution 7.[13]

July 2: a vote of 5 (Connecticut, New York, New Jersey, Delaware, Maryland) to 5 (Massachusetts, Pennsylvania, Virginia, North Carolina, South Carolina), with Georgia divided, on a resolution introduced by Ellsworth "allowing each state one vote in the second branch." [14] Maryland voted "aye" because "Mr. Jenifer not being present, Mr. Martin alone voted"; Georgia divided because Pierce and Few had departed, Baldwin had decided to act like the Connecticut man he was, and only Houstoun held firm behind Madison. Almost at once the Convention agreed to appoint a committee of one member from each state "to devise and report some compromise." [15] General Pinckney suggested the committee; Madison and Wilson opposed it (as did several of the small-staters); Randolph, Gerry, Gouverneur Morris, and other large-staters supported it. This was the first time the Convention had felt the need to fall back on such a technique, but as Sherman explained:

> We are now at a full stop, and nobody, he supposed, meant that we should break up without doing something. A committee he thought most likely to hit on some expedient.

Whatever expedient was hit on, it was clearly not going to be welcome to Madison and Wilson. The committee was "loaded," and the cool heads in the Convention, sensing the obstinacy of the small states and fearing the suicidal consequences of a thin victory (which they would have had with Jenifer back on the floor), had done the loading.[16] It was composed of adamant small-staters and malleable large-staters, with a few born compromisers thrown in to keep the peace: Gerry, Ellsworth (who, taking sick, was replaced by Sherman), Yates, Paterson, Franklin, Bedford, Martin, Mason, Davie, Rutledge, and Baldwin.

July 3–4: adjournment. While Philadelphia celebrated and sweated (the weather being all that could be expected of Philadelphia in July), the committee of eleven worked and sweated. According to Yates (who was there) and Madison (who was not, but from whom few secrets were kept), the committee worked out a plan based on a motion by Franklin.[17]

July 5: the report of the committee, which provided—to no one's surprise—for representation according to population in the first branch and an equal vote for each state in the second, and which tried to make the bitter pill tastier for the large states by placing the power to originate money bills exclusively in the former. It also suggested that cach state be allowed one member in the first branch for every forty thousand "inhabitants." [18]

July 6: appointment of a committee of five, on the motion of Gouverneur Morris, to fix the number of members for each state in the first branch.[19] The committee was expected to behave like statesmen rather than politicians, for all five were from large states (and two from the same state): Gorham, King, Randolph, Rutledge, and Morris himself.

July 9: the report of the committee, which doled out fifty-six seats among the thirteen states—no one, apparently, ever wanted to freeze out Rhode Island—and left it to the legislature to augment and adjust the representation of the states in the future "upon the principles of their wealth and number of inhabitants." [20] The second part of the report was handed over to Sherman's motion and with Morris's approval to yet another committee, whose members were King, Sherman, Yates, Brearly, Morris, Read, Carroll, Madison, Williamson, Rutledge, and Houstoun.

July 10: the report of the committee, which increased the seats to sixty-five and distributed them according to the formula finally adopted in the Great Compromise. After Madison had tried unsuccessfully to double the number—and General Pinckney to take away seats from Yankees and give them to the deep South—the formula was approved 9–2 (South Carolina and Georgia voting "no").[21] This was, more than incidentally, a historic vote, for it was the last time New York would be heard from as a state in the Convention. Here ended the contumacious labors of Robert Yates and John Lansing, jr.

July 11: a series of votes on related matters (such as the census and the three-fifths rule) that ended in a shambles when the delegates decided unanimously just before adjourning to undo everything they had done in the course of the most awkward day of the summer.[22] The Convention was once again "at a full stop."

July 12: a motion of Gouverneur Morris, who was never known to say die, tying in representation and direct taxation.

This motion, which was designed to quiet some of the fears of the South Carolinians, was passed unanimously, after which a brazen attempt by General Pinckney and his colleagues to have their slaves—"the productive peasants of the southern states," as his cousin hailed them—counted as whole men was defeated 8–2.[23] Among those speaking up for the three-fifths rule were Mason, Williamson, Gorham, and Sherman; among those opposing the representation of men who were denied the vote, and indeed all liberty, were King and Wilson. Dr. Johnson of Connecticut, a premature "Doughface," was the only northerner to support South Carolina in this secondary power struggle.

July 14: a vote on a motion of Charles Pinckney, which might be described as the last stand of the large-state nationalists, to apportion seats in the upper house on a scale running from one (Rhode Island and Delaware) to five (Virginia). The motion, which Wilson seconded and Madison approved as a "reasonable compromise," was defeated 6–4 by a combination of adamant small-staters and level-headed large-staters.[24]

July 15 (Sunday): a searching of souls?

July 16: adoption of the Great Compromise by a vote of 5 (Connecticut, New Jersey, Delaware, Maryland, North Carolina) to 4 (Pennsylvania, Virginia, South Carolina, Georgia), with Massachusetts divided. North Carolina had been swung over by Davie and Williamson, Massachusetts neutralized by Gerry and Strong (King and Gorham sticking with Madison and Wilson). Although the four states voting "no" far outnumbered the rest in population, in whatever ratio slaves might be counted, clear-eyed delegates must have realized that in a straight vote on this issue New Hampshire, New York, and Rhode Island would have voted "aye," and that Abraham Baldwin, if the game had still hung in the balance when the roll call reached Georgia, would very likely have repeated his performance of July 2. It may be argued plausibly that the real vote for the Great Compromise of 1787 was 8–3, with two states divided.

This bare recital of motions, votes, commitments, and reports gives only a faint idea of the whirl of events in these frantic weeks when passion wrestled with reason, defiance with forbearance, and brinkmanship with accommodation. As a struggle for power in which every contestant could speak, with no apparent feeling of hypocrisy, of the "simple justice" of his position, the hammering-out of the final compromise called forth emotions much deeper than those usually displayed in a game of political give-and-take. More than once on the floor—and who knows how often off it?—the tempers of men whose whole style of life was to display good manners came dangerously near the point of explosion. Gunning Bedford of Delaware, in particular, earned himself a dubious distinction as the angriest Framer when he replied on June 30 to a "dictatorial" lecture of King with a heated warning that the small states, if pushed out of the Union by the contumacy of the large, would "find some foreign ally of more honor and good faith, who will take them by the hand and do them justice." Called to order by King and Randolph, Bedford regained the floor several days later, blamed the "warmth" of his language on the "habits of his profession" (he was a lawyer), and retreated a step or two from this advanced but not implausible position.[25] Bedford, it should be acknowledged, had reason to be upset, for King, Morris, Wilson, Madison, and others had spoken roughly themselves about the "vicious" and "unjust" principle—calculated, Madison warned, to "infuse mortality into a constitution we wished to last forever"—on which the small-staters were standing fast.[26] Never were men so angry, never was the word "never" spoken so often and rashly in the Convention, as in these hotblooded days around July 4.

Although what follows may seem a dangerous over-simplification of the many positions taken and roles accepted during this "contest for power, not for liberty," especially since some men were constantly on the move, one may plausibly divide the delegates into five camps:

the irreconcilable large-staters like Madison, King, and Wilson, whose brand of nationalism compelled them to look upon any gesture toward compromise, even the lame one of July 14, as a surrender to injustice;

the reconcilable large-staters like Gorham, Mason, Morris, and Rutledge, who saw the justice in the small-state argument (or the impossibility of ignoring it) even if they could not bring themselves to accept it at the moment of decision;

the reconciling large-staters like Gerry, Davie, and Williamson, who changed their minds just enough to change their votes, and who spoke soothingly to their comrades-in-nationalism;

the three brokers from Connecticut, with whom might be joined Franklin and Dickinson, who had most to do with the process of accommodation on and off the floor;

the irreconcilable small-staters like Paterson, Dayton, and Bedford, who were no happier with the final arrangement than were Madison and Wilson. (To them might be joined the two irreconcilables from New York, who did not even wait for the decisive vote.) *

Stripped of all the sugar-coating about the census, direct taxation, and money bills, which sweetened the pill but made it no easier to swallow, the Great Compromise was a fifty-fifty accommodation between the confederate principles of the Articles of Confederation and the nationalist principles of the Virginia Plan. In arriving at this accommodation the delegates were not, as Franklin said in half-despair June 28, "groping in the dark." The notion of one house representing population and the other representing "equal" states emerged as early as June 2 from the wise old head of John Dickinson, and was suggested again and again by the Connecticut men as a natural, principled, and expedient solution to the dilemma of the Convention: by Sherman on June 11 and 20, by Johnson on June 29, and by Ellsworth, in the classic appeal of the "half-way man," at the end of the same day.[28] The problem, then, was not for constitution-makers to find the solution but for politicians to learn to live with it, and that process of learning, as we have seen, was a hard one. In the end, the process took place because enough large-state nationalists saw what Madison and Wilson, their necks never so stiff as at this moment of touch-and-go for the Union, refused to see: that when some men said "never" they meant "never"; that New Jersey was almost as real a political entity to Jerseyites as was Virginia to Virginians; and that, most important, the nationalists from Connecticut, New Jersey, and Delaware would continue to look with fear on the proposed national government until they, like the nationalists from Virginia and Pennsylvania, could imagine its power as their power. This they could never do under the terms of resolutions 7–8 of the report of the committee of the whole.

To Madison the solution of July 16 was a surrender rather than a compromise, and he was especially scornful of the alleged "concession" of the "exclusive privilege of originating money bills." [29] To most others in the Convention, however, the compromise seemed real, perhaps because they recognized better than the committed author of the Virginia Plan that the small-state men had already done their fair share of

* All by himself in a special category was Read of Delaware, who probably meant what he said when he proposed "doing away" with the states "altogether" and "uniting them all into one great society." Paterson and Brearly also proposed throwing the states into "hotchpot," but only to lay bare the difference between the no-state nationalism of Hamilton and Read and the large-state nationalism of the Virginia Plan, which, after all, took good care of Virginia. Madison and Wilson were both forced to admit openly that such a scheme was "totally impracticable." [27]

compromising, on June 11 and again on June 29, when they had submitted to the will of the majority in favor of proportional representation in the lower house. Compromise or surrender, pattern of distributive justice or enshrinement of fundamental error, this "half-way" meeting between the Articles of Confederation and the Virginia Plan was essential to the continued existence of the Convention. Indeed, except for an arrangement on representation with which only two or three of the Framers could have been entirely happy at the time, no constitution with a chance of being adopted would have been offered to the American people in 1787—nor for many years thereafter.

It would be a mistake to interpret this contest of will and nerve between the large-staters, all of whom were nationalists, and the small-staters, who were spread across the spectrum from the sanguine continentalism of Read to the crabbed particularism of Martin, as nothing more than a naked struggle for power. It was such a struggle, to be sure, and all the delegates must have realized that control of the proposed new government was at stake in the fierce in-fighting of Madison and Paterson. Yet it was other things as well: for Madison and his supporters a last opportunity, which they pushed to the brink of disaster, to "take out the teeth of the serpents," to do away with those petty "state attachments" that had been "the bane of this country";[30] for Paterson and his supporters a fight for the very lives of the communities that had sent them to Philadelphia. Sherman and Johnson, in particular, expressed the fear that anything short of "equality of voice" in one branch would mean an end to the state governments and, in time, to the states themselves.[31] No one but the absent Hamilton and the airy Read could imagine one consolidated regime governing justly and efficiently all through the United States.

The Great Compromise was a confirmation of the states as states, as communities that never had been and never would be sovereign nations, and yet always had been and still meant to be discrete, self-conscious, indestructible units of political and social organization. It was also a confirmation of the Union as union, as a nation that was more than a tight confederacy of sovereignties that shared a common destiny, and yet less than a consolidation of malleable components. Another man with a wise old head, Dr. Johnson of Connecticut, went to the root of the matter with the help of George Mason by reminding Paterson that America was, for many purposes, "one political society" composed of individuals, and by reminding Madison that the states, too, were political societies with "interests" all their own. And he pleaded with the men in both camps not to ignore the double-barreled "fact" of the one society and the many, but to make it the foundation of a lasting settlement. "The two ideas" that expressed this fact were not, he insisted, "opposed to each other." To the contrary, they were halves of a unique whole, and as such "ought to be combined" so that "in *one* branch the *people* ought to be represented, in the *other* the *states*." [32]

If this fifty-fifty accommodation had been simply an exercise in political arithmetic, it would never have stood up under the pressure of later events. It stood up in the early years, and stands up today, because it was indeed a projection, crude but effective, of one of the large facts of life in the new Republic. The Great Compromise, in sum, was the longest constitutional step ever taken in the process of creating a new kind of compound nation. While the provisions for proportional voting on a popular basis in one house of the legislature and for equal voting of the states in the other are not the only federal arrangements in the Constitution, they are, surely, the most essential, and without their support all others would fall to the ground. It is a delicious irony of history that the "invention" of American federalism should have been the result of an ill-tempered struggle for power, and that the man, James Madison, who first celebrated publicly the beauties of this unique system should have been the most irreconcilable of nationalists and the last to surrender. [33]

Paper-thin majorities rarely settle issues of consequence, and something more than the 5–4–1 decision of July 16 was needed to convince the large-state nationalists of both the necessity and propriety of surrender. Two incidents helped greatly. The first was a flurry that took place on the same day, and that Madison described in words so revealing of the mood of the Convention at this ticklish moment that they ought to be quoted:

> Mr. Randolph. The vote of this morning had embarrassed the business extremely. . . . He wished the Convention might adjourn, that the large states might consider the steps proper to be taken in the present solemn crisis of the business, and that the small states might also deliberate on the means of conciliation.
> Mr. Patterson thought with Mr. Randolph that it was high time for the Convention to adjourn, that the rule of secrecy ought to be rescinded, and that our constituents should be consulted. No conciliation could be admissible on the part of the smaller states on any other ground than that of an equality of votes in the second branch. If Mr. Randolph would reduce to form his motion for an

adjournment sine die, he would second it with all his heart.

Gen. Pinckney wished to know of Mr. Randolph whether he meant an adjournment sine die, or only an adjournment for the day. If the former was meant, it differed much from his idea. He could not think of going to South Carolina and returning again to this place. . . .

Mr. Randolph had never entertained an idea of an adjournment sine die; and was sorry that his meaning had been so readily and strangely misinterpreted. He had in view merely an adjournment till tomorrow. . . .

Mr. Patterson seconded the adjournment till tomorrow, as an opportunity seemed to be wished by the larger states to deliberate further on conciliatory expedients. On the question for adjourning till tomorrow, the states were equally divided.

Massachusetts, no. Connecticut, no. New Jersey, aye. Pennsylvania, aye. Delaware, no. Maryland, aye. Virginia, aye. North Carolina, aye. South Carolina, no. Georgia, no. So it was lost.

Mr. Broome thought it his duty to declare his opinion against an adjournment sine die, as had been urged by Mr. Patterson. Such a measure he thought would be fatal. Something must be done by the Convention, though it should be by a bare majority.

Mr. Gerry observed that Massachusetts was opposed to an adjournment, because they saw no new ground of compromise. But as it seemed to be the opinion of so many states that a trial should be made, the state would now concur in the adjournment.

Mr. Rutledge could see no need of an adjournment because he could see no chance of a compromise. The little states were fixt. They had repeatedly and solemnly declared themselves to be so. All that the large states then had to do was to decide whether they would yield or not. . . . Mr. Randolph and Mr. King renewed the motion to adjourn till tomorrow.

On the question. Massachusetts, aye. Connecticut, no. New Jersey, aye. Pennsylvania, aye. Delaware, no. Maryland, aye. Virginia, aye. North Carolina, aye. South Carolina, aye. Georgia, divided.

Adjourned.[34]

The second incident took place the next morning just before the regular session, and must have followed a long evening of pleas and threats at the Indian Queen. "A number of the members from the larger states, by common agreement, met for the purpose of consulting on the proper steps to be taken." Although the irreconcilables were still certain that "no good government could or would be built" on the "foundation" of the compromise, and were therefore prepared, so they said, to push ahead without the adamant small states, too many of their friends (to whom several small-staters were also present to lend encouragement) "seemed inclined to yield . . . and to concur in such an act, however imperfect and exceptionable, as might be agreed on by the Convention as a body." [35] And so, groaning or muttering or breathing more easily, the delegates went back to work as constitution-makers. No one, so far as we know, cheered, gloated, or sulked. The business had been too serious, the battle too dubious, and the spoils too meager for all of them, even the men of Connecticut.

Whatever compulsion Madison and Wilson may have felt to sulk must have vanished almost immediately, for the small-state nationalists, secure at last in the knowledge that they would have something attractive to sell their constituents, now outdid one another in arming the new government for its stupendous tasks. Madison himself, in later years, observed that from this day forward "they exceeded all others in zeal"; and, in an effort to dispel a gathering myth, he wrote Martin Van Buren that "the threatening contest in the Convention of 1787 did not . . . turn on the degree of power to be granted to the federal government, but on the rule by which the states should be represented and vote in the government." [36] The long awaited arrival of Langdon and Gilman from New Hampshire, which might have set off an explosion on July 2, caused hardly a stir on July 23. Both men were doubtless briefed on the nature of the compromise, and both began at once to vote as moderate nationalists.

The next nine working days, from Tuesday, July 17, through Thursday, July 26, were the most exemplary of the summer. Although the delegates ran around in circles looking for a viable answer to one question, on almost all others they proposed sensibly, debated intelligently, and decided conclusively—and decided, moreover, to confirm in convention the resolutions they had adopted in committee of the whole. The significant new departures of this period were:

to authorize Congress to legislate "in all cases for the general interests of the Union," which was done on a motion by Gunning Bedford, now anxious to prove that he had been a nationalist all along;

to extend the jurisdiction of the national courts "to cases

arising under laws passed by the general legislature," which was done on a motion of Madison, now trying to adjust to the consequences of the shattering defeat of July 16;

to strengthen the national government's guarantee of republicanism, good order, and territorial integrity to each state;

to give each state two members in the upper house, "who shall vote per capita," a distortion if not a mutilation of a principal feature of the Great Compromise;

to do away, over Madison's wounded protest, with the power of Congress to "negative" state laws. On the motion of Luther Martin, who for the time being was enjoying himself immensely, the supremacy clause was lifted from the New Jersey Plan and presented as a consolation prize to Madison.[37]

In a number of instances the Convention confirmed previous decisions only after being forced by uneasy members to reexamine its collective mind. Gorham and Wilson argued in vain against the selection of judges of the proposed "supreme tribunal" by the upper house, the former drawing on the constitution of his own state for a suggestion that appointments be made "by the executive by and with the advice and consent of the second branch." [38] Ellsworth, Paterson, and Gerry, for a variety of ideological and political reasons, proposed that the state legislatures be named as the ratifying agents of the new constitution; Mason, Randolph, Gorham, Gouverneur Morris, King, and Madison, for a variety of ideological and tactical reasons, held the fort for conventions "chosen by the people for the express purpose." [39] Morris, King, and Charles Pinckney spoke up bravely against the arrangement providing for impeachment of the executive, but so forceful were the arguments of Wilson, Mason, Davie, Franklin, Gerry, and Madison for the clause as it stood that Morris, impressed against his will by this irregular alliance of friends and foes of a strong executive, ended the game by confessing that his "opinion had been changed." [40] Two strong-executive men, Wilson and Madison, exhumed the plan for a council of revision and argued forcefully that the "aid of the judges" would "inspire additional confidence and firmness" in the use of the veto power. They were finally compelled to reinter it, not without tears.[41]

Perhaps most important in the sight of history, a sharp little struggle for power between the settled East and the empty West was resolved, thanks to the eloquence of several far-sighted men of the East, in favor of the West. Over the protests of Gouverneur Morris, Butler, Rutledge, and Gerry, who feared the day when "the western settlers" would swamp "the Atlantic states" in the councils of the nation, the Convention stayed with its decision to admit new states on essentially equal terms and "with the consent of a number of voices in the national legislature less than the whole." A wise speech of the venerable Sherman had much to do with forestalling an unwise move by an uneasy Convention. "If the event should ever happen," he mused, "it was too remote to be taken into consideration at this time."

> Besides, we are providing for our posterity, for our children and our grandchildren, who would be as likely to be citizens of new western states, as of the old states. On this consideration alone, we ought to make no discrimination.[42]

The question that had the delegates running around in circles—how should the executive be elected?—was so impervious to easy solution that a certain amount of disorder could hardly have been avoided at this otherwise orderly stage. It was, as they soon came to realize, one of the keys to the future of republican government as well as to the place of the states in the Union.

The resolution of the committee of the whole, it will be remembered, provided for election by the national legislature of an "executive to consist of a single person," who was to serve a term of seven years and then to be "ineligible a second time." This three-part arrangement had been approved by a clear and firm majority (8–3) as early as June 2, and was approved a second time by a vote of 7–3 on July 26. The second majority, however, was more clear than firm, and the vote was a way of suspending a debate that was getting nowhere rather than a final decision. Although most delegates were now persuaded of the impropriety of election by the legislature, they were persuaded for quite different reasons. Some were determined to reinforce the independence of the executive, others to bring the states into the process, still others (with eyes turned toward the man who was expected to fill this post under the new constitution) to find a way of rendering the executive eligible for two or more terms. The questions of length of term, reeligibility, and method of election were, in truth, so thoroughly mixed up that the debates on this resolution still read, as one historian has written, like a running account of a game of three-dimensional chess.[43] Most delegates agreed that an executive chosen by the legislature would have to be limited rigorously to one term lest he spend his time (and jeopardize his independence) courting reelection, and that in such case he should be given a fairly long term. Almost as many agreed, on the other hand, that the hope of reelection was an incentive to excellence that ought not to be lightly tossed aside, in which case the term must be shortened and the legislature thrust out of the picture.

Tugged this way and that by these considerations, as well as by the continuing tensions between nationalism and federalism and between large states and small, the delegates were for the moment unable to get together—and, more to the point, to stay together—on any acceptable alternative to the method of election by the legislature. Hopelessly mired in a swamp into which they had unwittingly stumbled, they sat and listened to all sorts of suggestions for getting themselves out: [44]

election by the "people at large," or at least by the "freeholders of the country," an astounding proposal put forward by Wilson and Gouverneur Morris, which appeared unworkable to some delegates and suicidal to others, and thus received only the vote of Pennsylvania;

election by electors chosen by the state legislatures, which was voted down July 17, in July 19, and out July 26;

election by the state governors or by electors chosen by them, neither a scheme that could muster any support;

nomination by the people of each state of "its best citizen," and election from this pool of thirteen by the national legislature (or by electors chosen by it), an unhelpful proposal of John Dickinson;

election by the national legislature, with electors chosen by the state legislatures taking over whenever an executive sought reelection, a proposal of Ellsworth that found favor with four states;

and, most astounding of all, election by a small group of national legislators chosen "by lot," an admittedly "undigested" proposal advanced and then withdrawn by Wilson as a way of expressing his low opinion, in which Morris joined vehemently, of the legislature as an electoral body.

Enough other delegates, Wilson was sure, now shared this opinion to give him "hope that a better method of election would yet be adopted." His hope was eventually to become reality, but not until confusion had been even worse confounded. "We seem," Gerry grumbled, "to be entirely at a loss on this head."

On Thursday, July 26, with a sigh of relief, the Convention adjourned until Monday, August 6, so that a committee of distinguished members could "prepare and report a constitution conformable" to the resolutions it had adopted in the past five weeks. Most of the delegates who lived nearby went home to attend to neglected business and to refresh lagging spirits; most of those who had come from afar stayed in Philadelphia and passed the time reading, writing, walking, talking, riding, dining, and, when they could not resist the temptation, giving free advice to the committee. The two Morrises and General Washington went fishing for trout up the river at Valley Forge, where the president "visited all the works" of the remembered winter of 1777–1778 and found them, so he recorded laconically, "in ruins." [45]

That a drafting committee would be the next necessary step in the proceedings had been anticipated almost from the outset. Several delegates, notably Gorham and King, had advised their colleagues to stick to "general principles" on the floor and to leave "precise and explicit" details to the committee.[46] To this committee of five were also referred the rejected "propositions" of Paterson, the hitherto ignored propositions of Charles Pinckney, and a last-minute resolution in support of some sort of "qualifications of property and citizenship" for officeholders in the new government; and to it were directed several informal but loud suggestions, the loudest of which was General Pinckney's warning not to leave out "some security to the southern states against an emancipation of slaves, and taxes on exports." [47]

The committee of detail—a label given to it by common consent—was well chosen. While the geographical spread was perfect—Rutledge (chairman) from the deep South, Randolph from the upper South, Wilson from the Middle States, Ellsworth from lower New England, and Gorham from the heart of New England—the posture of the committee was forcefully nationalist. The smallest state represented was the eighth largest in the Union, and no attempt had been made to strike one last blow for the Articles of Confederation by reserving a place for someone like Luther Martin, Sherman, or Paterson. Wilson had been, along with Madison, the most driving of nationalists; Rutledge, Randolph, and Gorham had been hardly less committed to the cause; and even Ellsworth had long since advanced to a position that would have startled Henry, Clinton, and other leading anti-nationalists outside the Convention. Learned in the law, rich in political experience, skilled at drafting, and laden with prestige, this committee of detail, each member of which had been heard from again and again on the floor, enjoyed the confidence and support of all but two or three doubters among the delegates. In view of the demanding character of its mandate and the short time set aside for its labors, the committee might need plenty of each before it was done.

We do not know much about the work of the committee of

detail, and it would almost seem as if these five men had adopted a secrecy rule of their own. From scraps of paper and wisps of memory we can reconstruct six stages.[48] First, the committee seems to have met in order to study the resolutions of the Convention, as well as to rummage for materials that might be borrowed from the Articles of Confederation, the best of the state constitutions, the Paterson and Pinckney plans, and other documents, reports, and laws with which all five members were acquainted. Then, while the others looked over his shoulder, Randolph wrote out a rough draft of a constitution, which was detailed at some points and merely suggestive at others, and which also contained a number of instructions and observations. One passage in particular catches the eye of the student of the Convention, for in its spirit the Constitution was written:

> In the draught of a fundamental constitution, two things deserve attention:
> 1. To insert essential principles only, lest the operations of government should be clogged by rendering those provisions permanent and unalterable, which ought to be accommodated to times and events; and
> 2. To use simple and precise language, and general propositions, according to the example of the several constitutions of the several states; for the construction of a constitution necessarily differs from that of law.[49]

After the Randolph draft had been discussed point by point, and the chairman had inserted various modifications in his own hand, the fourth and decisive stage was taken over by the most learned, experienced, and dedicated member of the committee, James Wilson. Working with the corrected Randolph draft, as well as with other materials that had appealed to the committee, Wilson produced a smoother and more detailed draft. This, too, was given a full review in committee, after which one member, probably Wilson again, wrote out a smooth copy and handed it to the prominent Philadelphia printers, John Dunlap and David Claypoole, who were asked to print just enough copies for the use of the delegates and otherwise to keep the colossal secret to themselves. Dunlap and Claypoole, who were also proprietors of the *Pennsylvania Packet,* must have been the most trusted men of their profession in the history of the Republic.

Although the constitution laid before the Convention August 6 was clearly the work of the whole committee, two men deserve special credit: John Rutledge, who kept his colleagues hard at work, reduced controversy to a minimum, and met the deadline with something to spare; and James

Wilson, who took upon himself the major responsibility for putting the resolutions of the Convention and the thoughts of his colleagues into the language of fundamental law. Whether Madison talked informally to the committee, or to any member of it, is not known; one suspects that he stayed punctiliously aloof in this stage. The inclusion of Wilson, who was as strong a nationalist, as committed a republican, and as able an "adept in political science," made it unnecessary for Madison, for at least a few days in the summer, to worry his head unduly. Indeed, in anticipation of the labors that still lay before him, he might have been well advised to go fishing with Washington and the Morrises—except that he was not the kind of man who cared much for fishing.

In the period of compromise and creativity between the decision in favor of the Virginia Plan and the appointment of the committee of detail, the Convention took on an even more distinctive style of doing both political and constitutional business. The new element in this style was, quite simply, a determination to succeed, which kept bringing the harried delegates back to the State House day after day in the heat of July to stumble toward the "half-way" solution of their harshest political problem. Whether as patriots, politicians, or men with reputations to win or lose, they saw clearly that they had marched, or had been lured or shoved, into an arena from which there was only one exit. Paterson may have been sincere in suggesting an "adjournment sine die" in the agony of July 16, but it is revealing that he never converted the suggestion into a formal motion. As the obscure Jacob Broom said in his moment of glory in the Convention, "such a measure" would have been "fatal" to the cause in which they believed. The one thing worse than presenting an imperfect constitution to the people of the United States would have been to present no constitution at all. From early June until the end of the summer, this seems to have been the pervading sentiment of all but three or four delegates.

The determination to succeed, the awareness of the underlying consensus of principle and purpose, and the ingrained deference and even timidity of the press all combined in this period to guard the Convention against the one development that could have destroyed it: a major breach in the rule of secrecy. Because no such breach was opened under the pressures of the struggle for power, the delegates were left alone —with no galleries to entertain, no scribblers to fence with, and no constituents to consult—to find a way they never could have found in the glare of publicity. The Convention's own awareness of the importance of privacy dictated a vote of July 25 forbidding "members of the house . . . to take copies of the resolutions which had been agreed to," [50] and also probably led to a "leak" to the Philadelphia newspapers in early July of a completely dissembling report that was reprinted all over the country:

> So great is the unanimity, we hear, that prevails in the Convention, upon all great federal subjects, that it has been proposed to call the room in which they assemble, *Unanimity Hall.*[51]

What then, some churlish reader of the *Pennsylvania Packet* might have asked as the weeks went by and no constitution appeared, what then are the delegates doing behind those closed and guarded doors? But no reader ever asked, no correspondent ever wondered, and no publisher ever complained; and so the Convention went on its private route to victory. Even the most imaginative newspapers confined themselves to reporting the barest details and to wishing the Convention well,* and even such a good friend and old comrade of half the delegates as Richard Henry Lee was shut out completely. The only information he could send home after a stopover of several days in Philadelphia on the way north to Congress was: "I found the Convention at Philadelphia very busy and very secret." [52]

The Convention presented a slightly different picture of leadership in July than it had in June. While Washington preserved his air of authority and Franklin his aura of benevolence, Madison, Wilson, Randolph, Charles Pinckney, and Dickinson failed to maintain the fast pace they had set at the start. Madison and Wilson, despite their dozens of valuable contributions as constitution-makers, had to be hauled back from the brink of political folly by men less brilliant but

---

* The kind of information one could glean from the press is evident in these two items from the *Pennsylvania Herald:*
July 28, 1787: The Federal Convention, having resolved upon the measures necessary to discharge their important trust, adjourned till Monday week, in order to give a committee . . . time to arrange and systematize the materials which that honorable body have collected. The public curiosity will soon be gratified; and it is hoped from the universal confidence reposed in this delegation, that the minds of the people throughout the United States are prepared to receive with respect, and to try with a fortitude and perseverance, the plan which will be offered to them by men distinguished for their wisdom and patriotism.
August 8, 1787: On Monday last the Federal Convention met, after their short adjournment; and we are told, that they are now debating by paragraphs, the plan which is to be submitted to public consideration.

more sensible than they; Randolph and Pinckney, delegates with less experience and nerve than they had appeared at first sight, gave way to tougher and steadier men; Dickinson, although an important figure in the construction of the Great Compromise, behaved more and more like a sick old man, which indeed he was.[53]

The new stars of this period were Gouverneur Morris, who returned July 2 bringing zest, wit, and wisdom to a weary gathering, and who reminded his colleagues that they were "representatives of the whole human race"; [54] Gorham, who celebrated his emancipation as chairman of the committee of the whole by making more than two dozen helpful speeches and motions in a vein of moderate nationalism; and the men of Connecticut, especially Sherman and Ellsworth, who took their stand early at the only possible meeting-point of prideful Virginia and tenacious New Jersey, and refused steadfastly to concede that no meeting was possible. Mason, Gerry, King, Rutledge, and Williamson all added to their stature in these tormented days; Hamilton showed himself in the best light just before his unfortunate retreat to New York; Davie and Baldwin proved that, while speeches may dazzle, votes count; and Read, Strong, Broom, Brearly, and even the overeager Bedford made contributions worthy of second rank (but not second-rate) Framers. Paterson set some sort of record for stubborn courage, Luther Martin for non-stop garrulity, and Johnson for talking only about important things.

Perhaps the most interesting development was the emergence of General Pinckney and Butler as special pleaders for their state and section. Although they were thoughtful, detached, and helpful on many issues, they were clearly more determined to "truck and bargain" for South Carolina than was, say, Gerry for Massachusetts, Jenifer for Maryland, Davie for North Carolina, or even Paterson for New Jersey. Perhaps that is because they had more to fear from a government armed with a conscience as well as with authority. In warning the committee of detail not to leave the peculiar institutions of the South unguarded, General Pinckney had also put the Convention on notice that another struggle for power might be in the making.

# 11 THE CONVENTION, AUGUST 6–SEPTEMBER 11: DETAILS, DETAILS, DETAILS

> *Every enterprise, public as well as private, in the United States . . . seems suspended, till it is known what kind of Government we are to receive from our National Convention. . . . The pulse of industry, ingenuity, and enterprise in every occupation of man now stands still . . . and every look and wish and hope is only to, and every prayer to Heaven that has for its object the safety of your country is only for, the present august National Convention.*
> PENNSYLVANIA GAZETTE, August 29, 1787

"THE most exact punctuality" having been "enjoined by the president when the Convention adjourned July 26,[1] most of the delegates were in their seats on Monday morning, August 6. As the session began, each man was handed the printed report of the committee of detail: seven folio pages, with comfortable margins for making corrections and additions, which presented a constitution of twenty-three articles "for the government of ourselves and our posterity."[2] In accepting twelve hundred words in the form of disconnected resolutions and reporting thirty-seven hundred in the form of an integrated plan, the committee of detail had done a remarkable job, one that blended faithfulness to orders, skill at borrowing, and the exercise of discretion in equal amounts, with several dashes of inventiveness and one of disobedience thrown in to prove that the members had minds of their own.

For the most part, Rutledge and his colleagues had acted prudently as agents of the Convention. The other delegates could tell in one careful reading that the reported constitution was a fair if far-ranging projection of their expressed wishes. Although James Wilson (we may assume that his leading role was known) might be accused of frigidity of expression, he had plainly not seized the occasion to carry the Convention even farther in the direction of a strong, consolidating, popu-

lar charter. Indeed, the one instance in which the committee
had acted contrary to the declared will of the Convention—in
providing that members of both branches of the legislature be
paid by the states—was a retreat from nationalism.

Many familiar words of the Constitution appeared for the
first time in the report of August 6. Major officers and organs
of government were designated as the President, Speaker,
Congress, Senate, House of Representatives, and Supreme
Court; engaging phrases such as "We the People," "state of
the Union," "privileges and immunities," and "necessary and
proper" twinkled here and there in the gloom; and even the
possibilities of "vacancies" in the House and Senate, "disability" in the Presidency, and "extraordinary occasions" on
which Congress might be assembled had been anticipated.
The committee had drawn on many sources—the resolutions
of the Convention, the rules of Congress, the crude plans of
Paterson and Pinckney, the constitutions of the states (especially those of Massachusetts and New York), and above all
the Articles of Confederation (as well as various proposals to
bolster the Articles)—for the phrasing of their draft, and the
familiarity of its language must have given these reform-
minded men a paradoxically comfortable sense of continuity
with the past.

Borrowing bits and pieces selectively, fitting them together
carefully, and filling in some of the cracks with notions of
their own, the members of the committee had moved a long
distance from generality to detail in many critical areas. They
had provided for the internal organization of both houses of
Congress, worked out the exact procedures of the qualified
veto, defined the jurisdiction of the courts, adjusted certain relations among the states, and armed the President with powers of guidance (of the legislature), appointment (of his own
aides), administration, command, ceremony, and mercy. In
some instances the committee had decided to make up the
Convention's mind: it placed the power to impeach in the
House and to convict in the Supreme Court, provided that
new states be admitted "on the same terms with the old" on a
two-thirds vote in both houses of Congress, fixed the ratio of
representation in the House at one member for every forty
thousand "inhabitants," and covered the constitutions as well
as the laws of the states in the supremacy clause. In others it
had handed over tough problems to future generations: it authorized Congress to establish property qualifications for the
members of both houses, and declared that all those eligible
to vote for "the most numerous branch of their own legislatures" in the states were likewise eligible to vote for members
of the House. And on one point that had hitherto been cir-

cled nervously the committee had decided to force the hand
of the Convention: Article XXI said simply and discreetly:
"The ratifications of the conventions of      states shall be
sufficient for organizing this constitution." What number
would fill that expectant space was anyone's guess; the
guesses ran from seven to thirteen.

The most important contribution of the committee of detail was to convert the general resolution on the law-making
authority of the proposed government to a list of eighteen
specific powers of Congress, to which it added the crowning
power "to make all laws" that appeared "necessary and
proper" to carry "into execution" these and "all other powers
vested" in the government by the Constitution. Although Wilson himself would have preferred a short, general statement
of the power of Congress to legislate "for the general interests" of the nation, most delegates expected—and several
must have demanded—an enumeration. The consensus of the
Convention on this issue was, Rutledge and Randolph were
sure, a sensible reflection of the wishes of most well-disposed
citizens on the outside. Among the specific grants to Congress
were the powers to "lay and collect taxes, duties, imposts,
and excises," regulate interstate and foreign commerce, establish uniform rules of naturalization, coin and borrow money,
"emit bills on the credit of the United States," establish post
offices, set up inferior courts, make war, raise armies, build
fleets, call forth the militia, "appoint a Treasurer by ballot,"
and "subdue a rebellion in any state, on the application of its
legislature." Although this enumeration was a long way short
of Hamilton's proposal to arm the national legislature with
"power to pass all laws whatsoever," it was also a long step
forward from the Articles of Confederation. Not only did the
proposed new Congress have more legislative powers than the
old; it was expected to bring these powers directly to bear
upon the citizens of the Republic.

The second most important contribution of the committee
was a series of prohibitions on the state governments. Encouraged by the precedent of the Articles of Confederation,
and disturbed by the hole left in their novel system by the
Convention's vote of July 17 against the power to "negative"
state laws, the committee forbade the states flatly to coin
money, grant "letters of marque and reprisal," make treaties,
or grant titles of nobility. It also forbade them "without the
consent" of Congress to print or support paper money, lay
duties on imports, "keep troops or ships of war in time of
peace," make agreements with other states and nations, or
"engage in any war" except under unusual circumstances.
Just how an unruly state was to be kept from doing these

things was not indicated. Most delegates, if asked their opinion, would doubtless have said something about the authority of the Supreme Court to declare obnoxious state laws "null and void." By granting some powers to Congress and forbidding others to the states, the committee of detail had come up with its own solution to the nagging problem of where to "draw the line" in the federal system.

Finally, this committee chaired by John Rutledge of South Carolina had responded to General Pinckney's threat of July 23 in behalf of South Carolina by placing the following clauses in the article dealing with the powers of Congress:

> No tax or duty shall be laid by the legislature on articles exported from any state; nor on the migration or importation of such persons as the several states shall think proper to admit; nor shall such migration or importation be prohibited.
> No navigation act shall be passed without the assent of two thirds of the members present in each house.

"Such persons" was a polite way of saying "slaves," "navigation act" a traditional label for laws that regulated foreign commerce—tariffs, quotas, embargoes, bounties, discriminations in favor of the ships of one's own country, and the like. Polite and traditional as the language may have been, these clauses were a challenge to many northerners, and even to some troubled southerners, that was certain to be taken up.

After adjourning for the rest of the day "to examine the report," the delegates reassembled the next morning, voted down an attempt to revive the committee of the whole, and plunged bravely into the business of picking this draft apart clause by clause, often even word by word, and then putting it back together for the instruction of yet another committee. This third major stage in the labors of the Convention ran exactly five weeks, from Tuesday, August 7, through Monday, September 10, and put the delegates to a severe test of nerve and endurance.

The precious record of these weeks kept by Madison, which is confirmed by letters written then and reminiscences engaged in long after, speaks of hard, dedicated, bone-tiring work, on the floor and off. It was a time, as the saying goes, to "separate the men from the boys"—or at least to separate the men who cared deeply from the men who did not. Most of the stalwarts of the earlier stages continued to dominate the proceedings by force of mind, will, or character. Although the weather went from hot to hotter, Washington thrust cool thoughts of the Potomac out of his mind and presided with tact and vigor, Franklin made his most relevant little speeches of the summer, and Dickinson regained some of the stature he had lost in the course of an indifferent July. Madison and Wilson once again took up their rightful positions at the center of affairs, Randolph and the younger Pinckney improved with age, Gouverneur Morris filled the roles of court jester and fountain of creative energy, and the men from Connecticut never flagged as brokers between large states and small, North and South, eager nationalists and reluctant ones. Gerry, Gorham, King, Read, Mason, Williamson, Rutledge, Butler, and General Pinckney, helped from time to time by one of the less verbal delegates, joined Madison, Wilson, and the others to keep the discussion at a high level of eloquence, relevance, and decision.

The record also speaks of growing restlessness. Although a few delegates behaved as if they had no other interests or obligations in the world, and were prepared to sit for months debating whether the supremacy clause should be directed to "the judges in" or "the judiciaries of" the states, most had heavy political and personal commitments; and every extra day in Philadelphia would make their affairs at home more difficult to unsnarl. John Rutledge, in particular, "complained much of the tediousness of the proceedings" and, seizing upon the "extreme anxiety of many members of the Convention to bring the business to an end," persuaded his colleagues on August 18 to extend their daily sessions to 4 P.M.[3] After a week of sitting down late to their dinners the delegates, doubtless prodded by the cooks at Mrs. House's and the Indian Queen, went back to the old hours, but Rutledge's point had been effectively made. Speeches got shorter,* votes were called for more readily, committees sprouted more thickly. State delegations, especially that of neighboring New Jersey, were caught "off the floor" more often than in June and July on roll calls, and four delegates sympathetic to the aims of the Convention—Strong, Ellsworth, Davie, and Alexander Martin—slipped off for home. Those who stayed behind showed themselves more disposed to compromise in small matters and less reluctant to trample on the dissenters in large ones. Their quest was for unanimity, but also for an end to toil.

By early September the pace of the nationalist majority had quickened so visibly that the last two members of the anti-nationalist minority, Luther Martin and John Francis Mercer, were home in Maryland girding themselves for the fight against ratification. Although one could be written off as

---

* As did also, alas, the weary Madison's notes of most speeches.

a bibulous eccentric and the other as a coxcomb, the fact that they spoke for the powerful Samuel Chase must have set the less sanguine delegates to worrying about the reception the Constitution would get when it was finally laid before the states. Unlike Martin, the delinquent Mercer had not been there in June and July to be coaxed step by step along the path of precedent-shattering reform. He and the draft of the committee of detail had arrived on the floor together, and Madison must have felt a small sense of disquiet as he jotted down the words: "Mr. Mercer expressed his dislike of the whole plan, and his opinion that it never could succeed." [4] Far more troubling to the Convention in its search for unanimity and repose was the growing uneasiness of three of its most active and respected members: Elbridge Gerry, Edmund Randolph, and George Mason. By the time of Martin's departure, September 4, each had suggested that, although he would not be a leave-taker, he might not be a signer. Yet Gerry's laments over the grave of old-fashioned republicanism could no longer deflect the course of the determined and impatient majority.

The majority had plenty of issues to settle in its own ranks. While many arrangements in the draft constitution found quick, unanimous confirmation on the floor, many others were targets for criticism, and the changes in detail and wording came especially thick and fast as August slid humidly into September. Some were suggested and adopted on the floor, others were thrust upon late-working committees (including the committee of detail, whose labors did not cease the morning of August 6). Although it would be a weariness to present a full catalogue of these changes, eight may be mentioned as examples of the kind of work in which the Convention was heavily engaged in this period:

After Madison had objected to the rigid requirement of one representative for every forty thousand inhabitants, Sherman moved that the words "not exceeding" be inserted in the formula. The motion having been adopted unanimously—or, as Madison liked to record such votes, "nem. con."—this generation of Americans was spared a House of five thousand members.[5]

After everybody had joined lustily in one last scrimmage over the exclusive power of the House to originate money bills, the Convention rendered the power rather less exclusive by knocking out the clause forbidding the Senate to "alter or amend." [6]

After several members, notably Mason, Gouverneur Morris, Sherman, and the Irish-born Butler, had complained of insufficient protection against "foreign habits, opinions, and at-

tachments . . . in public affairs," the requirements of three
years' citizenship for representatives and four for senators
were raised to seven and nine respectively—not without an-
guished complaints about "illiberality" from Madison, Franklin, Ellsworth, the Scottish-born Wilson, and (back in town
for a day or two) the West Indian-born Hamilton. At the
same time, the Convention decided wisely, over the protests
of its leading nabobs, to throw out any reference to
property-owning qualifications for service in the new government. Franklin had one of his finest moments of the summer
when he met the younger Pinckney head-on in this matter—
or as head-on as this shrewd and kindly old man ever met
anyone. Pinckney, who pretended to be twenty-four, asked
the Convention to consider a requirement of "not less than
one hundred thousand dollars for the President" and "half of
that sum" for judges and legislators; Franklin, who admitted
to being eighty-one, "expressed his dislike of everything that
tended to debase the spirit of the common people"; and "the
motion of Mr. Pinckney was rejected by so general a *no,* that
the states were not called." [7]

Ellsworth, Dickinson, Madison, Broom, and Carroll warned
their colleagues against leaving the new government "dependent" on the "prejudices, passions, and improper views" of
the state legislatures, whereupon they voted 9–2 to undo the
damage of the committee of detail and provide for paying
members of both houses "out of the national treasury." All
five members of the committee sat strangely mute throughout
this important debate.[8]

Egged on by Madison, Wilson, Carroll, Gouverneur Morris, and Williamson, the delegates voted 6–4, with Pennsylvania divided, to strengthen the President's hand by requiring
three-fourths rather than two-thirds of each house to override
a veto.[9]

Egged on by Wilson and Sherman, the latter of whom
"thought this a favorable crisis for crushing paper money,"
they voted almost unanimously to make the prohibition on
state emissions of bills of credit absolute, and then went on to
insert equally absolute provisions against "bills of attainder
and retrospective laws." [10]

The provisions governing the admission of new states were
rewritten almost completely under the prodding of Gouverneur Morris. The assurance of "equal terms" was struck out,
the price of admission was reduced from two-thirds to a simple majority of Congress, and the states were guaranteed
against fission or fusion without their express consent.[11]

After a debate that ranged over most of two days and
raised the emotional temperature to a level near that of early

July, the delegates voted by comfortable margins to strike two stout tactical blows for the system they were creating. Agreeing with Wilson that they, like the second Continental Congress, were agents of "the original powers of society," and refusing to place the fate of the nation in the hands of recalcitrant states like Rhode Island, they filled in the blank space in Article XXI with "nine"—a number, Mason acknowledged, that was "familiar to the people"—and decided not to ask for the "approbation" of Congress.[12] This decision to do away completely with the Articles of Confederation called forth the last angry protest from Luther Martin.

And so the days dragged on, and so the additions, subtractions, elaborations, and alterations piled up in such profusion that only the most alert delegates—and they were growing steadily fewer—had an exact knowledge of the details of the growing consensus. At the suggestion of Charles Pinckney the delegates voted to forbid public officials to accept presents or honors from foreign governments without the approval of Congress; on a motion by Rutledge they voted to strengthen the supremacy clause even further by giving everlasting precedence to "this Constitution"; and on a complaint of superfluity voiced by several of their fellows they struck out a complicated arrangement for settling squabbles between states over "jurisdiction or territory." [13] On many matters, of course, they stood fast on the recommendations of the committee of detail. Once again, this time somewhat highhandedly, they refused to listen to the stale arguments of Madison and Wilson for a council of revision, and once again they refused to give Congress any power, no matter how restricted, to censor state laws,[14] agreeing with Rutledge that, "if nothing else, this alone would damn and ought to damn the Constitution." * And while they played happily with the list of powers granted to Congress, adding here (for example, the helpful powers to "establish postroads" and to legislate on "the subject of bankruptcies") and subtracting there (for example, the naked powers to "subdue a rebellion in any state" and to emit bills of credit), they ended by accepting most of the recommendations of the committee of detail.[16] Their most fateful decision was made without debate or disagreement, indeed without even a passing thought: to tack the words "to pay the debts and provide for the common defense and general welfare of the United States" onto the clause granting Congress its taxing powers. James Madison, for one,

* Madison never did surrender on the latter point. As late as September 12 he was still lamenting the failure to provide for "a negative on the state laws." [15]

would come to regret the busy day of September 4, 1787, when he let this apparently innocuous clause steal into the Constitution.[17]

Certain that they had found workable solutions to all these major and minor problems, the delegates suspected rightly that the fate of their labors hung on the answers they finally gave to two explosive questions: How should the manifestly conflicting interests of North and South be balanced? How should the President be elected—and also empowered?

The committee of detail had raised the first question almost too brazenly in its draft constitution by giving General Pinckney everything for which he had asked in his menacing remarks of July 23: it had forbidden Congress to tax exports, to outlaw or even tax the slave trade, and to pass navigation acts except by a two-thirds majority of both houses. If John Rutledge expected his colleagues on the floor to swallow this dose of southern comfort without protest, he was quite mistaken. On August 8, in a discussion of the basis of representation in the House, Rufus King betrayed the uneasiness of many northern minds. It was one thing, he said, for states like Massachusetts to grant states like South Carolina additional seats under the three-fifths rule to represent persons who were, according to southern law and opinion, not really persons at all, quite another for South Carolina to import such persons freely and forever, and then expect the common government to rush to its rescue whenever they rose in revolt. "There was," he complained, "so much inequality and unreasonableness in all this, that the people of the northern states could never be reconciled to it." Gouverneur Morris agreed with him lustily in a speech that assailed slavery as a "nefarious institution" and "the curse of heaven"; but for the time being the southerners, secure in the knowledge that there could be no retreat from the three-fifths rule for representing slaves, said nothing.[18]

On August 21 the delegates reached the clauses so dear to General Pinckney and so offensive to King, and lurched into one of the angriest debates of the summer. Except for the fortunate fact that it was also one of the most confused, it might well have become too angry for the arts of compromise to resolve. Although Madison, Hamilton, and others had suggested from the beginning that the real division in the Union, and thus on the floor, was not between large states and small but between North and South, the debate brought on by the South Carolinians did not divide the delegates neatly into two opposing camps. There were northerners like Johnson and Ellsworth who apparently saw nothing much to worry about in slavery or even the slave trade, southerners like Mason and Madison who were worried sick, and men on both sides who simply wanted to finish the business and go home to their families. While the makings of another endless wrangle like that of June and July were on hand in full supply, on this occasion the necessary compromise was reached in short order. Something had to be done for the deep South, whose spokesmen warned bluntly that the price of union would be too high if it included any threat, open or implied, to its peculiar interests; something also had to be done for those men everywhere in the country who were troubled about slavery on political, social, or moral grounds, and who were loath to underwrite it in the charter of a republican nation. And so, Rutledge and the Pinckneys having said "never," Mason and Luther Martin having inveighed against the evils of slavery, Sherman and Ellsworth having predicted its natural death, and King and Langdon having cautioned against giving the deep South its very last wish, the Convention fell back August 22 upon a favorite technique. It handed to a committee of eleven—Langdon, King, Johnson, Livingston, Clymer, Dickinson, Luther Martin, Madison, Williamson, C. C. Pinckney, and Baldwin—the "whole subject" of the slave trade and navigation acts. "These things," Gouverneur Morris said in behalf of a fatigued Convention, "may form a bargain among the northern and southern states." "If we do not agree on this middle and moderate ground," Ellsworth added, two states would be lost to the Union, the rest would "fly into a variety of shapes and directions," and "bloodshed" would "most probably" follow.[19]

Two days later Governor Livingston reported the terms of the bargain: Congress was forbidden to do anything drastic about the slave trade until 1800; it could, however, tax the importation of slaves "at a rate not exceeding the average of the duties laid on imports"; the prohibition on export taxes was reaffirmed by implication; and the requirement of a two-thirds majority for navigation acts was struck out.[20] After the terms had been altered further, but only slightly, in the course of a tiresome debate on the floor—for example, the slave-traders were given eight more years in which to offer their wares—the bargain was struck on August 29, whereupon Butler sealed it with a flourish by persuading the napping delegates to give assent to a politely worded fugitive-slave clause borrowed from the Northwest Ordinance.[21]

The bargain was, in truth, a strange one, for it joined both ends (New England and South Carolina) against the middle in all the crucial votes, left the men of New Jersey, Pennsylvania, and Delaware unhappy about the propitiation of slavery, and mortified those southerners, notably Mason and Randolph, who suspected that the real threat of a national government to the South lay in the clear-cut power to pass navigation acts (which the other states would doubtless wield)* and not in some vague power to tamper with slavery (which they could not wield—except at the price of resistance or even revolution). Yet a bargain it was, and a bargain it remained. An attempt of Charles Pinckney, who was either poorly briefed or clumsily handled by his colleagues in the South Carolina delegation, to reinstitute the two-thirds requirement for such acts was defeated handily. Rutledge, C. C. Pinckney, and Butler, who knew that they had pushed other states to the limits of tolerance, threw buckets of water on the unexpected blaze. They would doubtless have voted for the young man's motion if it had been up for consideration on its merits alone, but they were now firmly committed to a compromise that might otherwise be smashed into ruins —with South Carolina at the bottom of the heap. While Butler agreed with his youthful colleague that the elimination of the two-thirds requirement was a huge concession on the part of the South, he described himself as so "desirous of conciliating the affections" of his brethren of New England that he was ready to grit his teeth and make the concession graciously. And so, after much gritting (and some grinding) of teeth on all sides, the second major compromise of the summer was embedded in the Constitution. If not so dramatic and hard-won and honorable a bargain as the first, it was an essential step toward constructing a government that delegates from every part of the country could take home to their constituents.

On August 31, having gone through the draft constitution clause by clause and still not decided how the President should be elected, the Convention responded to a "motion of Mr. Sherman" (whose name Madison had finally learned to spell correctly) and appointed a "committee on postponed matters" to bring in solutions to this issue and several others yet unsettled.[22] Chaired by the faithful Judge Brearly, and manned by Gilman, King, Sherman, Gouverneur Morris, Dickinson, Carroll, Madison, Williamson, Butler, and Baldwin, this admirable committee moved in as a rescue party to make up the Convention's mind. Beginning the very next

* Most other delegates from the South do not seem to have shared this fear, probably because they assumed, as did almost everyone in the Convention, that expansion of the nation to the south and west would sooner or later shift the center of gravity of political power away from the "carrying states" of the northern seaboard.

morning and continuing for several days, the committee tossed one useful suggestion after another onto the floor, and most found favor with the necessary majority of the delegates. Among these were: the fixing of certain slightly xenophobic qualifications to be met by the President, who, in addition to having reached the mature age of thirty-five, was to be "at least fourteen years a resident within the United States" and either a "natural born citizen" or, like eight of the delegates, a "citizen of the United States at the time of the adoption of this Constitution"; the transfer of the power to try impeachments from the Supreme Court to the Senate, with a two-thirds majority required to convict; the grant to Congress of several additional powers, including the power (which had originated with Madison) to "exercise legislation" over the "seat of the government of the United States";* and the clearing up of such questions as ineligibility of officers of the national government to membership in either house, the location of authority to regulate commerce with the Indian tribes, and a time limit on military appropriations.

The major contribution of this committee was an acceptable scheme for electing the President.[23] If some delegates found it rather too complicated, that was because the committee had been warned off the simple but unacceptable schemes of election directly by the people or election by a joint session of Congress, and also because in this area, too, it had to strike a politically viable balance between large states and small. The President, who was now given a four-year term and permitted to seek another and another and yet another, was to be elected by electors, who would be chosen in each state "in such manner" as its legislature might "direct"—and nothing forbade any legislature to bestow the choice upon the people. The electors of each state—equal in number to its total representation in Congress—would meet at home and "vote by ballot for two persons," of whom one could not be an inhabitant of the state. (This unusual arrangement was based on the assumption that electors would invariably vote for men from their own state.) The votes were then to be sent to the Senate for counting, and "the person having the greatest number of votes," provided that "such number" were a "majority of that of the electors," would be proclaimed President. If no person had such a majority, the Senate would choose the President "from the five highest on the list." The

---

* The clause dealing obliquely with "the common defense and general welfare" also emerged from the labors of the committee on postponed matters.

person with the second largest number of votes was to be Vice-President of the United States. In this capacity he would preside over the Senate (with a casting vote in case of ties), and, in the sad event of a vacancy in the Presidency or "inability" of the President, he would "exercise" the "powers and duties" of the office until the vacancy was filled or the inability "removed."

As if this ingenious mechanism were not enough for the delegates to digest, the committee gave them another surprise by recommending that authority to make treaties and appointments, including appointments to the Supreme Court, be vested in the President. He was requested to seek the "advice and consent" of the Senate in the use of these high prerogatives, and no treaty would be valid "without the consent of two thirds of the members present." He was also authorized to "require" written opinions of "the principal officer in each of the executive departments."

While even Mason was moved to express grudging admiration for the clever manner in which the committee on postponed matters had discharged its trust, the scheme for electing the President was still not one with which a majority could agree and the minority live comfortably. Most delegates seem to have doubted that, once George Washington had passed from the scene, the electors would be able to produce a majority for one man, and they feared that the Senate, authorized to choose among the five leading candidates, would thereupon take command of the process—and thus, quite probably, command of the President. Having worried all through the summer about the danger of senatorial oligarchy, they had responded favorably to the suggestion of the committee on postponed matters that the Senate be shorn, if not completely stripped, of its powers to make treaties as well as both diplomatic and judicial appointments. Now, after a debate in which Madison, Mason, Williamson, Wilson, Dickinson, and Sherman proved especially persuasive, the Senate was also shorn of most of its electoral power. In the event that no one person captured a majority of the electors, Sherman suggested, the House of Representatives, with each state's delegation casting one vote, was to choose the lucky man from the top five. This solution, acceptable alike to friends of the strong Presidency like Wilson, spokesmen for the small states like Sherman, and worriers about "the aristocratic influence of the Senate" like Mason, was thereupon placed in the Constitution by a 10–1 margin.[24] At the suggestion of King and Gerry, who were anxious to guard the process of election against "corruption and intrigue," this interesting clause had been added "nem. con." just before the decisive vote: "But no person shall be appointed an elector who is a member of the legislature of the United States, or who holds any office of profit or trust under the United States." [25] That prohibition, they hoped, would bar congressmen, postmasters, and customs officers from having a hand in the choice of a President, and also bar a President in search of reelection from toadying to congressmen, bullying postmasters, and bribing customs officers.

By the time the committee on postponed matters had come to the end of its short happy life, the outlines of the executive, so foggy in the early stages of the Convention and so fuzzy even in the middle of August, had assumed their final form, and the form must have been a genuine surprise, whether pleasant or unpleasant, to every last man on the floor. Considering the spirit of the age, which was still proudly and loudly Whiggish, the proposed Presidency was an office of unusual vigor and independence. As Hamilton was soon to point out in *The Federalist*, it joined energy, unity, duration, competent powers, and "an adequate provision for its support" with "a due dependence on the people" and "a due responsibility." [26] The President had a source of election legally separated if not totally divorced from the legislature, a fixed term and untrammeled reeligibility, a fixed compensation (which could be "neither increased nor diminished" while he was in office), immunity from collective advice he had not sought (whether tendered by the Court, the heads of executive departments, or a council of revision), and broad constitutional powers of his own. It would be his first task to run the new government: to be its administrative chief, to appoint and supervise the heads of departments and their principal aides, and to "take care" that the laws were "faithfully executed." He was to lead the government in its foreign relations, peaceful and hostile, and he was, it would appear, to be ceremonial head of state, a "republican monarch" with the prerogative of mercy. Despite the allegiance of the Convention to the principle of the separation of powers, it had by no means cut him off from the two houses of Congress. To them he could tender information and advice; over their labors he held a qualified but effective veto; at his request they were bound to convene "on extraordinary occasions." He was, in short, to be a strong, dignified, largely non-political chief of state and government.

Perhaps more to the point, he was to be George Washington. Washington was not a candidate for this or any other office on earth, but when Dr. Franklin predicted on June 4 that "the first man put at the helm will be a good one," [27] every delegate knew perfectly well who that first good man would be. We cannot measure even crudely the influence of the commanding presence of the most famous and trusted of Americans, yet we may be sure that it was sizable, that it pointed (as we know from Washington's recorded votes) toward unity, strength, and independence in the executive, and that the doubts of some old-fashioned Whigs were soothed, if never entirely laid to rest, by the expectation that he would be chosen as first occupant of the proposed Presidency, and chosen and chosen again until claimed by the grave. The powers of the President "are full great," Pierce Butler wrote the following year to a relative in England,

> and greater than I was disposed to make them. Nor, entre nous, do I believe they would have been so great had not many of the members cast their eyes towards General Washington as President; and shaped their ideas of the powers to be given a President, by their opinions of his virtue.[28]

Not every delegate was content with the shape of the proposed executive. Williamson admitted that the Vice-Presidency was an anomalous office, and had been "introduced only for the sake of a valuable mode of election which required two to be chosen at the same time." [29] Mason deplored the lack of a "privy council"—"the Grand Signor himself," he grumbled, "had his Divan"—and both Dickinson and Franklin supported him.[30] And Mason began to wonder out loud whether all this strength and independence might not lead in time to a "monarchy." The Convention was aware that any plan for a one-man executive would invite enemies of the new constitution to shriek this horrid word at the top of their lungs; and, in a timely move to muffle damaging rumors, someone "leaked" a piece of information in mid-August that was gobbled up and printed everywhere:

> We are well informed, that many letters have been written to the members of the federal convention from different quarters, respecting the reports idly circulating, that it is intended to establish a monarchical government, to send for the Bishop of Osnaburgh, etc., etc.—to which it has been uniformly answered, "Tho we cannot, affirmatively, tell you what we are doing; we can, negatively, tell you what we are not doing—we never once thought of a King."*

Other members of the Convention, untroubled by rumors

* The "Bishop of Osnaburgh" was in fact none other than the Duke of York, second son of George III.[31]

and unimpressed by threats of malice, could think of several ways to strengthen the Presidency. Gouverneur Morris, Hamilton, and Read remained partisans in theory of a tenure for life and advocates in fact of an absolute veto, while Wilson, Morris, Read, and Carroll regretted that the President was not to be elected by the people. Madison continued to insist that the judges of the Supreme Court, if given a share in the power of veto, would put backbone in a demoralized President under attack by an overweening Congress. James Wilson, from first to last the best friend of the Presidency in the Convention, still worried lest the President be "the minion of the Senate" rather than "the man of the people as he ought to be," and thus still hoped to cut down the "objectionable" power of a majority of the Senate to hold up appointments and of a minority to block treaties.[32] And several friends of orderly government were not quite convinced that Congress should have the authority—handed over casually by the committee of detail—to "appoint a Treasurer." Read had done his best on August 17 to strike out this clause, "leaving the appointment of the Treasurer as of other officers to the executive," but his motion had been defeated by the narrow margin of 6–4.[33]

For the most part, however, the friends of an energetic executive could be well satisfied with the course of events that had led, by no means inexorably, to the creation of the Presidency. Whether as a restraining hand on an impetuous Congress, which is the way Madison saw him, or as "the general guardian of the national interests," which is the way Morris described him, the proposed President was more splendidly armed than any delegate could have anticipated on opening day. When we stop to think that just two weeks before the end of the Convention the Senate still held exclusive authority to appoint ambassadors and judges and to make treaties, and also to recognize that a few really stubborn men could probably have insisted on election by the legislature, we must marvel at the happy ending of this meandering tale for Wilson, Morris, Read, Madison, Hamilton, and above all Washington. Piece by piece the Convention had put together an office worthy of its most celebrated member. In the twelfth year after the great rebellion against a "tyrant king," that was a good summer's work in itself.

A few loose ends remained to be tied up or tucked in. Randolph, with some help from Madison, persuaded his colleagues to authorize Congress to provide for succession to the Presidency, and Spaight, who had not been heard from in some time, persuaded them to give the President the power to

# THE PRESIDENT OF THE CONVENTION

## GENERAL GEORGE WASHINGTON

JULY 3, 1787. *"Sat before the meeting of the Convention for Mr. Peale, who wanted my picture to make a print or mezzotinto by.*

JULY 6, 1787. *"Sat for Mr. Peale in the morning. Attended Convention. Dined at the City Tavern with some members of the Convention, and spent the evening at my lodgings."*

*From the diary of George Washington*

# THE LEADING SPIRIT
# OF THE CONVENTION

JAMES MADISON

*"Every person seems to acknowledge his greatness. He blends together the profound politician with the scholar."*

*William Pierce, 1787*

# TWO PRINCIPAL ARCHITECTS
# OF THE CONSTITUTION

## JAMES WILSON

*"Government seems to have been his peculiar study, all the political institutions of the world he knows in detail."*

William Pierce, 1787

## GOUVERNEUR MORRIS

*"The finish given to the style and arrangement of the Constitution fairly belongs to the pen of Mr. Morris. . . . A better choice could not have been made."*

James Madison to
Jared Sparks, APRIL 8, 1831

# FOUR FRAMERS WHO
# MADE THEIR PRESENCE FELT

BENJAMIN FRANKLIN

RUFUS KING

NATHANIEL GORHAM

HUGH WILLIAMSON

# THE "NABOBS" OF SOUTH CAROLINA

CHARLES
COTESWORTH PINCKNEY

CHARLES PINCKNEY

JOHN RUTLEDGE

PIERCE BUTLER

# THE "HALF-WAY MEN" OF CONNECTICUT

## OLIVER ELLSWORTH

*"Let a strong executive, a judiciary and a legislative power be created; but let not too much be attempted, by which all may be lost. He was not in general a halfway man, yet he preferred doing half the good we could, rather than do nothing at all."*

Ellsworth to the Convention,
as reported by Madison,
JUNE 29, 1787

ROGER SHERMAN

WILLIAM SAMUEL JOHNSON

# BIG MEN FROM SMALL STATES

### JOHN DICKINSON

*Delaware*

### WILLIAM LIVINGSTON

*New Jersey*

## WILLIAM PATERSON

*New Jersey*

## GEORGE READ

*Delaware*

# DISAPPOINTMENTS IN THE CONVENTION, GREAT MEN OUTSIDE IT

### ALEXANDER HAMILTON

*"Without numbers, he is an host within himself."*

*Thomas Jefferson to James Madison,* SEPTEMBER 21, 1795

INDEPENDENCE NATIONAL HISTORICAL PARK COLLECTION

### ROBERT MORRIS

*"A merchant of great eminence and wealth, an able financier and a worthy patriot. . . . What could have been his reason for not speaking in the Convention I know not—but he never once spoke on any point."*

*William Pierce, 1787*

# THE EMINENT FRAMERS WHO REFUSED TO SIGN THE CONSTITUTION

### EDMUND RANDOLPH

*"He repeated that in refusing to sign the Constitution, he took a step which might be the most awful of his life, but it was dictated by his conscience, and it was not possible for him to hesitate, much less to change."*

*Randolph to the Convention,
as reported by Madison,* SEPTEMBER 17, 1787

## GEORGE MASON

## ELBRIDGE GERRY

# AN ENTRY FROM MADISON'S NOTES

THE CLIMACTIC EXCHANGE OF JULY 16, 1787

# THE PRESIDENT'S CHAIR

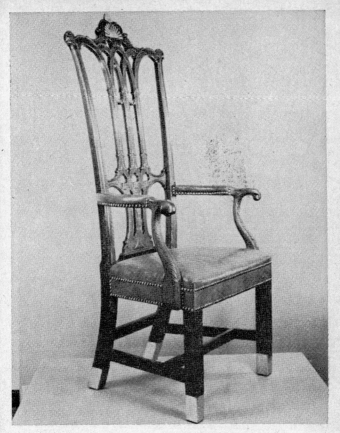

"*Dr. Franklin, looking towards the president's chair, at the back of which a rising sun happened to be painted, observed to a few members near him, that painters had found it difficult to distinguish in their art a rising sun from a setting sun. I have, said he, often and often in the course of the session and the vicissitudes of my hopes and fear as to its issue, looked at that behind the president without being able to tell whether it was rising or setting: But now at length I have the happiness to know that it is a rising and not a setting sun.*"

Madison's Notes, SEPTEMBER 17, 1787

# THE CONSTITUTION IS PRESENTED TO THE PEOPLE

The Pennsylvania Packet, *and Daily Advertiser.*

[ Price Four-Pence. ]   WEDNESDAY, September 19, 1787.   [ No. 2690 ]

WE, the People of the United States, in order to form a more perfect Union, establish Justice, insure domestic Tranquility, provide for the common Defence, promote the General Welfare, and secure the Blessings of Liberty to Ourselves and our Posterity, do ordain and establish this Constitution for the United States of America.

*The Front Page of the* Pennsylvania Packet,
SEPTEMBER 19, 1787

make recess appointments. Minor adjustments were made in the language of several complicated clauses, and Madison rescued his colleagues from a bog of confusion by suggesting an amending process that could be initiated by two-thirds of Congress or two-thirds of the state legislatures and brought to fruition by three-fourths of the states. After Rutledge had succeeded in freezing the sacred year 1808 in this amending clause, and Gerry, Randolph, and, of all people, Hamilton had failed in one last attempt to require "the approbation of Congress" for the Constitution, the Convention adjourned in the late afternoon of September 10 to await the report of a five-man "committee of stile and arrangement." [34]

The committee of style, a worthy successor to the committee of detail, had been appointed on Saturday, September 8,[35] and over the weekend had gone immediately to work on the task of producing a smooth, faithful, and final draft. While all five members were, despite lingering reservations, friends of the Constitution,* only four—Johnson (chairman), Gouverneur Morris, Madison, and King—could honestly be said to have earned their seats. The fifth man was that celebrated truant, Alexander Hamilton, who had been back on the floor only three working days, and whose very first remarks were a blunt expression of "dislike of the scheme of government" his weary colleagues had sweated out while he was in New York making love to his wife and money at the bar. Yet there he was on this trusted committee, and it speaks well of the reputation of "the stripling colonel" (who "meant to support the plan to be recommended, as better than nothing") that he was asked to join these four stalwarts.[36]

We know even less about the committee of style than we do about the committee of detail. The few existing scraps of evidence point to the ebullient Gouverneur Morris as the "penman of the Constitution." Abraham Baldwin told President Stiles of Yale in December that Morris had "the chief hand in the last arrangement and composition," [37] Morris assured Timothy Pickering in 1814 that the "instrument was written by the fingers which write this letter," [38] and Madison, who had no reason to be kind to Morris in later years, confirmed their testimony in 1831:

The *finish* given to the style and arrangement of the Constitution fairly belongs to the pen of Mr. Morris;

* Like the committee of detail, the committee of style counted four men trained in the law. Unlike that committee, it included no representatives of the deep (and anxious) South. The committee of detail was made up largely of men in their forties; the committee of style was a team of one Nestor (Johnson) and four comparative youngsters.

the task having probably been handed over to him by the chairman of the committee, himself a highly respectable member, and with the ready concurrence of the others.[39]

Whether Morris seized the initiative or had the job thrust upon him, whether he worked under the gaze of his four colleagues or went at it largely alone, whether the committee kept to itself or accepted help from other delegates*—these are questions to which, alas, we have no answers. We do know from the sound of the Constitution itself that, as Madison acknowledged graciously, "a better choice" than Morris "could not have been made."

> It is true, that the state of the materials, consisting of a reported draft in detail, and subsequent resolutions accurately penned, and falling easily into their proper places, was a good preparation for the symmetry and phraseology of the instrument, but there was sufficient room for the talents and taste stamped by the author on the face of it. The alterations made by the committee are not recollected. They were not such, as to impair the merit of the composition.[41]

By Wednesday morning, September 12, the committee had finished its labors. Once again Dunlap and Claypoole were called upon to lend their presses to the cause of freedom, and once again, now surely for the last time, the delegates prepared to go through their handiwork, this time skipping instead of slogging. Since the tasks of "comparing" the report of the committee of style "with the articles of the plan as agreed to" and of giving it "the final corrections and sanction of the Convention" could not begin until the printed copies were in hand, the impatient delegates used the rest of Wednesday to make the first of several last-minute changes and to reject the first of several last-minute motions.

The change was from three-fourths to two-thirds as the margin necessary to override a veto, and was, of course a reduction, sizable if hardly crippling, in the power of the Presidency. Pressed on the delegates by Williamson, Sherman, Gerry, Mason, and Charles Pinckney, and opposed by Morris, Hamilton, and Madison, the proposal for a two-thirds majority squeaked through by a margin of six states to four, with New Hampshire divided.[42] This was, incidentally, one of those occasions on which Madison recorded the individual votes in the Virginia delegation, and General Washington, to

---

* There is, for example, some reason to believe that Wilson was asked to run his practiced eye over the document.[40]

Madison's gratification, cast his ballot for the strong Presidency.

Since the rejection of the motion was to have enormous consequences in the struggle over ratification, it may be useful to set down the complete record of this incident of September 12:

> Col. Mason . . . wished the plan had been prefaced with a Bill of Rights, and would second a motion if made for the purpose—It would give great quiet to the people; and with the aid of the state declarations, a bill might be prepared in a few hours.
> Mr. Gerry concurred in the idea and moved for a committee to prepare a Bill of Rights. Col. Mason seconded the motion.
> Mr. Sherman was for securing the rights of the people where requisite. The state declarations of rights are not repealed by this Constitution; and being in force are sufficient . . .
> Col. Mason. The laws of the United States are to be paramount to state bills of rights. On the question for a committee to prepare a Bill of Rights New Hampshire, no. Massachusetts, absent. Connecticut, no. New Jersey, no. Pennsylvania, no. Delaware, no. Maryland, no. Virginia, no. North Carolina, no. South Carolina, no. Georgia, no.[43]

Having never considered it their business to write a bill of rights for the whole nation, having decided to keep the Constitution as free as possible of purple touches, and having sprinkled securities for personal liberty all through the text, the delegates turned a blind eye to the Whig tradition and gave short shrift to the proposal of the author of the Virginia Declaration of 1776. They were, moreover, in the home stretch, and whereas it would indeed have taken only "a few hours" for any one of a dozen candidates for immortality to draw up a bill of rights, it would have taken several weeks, not to mention some hard fighting and sharp bargaining, to get one accepted on the floor. And that, the Framers thought, was an end to that irrelevant issue.

# 12 THE CONVENTION, SEPTEMBER 12–17: LAST RITES AND RETROSPECT

*In all deliberations on this subject we kept steadily in our view, that which appears to us the greatest interest of every true American, the consolidation of our Union, in which is involved our prosperity, felicity, safety, perhaps our national existence. This important consideration, seriously and deeply impressed on our minds, led each state in the Convention to be less rigid on points of inferior magnitude, than might have been otherwise expected; and thus the Constitution, which we now present, is the result of a spirit of amity, and of that mutual deference and concession which the peculiarity our political situation rendered indispensable.*

THE PRESIDENT OF THE CONVENTION TO THE
PRESIDENT OF CONGRESS,
September 17, 1787[1]

THE REPORT of the committee of style was an adroit and tasteful rendering of the will of the Framers. By reducing the twenty-three articles of the amended draft to only seven (plus two resolutions dealing with the mechanics of ratifying the Constitution and inaugurating the new government), and by regrouping clauses and choosing words with an unerring touch, Morris and his colleagues had produced a masterpiece of draftsmanship. Although Morris liked to think in later years, as did some of his enemies in the Jeffersonian ranks, that he had taken certain "liberties" in order to give the national government even more strength and tone,[2] the fact is that he was a faithful servant of the committee and the committee of the Convention. In only two of a score of textual changes had Morris and his colleagues moved beyond the wishes of the Convention.

The most important single contribution of the committee appeared at the beginning of the Constitution. The preamble reported by the committee of detail on August 6 and handed over intact to the committee of style had read thus:

> We the people of the States of New Hampshire, Massachusetts, Rhode-Island and Providence Plantations, Connecticut, New-York, New-Jersey, Pennsylvania, Delaware, Maryland, Virginia, North-Carolina, South-Carolina, and Georgia, do ordain, declare and establish the following Constitution for the government of ourselves and our posterity.

The preamble reported back by the committee of style read rather differently:

> We the people of the United States, in order to form a more perfect Union, establish justice, insure domestic tranquility, provide for the common defense, promote the general welfare, and secure the blessings of liberty to ourselves and our posterity, do ordain and establish this Constitution for the United States of America.[3]

Although no one could find fault with this polished statement of the purposes of the Constitution, for which Morris had drawn on traditional sources, someone was bound to balk —and Patrick Henry balked with a bellow in the Virginia ratifying convention[4]—at the elimination of any mention of the separate states. We ought not attach too much significance to this change, for it had plainly been made necessary by the decision of August 31 that the new government should go into operation upon ratification by nine states. Since no one could tell for certain which states would ratify and which would stall or even refuse flatly to join, the sensible course was to leave out any mention at all of New Hampshire and her twelve sisters. Thus, somewhat fortuitously, "We the people of the United States" became the nominal as well as real sovereign source of the Constitution.

In addition to this largely unintentional contribution to the cause of American nationalism, the committee of style had made an intentional one to the cause of American property. Rufus King, having failed to persuade his colleagues on the floor in late August of the usefulness of some restraint on the power of the states to "interfere in private contracts," now persuaded his colleagues on the committee to add such a clause. When the Convention itself came on September 14 to consider this prohibition, it accepted the addition without a murmur, pausing only to tighten it slightly. No state, the Constitution now made clear, was to pass any "law impairing the obligation of contracts." Elbridge Gerry was so impressed by the wisdom of this unauthorized codicil that he tried, without success, to lay Congress "under the like prohibition." [5]

The Convention needed only four days, from Wednesday through Saturday, September 12–15, for its last review of the Constitution.[6] Yet even now, when the delegates were aching for release, they could not resist the temptation to tinker and polish, and even to reconsider decisions that were supposed to have been final. A full two dozen changes were made, another two dozen considered and then rejected.

The Presidency was the beneficiary of several important changes. Having taken away with one hand by agreeing to Williamson's motion to reduce the margin necessary to override a presidential veto, the delegates gave back with the other by agreeing to Rutledge's motion to deprive Congress of the power to "appoint a Treasurer." Since this "Treasurer" was intended to be, so far as we can tell, the chief financial officer of the new government, this was a fortunate decision in support of the principle of unity in the executive. Another interesting contribution from Rutledge, in which he was supported by Franklin, was a clause that forbade the President to receive any "emolument" other than his "fixed compensation," whether from "the United States" or from "any of them." Thus was the door shut and locked on the possibility of controlling the President (as some of the colonial legislatures had controlled or at least annoyed the royal governors) by tampering with his salary, and thus today are Rhode Island and Texas alike spared the temptation to reward the President for his kindnesses to them.

The only other changes of consequence, then or now, were a forceful rearrangement of the prohibitions that had been laid on the states; the addition of a few words to make certain that Congress, in regulating elections, would not be tempted to try its hand at shifting the capital of any state from one place to another; the granting of a restricted permission to the states to levy "incidental duties" on exports; the addition (or, to be exact, restoration) of a clause guaranteeing that "duties, imposts, and excises" should be "uniform throughout the United States"; the granting of a general power to Congress to "vest the appointment of such inferior officers as they think proper" in the President alone, the courts, or the heads of departments; and an addition to the amending clause that would make future conventions possible if not very probable. The last alteration proposed and accepted on September 15 was a faint echo of the memorable struggle of the large states for power and "justice" and the small for power and survival. Gouverneur Morris himself responded gallantly to "the circulating murmurs of the small states" by proposing "to annex a further proviso" to the amending clause, which ordained "that no state, without its consent, shall be deprived of its equal suffrage in the Senate." "No one opposing" the motion, "or on the question, saying no," the small-staters could now relax and look forward happily to the end of the affair.[7]

Not so those three leading members of the Convention who had already expressed serious doubts about the whole scheme. While some delegates sat quietly waiting for the last decisive vote and others tossed amendments cheerfully into the arena, Gerry grumbled, Mason prophesied calamity, and Randolph fell uncomfortably silent. Mason made the most determined attempt to put a few saving words into the Constitution, yet no matter what he proposed—a bill of rights, a denunciation of standing armies, the requirement of a two-thirds majority for navigation acts before 1808—he found himself thwarted by men who did not see the future through his apprehensive eyes. Williamson failed to get the size of the House increased, Rutledge and Morris to provide for suspension of impeached officers (a rather lucky failure, one guesses), Franklin to give Congress power "to cut canals," Madison to give it a general power of incorporation, Madison and Charles Pinckney to give it power to establish a model university, the generous Langdon to win more seats for Rhode Island and North Carolina, and the vigilant Sherman to win an everlasting guarantee of each state's power of "internal police," but since their allegiance to the new Constitution could not be doubted, they were able to take their little defeats with good grace.

On September 15, around three in the afternoon, the last small detail fell into place, and the Convention was ready to vote on the Constitution as a whole. Before the president could put the question, however, the eminent doubters insisted upon being heard.[8] First came Governor Randolph, the least doubtful yet most worried of the three. He had already stated his specific "objections to the system" on September 10,[9] but all of them together were not half so troubling as the uncertainty about what his constituents would think of this summer's work, or the certainty that Henry and Lee were lying in wait for him in Virginia.[10] After "animadverting on the indefinite and dangerous power given . . . to Congress" and "expressing the pain he felt at differing from the body of the Convention," he made the motion that everyone had been expecting all week: "that amendments to the plan might be offered by the state conventions, which should be submitted to and finally decided on by another general convention."

Should this proposition be disregarded, it would he said be impossible for him to put his name to the instrument. Whether he should oppose it afterwards he would not then decide but he would not deprive himself of the freedom to do so in his own state, if that course should be prescribed by his final judgment.

Mason arose at once to second the motion, and "followed Mr. Randolph in animadversions on the dangerous power and structure of the government, concluding that it would end either in monarchy, or a tyrannical aristocracy; which, he was in doubt, but one or the other, he was sure." A tougher and angrier man than Randolph—and one, more-over, quite uninterested in a political future—Mason made clear that a rejection of the motion for a second convention would put him unconditionally in the camp of the enemy. "As the Constitution now stands," Madison recorded him as saying bluntly, "he could neither give it his support or vote in Virginia; and he could not sign here what he could not sup-port there." [11]

Someone had to break in for the majority at this point, and the duty fell, for reasons we do not know, upon the younger Pinckney. Acknowledging the "peculiar solemnity" of the moment, he nevertheless ripped vehemently into the proposal of a second convention.

Nothing but confusion and contrariety could spring from the experiment. The states will never agree in their plans, and the deputies to a second convention, coming together under the discordant impressions of their con-stituents, will never agree. Conventions are serious things, and ought not to be repeated.

He, too, had "objections to the plan"—for example, the lack of a two-thirds requirement for navigation acts (Mason nodded agreement) and the "contemptible weakness and de-pendence of the executive" (Mason gasped)—but he would support it lest the "ultimate decision" on the future of the Republic be made "by the sword." Unmoved by Pinckney's rhetoric, Gerry then rose to have the last word. The word was "never"—or at least "never without a second conven-tion"—and it persuaded no one. Although he was a gentle-man for whom the other gentlemen on the floor had great respect, he was also, as someone noted a few weeks after the Convention, a "Grumbletonian" who was fond of "objecting to everything he did not propose." [12]

When all three bitter-enders had put their doubts on Madi-son's record, the president then stood to put the two final questions of the day.

On the question on the proposition of Mr. Randolph.
All the states answered no.
On the question to agree to the Constitution as
amended. All the states aye.
The Constitution was then ordered to be engrossed.
And the house adjourned.

The hour, Washington noted in his diary, was "6
oclock." [13] It had been the longest session of the summer, and
both he and his young friend from Orange County were glad
it was over. The idea of a second convention, which was certain to meet in a confusion of passion, publicity, and jarring
instructions, was so absurd to these tired men that they felt
no remorse about the beating they had just given to Randolph, Gerry, and Mason. Washington spent Sunday writing
letters and riding out with the Robert Morrises, Madison cop-
ied his notes, Franklin laid plans with his fellow delegates
from Pennsylvania, Dunlap and Claypoole printed several
hundred copies of the Constitution, and some competent penman, whose name we will never know, engrossed the Constitution on four sheets of the finest parchment.

When the Convention reassembled for the last time on
Monday morning, September 17,[14] forty-one of the fifty-five
Framers were in their seats: Langdon and Gilman; Gorham
and King; Johnson and Sherman; the lonely Hamilton;
Livingston, Brearly, Paterson, and Dayton; all eight of the Penn-
sylvanians; all the men of Delaware except Dickinson; Mc-
Henry, Jenifer, and Carroll; Washington, Madison, and Blair;
Williamson, Blount, and Spaight; all four South Carolinians;
Few and Baldwin; and the three dissenters, who were proud
of their perfect attendance records, anxious to see the end
with their own eyes, and unworried by the prospect of being
ghosts at a love feast. The sick, exhausted Dickinson had fled
home over the weekend after asking Read to sign his name.[15]
Someone, probably Major Jackson, read the engrossed
Constitution to these men who by now must have known its
every word by heart, whereupon Dr. Franklin "rose with a
speech in his hand." Unable to remain for long on his feet,
he handed it to Wilson to read, and then to Madison to copy.
It was, in many ways, the most remarkable performance of a
remarkable life. "Plain, insinuating, and persuasive," as
McHenry described it," [16] the speech was designed to create a
benign climate for the signing, to prevent any other doubters
from defecting, to lure at least the unsure Randolph back
into the majority, and, very probably, to "guard" his own
"fame" against popular disapproval of the Constitution. It

was vintage Franklin, and a few of its wise, gentle, disarming words should be heard:

Mr. President: I confess that there are several parts of this constitution which I do not approve, but I am not sure I shall never approve them: For having lived long, I have experienced many instances of being obliged by better information, or fuller consideration, to change opinions even on important subjects, which I once thought right, but found to be otherwise. It is therefore that the older I grow, the more apt I am to doubt my own judgment, and to pay more respect to the judgment of others. . . . Though many private persons think almost as highly of their own infallibility as of that of their sect, few express it so naturally as a certain French lady, who in a dispute with her sister, said "I don't know how it happens, Sister, but I meet with no body but myself, that's always in the right—*Il n'y a que moi qui a toujours raison.*"

In these sentiments, Sir, I agree to this constitution with all its faults, if they are such; because I think a general government necessary for us, and there is no form of government but what may be a blessing to the people if well administered, and believe farther that this is likely to be well administered for a course of years. . . . I doubt too whether any other convention we can obtain may be able to make a better constitution. For when you assemble a number of men to have the advantage of their joint wisdom, you inevitably assemble with those men, all their prejudices, their passions, their errors of opinion, their local interests, and their selfish views. From such an assembly can a perfect production be expected? It therefore astonishes me, Sir, to find this system approaching so near to perfection as it does; and I think it will astonish our enemies. . . . Thus I consent, Sir, to this constitution because I expect no better, and because I am not sure, that it is not the best. The opinions I have had of its errors, I sacrifice to the public good. I have never whispered a syllable of them abroad. Within these walls they were born, and here they shall die. . . .

On the whole, Sir, I cannot help expressing a wish that every member of the Convention who may still have objections to it, would with me, on this occasion, doubt a little of his own infallibility, and to make manifest our unanimity, put his name to this instrument.

The old fox then tossed in a motion dreamed up by a

young fox, Gouverneur Morris, which sought to "gain the dissenting members" by inviting all delegates to sign as witnesses to the fact of "the unanimous consent of *the states*" on the floor, and thus to create an illusion of concord.

Before the delegates could vote on Franklin's motion, Nathaniel Gorham moved that the 1:40,000 ratio in the House be changed to 1:30,000. After King and Carroll had seconded, Washington rose to put the question, and, to the astonishment of all, made his first speech since the day John Rutledge and Robert Morris had escorted him to the chair.

> He said that although his situation had hitherto restrained him from offering his sentiments on questions depending in the house, and it might be thought, ought now to impose silence on him, yet he could not forbear expressing his wish that the alteration proposed might take place. It was much to be desired that the objections to the plan recommended might be made as few as possible. The smallness of the proportion of Representatives had been considered by many members of the Convention an insufficient security for the rights and interests of the people. He acknowledged that it had always appeared to himself among the exceptionable parts of the plan; and late as the present moment was for admitting amendments, he thought this of so much consequence that it would give much satisfaction to see it adopted.

Having adopted the amendment unanimously—what else could they do?—the delegates then approved the engrossed Constitution and made ready to sign. The remarks of the patriarch had stung rather than soothed Randolph, however, and once again he rose to explain that by refusing to sign "he meant only to keep himself free to be governed by his duty as it should be prescribed by his future judgment." This was too much for Gouverneur Morris, Williamson, and Hamilton, all of whom sounded a theme that would become familiar in the fight over ratification. "The present plan," Morris said, was "the best that was to be attained," and since "general anarchy" was the "alternative," he would "take it with all its faults." "For himself," Williamson added, "he did not think a better plan was to be expected." And Hamilton, admitting candidly that "no man's ideas were more remote from the plan than his were known to be," asked nevertheless how it was "possible to deliberate between anarchy and convulsion on one side, and the chance of good . . . on the other." [17] After one last exchange among Randolph, Gerry, Franklin, General Pinckney, and the hitherto silent Blount and Ingersoll, Franklin's motion passed 10–0, with South Carolina divided.* The delegates then voted to keep up their guard against prying minds by "depositing the journal and other papers of the Convention in the hands of the president." Unsure what to do with all these materials, Washington sought guidance and was told to hold on to them tightly and wait for "the order of the Congress, if ever formed under the Constitution." Since Washington was sure to be President if Congress was "ever formed," this seemed a sensible arrangement. As to the far more explosive materials in the keeping of Madison, the delegates were apparently confident that he, too, could be trusted to guard their secrets.

While they were coming forward one after another to put their names to the engrossed copy, the patriarch got in the last word after all.

> Dr. Franklin, looking towards the president's chair, at the back of which a rising sun happened to be painted, observed to a few members near him, that painters had found it difficult to distinguish in their art a rising from a setting sun. I have, said he, often and often in the course of the session, and the vicissitudes of my hopes and fears as to its issue, looked at that behind the president without being able to tell whether it was rising or setting: But now at length I have the happiness to know that it is a rising and not a setting sun.

To this famous anecdote Madison then added the last words of his precious record:

> The Constitution being signed by all the members except Mr. Randolph, Mr. Mason, and Mr. Gerry who declined giving it the sanction of their names, the Convention dissolved itself by an adjournment sine die.

"The business being thus closed," Washington wrote in his diary in a mixed mood of pride and relief, the delegates walked over to the City Tavern on Second near Walnut, "dined together, and took a cordial leave of each other."

> After which I returned to my lodgings, did some business with, and received the papers from the secretary of the Convention, and retired to meditate on the momentous work which had been executed.

And perhaps also to meditate on its chances for approval, which were thought to be excellent in some states, doubtful in others, and poor in at least two. (I use the phrase "thought

---

* Madison's explanation of this division makes sense: "General Pinckney and Mr. Butler disliked the equivocal form of the signing and on that account voted in the negative."

to be" with clear intent, for even Madison had to confess at this stage that, as "the public" was "certainly in the dark" about the proceedings in the Convention, the delegates were "equally in the dark as to the reception" which would be given to the Constitution.) [18]

As the delegates set out for home by stage, horseback, or packet (nine of them by way of Congress in New York), their heads were spinning with fatigue and confusion. They could recall where they had begun, and they could see where they had come out; but many must have wondered how they had ever managed to move from the good intentions of May 25 to the sensible conclusions of September 17. As fatigue gave way to composure and cheer, however, so did confusion to understanding, and some of them began to suspect that they had taken part in one of the most purposeful, skilled, and, they hoped, successful meetings of public men in the history of the Western World.

We of a later generation know what they could only suspect: that the Grand Convention was indeed a model gathering of statesmen-politicians, the archetype of the constituent assembly. The Framers continue to earn the acclaim of a grateful people, and also to deserve the attention of a curious world, not alone because they ordained and established an enduring constitution, but because they did it in such a resourceful way. The creation is exemplary; so, too, was the act of creation. Whatever one may think of the Constitution, it would not be easy to imagine a more effective process of constitution-making.

Many of the circumstances under which the Framers had gathered to transact their solemn business were, to be sure, extremely favorable. Their will to succeed was overpowering, nourished as it was by both a sense of the urgency of the hour and a spirit of mission for all mankind;* their experience, much of which they had won in common, was exceptional, as was also their learning; their style of political life was self-disciplined, courteous, moderate, and healthily skeptical. They had a sense of the limits of their wisdom, a sense of the limits of the whole endeavor. And they represented, as we have seen, a consensus of principle and purpose that made it possible for them to keep talking across the barri-

---

* This spirit was most straightforwardly and thoughtfully expressed on June 26 in a discussion of the necessity of a second house. Madison recorded himself as having "observed . . . that it was more than probable we were now digesting a plan which in its operation would decide forever the fate of republican government," and Hamilton as having at once "concurred with Mr. Madison in thinking we were now to decide forever the fate of republican government." [19]

cades even in their most gladiatorial moments. Although the struggle for political power was sharp, it was never ferocious or malevolent. Since neither the existence of a religion nor the supremacy of a class nor the fortune of a party was at issue on the floor, the Framers could afford to set their sights on something less than total victory for the states, sections, and interests they represented. Since the process of selection had encouraged only a handful of committed anti-nationalists to appear in Philadelphia—all of whom bowed out before the end—they could abandon the sinking ship of the Confederation with few feelings of guilt or pity. And since the one great interest that lacked the nation-building instinct at this stage of American history—the small farmers of the back country—was only vaguely represented, the troubled leaders of the one great interest that had this instinct in abundance —the merchants and lawyers and planters in the more settled areas—could go about the task of laying a political foundation for the nation with some hope of adjusting their own differences and thus some hope of achieving success. I do not mean to draw too sharp a line between these two interests, in particular to suggest that all yeomen of the West were indifferent or hostile to the nationalist thrust and all gentlemen of the East caught up in it. Yet it must be understood that a majority of the continental elite was ready, for the sake of the Republic and also for the sake of its own power and prosperity, to move rapidly toward nationhood in the 1780's, while a majority of the yeomanry preferred, for the sake of "liberty" and also out of indifference or apathy or antipathy for the elite, to go on as before. If a dozen spokesmen of this interest had shown up in Philadelphia and then stuck to their guns, it is hard to see how Madison and his friends could have pieced together a nationalist charter.

Once the Framers had gathered, they thereupon created for themselves, as we have also seen, the best possible circumstances under which to work. Their sessions were orderly but not stagy, decorous but not stilted, flexible but not flighty, secret but not conspiratorial. They worked hard, some almost too hard; and those who remained in Philadelphia attended faithfully. The standard of their debates was high—principally, one suspects, because they were talking only to each other and to posterity—and both long-windedness and irrelevance were at a discount except on a few painful days. The standard of leadership was equally high, and they seemed to know instinctively when to slog ahead blindly, to leave something to chance (which they never did on crucial matters), or to accept guidance from one of their more knowledgeable, committed, or commanding colleagues. Some of the best

work of the Convention was done off the floor in private con-
versations, state caucuses, and informal conferences of like-
minded, other-minded, or open-minded men. While the Indian Queen was the focus of this sort of activity, other scenes
of discourse and persuasion were Mrs. House's public rooms,
the City Tavern, Robert Morris's parlor, Dr. Franklin's library, the yard of the State House, the well-paved streets of
the city, and the trout stream at Valley Forge.

Perhaps the most impressive aspect of the Convention as a
decision-making body was the confident, imaginative, and
measured use of committees. At least four were as essential
to the process of constitution-making as were the debates on
the floor—the self-appointed Virginia caucus of May, the
committee of detail, the committee on postponed matters,
and the committee of style—and all were manned with delegates well qualified to act creatively for the whole Convention. Two others were essential to the resolution of harsh
political problems—the compromising committees of eleven of
July 2 and August 22—and they, too, were manned (in the
first instance "loaded") to excellent purpose. While the Convention was quite willing to resort to this technique to help it
over rough spots—five times in August alone[20]—it did not
work it to death, for plenty of "motions to commit" failed to
win a majority. And while it gave each committee a confident
mandate, it did not propose to swallow the medicine offered
without a good look at the prescription. Every report of
every committee received the compliment of unruffled scru-
tiny.

One can think, of course, of small improvements in timing
and technique that would have made the Convention an even
more effective body. A few less hours might have been spent
on the problem of representation and a few more on the judiciary, which was, in a sense, the taken-for-granted stepchild
of 1787. There ought, perhaps, to have been some arrangement under which the voluble Martin could be cut off and
the silent Livingston, Blair, and Robert Morris encouraged to
speak. And it cannot be denied that this assembly, like all
hard-working assemblies, rolled a little too fast as it neared
the end. "It was not exempt," Madison acknowledged in later
years, "from a degree of the hurrying influence introduced by
fatigue and impatience in all such bodies," [21] and as a result
several critical questions went unanswered and several important arrangements unrefined. Yet these, surely, are minor
blemishes on a splendid record of both performance and
achievement. The political process of the liberal West, it bears
repeating, had one of its finest moments in the intense, hardheaded session of give-and-take among independent gentlemen

at Philadelphia in the summer of 1787. Imagined philosopher-kings might have done this work more efficiently than the Framers, but not real men with concrete interests— and with constituents waiting for them at home.

Those constituents—the legislators who had sent them, the voters who would elect (and presumably instruct) delegates to the ratifying conventions, the delegates themselves with their power to give or deny life to the Constitution—were much on the minds of the Framers, even in their most detached moments; and the longer the Convention ran, the more forcibly the thought of their constituents pressed upon them. That, of course, is exactly the way things should have been, for they had assembled to write rules not for Athens or Geneva or Utopia, but for the United States of America, an existing county made up of other real men with concrete interests. Since the men had principles as well as interests, and were indeed the most proudly self-governing in the world, the rules had to win the happy approval of the majority, the not unhappy sufferance of the minority, and the unforced obedience of all. At the same time, the Framers were members of an elite, gentlemen who had been taught to lead, although never to bully, and they had no intention of offering a constitution that was simply the lowest common denominator of the wishes, prejudices, and anxieties of the people. Moreover, they could sense that the only half-formed state of opinion in the country would never be more favorable to an imaginative exercise of the arts of political and intellectual leadership.

The search of the Convention, it seems in retrospect, was for solutions that would strike a subtle balance among four principal considerations that framers of constitutions must keep in mind, shifting them about on their personal scales in response to changing pressures of conviction and circumstance. The first is what their constituents have directed them to do, and the Framers were fortunate (or foresighted) enough to have imprecise directions that encouraged them to make the necessary gamble on an entirely new constitution. When Paterson reminded his colleagues on June 16 that their "object" was "not such a government as may be best in itself, but such a one as our constituents have authorized us to prepare," Wilson and Randolph were able to argue plausibly that the Convention, while it was "authorized to *conclude nothing,*" was "at liberty to *propose anything.*" [22]

Anything, they meant to add, that the people would approve, for this is, of course, another principal consideration of would-be framers. The Framers of 1787 never forgot their constituents, "the people of America." "We must consult their rooted prejudices," Gorham advised his colleagues at one critical moment, "if we expect their concurrence in our propositions." "The plan must be accommodated to the public mind," Paterson warned them at another; it must "consult the genius, the temper, the habits, the prejudices of the people." "The genius of the people," Mason, Dickinson, and a half-dozen others echoed, commanded republicanism, forbade monarchy, expected bicameralism, and approved the separation of powers. "We must follow the example of Solon," Butler said in behalf of all his colleagues, "who gave the Athenians not the best government he could devise, but the best they would receive." [23]

The best they would receive, however, was something different from the least they would expect. Throughout the Convention the delegates spoke admiringly of their constituents as men who were rightly tenacious about principles and sensibly flexible about details, and thus as men who were open to explanation and persuasion—especially, it would seem, in the critical area of nationalism. In some things, they recognized, they would have to "follow the people," but in others, they guessed and gambled, the people would follow them.[24] Hamilton, in particular, was convinced that "the public mind," if properly instructed, would rouse to the challenge of nationhood and "adopt a solid plan." [25]

However they may be instructed, and whatever they may hazard on the probabilities of public opinion, men who would write a long-lived constitution must also worry their heads over the practical question: will it work? Certainly the Framers kept this consideration firmly in mind. They sought not merely immediate approval but continuing viability for their charter, and they got it, one likes to think, because they understood—or came to understand in the course of the summer—what would and would not work in a country with the circumstances, traditions, prospects, and problems of the United States. While some of their attempts to be at all costs "practical" were destined to founder on the shoals of developments they could not anticipate—for example, their ingenious scheme for electing the President—most were to be successful beyond their fondest hopes.

Finally, would-be framers must occasionally raise their eyes above the real to contemplate the ideal, lest their style become that of narrow-minded cynics, and this the Framers of 1787 seemed able to do at the right times and in the right proportion. In a debate of June 22 over the question of how to pay legislators, Randolph sounded one of his truest notes of the summer.

Mr. Randolph feared we were going too far, in consulting popular prejudices. Whatever respect might be due to them, in lesser matters, or in cases where they formed the permanent character of the people, he thought it neither incumbent on nor honorable for the Convention to sacrifice right and justice to that consideration.[26]

The choicest story in this vein is one for whose veracity we must rely on the word of Gouverneur Morris. Since Morris told it in "an oration upon the death of General Washington," perhaps we can. Describing the discussions that took place just before the opening of the Convention, Morris saluted the shade of the great man—and drew a stern moral:

Men of decided temper, who, devoted to the public, overlooked prudential considerations, thought a form of government should be framed entirely new. But cautious men, with whom popularity was an object, deemed it fit to consult and comply with the wishes of the people. AMERICANS!—let the opinion then delivered by the greatest and best of men, be ever present to your remembrance. He was collected within himself. His countenance had more than usual solemnity—His eye was fixed, and seemed to look into futurity. "It is (said he) too probable that no plan we propose will be adopted. Perhaps another dreadful conflict is to be sustained. If to please the people, we offer what we ourselves disapprove, how can we afterwards defend our work? Let us raise a standard to which the wise and the honest can repair. The event is in the hand of God."—this was the patriot voice of WASHINGTON; and this the constant tenor of his conduct.[27]

The triumph of the Convention of 1787 is that in raising a standard to which the wise and honest could repair, it also raised one that met the threefold test of legitimacy, popularity, and viability.

One reason the Convention was able to strike the right balance between the urge to lead the people and the need to obey them, and between the urge to be noble and the need to be practical, was the disposition of most delegates to be "whole men" on stern principles and "half-way men" on negotiable details. Another was the way in which it worked with familiar materials—the state constitutions, the Articles of Confederation, the best of the colonial experiences—and thus presented the people with a constitution that surprised but did not shock. Rejoicing in philosophy but despising ideology, putting a high value on "reason" but an even higher one on "experience," interested in the institutions of other times and peoples but confident that their own were better, unafraid to contemplate the mysteries of the British Constitution but aware, in Wilson's words, that it "cannot be our own model," [28] the Framers kept faith with the American past even as they prepared to make a break with it. Indeed, the excellence of their handiwork is as much a tribute to their sense of continuity as to their talent for creative statesmanship. The Constitution was an ingenious plan of government chiefly in the sense that its authors made a careful selection of familiar techniques and institutions, then fitted them together with an unerring eye for form. It had very little novelty in it, and that, we see with the aid of hindsight, was one of its strongest points.

A final reason—and also perhaps the most heartening lesson the Convention presents to supporters of constitutional democracy—was the process of give-and-take through which these masterful public men managed to create a constitution that could be carried home with some confidence to every part of a sprawling country. While the process may have often seemed unnecessarily erratic and time-wasting to those trapped in its midst, we can see that it was the only way in which self-respecting representatives of free men could have pieced together a set of operational rules of government and, at the same time, settled their outstanding political differences. In doing these things so well, and so acceptably to all but a handful of their colleagues, the men of 1787 met the supreme test of the democratic assembly: they proved beyond a doubt that the whole was wiser than the parts, that the collective was more creative than any individual in it. No single man, nor even the most artfully constructed team of four or five, could have provided so wisely for the constitutional needs of the American people as did "the cunning of reason" that operated through the whole Convention.

The Convention passed this test and became the archetype of the constituent assembly by acting both negatively and positively to demonstrate its collective wisdom. On one hand, it voted down a string of pet proposals that would have loaded the Constitution with weak, clumsy, or simply unacceptable techniques. Consider, for example, some of the serious suggestions made by serious men to improve the Presidency: Madison wanted to give the Supreme Court a share of the President's veto; Morris favored the Chief Justice as successor to the President; Mason proposed that "maladministration" be added to the list of impeachable offenses; Martin and Gerry wanted to fix the size of the army in the Constitution itself; Charles Pinckney would have set a property qualification so high as to bar the Presidency to anyone not as rich as he; and Williamson agreed with Mason that three executives would be three times as good as one.[29] Every one of these proposals, it should be noted, was thoroughly digested; every one was made, not in the early stages when men were lobbing ideas back and forth for practice, but in the late stages when they were passing on the final plan. Surely the Convention showed itself wiser than these men in rejecting such proposals.

On the other hand, and in a far more important demonstration of the power of collective wisdom, the Convention acted positively to produce those familiar compromises of July 16 and August 25 without which the Union would have collapsed, decayed, or been rent asunder. Especially in the matter of federalism—in drawing the line between nation and states and in adjusting the balance of large states and small —the whole body proved itself more astute than the men who were, in most things, its guiding spirits. If Wilson and Madison had had their way on the issues of representation, the powers of Congress, and the review of state legislation— and they did everything they could to have it—the Constitution could not possibly have won approval in more than a handful of states. By muddling through to "half-way" solutions, and by shaping the solutions to the "genius" of the country as it was interpreted through the prism of a collective mind, the Convention moved up step by step to the outer boundaries of the politically possible in a dozen critical areas, and then refused prudently to move one step beyond. All in all, it was a convincing demonstration of the truth that the highest political wisdom in a constitutional democracy lies in the assembly rather than in the individual lawmaker. The assembly must be of the right size and composition for its purpose, and it must be organized on sound principles and led in a skillful way; but if those conditions are met, as they were met with something to spare in 1787, it has a better chance to find the workable solution than any one man in it.

This is not at all to disparage the importance of the individual, for the wisdom of the assembly is of necessity a projection, if not a simple sum, of the wisdom of those who sit in it. The collective triumph of 1787 was nourished on the experience, learning, dedication, and industry of remarkable individuals, and we might therefore end this review of the labors of the Convention by distributing our gratitude and admiration according to the several contributions of the delegates. Although "Ranking the Framers" will never be as popular an indoor sport as "Ranking the Presidents," a student of American history can always play it with pleasure. As I look back once more at all the Framers, limiting my gaze rigidly to their activities between May 14 and September 17, 1787, they seem to fall into eight fairly distinguishable groups, which might be labeled the Principals, the Influentials, the Very Usefuls, the Usefuls, the Visibles, the Ciphers, the Drop-outs and Walkouts, and the Inexplicable Disappointments.

*The Principals:* James Madison. Although even Madison's admiring biographer reminds us that none of the men of 1787 would have dreamed of calling him (or anyone else) the "Father of the Constitution," he was, beyond a doubt, the leading spirit and, as Major Jackson could testify, "most efficient member" in this conclave.[30] His foresight in drafting the Virginia Plan and making it the agenda of the Convention, his willingness to debate great issues and small with courteous and learned intensity, his dozens of suggestions of ways for his colleagues to extricate themselves from thickets, his membership on three of the four essential committees, even perhaps his doggedness in the major struggle for power —these are the solid credentials of the one Framer who stands, modestly and eternally, first among his splendid peers. And as if all these services were not enough, there remains the precious manuscript, written in blood as well as ink, that tells us most of what we know of the Great Happening.

James Wilson. Second only to Madison—and an honorable second—was the learned, inventive, painstaking lawyer from St. Andrews. As brother-in-arms to the Virginian in the cause of reform-minded nationalism, Wilson debated, drafted, bargained, and voted with unremitting zeal. He did most to give strength and independence to the executive, and to lay the foundations of the new government "broad and deep" upon the sovereign people of the United States.

George Washington. Washington's contribution was of a different kind from that of Madison and Wilson, but certainly we can imagine a far less pleasant outcome for a gathering that he had refused to grace or—this, admittedly, is hard to imagine—from which he had withdrawn in sorrow or fury. By lending a constant presence (he did not miss a single day), by presiding with dignity and understanding, by serving willy-nilly as the probable first President, and by giving the quiet support of his influence and vote to Madison, Washington helped mightily to make the Convention a success. Moreover, he did his uncomplaining duty as semi-official chief of state to the American people. He drank tea with the ladies of Philadelphia, dined with the Sons of St. Patrick, visited farms and museums and historic sites, sat through orations, reviewed troops ("at the importunity of General Mifflin"), received visiting dignitaries, and had his portrait painted by

Charles Willson Peale. He even went, man of grace and tolerance that he was, "to the Romish Church to high mass." [31]

Gouverneur Morris. The credentials of Gouverneur Morris
as a giant of the Convention will always be slightly suspect to
those who see him as a man too clever, too fickle, and too
cynical "by half." Yet anyone who has traced and retraced
his trail through the Convention—noting the frankness and
superb timing of his important speeches, watching him shoulder most of the burden of committee work for his fellow
Pennsylvanians, reading over his final draft of September
12—must recognize a magnificent contribution. Since the
contribution was also quite unexpected, he stands out as the
Framer whose reputation received the largest boost in this period. And if he had done nothing else, he would have earned
our gratitude for making the Convention chuckle, and also
think, with his pointed jokes about overhospitable Indians,
hypocritical slavers (the South Carolinians thought, but did
not chuckle) and restless Vice-Presidents.*

*The Influentials:* John Rutledge, who spoke often and usefully, sat on five committees, guided the labors of the committee of detail, was the gadfly of the Convention in August
and September, and served the cause of moderate nationalism
with intelligence and devotion.

Benjamin Franklin, who poked fun along with Morris,
spun out compromises and soothed hurt feelings along with
the men of Connecticut, spoke up for the people even more
confidently than Wilson and Madison, and joined Washington
in fortifying both the prestige and the self-confidence of the
Convention. (Franklin was one of the few delegates who
were sorry to see it all come to an end. "Some tell me I look
better," he wrote of his health to his sister, "and they suppose
the daily exercise of going and returning from the State
House has done me good.") [33]

Roger Sherman, probably the most useful and certainly the
most voluble delegate from Connecticut, who had a longer
intellectual pilgrimage to make than any other man in the
Convention, and who made it without surrendering a single
one of his Yankee principles.

Charles Pinckney, who spoke often and earnestly, and who
was at his best filling in the holes of the grand design that
was taking shape on the floor.

---

* Madison's tribute to the "able, eloquent, and active" Morris, delivered more than forty years after the event, is worth recording:

"To the brilliancy of his genius he added, what is too rare, a candid
surrender of his opinions, when the lights of discussion satisfied him,
that they had been too hastily formed, and a readiness to make the
best of measures in which he had been overruled." [32]

Rufus King, who turned suddenly, perhaps under the influence of Hamilton, into an enthusiastic, sharp-witted, persuasive nationalist, and who was the champion committee-man of the summer.

Charles Cotesworth Pinckney, whose single-minded devotion to the interests of his class, state, section, and way of life did not prevent him from lending a powerful hand to the cause of a strong and stable government.

Oliver Ellsworth, the "half-way man" of the century, who may have done more in Philadelphia for the Union than Hamilton, Wilson, and the two Pinckneys together.

Nathaniel Gorham, who chaired the committee of the whole, sat on the committee of detail, and debated helpfully in the spirit of moderate nationalism.

George Mason, unhappily a non-signer, but always a faithful, industrious, honest exponent of old-fashioned republicanism.

Edmund Randolph, also a non-signer, whose performance was erratic, yet who gets considerable credit for the decision to enumerate the powers of Congress.

Elbridge Gerry, the non-signing "Grumbletonian," who never let the Convention forget that "the genius of the country" was indeed republican.

*The Very Usefuls:* John Dickinson, a victim of old age, poor health, and an unfortunate lack of perspective, whose overall performance, despite flashes of brilliance, failed to match his considerable reputation.

Hugh Williamson, the ablest and hardest-working of the North Carolinians, a member of five committees and a thoughtful participant in key debates.

William Samuel Johnson, the least talkative but by no means least persuasive member of the Connecticut delegation, who may have had more to do with the success of the committee of style than we think.

George Read, that admirable small-state man with prophetic big-nation ideas.

Pierce Butler, like General Pinckney a little too anxious to serve the interests of those who had sent him, yet also like Pinckney a man worth having in the ranks of the nationalist caucus.

William Paterson, the stubborn and successful advocate of state equality, whose departure in late July may have robbed him of a much higher ranking.

Luther Martin, garrulous, sour, and pigheaded, yet an influential pricker of egos and consciences.

*The Usefuls:* David Brearly, most faithful of the Jerseyites, supporter of Paterson, and chairman of the committee on postponed matters.

William Livingston, like Dickinson something of a disappointment, who did his best work on committees.

Richard Dobbs Spaight, who had several small triumphs as a plugger of holes.

Gunning Bedford, jr., who proved explosively that Framers were not really demigods, and who was an interesting example of the small-state nationalist.

Abraham Baldwin, far and away the best of the Georgians, an able committeeman and a force for intelligent compromise.

Daniel Carroll and John Langdon, each of whom spoke up on two dozen occasions for the cause of moderate nationalism.

William R. Davie, an agent if not an architect of the Great Compromise.

*The Visibles:* John Blair, who never spoke and never sat on a committee, but whose vote several times provided the margin of victory within the Virginia delegation for Madison and Washington against Mason and Randolph.

Daniel of St. Thomas Jenifer and William Few, who also made their presence felt by voting the right way at critical moments.

Jacob Broom, Caleb Strong, William Houstoun, George Clymer, Jonathan Dayton, and James McHenry, each of whom opened his mouth just often and sensibly enough to catch the ear of history.

James McClurg, who opened it three times, put his foot in twice, and went home to his patients.[34]

*The Ciphers:* Richard Bassett, who somehow managed to sit through the entire summer without making a speech, serving on a committee, or casting a decisive vote, and who did not make even a single convert to Methodism.

Thomas Mifflin, whose only recorded action was to second a motion of Charles Pinckney.

William Blount and Jared Ingersoll, who spoke up for the first time, and did it feebly, on the last day, and who served on no committees.

Thomas Fitzsimons, Nicholas Gilman, and Alexander Martin, none of whom made any recorded contribution to the proceedings.

*The Dropouts and Walkouts:* William Churchill Houston, William Pierce, and George Wythe, the last of whom might have been an Influential if fate had permitted him to remain in Philadelphia.

John Francis Mercer, the indignant blade, who could spare

the Convention only two weeks and two score ill-tempered observations.

Robert Yates and John Lansing, jr., the obstinate men from Albany, whose devotion to Governor Clinton forced them to withdraw huffily and rather ingloriously.

*The Inexplicable Disappointments:* Robert Morris. While in May no one expected the financier to be a Wilson or Madison, in October everyone must have wondered why he had made such a small splash in the proceedings. He had the political and forensic talents, as he had proved in the old days in Congress, to lend a powerful hand to the cause of nationalism, yet he spoke up only twice—to nominate Washington and to second a motion by Read to give Senators a life term —and served on no committee. One can think of many possible explanations for his cipherlike behavior—for example, the pressures of business, the eagerness of his junior colleagues Wilson and Gouverneur Morris, a realization that a new generation was taking over, a desire to mask his vast yet always suspect influence—yet none of them rings quite true. There must always be something a little pathetic in the contrast of the recorded activities of Robert and Gouverneur Morris. The former made no speeches, which puts him in a class with Blair, Few, Gilman, and Mifflin; the latter made 173, which puts him in a class by himself.*

Alexander Hamilton. Far and away the most disappointing man was the brilliant New Yorker who had done so much to bring the Convention to life. The wide gap between the possible and the actual in Hamilton's performance at Philadelphia comes as an unpleasant shock to the historian of the Convention, and leads him to wonder if there were not personal reasons for his lackluster showing that have never been revealed. Even when we take into account his eccentric hopes for a high-toned government and his anomalous position on the New York delegation, we are left with the feeling that he could have been a Principal, or at worst an Influential, if he had simply behaved like the man he had been in 1783 or 1786 and was to be again in 1788 and 1790—and even was for a few exciting moments in June and September of 1787. He had so much to give, and he gave so little—that is the cheerless appraisal one is bound to make of Hamilton the Framer.

One cannot help wondering, as he runs an eye over this list, whether the proceedings would have taken some radically

---

* Perhaps not quite, since Wilson made 168 and Madison 161. Other irrepressible Framers were Sherman (138), Mason (136), and Gerry (119).

different turn if, let us say, the five most notable of the "should-have-been-Framers" had managed to get to Philadelphia. My own guess is that the Convention would have had pretty much the same history, and that the Constitution would read almost exactly as it does. Jefferson would have been an even-tempered cross between Madison and Mason; Richard Henry Lee would probably have gone along with Jefferson and Madison despite misgivings; Jay would have been a dull edition of Gouverneur Morris; and Henry would have walked out with Mercer or Martin. Although John Adams, that prince of constitutionalists, would have begged for a few more checks and balances, one cannot imagine him standing anywhere but in the middle of the emerging consensus. One can, however, imagine him speaking more often than Morris and serving on more committees than King, and thus, single-handedly and single-mindedly, adding two or three weeks to the life of the Convention. There is, in any case, little doubt that his otherwise unfortunate absence gave Madison, Wilson, Gouverneur Morris, and especially King an extra chance to shine.

It should be plain that some states had rather more to do than others with framing the Constitution of 1787. Every delegation had its moments of glory when it voted for liberty, justice, and union, but not every one played a steady and creative role. Indeed, if we are entirely honest, and prepared to endure the wrath of several state historical societies, we may well conclude that five states—Virginia, Pennsylvania (thanks to the dutiful zeal of three men), Connecticut, South Carolina, and Massachusetts, in that order—produced 95 per cent of the thoughts, decisions, and inventive moments that went into the document, and that the others were largely along for the ride. For a tiny state, Delaware did remarkably well; for a neighboring state, New Jersey was painfully delinquent; for a major state, Maryland showed itself unenthusiastic in intent and undistinguished in action. As for New Hampshire, Georgia, and North Carolina, perhaps we should be grateful that they arrived sooner or later and stayed to the end, and that each produced one admirable man. As for New York and Rhode Island, perhaps the less said the better. Or is it possible that the Constitution was a more sensible and acceptable plan of government because one walked out and the other never appeared at all? The faithful delegates were able to take the existence (and even the best interests) of these self-willed states into account without having to expose themselves to a rattling fire or their consensus to severe stress—a happy arrangement.

In the end, the two dozen truly eminent Framers and the

five truly influential states merge into the larger reality of the Grand Convention as a collective, national endeavor. It was healthily collective, as we have seen, because self-propelling individuals gained new wisdom and strength from being thrown together, and went on to build an edifice that no one of them could have built alone. It was healthily national because self-interested states came sooner or later to see that their problems could best be solved, and their existence most effectively guaranteed,* by placing the edifice in the keeping of the whole people. The "greatest single effort of national deliberation that the world has ever seen" had led to the discovery of a new kind of nation.

* The North Carolinians provide amusing proof of this truth. Having voted and worked, to the best of their limited abilities, for the new nationalism, they dispatched a copy of the Constitution to Governor Caswell on September 18, and covered it with the words: "When you are pleased to lay this plan before the General Assembly, we entreat that you will do us the justice to assure that honorable body that no exertions have been wanting on our part to guard and promote the particular interest of North Carolina." [35]

# IV

## Consequences

## 13 THE FINISHED WORK

> *The example of changing a constitution by assembling the wise men of the state, instead of assembling armies, will be worth as much to the world as the former examples we had given them. The constitution, too, which was the result of our deliberation, is unquestionably the wisest ever yet presented to men.*
>
> JEFFERSON to DAVID HUMPHREYS,
> March 18, 1789[1]

THE DETAILS of the convenant "secretly arrived at" during the long weeks in Philadelphia were now disclosed to the American people. In the early morning of September 18 Major Jackson set out by stage for New York "in order to lay the great result . . . before the United States in Congress." A few hours later in the State House, under the prodding of Franklin and on the motion of the long silent Fitzsimons, General Mifflin rose to read the Constitution to the members of the Pennsylvania Assembly, several of whom did not care much for what they heard.[2] The newspapers of Philadelphia printed the text in their issues of September 19, 20, or 21; newspapers in Germantown and Lancaster needed only a day or two longer to translate "We the people" into *"Wir das Volk,"* "Senators" into *"Ratsherrn,"* and George Washington into Georg Waschington; and printers all over America (even in Newport and Providence) followed on during the next two weeks, several of them publishing special editions in order to inform, comfort, or shock their readers.[3] Delegates sent off copies in every direction—the committed Washington to Jefferson and Lafayette, the hostile Gerry to John Adams, the faithful North Carolinians to Governor Caswell—and by early November it was a lonely or uncaring American, whether a merchant in Paris or a trapper in the Kickapoo country, who had not read the proposed Constitution.

To read, however, was not necessarily to understand, especially when most readers had to guess unaided at the intentions and methods of the authors. Since many of the authors themselves would have been hard pressed to give a logical explanation of the course of events in Philadelphia—and were, indeed, to be pressed to little avail in the ratifying conventions—it seems plain that the Constitution was offered, resisted, and finally accepted in a climate of half-certainty about the purposes to which it might be put. Still, a sharp-eyed, coolheaded, well-meaning citizen on the outside could learn a great deal, and guess shrewdly about a great deal more, simply by picking the Constitution apart clause by clause. We may find it useful, in Frederic Maitland's dramatic phrase, to "think ourselves back into the twilight" of the late fall of 1787 and to see the Constitution as such a man might have seen it.

At first reading, the most impressive feature of the document must have been the language itself. The Constitution, I repeat, was a masterpiece of draftsmanship, probably the most artfully constructed charter of government the Western World had seen, certainly a vast improvement in mode of expression over the best of the state constitutions. Plain to the point of severity, frugal to the point of austerity, laconic to the point of aphorism, the Constitution was, as Randolph had recommended in his observations on the rough draft of late July, a statement in "simple and precise language" of "essential principles only" that could be "accommodated to times and events" no living man could foretell.[4] What is acceptably "simple and precise" to one man may, of course, seem unnecessarily tangled and obscure to another, and plenty of first readers joined with Thomas B. Wait of Maine in finding "a certain darkness, duplicity, and studied ambiguity of expression" in the Constitution.[5] Most such readers, however, were ready to find duplicity in any combination of words the men of Philadelphia might produce, and other readers seem to have agreed with Caleb Strong, who met the charge of ambiguity in the Massachusetts ratifying convention by insisting that the commands of the Constitution were "expressed in the plain, common language of mankind."[6]

Some men of advanced literary tastes may have found it too plain and common. Although at least a dozen of the Framers had soared high and far in print during their careers, they and their more prosaic colleagues seem to have agreed from the beginning to eschew eloquence and to pitch their appeal to the ages in a low key. John Adams had proclaimed the principle of the separation of powers with an explicit flourish in the Massachusetts Constitution of 1779–1780; the Framers thought it more fitting to honor the principle implicitly in the opening words of each of the first three articles. George Mason had saluted the inalienable rights of man passionately in the Virginia Declaration of 1776; his stubborn colleagues of 1787 would do no more than sprinkle a few dispassionately stated legal rights through the body of the Constitution. One state constitution after another had announced the importance of civil supremacy; the Constitution of the United States gave supreme command to a civilian chief executive without pausing to admonish him, and let it go at that. Even the preamble, in which one might have expected the Framers to wave the flag of liberty and union, is a model of restraint. No one has ever accused them of padding their document with froth or fustian.

So plain and chaste is the language of the Constitution that, in this first reading, it must have struck the eye as a remarkably indulgent charter, one that invited future generations of Americans to govern themselves both imaginatively and expansively. The prohibitions were explicit but few, especially those directed toward the proposed common government; and some of the delegations of power suggested a half-dozen interpretations. "The executive power," "common defense and general welfare," "commerce . . . among the several states," "necessary and proper"—who could say what uses clever men might make of these short, vague, inflatable phrases? No constitution, it was agreed on all sides, could anticipate the public needs of a potentially great people except in general terms, but this one showed an unusual passion for the general and distaste for the specific.

If the truth had been known, the Framers themselves were not sure what they meant by some of their neatest phrases. There were, one suspects, fifty-five different understandings of several key phrases of the Constitution; and there was, one reads in the records of the Convention itself, no understanding at all of several others. For example on August 20, according to Madison, "Mr. King asked what was the precise meaning of *direct* taxation," and "no one answered." Then, on August 27, in a desultory discussion of the problem of succession to the Presidency, Dickinson complained that the proposed language was vague. "What is the extent of the term 'disability'?" he asked plaintively, "and who is to be the judge of it?" [7] Again, alas, no one answered, and men are still asking this question plaintively 175 years later. Baldwin of Georgia spoke an honest word on the question of vagueness in the House of Representatives in 1796:

> He said it was not to disparage the instrument, to say that it had not definitely, and with precision, absolutely settled everything on which it had spoke. He had sufficient evidence to satisfy his own mind that it was not supposed by the makers of it at the time, but that some subjects were left a little ambiguous and uncertain. . . . When he reflected on the immense difficulties and dangers of that trying occasion—the old government prostrated, and a chance whether a new one could be agreed on—the recollection recalled to him nothing but the most joyful sensations that so many things had been so well settled, and that experience had shown there was very little difficulty or danger in settling the rest.[8]

In 1787, needless to say, all this "experience" lay in the future, and some of it was to prove more full of "difficulty" and "danger" than the kindly Baldwin would ever admit.

Precise and vague at one and the same time, the words of the Constitution were, as almost every Framer began at once to tell his friends and constituents, the visible signs of a painful process of bargaining among proud, committed, and yet not unbending men. No one who had not taken part could imagine the toils of the process, and the result was inevitably, in the understanding phrases of later generations, "a bundle of compromises" and "a mosaic of second choices." [9] "Look through that instrument from beginning to end," Dayton of New Jersey begged his colleagues in the Senate in 1803, "and you will not find an article which is not founded on the presumption of a clashing of interests." [10] The Constitution was, in truth, a shrewd armistice among men who had become convinced that their common interest would never be realized unless their special interests were compromised; and only such an armistice, the creation of politicians who had a genius for inventing "half-way" solutions, could have been proposed to the citizens of a continental republic.

In the end, the familiarity of the wording of the Constitution recommended it most strongly. Wherever they looked, readers found words they had learned to live with in the constitutions of the states and in the Articles of Confederation. It might, for example, have been judged an overly bold gamble to designate the President of the United States as "commander in chief"—except that the governors of New York, Massachusetts, and South Carolina had already been so designated in the freely adopted and painfully tested charters of those leading states. Such phrases as "the executive power," "full faith and credit," and "general welfare" may have been pregnant with confusion, but at least they were old friends to most Americans.

At second reading, the Constitution must have appeared to our sharp-eyed, coolheaded, well-meaning citizen as a kind of registry of critical decisions about the nature and destiny of the United States of America. It was not so much the decisions on the surface—the choice of a single-headed executive, the creation of a two-chambered legislature, the prohibition on titles of nobility—that would have intrigued such a man, but the more fateful confirmations of the past and gambles with the future that he could find for himself only after an intense exercise in constitutional exegesis.

We tend to forget today how important the Constitution was in the circumstances of 1787 as an act of confirmation: a solemn pledge of the continental elite that certain decisions taken by and for the American people were closed forever. The Constitution was designed to be the last formal act of the Revolution, and it put the stamp of irrevocable legitimacy on the three great legacies of 1776: independence, republicanism, and union. From these three commitments there could now be no turning back; to these the people of the United States would henceforth be bound so tightly that only another, far bloodier revolution could reopen them for consideration.

Although the Constitution is a whole series of gambles in the unpredictable game of republican self-government, two in particular must have caught the eye of the citizen who read it through with an open mind in late September, 1787. The first was a short-range bet that a majority of politically conscious Americans was disenchanted with the Articles of Confederation, and that trusted leaders might therefore propose an alternative with some hope of success. Four separate decisions had gone into this bet, and each was certain to stir the anger of those to whom the idea of a constitutional convention had been suspect: first, the decision of the delegates to become Framers, that is, to go beyond their instructions and to write a new constitution; second, the decision, which was not made firmly until the last days of the Convention, to send the Constitution to the people by way of Congress without asking for an act of formal approval; third, the decision, which was never in doubt, to designate special conventions rather than the legislatures as the ratifying agents in the states; and finally, the determination that the new government should come into being when nine conventions had acted affirmatively.

While it may be argued that these things were done on a pragmatic basis—because only a convention "unknown to the Confederation" could give the nation a national government,[11] or, to reduce one of Madison's motives to starkest terms, because the legislature of Rhode Island could no longer be permitted to block the path of continental destiny—we should recognize that these principled men were also honoring two great commands of their political tradition. As George Mason himself had expressed them in the Virginia Declaration of Rights:

> That all power is vested in, and consequently derived from, the people; that magistrates are their trustees and servants, and at all times amenable to them.
> That government is, or ought to be instituted for the common benefit, protection and security of the people, nation or community; that of all the various modes and forms of government, that is best which is capable of producing the greatest degree of happiness and safety, and is most effectually secured against the danger of maladministration; and that, when a government shall be found inadequate or contrary to these purposes, a majority of the community hath an indubitable, unalienable, and indefeasible right to reform, alter or abolish it, in such manner as shall be judged most conducive to the public weal.[12]

In proposing this Constitution in this way to their fellow citizens, the Framers meant, Wilson pointed out, to "go to the original powers of society," [13] and "the fountain" of all such power, Madison added, was the people of the country. By "resorting to them"—and not to Congress and the state legislatures—"all difficulties" about the legality of the Convention could be safely "got over." [14]

If not all difficulties, one must scold Madison's ghost gently, certainly enough to clear him and his colleagues of the charge of staging a counterrevolutionary *coup d'etat*. Their actions were, in the narrow sense, illegal under the terms of the Articles of Confederation; they also were, in the broad sense, legitimate under the principles of the American Revolution—and were in fact sparked by a desire to bring it to fruition. What Massachusetts had done in 1779–1780 and New Hampshire in 1784 with their new techniques of constitution-making, the United States must surely be able to do in

1787–1788. The people, in any case, would decide in their own good time whether to give the stamp of legitimacy to the Constitution and thus to the Convention, and the Framers hoped that the people would prove themselves good enough Lockeans to recognize two facts clearly: that they were indeed the purest source of political authority, and that the Articles of Confederation lacked the essential touch of legitimacy because, in addition to other defects of structure and function, they had not arisen from this source. If the new Constitution were to find favor with the conventions in the states, it would thereupon become an act of the sovereign people.

The second gamble had been made as subtly as the first—and also, we now see, as finally. Although the word "national" did not appear in the Constitution, those who read it carefully must have understood that it was meant to be the charter of a nation. Since the nation was more incipient than established in 1787, the Framers were assuming that they sensed the mood and aspirations of the American people better than did the honestly fearful or merely self-interested anti-nationalists. The people, they guessed, were ready for a forceful shove toward emotional and political unity, and this Constitution, they hoped, would provide most of the shove. In the articles creating the three main branches, in the phrases delegating the responsibilities of sovereignty to Congress and the President, in the prohibitions fixed absolutely or conditionally on the states, and above all in the sententious clause that established the supremacy of the Constitution and of all laws and treaties to be made under it, the Framers provided for a common government far more consolidated and authoritative than any that could have developed under the Articles of Confederation. Like most great principles of the Constitution, the centralizing "principle of legislation for the individual citizens of America" was nowhere stated directly, and thus had to be read between the lines with the aid of teachers like Madison, Hamilton, and Wilson. Yet even those readers who had no such teachers could recognize that the Convention had moved a long way forward from the confederate "principle of legislation for states or governments in their corporate or collective capacities." [15]

All things considered, it was fortunate for the Framers that they had decided not to move even farther in this direction by agreeing to Madison's proposal of a national "negative" on state laws. Indeed, the whole of clause 6 of the Virginia Plan would have been too large a dose of nationalism for most Americans to swallow. Few who wished the Constitution well could have joined Hamilton and Read in contemplating the redrawing of regional and local boundaries under the benevolent gaze of a consolidated national government, and most must have been relieved to learn that the states, although they could no longer pretend to "sovereignty, freedom and independence," would continue as half-sovereign communities charged with large responsibilities for the safety and happiness of their citizens. More than that, the state legislatures were intended to play a critical role in the choice of men to conduct the affairs of the new government—whether as primary instruments (in the case of the Senate) or secondary (in the case of the President) or tertiary (in the case of the House). The Constitution of the United States provided a national government for an incipient nation, but the nation itself was to be compound rather than consolidated in structure. As a Chief Justice was to write three generations later, "the Constitution, in all its provisions, looks to an indestructible Union, composed of indestructible states." [16] That the state governments would endure as healthy political entities was almost as fond a wish of the Framers as that the national government would be able to bear up under the strains of what struck both Madison and Hamilton as a naturally centrifugal arrangement.

In the course of his second or third reading, our model citizen of 1787 would have begun to notice that the Framers had left critical decisions to other men and other times; and they had done this, he could guess, not simply because they preferred to keep their precious charter free of what Morris had called "minutious regulations" and Hamilton "embarrassing restrictions." [17] We of a later generation, who do not have to guess, can find many postponed or evaded decisions in the text and between the lines that were the consequence of dissension or apprehension or a lack of imagination among the Framers. Undecided about how much or what parts of the Revolutionary debt the new government should be obligated to pay off, they had handed over this delicate problem to the proposed Congress with an expression of confidence that "all debts contracted . . . before the adoption of this Constitution" would be as "valid against the United States under this Constitution, as under the Confederation." [18] Unable to fix upon a rule of suffrage that would be viable for all thirteen states, they had struck at least a glancing blow for old-fashioned federalism by declaring that every American eligible to vote for "the most numerous branch" of his state legislature would be likewise eligible to vote for the House of Representatives. [19] Unwilling to give the whole game away by providing specifically for the high-toned technique of judicial review, they (or rather the dozen or more who had begun to flirt seriously with this developing idea)[20] had left an inviting hole to be filled in by judges made brave by ambition or popular pressure. To Congress they gave an explicit power to act in place or even defiance of those states that fudged their primary duty to prescribe "the times, places, and manner of holding elections for Congress"; upon the President they laid an implicit charge to compete with the Senate for authority to remove incompetents or malcontents from positions in the executive branch. What major departments ought to be created, whether the President was to have a council, on what terms new states should be admitted, how many judges should sit on the Supreme Court—all these were questions the Framers might properly have answered in a charter limited to "essential principles," all were passed along out of uncertainty or prudence or fatigue to those who would hold power in the immediate or distant future. The Framers did not, it should be noted, make a conscious decision against adopting the parliamentary system. The celebrated form of "responsible government" of which Britain is the archetype had not developed sufficiently by 1787 for Americans to recognize an alternative to the separation of powers, and one is bound to wonder what choice they would have made fifty or sixty years later.

The most fateful decision *not* taken in the Convention—or so it appears to men of the 1960's and must have appeared to men of the 1860's—was to do something imaginative about Negro slavery, which had long been recognized in at least half the states as a monumental injustice to the slaves themselves, a mockery of the principles of 1776,[21] and a menace to free government. That slavery was a problem for many leading Framers is clear in the remarks of Madison, Luther Martin, Mason, King, Gerry, and Gouverneur Morris; and there is something unconvincing in the apparently sanguine predictions of Ellsworth and Sherman that it would someday be no more than "a speck in our country."[22] The Framers, like almost all men of their time, may have had trouble thinking of slaves as persons, but they were, with few exceptions, oppressively aware of slavery as an institution.

What the Convention did about slavery is beyond dispute: at four scattered points in their charter the Framers confirmed its existence in opaque language—the "three-fifths clause" in Article I, section 2; the "1808 clause" in Article I, section 9; the provision for extradition of an escaped "person held to service or labor" in Article IV, section 2; and the extra protection given to the "1808 clause" in Article V. In addition, the second of these arrangements was, on any sensible construction of its wording, an acknowledgment that Congress would have power under the commerce clause to suppress the slave trade once this twenty-year period of grace (if that is the proper word) was up. What they did not do is also beyond dispute: they did not themselves outlaw slavery, nor in any way seek to mitigate its effects; they did not give Congress the power to outlaw slavery in the states; they made provision neither to help nor hinder free Negroes in the attempt to win the status and rights of citizenship.

What the Framers could have done is, of course, a more hotly disputed question. Many Americans have insisted that the Convention of 1787 missed a splendid opportunity to settle the issue once and for all. Most such persons have wished that the Framers, in some manner that is never stated precisely, could have provided for emancipation of all slaves, either immediately or by stages, and also perhaps for their incorporation in the American community. A few, of whom not many are still living, have wished that the Framers, in some short provision, could have guaranteed to each state (and even to each territory) the exclusive right to deal with slavery in its own time and way, which might have included the right to nourish as well as to abolish.

All such persons, in my opinion, have failed to "think themselves back into the twilight" of 1787 and to understand the limits under which the Framers were operating in this matter—limits that permitted them as builders of a nation to do nothing positive and only a few things negative about their potentially most explosive social problem. On one hand, a blow at slavery, however masked and glancing, in the Constitution itself would have invited certain rejection in the southern states; and even the implicit acknowledgment of a delayed power to suppress the slave trade was a gamble with opinion in South Carolina. On the other, any additional display of tolerance toward what Morris called this "nefarious institution" and "curse of heaven," [23] indeed the very mention of the word "slaves" or "slavery" or "slave trade" in the Constitution, [24] would have invited rejection in the North; and even the concession that a slave might be considered as three-fifths of a man (for the political purposes of the white South) was a gamble with both the conscience and self-interest of Massachusetts or Pennsylvania. Here, as in the attempt to work out an adjustment of representation acceptable to both Delaware and Virginia, the Framers were searching for the viable middle; here, as in every decision, their principal concern was to give the nation a new government, one that could win support in all parts of the Union. Their strongest fear of the moment was that certain key states would reject

their proposal, and at least three of these states had econo-
mies built squarely on slavery. And so they believed John
Rutledge when he said that the question of what to do about
slavery was at bottom a question of "whether the southern
states shall or shall not be parties to the Union," and believed
General Pinckney when he warned that the elimination of
the twenty-year period of grace would mean "an exclusion of
South Carolina from the Union." [25]

The decisions and non-decisions of 1787 about slavery
and the slave trade were, to be short about it, decisions for
the Union. Those who criticize the Framers for not acting
boldly in this matter see them as men they never were or
could have been—audacious heralds of a social revolution—
rather than as the men they were—prudent builders of a nation. Both the angry men of the North and the troubled men
of the South, who went along with the four offensive clauses
and the silences of the Constitution in defiance of principle
and disregard of conscience, were blocked by a whole array
of circumstances—inertia, tradition, sectionalism, poor timing, lack of imagination, the preference for "essential principles only," and above all their passion for nationhood—from
striking for the emancipation of a misunderstood and, for
that matter, feared description of men. This was, they were
certain, their last chance to forge a political unity out of the
thirteen semi-sovereignties that stretched from Canada to
Florida, and they were not disposed to lose it—and to court
the hazards of disunion—by gambling that the southern states
would now see a light where they had never seen one before.
The United States of America, which has repeatedly paid a
high price for its precious Union over the years since 1776,
laid out a huge sum of moral and political currency for the
charter upon which the Union was to rise. Yet the sum,
surely, was not too huge, for we must recognize, despite our
misgivings, that any determined step against slavery in the
Constitution—assuming that any Framer was disposed to
take it—would have been an act of sheer political quixotism.
Simply to have made it possible for the new government to
move against the slave trade in twenty years (and to tax it in
the meantime) was as decisive a victory for human decency
as men who loved the Union and hated slavery could have
won at Philadelphia.

Even those Framers who answer this description were
something less than abolitionists. Indeed, it would be hard to
point to a single man in the Convention who thought that the
national government could or should have authority to control slavery; who could suggest how the government, if ever it
were to be granted such authority, would proceed with the

stupendous task of giving the slaves both the substance and fact of freedom; or who could imagine a society in which, as Jefferson was later to put it, "the two races, equally free" could live peaceably "in the same government." [26] And even those Americans of the 1780's who hated slavery so passionately as to care nothing for the Union—there were no such men in the Convention—must have suspected that Patrick Henry was not entirely wrong when he warned that to liberate all slaves suddenly in any state south of Delaware would be to invite "the most dreadful and ruinous consequences." [27] In the political and emotional circumstances of 1787 it was possible and therefore proper for Congress to exclude slavery from the Northwest Territory; in the same circumstances it would have been impossible, and therefore both fatuous and suicidal, for the Convention to have attempted to outlaw or even control slavery in the old states. If it should ever be proved, as one imaginative scholar hopes it will be,[28] that the somewhat contradictory dispositions of the problem of slavery in the Ordinance and the Constitution were the fruits of a complicated "deal" between leading men in Congress and the Convention, the proof would only confirm this proposition about the climate of American opinion in 1787, which smiled guardedly upon would-be builders of a nation and frowned coldly upon would-be emancipators of slaves.

Although the word "conservative" was not in circulation in 1787, and although it has been abused dreadfully in recent years, no other word—which I use in this instance as a synonym for "preservative"—expresses the essence of the Constitution so purely and comprehensively. The gingerly way in which the Framers dealt with slavery is the leading case in point for it reminds us of the vital yet easily forgotten fact that the Constitution is the result of a grand exercise in political, not social engineering. The principles of the delegates, their positions in the structure of status and power, and their explicit and implicit mandates set clear limits upon the creative energies of the Convention. The Framers came together in 1787 just as most of them had gone to war in 1776: not to make the world over but to make their corner of it secure, not with hearts full of envy or pity but with minds full of apprehension and prudence, not dazzled by schemes for paradise but spurred by a modest intent to make the happiest country on earth even happier. The Constitution they wrote was not the first act of a second revolution; it was, rather, a prudent set of rules for peaceful evolution in pursuit of large ends upon which all men of good will would agree. It did not demand, it did not even anticipate an upheaval in the social order or a forced redistribution of property; it did not challenge any existing institution or arrangement in the American economy, society, culture, or pattern of religion. It was, I repeat, a conservative document, and the Framers were, although they did not know it, men of conservative style and temper. The refusal to engage in social engineering, the continuity of experience with the English and American pasts, the continuity of principle with the teachings of Cicero and Locke, the self-identification of the Framers as members of a ruling and serving aristocracy, the moderately pessimistic view of human nature that pervaded the debates, the cautiously optimistic view of human destiny that had persuaded these men to come together—all these qualities of the Convention lead me inexorably, and rather against my will, to describe the Great Happening of 1787 as a triumph for the best kind of conservatism.

Yet it was also, we now see from the perspective of almost two centuries, a triumph for the best kind of liberalism—a word I also use cautiously, as a synonym for "progressivism." If the Constitution was not an act of revolution, neither was it a summons to counterrevolution. If it did not challenge the existing order, neither did it underwrite any part of that order on a permanent basis, with the possible exception of the right of individuals to own private property in reasonable amounts. And while it made a comfortable peace with most of the American past, it did not foreclose the future. By opening up a prospect of steady progress to their descendents, and by doing it through the techniques of the popular assembly, the Framers won a secure place for themselves in all histories of political liberalism.

Certainly the Constitution erected no impenetrable barrier to the march of democracy across the American landscape. Although it is full of what we might describe euphemistically as sensible precautions against the unfettered rule of the untutored majority—the checks and balances, the staggered terms of office, the prohibitions on the states—it has enough popular features to give it the air of a stoutly republican charter. The Framers had no argument with the doctrine of majority rule; they simply wished to insist, as their document still insists today, that the majority be clear-cut and cool-headed on all occasions, extraordinary on extraordinary occasions, and powerless on occasions when the consciences of men were at issue. Those critics who like to go rummaging through the Constitution for signs that the Framers had no use for democracy might also consider such arrangements as the provisions for representation in the House, the prohibitions on titles of nobility and on religious tests for officeholding, the absence of property qualifications for political participation, the machinery for admitting new states, the protections for personal liberty, and the prudently permissive process of amendment—far more permissive, it should be noted, than the thirteenth Article of Confederation. The Framers had done their best to create a diffused, limited, balanced form of government in which gentlemen like themselves would fill the leading offices, but they had allowed each state to decide for itself how democratic it wished to be in choosing electors for the Presidency and Representatives in the House. All but a handful of states were soon to decide in favor of popular participation on the broadest footing then conceivable to enlightened men.

If our model citizen of 1787 had been privileged to read through Madison's record of the debates in the Convention, he might have concluded that some delegates had been too harsh in their judgments on the political competence of the American people. Although he would have agreed with Madison himself that "direct democracy" was an invitation to disaster, and that the Constitution should therefore embody "the policy of refining the popular appointments by successive filtrations," he would have been troubled by the remarks about the "excesses of democracy," the "dangers of the levelling spirit," and the "turbulence and follies" of popular assemblies that fell from the lips of men like Sherman, Randolph, Butler, Hamilton, and Gerry.[29] Yet if he had taken account of the context in which such remarks were made, noted that most were no sooner made than qualified, and gathered together all the hopeful things that were said about the people, he might also have concluded that the Framers were remarkably friendly to the claims of plain men to a hand in governing their own affairs. The Constitution they wrote was neither democratic nor undemocratic nor anti-democratic. It was a half-popular, half-aristocratic charter of republicanism, an exciting gamble by a liberty-minded elite that men were ready for the first time in history to be governed rationally and constitutionally on a continental scale. Such men, the Framers insisted, would have to be tutored, exhorted, and restrained, and also persuaded to raise the wisest and most virtuous of their number to the seats of power; and so they designed their charter of ordered liberty with these large purposes in mind.

The men of 1787, who distrusted plebiscitary democracy, deserve much credit for the success of the constitutional democracy that was to establish itself in America within two generations. Lacking an overpowering faith in the wisdom and steadiness of the people, they nevertheless rested the new government upon the broad base of popular sovereignty.

Placing faith in government by the gentry, they nevertheless raised a structure that could be converted without bloodshed into government of, by, and for the people. The Framers insisted in 1787, and their document insists today, that order is the price of liberty, duty of happiness, deliberation of wise decision, and constitutionalism of democracy; and who can deny that the Constitution, conceived in this tough-minded philosophy, has made it possible for a restless race to have its stability and its progress, too?

If this description of 1787 as a triumph of both conservatism and liberalism strikes some readers as an attempt to have the best of two worlds, let it be remembered that there is just as much kinship as antagonism, whether historical or logical, between these two ways of life and thought. In the best of Western liberalism one has always found sober strains of prudence, tradition, and the sense of continuity, in the best of Western conservatism piquant strains of hope, adventure, and the will to progress. The achievement of 1787 is a piece of stunning evidence in support of the grand truth about liberalism and conservatism to which Emerson pointed, and to which far too many of us remain oblivious: "Each is a good half, but an impossible whole. . . . In a true society, in a true man, both must combine." [30] In 1787 at Philadelphia, in the preserving, creating minds of Madison, Wilson, Washington, and their colleagues, both did combine to produce the precepts of a society in which order and progress could be cherished with equal fervor.

# 14 THE STRUGGLE FOR RATIFICATION

*The plot thickens fast. A few short weeks will determine the political fate of America for the present generation, and probably produce no small influence on the happiness of society through a long succession of ages to come.*

WASHINGTON to LAFAYETTE, May 28, 1788[1]

THE NEXT STEP toward a new government was to persuade the old one to send the Constitution on to the states without delay "for their assent and ratification." So lethargic was the Congress of 1787, however, and so suspicious of the Convention were several of its most respected members, that no one could take this step for granted. While Congress had struggled manfully to rise up out of its Slough of Despond on several occasions during this year—notably on July 13 when eighteen men from eight states had presented posterity (and the Ohio Company) with the Northwest Ordinance*—it had failed to muster a quorum on more than half its working days. And while it counted some members who had wished the Convention well from the beginning, it counted others—notably Richard Henry Lee and William Grayson of Virginia, Nathan Dane of Massachusetts, and Melancton Smith of New York—who were certain to grumble, and who might even attempt to block transmission.

Anticipating trouble, and determined to avoid it, almost all those Framers who were members of Congress now followed Major Jackson to New York, changed their hats, and made ready to welcome the charter they had dispatched from Philadelphia. Of the thirty-three men who took part in the events of September 26–28 that led to a resolution for transmission, nearly one-third—Langdon, Gilman, Gorham, King, Johnson, Madison, Blount, Butler, Few, and Pierce—had been delegates to the Convention; and by their votes, speeches, and private assurances they were able to carry the Constitution handsomely over this first hurdle. On September 28, in the

---

* Three Framers—Blount, Few, and Pierce—were in New York on detached duty, and all voted "aye" on the Ordinance.[2]

truculent absence of Rhode Island and over the oblique opposition of New York, Congress voted that the Constitution "be transmitted to the several legislatures in order to be submitted to a convention of delegates chosen in each state by the people thereof." [3]

Some of the men of Philadelphia, who were beginning to feel quite paternal about their little bundle of compromises, wished that the hurdle could have been cleared even more handsomely. What they had wanted was transmission with a recommendation that the Constitution be ratified; what they got, after some jockeying, was transmission pure, simple, and non-committal. Lee and his colleagues were too weak in numbers to persuade Congress to attach a list of restrictive amendments, most of which seem to have originated with George Mason, but they were strong enough in nerve and formidable enough in reputation to force the friends of the Constitution to buy unanimous approval for the resolution of transmission at the price of omitting any word of approval or advice.

And so the Constitution went forth to all thirteen states, even to uncaring Rhode Island, and so Congress sank again into a sleep that seemed to anticipate death. Toward the end of October only four states could muster delegations, and in November there were days when not a single member attended. One hard-working member did manage to look in November 22,[4] but his name was James Madison and "his faith unfaithful." He had already transferred this faith to an object more worthy of it, and was biding his time in order to return to Virginia at just the right moment in a contest over ratification that promised to be boisterous.

If death were to be the fate of Congress, some men might judge that suicide had been a principal cause. Although the Convention was indeed "unknown" and even hostile in intent to the Articles of Confederation, Congress had proved to be remarkably obliging toward it. Not only had it summoned the states to send delegates to a convention "on the second Monday in May next," fought off the temptation to move to Philadelphia and keep an eye on the proceedings,[5] and then transmitted the creation of this Convention promptly to the states; it had reached into a purse that was emptier than empty to find $1165.90 to pay the salaries of the secretary, doorkeeper, and messenger, as well as expenses incurred in transcribing and engrossing the Constitution. It had even, far back in April, extended the franking privilege "to the members of the Convention . . . in the same manner as is allowed to the members of Congress," something no assembly need do for another assembly that wishes it a quick demise. Congress, it would seem, lent its palsied hand rather too eagerly to the eminent men who were engaged in digging its grave.[6]

The resolution of September 26, 1787, launched a political contest that was not resolved until July 26, 1788, when New York agreed sulkily to ratify the Constitution, and was not concluded until May 29, 1790, when Rhode Island decided at last to join the Union. That it was a contest, a fierce struggle that might have gone either way, is plain in the records and newspaper accounts of the state conventions, and that most of the Framers were prepared for a contest is plain in the worried letters with which, after a brief bout of optimism, they began to exhort each other and to damn their opponents. Although the least sanguine among them expected New Jersey, Delaware, and Georgia to approve the Constitution quickly and happily, the most sanguine were reluctant to predict victory in Massachusetts, Virginia, and New York, reluctant even to guess about the mysterious ways of North Carolina and New Hampshire. In these ten months in 1787–1788 when Americans had an unparalleled opportunity to "make history," both advocates and enemies of the proposed charter were aware of the magnitude of the opportunity laid before them. We should not blame them for taking themselves too seriously on occasion, indeed for sounding as if the fate of all nations lay in their hands: as self-conscious makers of history for themselves and posterity they had a great deal to be serious about.

The history made between September 26, 1787, and July 26, 1788, was of a quite different texture from that made in the summer of 1787. The labors of the Convention were focused on one place and time; the struggle over ratification was sprawled all across the map of America, and seemed, at least to Madison and Hamilton, to have no end. In the political and physical circumstances of the young Republic, the campaign for the Constitution was really thirteen campaigns. Each one had to move at its own pace and under its own head of steam; each had to grapple with local issues, many of them intensely personal in nature, that had little to do with the life or death of the Union. No man or committee could sit in New York or Philadelphia or Richmond and coordinate, much less direct, the efforts of either the friends or the enemies of the Constitution in each state; only by sending along news of major steps toward ratification or rejection could men in one state influence the course of events in any other state. Although an informal network of contacts among Washington, Madison, Hamilton, Langdon, Wilson, and other nationalists operated throughout these months, and although a dedicated group of Clintonians in New York City ran a kind of clearinghouse for the opposition, nothing resembling a national organization had a hand in this fateful contest over the destiny of a nation. While the issue was dualistic—to ratify or to reject—the forces called upon to decide it were pluralistic beyond anything we of a far more politically, administratively, and emotionally integrated America can imagine.

Thanks to the underlying dualism of an otherwise apparently formless event, one can make several useful generalizations about the friends and enemies of ratification. In the first place, in every state the leadership of the forces that favored the new Constitution fell to members of the continental elite. Although a healthy minority of this elite fought doggedly against the Constitution, and although the nationalists depended heavily upon the support of thousands upon thousands of craftsmen and farmers of "the middling sort," the drive for ratification, like the drive to call the Convention in the first instance, was managed by a small group of men who owned a disproportionate amount of power and prestige. To Framers like Madison, Hamilton, Wilson, Langdon, and Rutledge, and to "might-have-been-Framers" like John Jay, Edmund Pendleton, and John Sullivan, goes most of the credit for victory in the thirteen largely unrelated campaigns that gave the United States its first national government.

Second, this elite—or series of elites—did as effective a job of arguing and manipulating as could have been done in those days of slow-paced communications and primitive organization. The advocates of ratification began their campaign in a "one-up" position: they had a program—the Constitution—for the reform of a sick system, and their opponents, many of whom agreed that something must be done to strengthen the common government, had none. They had sent out a compelling challenge to a climactic game of high politics for which they themselves had written the rules, including the critical rule that reduced each state legislature to the status of a transmitting agent. From these happy beginnings, which were blessed by the signed approval of America's only two national heroes,* they moved into an even stronger posi-

---

* At least two anonymous opponents of ratification expressed irritation over the Federalist argument that what was good enough for Washington and Franklin should be good enough for every American. A sharp-tongued man called "Centinel" told the citizens of Philadelphia that, in effect, a distracted and inexperienced Washington and an aged Franklin had been led astray by "wealthy and ambitious" schemers. "I doubt much," a "Farmer" wrote of his countrymen to the *American Herald* in Boston, "whether they have carefully examined the Constitution. The hypothesis that General Washington and Dr. Franklin made it, is too strong an argument in the minds of many to suffer them to examine, like freemen, for themselves." [7]

tion by capturing the honored title of "Federalists," thus
forcing the original federalists to call themselves "anti-Federalists"; and they went on to plan, correspond, campaign, and
debate, as well as to bring pressure and make threats and
play tricks, with the special enthusiasm of men who know
what they want, have spent years trying to get it, and feel
that at last it is within their reach. If the struggle had been
directed from a central command-post, and carried on with
the aid of all the fine political arts that were soon to flourish
in America, it could not have been much more successfully
fought than it was by the fragmented yet fraternal elite of
1787–1788.

The purpose of the Federalists, as we must now agree to
call them, was much the same in every state: to get the Constitution ratified unconditionally, quickly, and painlessly.
Once they had been through the labors of creation, the Framers could not surrender to demands for revision that would
require the calling of a second convention. Once they had
placed the fruit of these labors before the people, they could
not suffer the kind of delay that had drained the vitality out
of the Articles of Confederation long before they had gone
into force. And, however hard some of their nine separate
victories might come, they had to win them without disgracing or estranging the anti-Federalists. Thin margins of victory
over bitter men would not be enough. Sooner or later, if the
Constitution were to last, the legitimacy of the new government would have to be conceded by those who had opposed
it vigorously. More than that, some ratifications were absolutely necessary to win; just any nine were not enough to
bring the Constitution to life. Any one of at least four states
—Massachusetts, New York, Pennsylvania, and Virginia—
was in a physical and political position to wreck the whole
scheme by holding out.

Finally, the Federalists were in a somewhat less favorable
position in the blustering war of words that went on during
these months than in the rough-and-ready contest for votes that
would bring life or death to the Constitution. For one thing, they
were forced to meet the opposition on its own ground, which
was almost always and everywhere well below the level of the
debates in the Convention, and thus to defend their grand design with some of the most petty arguments ever heard in
America. For another, they were rhetorically "one-down" to
the anti-Federalists, who made much—and who can blame
them?—of the Revolutionary slogans that equated liberty
with localism and tyranny with consolidation. To the anti-Federalists the Constitution appeared as a betrayal rather
than a fulfillment of the Revolution. In the end, the Federalists won this war because they numbered among their leaders

an overpowering majority of the word-makers—preachers, teachers, pamphleteers, editors, and lawyers—of republican America, and because there was a compelling tone of authenticity about the three principal changes they rang from the first day of the struggle to the last: only those men who had been in the Convention could understand the difficulties of writing a legitimate charter for a "numerous and various people"; in the light of these difficulties, the Convention had produced the best of all possible charters, and there was "no prospect of getting a better"; [8] rejection of this charter, or even a lengthy delay in ratifying it, would mean disunion, disorder, and finally disaster for the United States. "The question on which the proposed Constitution must turn," Madison wrote to Virginia from New York, "is the simple one whether the Union shall or shall not be continued. There is, in my opinion, no middle ground to be taken." [9] "It was done by bargain and compromise," Nicholas Gilman had already written to New Hampshire from Philadelphia, "yet notwithstanding its imperfections, on the adoption of it depends (in my feeble judgment) whether we shall become a respectable nation, or a people torn to pieces by intestine commotions, and rendered contemptible for ages." [10] This was the theme—stated with hundreds of variations—on which the Federalists placed their fondest hopes of victory.

Even during the climactic struggles in Virginia and New York, the anti-Federalists never did muster as large, enterprising, and high-spirited a band of brothers as the outriders of nationalism, but they suffered from no lack of able leaders. Madison was only one of many Framers who were both upset and surprised "to find so many respectable names" on the "list of adversaries to the Federal Constitution." [11] In states like Massachusetts, New York, Maryland, Virginia, and South Carolina, certified members of the continental elite stood ready to declaim upon the vices of the proposed Constitution and to use their sizable influence to have it defeated; and in every state of the Union politicians whose interests and loyalties were casually or fiercely local could be counted on to oppose the adoption of a system that might strip them of power. "They will not cherish the great oak which is to reduce them to paltry shrubs," Randolph had predicted of the state politicians and officeholders at an early stage of the Convention,* and he and his fellow Framers were alto-

---

\* In this speech Randolph was paying particular attention to the state governors, only three of whom, in the end, were opponents of ratification, and a full nine of whom took a leading part in seeing the Constitution safely through the conventions in their states. The opposition among state and local politicians was concentrated on the middle and lower levels of power.

gether right in anticipating that the opposition in several doubtful states would group itself around "the local demagogues." [12] Whether long-committed foes of any extension of national authority or shortsighted advocates for the interests of their states and sections, whether dissembling men of property who were doing well in the confusions of the decade or honest men of principle who could not imagine a government both national and republican, the leaders of anti-Federalism were strong enough in will and numbers to give the friends of the Constitution the stiffest kind of fight, and this fight, unlike the one carried on privately in Philadelphia, was scheduled to take place in the light of day.

Behind the "respectable names" of which Madison wrote, and helping to give the anti-Federalists a look of power they may never have had, loomed a vast array of Americans, some of them city-dwellers but most of them farmers, whose attitude was one of apathy rather than hostility, and who, if they could be mobilized at all, would vote to reject the Constitution outright. Every state, even Delaware and New Jersey, had its share of men who could not make the kind of mental effort that would persuade them of the need for such a drastic gamble with the future as this high-toned, consolidating, almost overbearing charter of nationalism. In states like New Hampshire and North Carolina these men were so clearly in the majority that they might well do the Constitution to death simply by doing nothing.

In the end, the anti-Federalist leaders failed to form an unbreachable front out of these elements of hostility, suspicion, indifference, and apathy because they lacked the unifying sense of purpose of the Federalists. Although they were manfully united in opposing this plan of reform, which had been presented so high-handedly on an all-or-nothing, take-it-or-leave-it basis, they were uncomfortably divided in proposing a workable alternative. Some were die-hards who insisted that the Articles of Confederation could still be rescued by the addition of a few prudent amendments; others were skeptics who were ready to let the Union dissolve and then regroup into three or four viable confederacies; still others were moderates who, after much searching of souls, were prepared to accept the Constitution on condition that a second convention be called to amend the most objectionable parts and to add further protections for the rights of citizens and the authority of the states. The trouble was, as Madison recognized and even Lee must have admitted in his heart, that a second convention could never have succeeded where the first one had failed, and that every changed or added line would lose as many friends of the Constitution as it would convert enemies. As the struggle went on, and the opposition began to show its power in states like Virginia, New Hampshire, and New York, the Federalists pulled back prudently from an adamant demand for unconditional ratification and opened their minds, wherever this proved necessary, to the notion of "ratification with recommendations"—recommendations, that is to say, for the consideration of the new Congress under the Constitution. To the notion of "ratification with conditions," especially if one condition was the calling of a second convention, they kept their minds tightly and correctly shut.

History wastes little time on losers in political struggles (as contrasted with the attention it pours upon losers in civil wars), and we have been able only recently to close our ears for a few moments to the voices of Hamilton, Madison, Wilson, Ellsworth, and other polemicists for the Constitution in order to listen with respect, and perhaps even a touch of admiration, to the arguments of the anti-Federalists. In every state where the issue was in doubt, the case against the Constitution was put with eloquence and passion, and some historians believe that the Federalists were the victors in the war of words only because they were the victors in the contest for votes. Remembered men like Lee, Mason, Gerry, Martin, Melancton Smith, and Henry, forgotten men like Amos Singletary of Massachusetts and William Goudy of North Carolina, and unknown men like Brutus, Helvidius, John Humble, Rough Hewer, Tar and Feathers, and a Friend to Liberty all joined to give the Constitution a savage mauling. If the essence of democracy is open and nearly endless debate, the struggle over ratification in all but the two or three most easily won states was a searching test of this famous pattern of politics.

Since the embattled anti-Federalists could hardly be expected to emulate our model citizen of Chapter 13 and stay cool and punctilious, many attacks on the Constitution—like that of the North Carolina preacher who imagined the proposed federal district as ten square miles of debauchery and tyranny[13]—were downright silly and dishonest; and since these anti-Federalists were scattered all over the map of America, and all up and down the social ladder, they often seemed to be shooting at each other over the heads of the Federalists in between. Hard-minded planters in South Carolina assailed the Constitution for failing to give full security to slavery; tender-minded Quakers in Pennsylvania were appalled to learn that Congress could not move against the slave trade for twenty years. Pious Baptists in North Carolina wanted a clear statement of religious freedom; pious Congregationalists in Connecticut wanted a clear statement (in the preamble and not as an afterthought) of belief in "the being and perfections of the one living and true God." [14] Yet, for all their pettifogging, name-calling, and mumbling in a confusion of tongues, the anti-Federalists did make a discomfiting case against the Constitution. In the best of their letters, pamphlets, and speeches, they exploited several common and endlessly recurring points, the most nearly persuasive of which were:

1. The Federalists were trying to stampede the country into adopting an untested, unpredictable, highly novel system —"so new," Patrick Henry complained, "it wants a name" [15] —by painting a picture of troubles that did not exist and horrors that would not arise. "To say that a bad government must be established for fear of anarchy," Richard Henry Lee wrote publicly to the unsure Randolph, "is really saying that we should kill ourselves for fear of dying." [16]

2. Possessing no mandate to write a new constitution, they had acted contrary to both the law and spirit of the Articles of Confederation, and had done this—a damning and symbolic piece of evidence—as a "Dark Conclave" under a "thick veil of secrecy," [17] a shocking and "unaccountable insult . . . to the majority of the people." *

3. The Constitution was a long step toward monarchy and aristocracy, and was thus a repudiation of the Revolution of 1776. It was, indeed, in Henry's words, an affront to the "spirit of republicanism" and the "genius of democracy." [18] Four decisions of the Convention drew fire in every state, even from men who had wished it well: the failure to include a bill of rights ("Should not such a thing have preceded the model?" Adams asked Jefferson); [19] the creation of a powerful and virtually irresponsible executive ("a bad edition of a Polish king," Jefferson warned Adams); [20] the provision for an inevitably aristocratic upper house ("this host of influence and power," George Clinton described it); [21] and the narrow scale of representation in the House of Representatives (which would make it simply an "assistant aristocratical branch," wrote an outraged Bostonian). [22]

4. The Constitution created, again in Henry's words, "one great, consolidated, national government," and thus doomed the states to a long decline and degrading death. The

* The veil of secrecy never did get lifted more than an inch or two during the struggle over ratification. No records or notes or transcripts of speeches—except Franklin's little sermon of September 17— found their way into print, and none of the contrary-minded delegates, not even the outraged Luther Martin, revealed more than a few scraps of information about the doings in Philadelphia.

taxation clause, Mason warned softly, "clearly discovers that it is a national government, and no longer a confederation." [23] The supremacy clause, Robert Whitehill of Pennsylvania echoed angrily, "eradicates every vestige of state government —and was intended so—it was deliberated." [24] Even if the new government were perfect in form, it could not govern fairly and benevolently over so vast a territory. Thomas Wait of Maine, one of a thousand anti-Federalists who summoned Montesquieu to witness, denied that the "vast continent of America" could be ruled on principles of freedom if "consolidated into one government." "You might as well attempt," he wrote a friend, "to rule Hell by prayer." [25]

Through all the arguments against the Constitution—solemn and shrill, sensible and absurd, clever and vulgar—ran the ancient and honorable theme, so dear to the hearts of freedom-loving Americans, of the corrupting effects of political power. The size, number, and vagueness of the delegations in Article I, section 8 gave every anti-Federalist a knobby stick with which to belabor the Framers for betraying either a wicked urge to wield power themselves or a quaint naïveté about the springs of human conduct. "Look at the predominant thirst of dominion," Henry thundered, "which has invariably and uniformly prompted rulers to abuse their power." "I suspect my own heart," General Thompson of Massachusetts confessed openly, "and I shall suspect our rulers." [26] Power granted without adequate restraints, power asserted in cryptic words, power taken from the states and lodged in a distant government—this was the sum of the evils the anti-Federalists found in the Constitution, this was the parade of horrors the Federalists had to argue away logically or conjure away derisively. "I think power the hinge on which the whole Constitution turns," Isaac Snow of Massachusetts said in behalf of all the Federalists,[27] and he and his colleagues went on to win this great debate because they were able to prove, as Hamilton did in *The Federalist*, numbers 23–28, that no national government ought to have any less power than the total agreed upon in Philadelphia, and that, moreover, the men who would hold it in the future could be persuaded to use it wisely. It is an odd quirk of American intellectual history that even the most democratic anti-Federalists of 1787–1788 should have been driven to cast themselves as "men of little faith," as exponents of a grotesque Whiggery that fed on a degrading view of human nature.[28] The hopeful men of 1787–1788 were the Federalists, and that may be one reason why they got their charter ratified.

Distracted only slightly by the din and smoke of the war of

words, indeed moving into action before the war was fairly begun, the Federalists pressed for quick approval in states that were thought to favor the Constitution. By early January of 1788 they had five instruments of ratification in their bag, and had gained a momentum they were never to lose. In four of the five states—all small ones—they had won almost too easily: helpless Delaware, which, in the acid words of an anti-Federalist in Pennsylvania, "reaped the honor of having first surrendered the liberties of the people" by ratifying unanimously (30–0)*—and also "fully, freely, and entirely"—after only five days of friendly and desultory discussion; [29] hapless New Jersey, whose convention gave the Constitution the courtesy of a full week, then voted unanimously (38–0) to ratify December 18; [30] defenseless Georgia, where the menace of the Creeks cast a pall over what could have been a lively debate and produced another unanimous ratification (26–0) January 2; [31] and sensible Connecticut, where the political struggle was sharper, the war of words much more clamorous, and the approving vote of January 9 divided (128–40). [32] Many of these forty dissenting votes were cast by lawyers, merchants, and farmers who held rewarding state offices; not even the orchestrated eloquence of the three Framers from Connecticut could persuade them to raise their eyes above the rooftops of Simsbury, Enfield, Sharon, and East Haven.

The second in order of this first batch of ratifications was an entirely different experience. The margin of victory in the Pennsylvania convention was handsome enough (46–23), and the date was early enough (December 12); but the manner in which the Federalists had won this important battle—one they clearly could not afford to lose—raised serious doubts about their claims to wisdom and virtue. [33] Anxious to throw the weight of their famous state quickly into the scales, and anxious also to see the new federal capital located on the west bank of the Delaware, they had used every trick of politics and propaganda to win over wavering anti-Morris men in Philadelphia and to beat down obstinate ones in the western counties. When the opponents of ratification, who were not averse to playing tricks themselves, tried to block action in the outgoing legislature by absenting themselves from the floor, two of them—the exact number needed to produce a bare quorum—were hustled by a mob from their lodgings, deposited in their seats, and forced to bear witness to the call-

---

* Delaware has always viewed the honor in a rather different light, as one may read for himself when stuck in traffic behind a car bearing a Delaware license plate.

ing of a ratifying convention. And although the case against the Constitution was stated with spirit by home-grown orators like John Smilie and William Findley and imported pamphleteers like Mason and Lee, it could scarcely be heard amidst the din of the voices raised in behalf of ratification.

The leading voice in the Federalist camp was that of James Wilson, who alone among the eight Framers from Pennsylvania was willing and able to be elected as a delegate to the convention. At a large outdoor meeting in the yard of the State House on October 6, and in the convention itself (which sat from November 21 to December 12), Wilson surpassed even his efforts of the summer, beating back every sensible argument against the Constitution—and a number of silly ones as well—with the measured eloquence one would expect of the best of the Philadelphia lawyers. While Wilson reasoned patiently on the floor of the convention, his friends worked cleverly to see that his words were reported favorably and at length and those of his opponents unfavorably or not at all.

Although many of these words were no doubt memorable, they had almost no influence on the final decision to ratify. The elections of November 6 produced a convention of forty-six Federalists (including Wilson, Thomas McKean, Dr. Benjamin Rush, F. A. Muhlenberg, Timothy Pickering, and General Anthony Wayne) and twenty-three anti-Federalists, and three weeks of debate changed not a single mind. The Federalists won in Pennsylvania because, fearing what the younger Morris called "the cold and sower temper of the back counties," [34] they threw all the ample resources and finely-honed skills of the Republican party into the contest for votes. Whether they had been perhaps too ruthless in the contest, and thus had hardened the hearts of otherwise moderate men in the opposition, remained to be seen. The news that a crowd in Carlisle had greeted the report of ratification by rioting in the town square and burning "James the Caledonian" in effigy was a shock to the Federalists and a shot in the arm to the anti-Federalists, who acted as if the struggle were only beginning in Pennsylvania by continuing to belabor the Constitution and its leading friends.

If Pennsylvania was a model for those who like to win political victories at almost any price—even the price of a grievously disaffected minority—Massachusetts was a model for those who like to win by fair methods and a reasonable margin, and then to send everyone home happy.[35] When the convention met in Boston on January 9, 1788, a narrow majority of the 350-odd delegates elected in the towns, many of which were still torn by the passions of the Shays Rebellion, was opposed to ratification. When the decisive vote was taken on February 6, enough unsure minds had been made up and enough skeptical minds changed to produce a margin of 187–168 for the new Constitution. An unsure delegate named Samuel Adams had been helped to make up his mind by a mass meeting of Federalist mechanics and tradesmen in Boston under the leadership of John Lucas and Paul Revere; a skeptical delegate named John Hancock had been persuaded to change his by promises of support for the governorship, the Vice-Presidency, or even, if Virginia were to hold itself aloof, for the Presidency. Most important, the sensible Federalists and the flexible doubters had found a formula for ratification that softened the harsh line hitherto drawn between the "ayes" and the "noes." At the suggestion of Hancock himself, who, with the help of Theophilus Parsons, made his share of history at this perilous moment, Massachusetts ratified unconditionally but with a strong expression of "opinion" that "certain amendments and alterations in the said Constitution would remove the fears and quiet the apprehensions of many of the good people of this Commonwealth." Nine recommendations—the first of which was, in effect, a rough draft of the Tenth Amendment—were laid before the people of the United States, and future Congressmen from Massachusetts were enjoined to "exert all their influence" in order to get them adopted as amendments to the Constitution.

The victory in Massachusetts, in which Gorham, King, and Strong all had a hand, was an essential one for the Federalists. If the Constitution had lost in this large and powerful state, it would probably have failed to win approval in New Hampshire, New York, and Virginia. By fighting hard but fairly, by giving the opposition (which included thirty Shaysites) every opportunity to express its doubts and fears, and by discovering a formula for ratification that would prove attractive in other divided states, the Federalists of Massachusetts carried the Constitution safely through a severe test. Their margin of victory was a good deal smaller than that rung up in Pennsylvania, but it was the kind of victory that puts an abrupt end to the game. The most revealing passages in the record of the convention at Boston are at the end, when one delegate after another who had voted "no"—Abraham White of Norton, Daniel Cooley of Amherst, William Widgery of New Gloucester up in Maine, and a half-dozen more —rose to pledge their faith to the new Constitution. In the words of the last two men to speak in the convention, Benja-

min Randall of Sharon and Major Benjamin Swain of Marl-
borough:

> Mr. Randal said, he had been uniformly opposed to the
> Constitution. He had, he said, fought like a good soldier;
> but, as he was beaten, he should sit down contented,
> hoping the minority may be disappointed in their fears,
> and that the majority may reap the full fruition of the
> blessings they anticipate. In the hope that the amend-
> ments recommended by his excellency, the president,
> will take place, I shall, says he, go home and endeavor
> to satisfy those that have honored me by their choice, so
> that we may all live in peace.
>
> Major Swain declared, that the Constitution had had a
> fair trial, and that there had not, to his knowledge, been
> any undue influence exercised to obtain the vote in its
> favor; that many doubts which lay on his mind had been
> removed; and that, although he was in the minority, he
> should support the Constitution as cheerfully and as
> heartily as though he had voted on the other side of the
> question.[36]

Such gracious remarks promised legitimacy to the Constitution, and the Federalists of Massachusetts had reason to smile
when they heard them.

It was just as well for the morale of the Federalists that
they had won a happy victory at this moment, for in neighboring New Hampshire, the next state to consider the Constitution, the march into the future came to a sudden if temporary halt.[37] When the convention assembled in Exeter on
February 13, so many delegates from distant towns had firm instructions to reject the Constitution that a favorable vote was
out of the question, and the best the Federalists could do was
to win an adjournment from February to June. In the inter-
vening months they hoped to mount an effective campaign to
rescue the Constitution from the clutches of ignorance and apathy, especially by sending converted delegates home to persuade their constituents to issue new instructions. This strategy
paid off on June 21 with a 57–47 margin for an instrument of
ratification that recommended twelve amendments to the Constitution according to the Massachusetts formula. Only the
strongest efforts of John Langdon and John Sullivan, who
suspended hostilities for a few months in an effort to win a victory they both wanted badly, were able to overcome the suspicion with which New Hampshire had first greeted the Constitution. Federalists all over the country were relieved to see
this stubborn and unpredictable state line up on their side.

By the time that Langdon and Sullivan had done their duty as members of the continental elite, two more states were in the fold. Over the wounded protests of Samuel Chase and his faction, for whom Luther Martin did yeoman service when he accused his fellow Framers of "forging chains" for their countrymen and washed a good deal of their private linen in public,[38] Maryland accepted the Constitution on April 26 by a margin of 63–11.[39] The voters of the state had shown such enthusiasm for the Constitution in the election of delegates that the Federalists in the convention, who had already had their say in the press and in the legislature, decided to sit quietly while the anti-Federalists talked on and on about the dangers of a too perfect Union. Then, when Chase, Martin, and Mercer had worn themselves down, they called for a vote and adjourned without delay. This process of attrition-by-silence took only four working days, and produced, to the distress of the minority, the last ratification of any state that made no recommendations for amendment. Although the feelings of Chase's men were not quite so injured as those of the anti-Federalists in Pennsylvania, the tactics of the victors do seem to have been unnecessarily rude and contemptuous—unless, of course, one remembers that this was the way men liked to play politics in steamy Maryland.

In South Carolina, where things have always moved at a more leisurely pace, the convention met on May 12, 1788, gave two weeks to those gentlemen who wished to parade their talents, and then voted 149–73 to ratify the Constitution with four recommendations, of which the most important was another rough draft of the Tenth Amendment.[40] In the convention, as in the session of the legislature that had voted to summon it, the Pinckneys and Rutledge took the lead for the friends of the Constitution. General Pinckney was especially useful in defending the "1808 clause" as the "best terms for the security of this species of property it was in our power to make," [41] and even Rawlin Lowndes, who summoned "the principles of religion, humanity, and justice" to sanctify the slave trade, finally had to admit that Pinckney was probably right.

By June 2, 1788, when Virginia assembled at last in convention at Richmond,[42] eight states were known to have ratified the Constitution, and news from the ninth, New Hampshire, was getting better all the time. A nine-state Union without Virginia, however, would be no union at all, and even at this late hour the anti-Federalists hoped to prevent the new government from coming into being, either by withholding the approval of this essential state or by insisting that the other states join with it in a second convention. Certainly they did their best in Virginia to defeat the Constitution, or at worst to load it with amendments that would have crippled it as an instrument of nation-building. In the war of words, which raged throughout the winter and spring, Mason, Richard Henry Lee, and others were more than a match for the Federalists, many of whom seemed to be saving their breath for the showdown in Richmond; and in the contest for votes, one of the liveliest ever held in the state, they did better than the Federalists had expected them to do and came into the convention with just about half of the 170 delegates.

In no convention were the opponents of the Constitution able to meet the friends on such equal terms. While the Federalists rallied behind Madison, Wythe, John Marshall, Henry Lee, Edmund Pendleton, and, sure at last in his inconstant mind, Governor Randolph, the anti-Federalists delighted in the leadership of Mason, William Grayson, Theodorick Bland, James Monroe, Joseph Jones, and, mighty of voice and influence, Patrick Henry. The debates, which lasted the better part of four weeks, were the most searching, exciting, and well-reported of any convention. By the time of the decisive vote of June 25, which went 89–79 for ratification with recommendations, neither the wildly slashing Henry nor the neatly parrying Madison, who rose to heights as lofty as those he had reached in Philadelphia, could deny that every potential defect and every real merit of the Constitution had been candidly exposed. The rhetoric of Revolutionary liberty burst forth from Henry in passage after passage that even today sends chills (and an occasional twitch of irritation) down the spine; the rhetoric of Union as the consummation of the Revolution and the guardian of liberty, in which Madison and his colleagues proved quietly adept, brought wavering delegates and bedazzled spectators time after time back to their senses. The confrontation of Madison and Henry was direct, for the latter simply did not recognize the two fears about the American pattern of constitutional government that had stalked Madison ever since 1785: that a legislature was "naturally" stronger than an executive and state governments "naturally" stronger than a national government. Henry, indeed, was certain that power and prestige would flow in quite the opposite direction: from Congress to President, from states to nation.

Virginia ratified the Constitution and gave new life to the Union because of a whole series of accidents and incidents that mock the crudely economic interpretation of the Great

Happening of 1787–1788. In no state, for example, was timing so important; for, as Randolph himself insisted in the last speech of the convention, "the accession of eight states reduced our deliberations to the single question of *Union or no Union.*" [43] In none were the friends of the Constitution so willing to let the other side, both the enemies and the skeptics, load the instrument of ratification with recommendations to the new Congress for amending the Constitution. And in none were the preferences and activities of leading men more influential. It may be argued that Virginia came down at last on the side of the more perfect Union because of the mere existence of Washington, who was waiting with mixed emotions at Mt. Vernon to learn if he would be eligible to be the first President under a Constitution that he had now come to cherish; * because of the belated but firm decision of the popular Randolph to support in Richmond what he had not signed in Philadelphia (a decision in which both Washington and Madison played influential roles); because of the benevolent neutrality of the faraway Jefferson, who might be quoted as a critic of the Constitution but not as an enemy; because of the skill of Henry Lee, "Lighthorse Harry" himself, in spraying Patrick Henry with some of his own invective in the rough-and-tumble on the floor; and above all because of the total commitment of James Madison to his personal vision of a Union both strong and free. In the end, Virginia rose above the hostility, parochialism, and suspicion that gripped many of its citizens and accepted the Constitution largely because it saw itself as the leading state in any union that Americans might form. While Patrick Henry might frighten some Virginians with his description of the proposed Presidency as an "awful squinting . . . towards monarchy," most were persuaded otherwise by the assurance that the first holder of this splendid office would be one of their own—if, of course, Virginia acted with sufficient vigor and dispatch.

If the more perfect Union could not do without lordly Virginia, neither could it do without rich, growing, and strategically placed New York. The fate of the Constitution, which had so often been in jeopardy in 1787–1788, now hung upon the decision that would emerge sooner or later, in George Clinton's good time, from the clash of his will with that of Alexander Hamilton. Because of a series of delays engineered by the hostile Clintonians (whose power lay in the upstate

* "Be assured," James Monroe wrote to Jefferson shortly after the convention, "his influence carried this government; for my own part, I have a boundless confidence in him." [44]

counties) and endured by the impatient Federalists (who had a firm grip on the city), New York did not meet in convention to consider the Constitution until June 17, 1788. Although only nineteen of the sixty-five delegates had been elected as open friends of the new Constitution, so many things worked in their favor that the final vote of July 26 (30–27 in favor of ratification with recommendations) bears in retrospect the stamp of inevitability.[45] They had already won, thanks to the brilliant contributions of Hamilton, Madison, and Jay to *The Federalist,* a moral victory in New York's splendid little war of words; they expected good news from New Hampshire and Virginia, and they got it (thanks to Hamilton's foresight and willingness to dig into his own pocket) from Exeter on June 24 and Richmond on July 2; and they could count enough troubled spirits in Clinton's ranks—including, in an odd way, the redoubtable Clinton himself—to hope for a reversal in convention of the harsh verdict on the Constitution registered by the people of New York in the elections of April.

Most of all, they had Alexander Hamilton, and he posed a threat that was impossible to laugh off. While it is pleasant to think that his dazzling oratory on the floor of the convention persuaded Melancton Smith, Gilbert Livingston, and nine other sensible anti-Federalists to change their minds and vote for the Constitution (but not those two obstinate Framers, Robert Yates and John Lansing, jr.), the fact is that New York ratified principally because Hamilton raised the specter of a secession by the city and southern counties, which would choose, he suggested, to join the slowly perfecting Union and close the worrisome gap between New England and the Middle States. Knowing then as well as we know now that there could be no Union without New York, Hamilton turned this truth around to convince the anti-Federalists privately that there might be no New York without the Union. Although the ratification was a grudging one, accompanied as it was by sixteen passionately declared rights, seven "impressions," four "reservations," thirty-two amendments, and a circular letter to "our sister states" calling for a second general convention, it was more than Hamilton and his friends could have obtained before Virginia had acted favorably. They had full reason—although they would have been either more or less than human to voice it—to thank Governor Clinton for having stalled his unseeing way into a situation in which to reject the Constitution would have been to invite disaster for New York.

By the end of July the Federalists could be sure that they had won the struggle for ratification. Although the convention in North Carolina, unimpressed by the actions of its lofty neighbors and unaware of the decision in New York, voted 184–84 against unconditional ratification on August 2,[46] and although the legislature of Rhode Island refused even to call a convention, an eleven-state Union that included Massachusetts, New York, Pennsylvania, and Virginia provided a solid foundation for a new government. The business of forming that government, in particular of fixing a temporary seat and of electing a President and a Congress, could now go forward. It had been a struggle, no doubt of that— long, passionate, exhausting, and dubious—and men like Washington had reason to believe humbly that the result had been a victory "for all mankind."

Millions of words have been written, and at least a million more are even now laboring their way into print, about the economic, social, and political make-up of the two camps in the struggle over ratification: the friends and the enemies of the Constitution in the conventions and among the people at large.[47] Rather than add a superfluous ten or twenty thousand of my own, let me say simply that the evidence we now have leads most historians to conclude that no sharp economic or social line can be drawn on a nationwide basis between these two camps, and that it most certainly was not—neither in the subtle Beardian nor vulgar Marxist sense—a contest between the haves and the have-nots of post-Revolutionary America. In several states, to be sure, most men of wealth and status —established lawyers, enterprising merchants, planters or large-scale farmers—favored the new Constitution, while the opposition drew heavily on the support of small farmers, debtors, and paper-money men. Yet even in Massachusetts, perhaps the best example of such a state, plenty of the well-to-do and well-placed fought as hard as Gerry against ratification, and plenty of unimportant people lined up enthusiastically behind King, Gorham, and Strong. In New Jersey, Delaware, and Georgia the Constitution found such favor with men in all walks of life that no meaningful line can be drawn between the many who were for and the few who were against. In New York and Virginia so many leading men could be found on both sides (or in the middle) that one must describe the principal line of demarcation as political rather than social or economic. In these crucial states, as also in more easily won Connecticut and Maryland, it was a case of faction pitted against faction without too much regard for property-holdings and claims to prestige.

Factional politics was more often than not sectional politics in early republican America, as indeed it had been at the height of the colonial period, and I would therefore go one step further to suggest that the real line between the two camps in 1787–1788 was geographic. In state after state the advocates of ratification were concentrated in the ports, market towns, and settled areas, as well as along the navigable rivers and the well-traveled roads, while the opponents were scattered through the newer, less developed, more isolated sections. Where men were busy in trade, where pamphlets were printed and newspapers delivered, where dollars and ideas were spawned and circulated, there one found friends of the Constitution among the better sort, the middling sort, and even the meaner sort. Where men farmed largely for subsistence, where the printed word penetrated laboriously, where life was hard and horizons limited, there, in a land in which few of the better sort had settled and even fewer had arisen to prosper, one found apathy, lethargy, and suspicion. Since one also found, in every state but three, skilled political leaders who disliked the proposed new government out of fear or envy or principle, and could therefore be counted on to attempt to convert "the cold and sower temper" of the back country into active hostility, the wonder is that the friends of the Constitution managed to secure ratification in eleven states in ten months. The burden was on them to prove the need for so apparently drastic a reform, and if they had not cared enough to shoulder this burden, the Constitution must surely have perished of attrition.

The Federalists won their eleven games of propaganda and politics, at least four of which they could easily have lost, because the Constitution seemed to be a shrewd and honest projection of the fact of incipient nationhood, the sign of an economic, social, and emotional reality that more and more Americans were coming to cherish as a legacy of the Revolution, an open door to prosperity, and a shield to independence. The friends of the Constitution could hardly have argued for the establishment of a national government if there had been no nation for it to defend and serve. They could hardly have persuaded governors and legislators to lay the Constitution before the people if such men had really believed that the states were sovereign and the United States a league of convenience. And whatever aspersions may be cast at the methods of the Convention of 1787 itself, the process of ratification was open, legal, and, certainly as the word was understood in those days, democratic. Defective in membership and arrogant or stumbling in procedure as some of them may have been, the elected conventions of 1787–1788—whose galleries were open to the public and whose doings were, in most instances, well reported—were a major event in the history of popular government and perhaps the most severe test to which such government had ever been put. By the time the test was finished, Madison and Wilson were convinced that the Constitution was indeed the act of the sovereign people. It is, more than incidentally, an idle exercise to try to count up the votes for and against the Constitution in the elections of delegates to the ratifying conventions. In many districts the question was not (and could not be) that simply put, and from many the delegates came to the conventions without benefit of (and thus unshackled by) clear instructions.

The Federalists also won because, in most of their decisions and dealings, they showed good judgment in distinguishing the possible from the unacceptable, in knowing when to hold fast and when to give way. By adding any one of a half-dozen techniques and arrangements to their Constitution —a veto on state laws, property-owning qualifications for the suffrage, judicial review, a flat guarantee of assumption of state obligations, additional powers for either the Senate or the President—the Framers might have tipped the delicately balanced scale of opinion against their cause. By failing to respond positively to the honest doubts and fears of the anti-Federalists, the leaders in the drive for ratification, who included almost every one of the forty-nine approving Framers,* might have proved the point of their most savage critics: that they had to have things their own way and were therefore not to be trusted. But the Framers, as we learned in Part III, had a good collective sense of what the people, if properly instructed, would accept; and the Federalists, as we have just seen, made enough concessions to carry the day but not so many as to spoil it. In every one of the eleven ratifying states they had put the Constitution squarely before the electorate; in every one they had been forced to give the opposition, if it existed at all, a fair hearing; in all but one, divided and mishandled Pennsylvania, they had won victories with which their defeated foes could live peaceably if not entirely happily.

Most important for the morale of a fledgling nation and for the health of its politics, they had persuaded majorities of delegates in eleven states that they, not Gerry and Clinton

---

* Thirty Framers were elected as delegates to ratifying conventions, five of this number (Luther Martin, Mercer, Mason, Yates, and Lansing) as leaders of the opposition. For most of the others it was either unnecessary (Dickinson, Read, and Livingston) or impolitic (Washington and the two Morrises) or quixotic (Gerry) to stand for election. Only one Framer, Martin of North Carolina, sought election openly and suffered defeat.

and Henry, were the true friends of the Revolution. Since only a handful of the forty-three living signers of the Declaration of Independence had fought with any zest against the Constitution, and indeed a full thirty had helped in one way or another to bring it to life, the Federalists could make this point with entire sincerity. Perhaps it is time for those who still cannot warm to the Federalists of 1787–1788 to drop the tired old charges of "counterrevolution." The conventions from New Hampshire to Georgia, like the Convention in Philadelphia that called on them to "assent and ratify," were instruments of the Revolution every bit as legitimate as the meetings and battles of 1776. The Constitution was indeed the Revolution brought to fruition.

# 15 THE FIRST YEARS OF THE CONSTITUTION

*My malady renders my sitting up to write rather painful to me; but I cannot let my son-in-law, Mr. Bache, part for New York without congratulating you by him . . . on the growing strength of our new government under your administration. For my own personal ease I should have died two years ago; but, though those years have been spent in excruciating pain, I am pleased that I have lived them, since they have brought me to see our present situation.*

FRANKLIN to WASHINGTON, September 16, 1789[1]

A CRITICAL STAGE in the life of a constitution is the conversion of what is, after all, only a spider's web of words into the solid reality of a political system both operational and legitimate. To agree upon the rules for governing a nation and to win consent for a test of their viability are achievements that call for judgment, tact, nerve, and vision; to meet this test in the form of policies that work, laws that are obeyed, and officers who govern fairly and effectively is an achievement that calls for all the arts of statesmanship. For the Constitution of the United States this stage began in the summer of 1788, when the old Congress prepared to set the machinery of the new government in motion, and ended in March of 1801, when Thomas Jefferson and his friends took over the machinery with hardly a hitch or a stutter; and it was a triumph of statesmanship with few equals in the annals of freedom. A time of danger and passion, the administrations of Washington and Adams were also a time of achievement. If these years had not been lived in a brave and imaginative style, we might now be looking back to 1787 as a year of frustration or even disaster, not as a year of creation.

On July 2, 1788, when "the ninth ratification" had been "transmitted and laid before them," the members of Congress voted to appoint a committee of five (one of them the faithful Baldwin) to "report an act . . . for putting the new Constitution into operation." On September 13, after more than two months of pulling and hauling over the location of the capital, they signed the death warrant of the Articles of Confederation by setting a timetable for the election of the first President and both a date ("the first Wednesday in March next"—March 4, 1789) and a place ("the present seat of Congress"—New York) for "commencing proceedings" as a more perfect Union.[2] Warmed by the pleasantly Federalist climate of New York City, excited by a dazzling parade down Broadway in honor of the new Constitution,* and prodded by Framers like Baldwin, Few, Dayton, Gilman, Madison, and Hamilton as well as by artisans of ratification like Jeremiah Wadsworth and Henry Lee, Congress did its final duty to the American people and then sank into a well-earned oblivion. It mustered a quorum for the last time on October 10,[4] and from that day until its formal death April 30, 1789, lived on principally in the sturdy person of its secretary, Charles Thomson.[5]

The eleven ratifying states did their second duty to the new Constitution by choosing electors for the purpose of choosing George Washington as President, and also—except in agitated New York where the legislators could not get together on the names of two senators—by electing their share of members to the two houses of the new Congress. Since all but a few of these men had been active Federalists in the events of 1787–1788, the first hands to be laid on the Constitution were certain to be those of its friends.

Roads being what they were in the young Republic, and winter being what it still is on the Atlantic seaboard, a quorum in both the House and Senate was not assembled until April 6. It was April 23 before Washington, who had to wait at Mt. Vernon for Secretary Thomson to notify him officially of his election, could get to New York and be given the welcome of his life by a cheering city, which was to be expected, and a smiling Governor Clinton, which augured well for the success of the new government.[6] It was April 30 before the chancellor of the host state, Robert R. Livingston, could swear him in as President. Under the experienced guidance of James Madison, whom the vengeance of Patrick Henry could bar from the Senate but not from the House of Representatives, Congress had already gone to work on measures to

---

* The highlight of this parade of July 23, which would not even wait upon official word from Poughkeepsie, was a miniature frigate of "thirty-two guns and twenty-seven feet keel" named the *Alexander Hamilton*. Other cities that celebrated ratification with colorful (and persuasive) "Federal Processions" were Charleston, Baltimore, Boston, Philadelphia, and New Haven.[3]

produce revenue. Washington, too, was soon at work sifting out the names of other friends of the Constitution—some of long standing, others recent converts—who were being pressed on him for offices not yet created.

By September 17, 1789, the second anniversary of the signing of the Constitution in Philadelphia, it must have been clear to all citizens of the United States, even in temporarily detached North Carolina and Rhode Island, that the new government of which men had been talking for years was on the way to becoming a peace-keeping, commerce-regulating, mail-carrying, tax-raising, and money-spending reality. The first session of the first Congress had acted almost as a second constitutional convention, in which eleven Framers sat as senators (Langdon, Strong, Ellsworth, Johnson, King, Paterson, Robert Morris, Read, Bassett, Butler, and Few) and eight as representatives (Gilman, Sherman, Clymer, Fitzsimons, Carroll, Madison, Baldwin, and, having made a sort of peace with the Constitution, Gerry) from the eleven participating states. In its five months of activity (it adjourned September 29)[7] Congress had absorbed the remnants of the government to which it was the legal successor; provided for carrying on the government of the Northwest Territory; established a system of federal courts, including a six-man Supreme Court, and outlined its relations to the state courts; created the Departments of State, Treasury, and War (and thus created a parcel of offices for Washington to fill); fixed the salaries of officials ranging from the President down to clerks; found sources of revenue with which to sustain the functions of the new government; and resolved some of the constitutional questions that were left unanswered in 1787. Perhaps the most important of these was the location of the power to remove high officers like the Secretary of State. After many days of discussion,[8] during which at least four major answers to the question were proposed, Congress did the sensible thing by confirming the existence of this power as part of the apparatus of the Presidency. The first "great debate" in the Congress of the United States, which was led and won by James Madison, was as candid, learned, and penetrating as any in the Convention of 1787.

The most significant action of the first session of the first Congress was fully constituent in nature: it honored the unwritten but unequivocal pledge of the Federalists in Massachusetts, South Carolina, New Hampshire, Virginia, and New York to add guarantees of the rights of individuals to the Constitution, as well as to confirm the states in possession of all powers not delegated to the federal government or prohibited to them.⁹ Although almost no one expected Congress to give serious consideration to the many dubious suggestions of the five conventions that had ratified "with recommendations," almost everyone expected it to respond to the widespread complaint about the absence of a bill of rights that would shield citizens and states against the grasp of the new government. At the delicate prompting of Washington and under the masterful prodding of Madison, Congress responded finally, after much discussion and manipulation, with twelve proposals for amending the Constitution under the terms of Article V. These were framed, like the Constitution itself, in plain, frugal, and laconic language that contrasted sharply with the purple prose of the state declarations of rights.

Madison may still have agreed privately with Wilson and Hamilton (who had made the point forcefully in *The Federalist*, number 84)¹⁰ that a declaration of rights was irrelevant in a constitution of delegated powers, but he recognized that the addition of such a declaration could enhance the legitimacy of the new government "without weakening its frame or abridging its usefulness in the judgment of those who are attached to it."¹¹ No one who read the proposed amendments could deny—least of all the angry anti-Federalists like Patrick Henry who had asked for real bread in the form of restrictions on Congress and been given an apparent stone in the form of several hundred colorless words—that Madison and his colleagues had succeeded admirably in their noble and also highly political purpose. The first two of these twelve proposals, which dealt with the troublesome issues of the scale of representation in the House and the compensation of members of Congress, fell mercifully by the wayside on their journey through the state legislatures. The remaining ten, the most important of which defended the ancient rights of persons against Congress and acknowledged the reserved powers of the states, became part of the Constitution December 15, 1791,¹² when the Virginia legislature swallowed its disappointment and added its approval to those of the ten other states, including recently admitted Vermont, that had already ratified. In 1941 the states of Connecticut, Massachusetts, and Georgia celebrated the sesquicentennial of the Bill of Rights by giving their hitherto withheld and unneeded assent.

The redemption of the promises of 1788 helped to perfect the still feeble Union and to reinforce the still dubious Constitution in three ways. In the first place, it was the juiciest carrot—threats of commercial reprisal were the crudest stick —with which to bring the two delinquent states into line.

North Carolina, in which Williamson, Davie, James Iredell, and other zealous Federalists had refused to accept the defeat of 1788, ratified the Constitution in convention at Fayetteville on November 21, 1789, by the comfortable margin of 194–77.[13] Rhode Island, in which the town of Providence went even further than the city of New York had gone in 1788 and voted to secede from the rest of the state, ratified in convention at Newport on May 29, 1790, by the ungracious margin of 34–32.[14] Both states loaded their instruments of ratification with declarations, reservations, and recommendations of amendments, but both appeared to be content with the proposals worked out by Madison and his colleagues—more content, it is plain, than cantankerous Virginia, which finally gave its assent to the Bill of Rights a full eighteen months after Rhode Island. Uncomfortable in growing isolation from the sisters and unmenaced by ravening armies under orders from New York City, Rhode Island and North Carolina found the Bill of Rights a commodious bridge over which to march back into the arms of the Republic. If the whole Republic did not exactly thrill to the news of the accession of Rhode Island, the President of the United States was the perfect gentleman—and the perfect Federalist. As he wrote to Governor Arthur Fenner in acknowledgment of the news of ratification:

> Since the bond of Union is now complete, and we once more consider ourselves as one family, it is much to be hoped that reproaches will cease and prejudices be done away; for we should all remember that we are members of that community upon whose general success depends our particular and individual welfare; and, therefore, if we mean to support the liberty and independence which it has cost us so much blood and treasure to establish, we must drive far away the demon of party spirit and local reproach.[15]

Second, the mere proposal of twelve amendments to the Constitution cut the ground from under those anti-Federalists who were still hoping for a second constitutional convention. Madison suspected and Henry feared that the ratification of some or all of these amendments would smother demands for more radical alterations (such as the requirement of a two-thirds majority in Congress for passing any navigation act) —with the strange result that in Virginia and several other states the Federalists were the chief advocates of the Bill of Rights and the anti-Federalists the chief opponents. Whether a second convention could ever have been called is to be doubted; that it would have failed to write a more acceptable charter for the nation cannot be doubted at all. James Madison served the Constitution well by agreeing to a line of action in 1789 that put an end to the reckless, largely hopeless campaign that Randolph had launched in his speech of September 10, 1787.

Finally, the redemption of the promises of 1788 did much to hasten acceptance of the Constitution as fundamental law by all those who had opposed it in 1787–1788, whether from fear, doubt, apathy, or ignorance. The process of acceptance had already begun in the popular and legislative elections to the new Congress. Dozens of outspoken anti-Federalists had been put up and a small galaxy elected, of whom Representative Gerry of Massachusetts, Representative Aedanus Burke of South Carolina, and Senators Grayson and R. H. Lee of Virginia were perhaps the brightest stars. It had moved further toward a happy ending with some judicious appointments by President Washington, for example, Jefferson as Secretary of State, Randolph as Attorney General, and General John Lamb, a partisan of George Clinton and strenuous organizer of the forces of anti-Federalism, as collector of customs in the port of New York. And it reached that ending sooner than expected with the adoption of the Bill of Rights. The Constitution was not more than three or four years old when men of all political faiths began to acclaim it gladly. They might argue with one another strenuously, as their political descendants argue today, over the meaning of this or that "plain and simple" clause, but for the Constitution itself —as act of the sovereign people and earthly projection of the higher law—there would hereafter be a virtually universal respect that spilled over into veneration. The way in which the opponents of the Constitution, once they knew they were beaten, rushed to get into the old game under the new rules is one of the most reassuring stories in American political history.* If someone had told William Findley, John Smilie, Robert Whitehill, and John Whitehill of Pennsylvania in 1788 that they would end up sitting in James Wilson's proposed Congress of the United States, they would have laughed bitterly in disbelief. Yet all did sit usefully as politicians who claimed to know and love the Constitution better than he or any other Federalist. The willingness of men as far apart politically as Wilson and the Whitehills to serve the Constitution

* The adoption of new rules for the nation stirred leading men (including several of the Framers) to push for new rules in the states. Georgia (1789), South Carolina (1790), Pennsylvania (1790), Delaware (1792), New Hampshire (1792), and Vermont (1793) all rewrote their constitutions in the aftermath of 1787.

of 1787 is the surest evidence we have of its well-earned legitimacy.

The Framers did not secure the legitimacy of their Constitution by letting other men take over once they had set it in motion. To the contrary, they provided a good deal of the manpower for the government during the first years of its existence. From George Washington in the Presidency down to Jacob Broom in the postmastership in Wilmington, from Gouverneur Morris, minister in Paris, across the map to William Blount, territorial governor of Tennessee, thirty-nine of the Framers did service at one time or another under the Constitution. If a knowledgeable citizen had looked about him in New York in the summer of 1790, for example, he could have counted more than two dozen of these now celebrated men at work for the Union: Washington, Hamilton (Secretary of the Treasury), and Randolph (Attorney General) in the executive branch; Bassett, Butler, Ellsworth, Few, Johnson, King, Langdon, Robert Morris, Read, and Strong in the Senate (Paterson had just resigned in order to succeed Livingston as governor of New Jersey); Baldwin, Carroll, Clymer, Fitzsimons, Gerry, Gilman, Madison, Sherman, and Williamson in the House; and Blair, Rutledge, and Wilson on the newly formed Supreme Court. Over the horizon of space the eye of his imagination might have caught a glimpse of Gouverneur Morris on a special mission to London, Blount tending to his own and the public's business in Knoxville, Bedford and Brearly dispensing justice in the lower courts, and Broom deciphering badly written addresses on letters and packages. Over the horizon of time, if this citizen's talents had included prophecy, he might have seen Dayton joining his old colleagues in the House and rising to be Speaker, Sherman and others (including Dayton) moving from the House to the Senate, Paterson and Blair taking seats on the Supreme Court, Ellsworth becoming Chief Justice in place of a rejected Rutledge, Ingersoll serving as a district attorney, and seven early laggards—Davie, Alexander Martin, Mercer, McHenry, the two Pinckneys, and Spaight—giving in to the importunities of friends and serving as legislators, diplomats, or soldiers. Of all the Framers who lived more than a year after the launching of the new government, only ten—Dickinson, Gorham, Houstoun, Lansing, McClurg, Luther Martin, Mason, Mifflin, Wythe, and Yates—refused, in most instances for compelling reasons, to seek or accept service in the new government of the United States.

Of all those who served, the one who did most to convert the Constitution from word to reality—and to reality as he understood it—was Alexander Hamilton, Secretary of the

Treasury under Washington from September 11, 1789, to January 31, 1795. To Washington himself must go vast credit for serving two reluctant terms as the best of all possible first Presidents. It is not pleasant to imagine the fate of this experiment in continental republicanism if he had stayed at Mt. Vernon and let some other man of less prestige—John Adams or John Hancock or John Jay—try to fill a mistrusted office in pursuit of an unclear mandate. To Madison must go hardly less credit for his four terms (1789–1797) in the House of Representatives. As the chief guide in that first constructive year, as the man who raised the most serious questions about Hamilton's view of constitutional reality, and as the partner of Thomas Jefferson in the struggles that gave birth to the American party system, Madison was a model of the congressman who combines the politician, the constitutionalist, and the statesman in one public-spirited person. And upon other men, too—old hands like Jefferson, Adams, Ellsworth, Jay, Wilson, King, and Langdon and new faces like Fisher Ames, Theodore Sedgwick, James Monroe, and William L. Smith—we may bestow praise for having contributed in their diverse ways to the early development of the Constitution. Yet none of these men, not even the essential Washington, left a more visible mark than the "inexplicable disappointment" of the Convention of 1787 on the nation-sustaining charter that Jefferson and his colleagues inherited in 1801.

Hamilton worked his principal influence upon the Constitution by launching a many-sided program to rescue the finances of the United States (and those of its more enterprising men) from the doldrums and petty squalls of the post-war years. The acknowledgment of the Revolutionary debt, the assumption of the state debts, the funding of all these debts and provision for their reduction, the tapping of old sources of revenue and discovery of new ones, the insistence upon honesty and efficiency in the Department of the Treasury, the creation of the Bank of the United States, and above all the establishment of the public credit of a shaky and virtually friendless government—these were the brightest pages in a record of achievement in the field of public finance that no other American has ever come close to matching. In all these matters he had the support, so necessary to his high purposes, of the large-minded Washington, who was never his dupe and often his "aegis";[16] and in most he earned the enmity, so galling to his eager spirit, of the tormented Madison, with whom he had broken forever by 1792, and the worried Jefferson, with whom he had never enjoyed more than respectfully formal relations.

If Madison was tormented and Jefferson worried by Hamilton's reports to Congress and his influence upon the President, it was in large part because his proposals—wrongheaded enough, in their opinion, simply as a program for economic development—also called for a reading of the Constitution and that the one had backed away from in confusion and the other had never entertained at all. The Bank of the United States, the rock of the Hamiltonian scheme, was a mischievous instrument of national policy because it promised to line the pockets of the few at the expense of the many; it was also mischievous because its incorporation could be justified only on an interpretation of the authority of Congress that, in the words of the Madison of 1791, leveled "all the barriers which limit the power of the general government, and protect those of the state governments." [17] The Bank Act of February 25, 1791, was perhaps the longest step ever taken in the direction of the indulgent Constitution under which we live today, and Hamilton was beyond any doubt the person who forced the step. He came up with his scheme for a national bank to serve a strong government and an expanding economy on December 13, 1790; he kept after his friends in Congress so relentlessly, and supplied them with ammunition to fire back at Madison so lavishly, that he won a nearly 2–1 majority in the House and 3–1 in the Senate for the bill incorporating the bank; and then, learning that Madison, Jefferson, and Randolph were pressing Washington to veto the bill, he produced the famous Opinion on the Constitutionality of the Bank and persuaded the President to take an "enlarged view" of the powers of Congress.[18] He did all this, as he did his countless zestful deeds as the driving force in the domestic affairs of the young Republic, without weakening the hold of the Constitution on the allegiance of men in every walk of life and every part of the Republic. Neither the restrictive opinion of Secretary of State Jefferson about Hamilton's bank in 1791 nor the defiant campaign of the Whisky Rebels against Hamilton's excise tax in 1794 was aimed at the Constitution itself—only at the "unconstitutional" exploits of the "King of the Feds." To Hamilton and his friends the Constitution was a charter of national supremacy to be "construed liberally in advancement of the public good." To Jefferson, Madison, and theirs it was a charter of true federalism to be construed narrowly in defense of the rights of states and individuals. To all it was a sheltering oak, a bright shield, a compendium of wise instructions that had only to be read correctly in order to assure freedom and prosperity for every American who deserved them.

Although as Secretary of the Treasury, even the most wide-ranging and officious in history, Hamilton could not expect to have the influence on foreign policy that he had in domestic affairs, in this field, too, he had his victories, and one consequence of them was yet another reading of the Constitution that drove Jefferson and Madison to the brink of political despair—without, however, weakening their dedication to the Constitution. The greatest of these victories took place in early 1793, when a renewal of the long war between France and Great Britain forced the United States to adopt a posture of strict neutrality. This, in turn, raised the kind of constitutional question that no one seems to have anticipated in 1787: which branch of the government, President or Congress has authority to make a declaration of American neutrality in a foreign war? Men of all shades of opinion, Jefferson as well as Hamilton, agreed that such a declaration should be made, but they could not agree, thanks to political animosities and the silence of the Constitution, on how to make it. To Jefferson the only possible answer was Congress: since it alone had the power to declare that the Republic was at war, it alone must have the power to declare that the Republic was not.[19] To Hamilton, on the contrary, the only possible answer was the President: since the conduct of diplomacy had always and everywhere been the business of executives, the officer in whom the "executive power" was "vested" must act for the nation.[20]

Washington, who was faced with the two-edged situation of a war that had just erupted and a Congress that had just left for home, behaved exactly like Washington: he "consulted much, pondered much, resolved slowly," and, in the end, "resolved surely" in favor of Hamilton's expansive view of Article II.[21] Out of a series of intense sessions with his Cabinet, in one of which Hamilton and Jefferson argued the constitutional question face to face,[22] came the famous proclamation of April 22, 1793.[23] Except for the fact that the President had tried to soothe Jefferson by declaring American neutrality without actually using the prickly word, it was all that Hamilton, the expounder of a bold Constitution, could have asked for. The events of 1793, which were a gratifying victory for Hamilton as politician and constitutionalist, were a consequential victory for the United States as a continental republic. Thanks to the steadfast Washington and the men around him, including both Hamilton and Jefferson, the Presidency emerged from this ordeal as a tempered instrument of national policy, the Constitution as a tested charter of popular government, and the Republic as a nation that could at last take care of itself amidst the clash of mighty powers.

Hamilton's service to the Constitution in this crisis was literary as well as political. Irritated by the cries of "unconstitutionality" that greeted Washington's action, he took up his pen, as he so often did at such moments, and wrote a series of sharp letters over the pseudonym Pacificus in defense of both the propriety and constitutionality of this declaration of neutrality.[24] Jefferson, who had no stomach for a literary duel with Hamilton, persuaded Madison to write five articles as Helvidius, four of which dealt with the constitutional question and branded the interpretation of Pacificus as "vicious in theory." [25] To such a violent disagreement had the sharpening zeal of the Secretary of the Treasury and the growing doubts of the Representative from Virginia brought these two old comrades of Princeton, Philadelphia, and New York.

I do not mean to draw a picture of Hamilton as a policymaker and constitutionalist who managed everyone to death and swept everything before him. While he was the liveliest figure in the early years, there were plenty of other first-rate men, including his old chief Washington and his old mentor Robert Morris, who lent their talents and reputations to the cause. While he was professor of constitutional law to all the Federalists from Washington and Jay to Ames and King, these men were already disposed to read the Constitution "liberally in advancement of the public good." And while he got his way, not without a contest, as stabilizer of public finance, he most certainly did not get it as director of economic and social development. The Report on Manufactures of December 5, 1791,[26] a daring set of recommendations for encouraging the growth of commerce and industry under the benevolent leadership of the national government, was too visionary for his friends and too fearsome for his enemies. It would be many generations before Americans would be ready to accept—and then somewhat shamefacedly—the advanced opinions about the role of government that Hamilton expressed so confidently in this celebrated report.

Still, if Hamilton was only one of a team of excellent men who brought the Constitution to life in these first shaky years, he was second only to Washington in presence and second to no one in creative genius. It was almost as if, recognizing how little he had helped in writing the rules of the game in Philadelphia, he had decided to atone for his weak performance by showing what remarkable things forceful men could do with these rules. If many key words in the Constitution were considerably less vague in 1795 than they had been in 1787, that is because Hamilton seized them and put them to work for the public good as he understood it. If Madison and Jefferson refused to accept Hamilton's views and proposed to replace them with their own at the earliest opportunity, that, according to their rules, was their undoubted right. The fact of most consequence is that Jefferson and his friends proposed to undo the damage Hamilton had done not by scrapping the Constitution or even loading it with crippling amendments, but by taking it over legally and then governing fairly in accord with their more restricted views. Interpretation of the Constitution was to be the juiciest bone of contention in American politics for generations to come. The Constitution itself, already well on the way to apotheosis, was no longer at issue, and thus no longer in danger of being abandoned or altered. Not even in 1798–1799, when the Federalists went beyond the fringe of political decency with the Alien and Sedition Acts, and Jefferson and Madison responded with those mischievous expressions of anti-nationalism, the Virginia and Kentucky Resolutions,[27] did men suggest seriously that another convention review the decisions of 1787.

Although the men of the opposition do not seem to have known what they were doing until the process was irreversibly under way—they had, let us remember, no models to copy—they engaged in their own act of political creation during these turbulent years. While the new Federalists of the 1790's (as distinguished from the old Federalists of 1788 and the even older ones of the mid-1780's) behaved more and more like a party while insisting that they were nothing of the sort, the men around Jefferson slowly forged an instrument, the Democratic-Republican party, for winning control of the government peacefully and then exercising it purposefully. It is hard to say which national election first found Republicans contesting openly with Federalists for partisan command of the new government, but certainly by 1800 the politicians and voters who supported Jefferson were a party in every meaningful sense of the word—as were also, despite the state of demoralized confusion brought on by Hamilton's gratuitous feud with Adams, those politicians and voters who fought to keep Jefferson out of the Presidency. Because of the traditional "court-country" cleavage in American politics, the impact of Hamilton's financial program, the suspicions entertained by many southern planters of the mercantile interests of the North, the sharpening differences of opinion about the meaning of the Constitution,* the Republicans were a tendency in the country from the beginning, an identifiable group in Congress in 1792, a governmental party in

---

* Contrary to the expectations of many of the Framers, the one line that was not drawn in this period (and, indeed, has never been drawn in American politics) was between large states and small.

1795, an election-fighting alliance in 1796, and an organization functioning on a national scale in 1800. Outwitted by Hamilton and badgered by Adams, the Republicans spawned politicians by the dozen to destroy their power. Jefferson, whether reluctant as in 1794–1795 or eager as in 1797–1800, was the kind of leader around whom men rally for battle. Madison, whose critical role in the political maneuvers of the first decade is just now coming to be appreciated, was the skillful architect of the opposition party in Congress. Men like Albert Gallatin and William Branch Giles wrung the last ounce of partisan usefulness out of the controversial Jay's Treaty of 1795–1796; men like Wilson Cary Nicholas and John Breckinridge did the same with the Alien and Sedition Acts of 1798; and John Beckley, Aaron Burr, George Clinton, James Monroe, and John Francis Mercer worked shrewdly to build a scatter of republican societies and other local groups into the organization that smashed the Federalists in the election of 1800.

The line between Federalists and Republicans in 1800 was not, be it noted, a direct projection of the line between Federalists and anti-Federalists in 1787–1788. The fact that such committed Framers as Baldwin, Langdon, Madison, Mifflin, Charles Pinckney, and Spaight became active Republicans should warn us against jumping to the easy conclusion in this matter. At the same time, we should take note that the acknowledged Federalists among the surviving Framers outnumbered the acknowledged Republicans by two to one.

The election of 1800 was a historic event in the life of the Constitution for at least four reasons. In the first place, it introduced a piece of equipment into the American constitutional system for which the Constitution itself had made no provision. The Framers refused stubbornly in 1787 to think about organized political parties as both dynamic and stabilizing elements of the constitutional process, and it remained for the savage clash of interests in the 1790's to convince most men—although never Washington[28]—that the Constitution could not function effectively without the help of such machinery. Even as it was being constructed, this machinery began to work vast influence on the Constitution itself. To the Republicans and Federalists of 1796–1800 must go the blame or credit for having frustrated some of the fondest hopes of the Framers, for their activities altered the ingenious system for electing a President almost beyond recognition.

Second, the election of 1800 was a happy sign of the early maturity of this new system of government and thus of the dedication of most Americans to the Constitution. The voluntary retirement of Washington from the Presidency in March,

1797, was a splendid demonstration of the virtues of republican government; the involuntary retirement of Adams in March, 1801, was, if anything, an even more splendid demonstration. That an election on a continental scale could be fought so fiercely without inviting the losers to appeal the verdict on the field of battle was a startling lesson to the world at large—or at least to that part of it which took America seriously. Adams may have been ungracious in transferring power to Jefferson, but the significant fact is that the transfer took place in response to the stated will of a majority of the electorate, and that the public business of the United States went forward without interruption.

It did more than that: it went forward in much the same direction that the Federalists had been traveling for twelve years. In spite of all his complaints about the naughty deeds of Hamilton, Adams, and even the venerated Washington, Jefferson seems to have been conscious of no hypocrisy when he stood up on March 4, 1801, and expressed his delight over inheriting a "republican government . . . in the full tide of successful experiment";[29] and in disregard of the expectations of his followers that he would dismantle the Hamiltonian structure, he left it virtually intact. He accepted the Constitution gratefully, struck for peripheral reforms that were long overdue, and failed, except in the repeal of the ill-timed Judiciary Act of 1801 and repudiation of the ill-considered Sedition Act, to make any real dent in the Federalist legacy. Before his two terms were over, the author of the Kentucky Resolutions was forced to behave like a Hamiltonian by purchasing the Louisiana Territory in 1803 and jamming through the Embargo Act in 1807. Before the faithful successor, James Madison, was finished with his own two terms, he had exhumed the Madison of 1787, and, to the disgust of doctrinaire Republicans like John Randolph, had "out-Hamiltoned Alexander Hamilton" by endorsing the movement to incorporate the Second Bank of the United States.[30] Both Jefferson and Madison, once they had come to power, proved beyond a doubt that if the United States were to be a true nation, it would have to be served by a truly national government. Although neither man would admit it to the end of his long life, they also proved that an "enlarged view" of the Constitution—if not the fully inflated view for which Hamilton had contended—was both an essential instrument and a faithful expression of American nationhood.

Finally, the election of 1800 left an exasperating legacy for Jefferson and his political heirs to contemplate in the sturdily Federalist person of Chief Justice John Marshall. A series of fortuitous events—the retirement of an ailing Ellsworth, the reluctance of a battered Jay to be named (or rather re-named) to succeed him, the refusal of a stubborn Adams to promote William Paterson, the availability of a moderately successful lawyer-politician who was both a Federalist and a Virginian—combined to open the way to Marshall, who took his seat February 4, 1801, and died in it July 6, 1835. His celebrated tenure did for the hitherto sleepy Court what Washington had done for the Presidency and men like Madison had done for Congress. By the time Marshall was gathered still unyielding to his fathers, the Court was a fully legitimate, fully operational organ of republican government, and even his detractors had to admit privately that his decisions in defense of national supremacy (*Gibbons* v. *Ogden*), broad construction (*McCulloch* v. *Maryland*), and private property (*Fletcher* v. *Peck*) were brilliantly executed maneuvers in be-half of a supposedly discredited view of the Constitution.[31] Marshall's chief contribution to the Constitution for which he had fought in the Virginia convention of 1788 was the doc-trine of judicial review, toward which his friends among the Framers had been groping in Philadelphia and of which his friend Alexander Hamilton had first spoken pointedly in *The Federalist,* number 78. By asserting the power of the Court to ignore and thus invalidate laws judged to be unconstitutional, he put the last stone in place in the foundation of 1787. When Marshall had finished reading his opinion in *Marbury* v. *Madison* on February 24, 1803,[32] the Grand Convention stood at last adjourned.

# 16 THE LAST YEARS OF THE FRAMERS

*Whatever may be the judgment pronounced on the competency of the architects of the Constitution, or whatever may be the destiny of the edifice prepared by them, I feel it a duty to express my profound and solemn conviction . . . that there never was an assembly of men, charged with a great and arduous trust, who were more pure in their motives, or more exclusive or anxiously devoted to the object committed to them.*

JAMES MADISON, Last of the Framers, in a "sketch never finished" of 1835 or 1836[1]

AMERICANS who think of the Convention as an assembly of demigods, like those who expect heroes to live happily ever after, would do well not to look too closely at the lives of the Framers in the years that followed the Great Happening of 1787. Although many of them prospered in estate and influence along with the nation they had helped to build, and then went to their graves with feelings of a life well lived and an esteem truly earned, a surprising number fell victims to misfortune, shame, and even violence. When ten of an elite group of fifty-five come to financial grief or fall over the edge into bankruptcy, a half-dozen suffer for years in shattered health, two die in duels, one is poisoned by a greedy heir, one disappears without a trace, one becomes a memorable drunkard, one goes mad, and two dabble in treason, there is reason to wonder whether the gods of politics are not harder on persons who are nominated as half-gods than on those who are classed as ordinary men.

Even the Framers who invested their money wisely, enjoyed good health, and kept their wits sharp and records clean were not accorded, while they lived, the kind of veneration that is assumed to be the prerogative of founding fathers. Few of them died, as did Franklin and Washington, legendary figures mourned by all but a handful of cranks or rascals; few of them felt, as did the long-lived King and Madison in their last years, that they had been brothers in the noblest fraternity of statesmen ever assembled to fix the destiny of a great people. The first years under the Constitution were a time of passion, and too many of the Framers were too active in the political wars over assumption, the Bank, Jay's Treaty, and the Sedition Act to invite or expect veneration. Too many, for that matter, were leaders in opposing camps, and it would have been asking a great deal of the human spirit for Hamilton to have continued to entertain brotherly feelings about Madison, Madison about Wilson, Wilson about Langdon, and Langdon about the Morrises. The Constitution did not settle any of the outstanding social issues that had been agitating the young Republic since 1776; it set new rules for the contestants and moved the arena of combat to somewhat higher and firmer ground. The fight went on as vigorously as before, and into this fight most of the Framers entered with a will. The cult of the Constitution, whose rites were being celebrated in almost every part of the country before 1801, did not spawn the associated cult of the authors of the Constitution until many years after the last of them had died. Since few citizens of the young Republic were driven to argue over the meaning of the Declaration of Independence, it was generally considered a more noble achievement to have been a Signer of 1776 than a Framer of 1787. Jefferson and Adams, as one would expect of patriots who had been Signers but not Framers, did nothing to disabuse their large followings of the assumption that the men of 1776 had shaken the earth while the men of 1787 had only helped to settle the dust.

Whatever might be thought of the Convention by men who had not been there, the Framers themselves, with a few crabbed exceptions, were proud of the part they had played at this fateful turn in the history of freedom. They knew how far they had traveled in search of success and how near they had come to failure; they also knew that the labors of statesmen, like those of husbandmen, are best judged by persons who are nourished by the fruits of these labors. And those who lived on to be very old men therefore had every cause to rejoice—as rejoice they did in a becoming manner—that they had been charged, in Madison's own words, "with a great and arduous trust," and had honored it by writing a Constitution that all parties and interests could join in admiring and obeying.

By March 4, 1801, when Jefferson and his colleagues converted the Constitution into a national monument by accepting its mandate gratefully and acknowledging its glories cheerfully, seventeen of the fifty-five Framers were already beyond caring. Six of this number had passed from the scene even before Hamilton could lay his hand upon their charter and prove to a doubting public that it hid more seeds of power within its austere shell than either Madison or Wilson had imagined. Houston of New Jersey, whom mortal illness had driven from the Convention after only a week of quiet service, died of tuberculosis on his way south in search of rest in August, 1788. Pierce of Georgia, who had hoped to pick his way out of the morass of bankruptcy with the aid of a federal post in Savannah, died in that city in December, 1789. The faithful Brearly, the long-suffering Franklin, the once quixotic Livingston, and the amiable Jenifer all followed Houston and Pierce to the grave in 1790. Brearly had been the only one of this number to accept office under the Constitution, and his tenure as a district judge was so undemanding that he could give most of his public energies to the Cincinnati, the Masons, and the Episcopal church.

The next two men to die, the complete Virginian and the complete Yankee, went almost as quietly as Brearly or Jenifer. The Virginian was George Mason, who showed what he thought of public life in general and of the Constitution in particular by refusing to accept an appointment to the Senate proffered by Governor Beverley Randolph in 1790, and who lived on in cherished privacy until October, 1792, with his ample wealth, his three hundred slaves, and his unfair share of aches and pains. Just before his death he had the grim satisfaction (which was the sort he enjoyed) of telling Jefferson that Hamilton's activities in behalf of the "moneyed interests" in the North had made a harsh reality of his suspicions of 1787.[2] As to the complete Yankee, Roger Sherman of Connecticut, he lived the last four years of his life as he had lived ever since moving to Connecticut as a young man: serving faithfully in public office and managing to scrape along—in this period just barely—on the salary that went with it. After two useful years as a member of the House of Representatives, he succeeded William Samuel Johnson in the Senate in 1791, voted consistently if not blindly for the Federalist program, and died in New Haven in July, 1793, a much honored symbol of the continuity of Connecticut history.

The deaths of Daniel Carroll in 1796 and George Read in 1798 were serene in manner and untarnished in circumstance. Each served a stint as a dedicated Federalist in Congress, and then returned home—Carroll as commissioner to lay out the boundaries of the District of Columbia, Read as chief justice of Delaware—to pass his last few years among loving friends and admiring neighbors. The deaths of Nathaniel Gorham and James Wilson, however, were pitiful

reminders of the fate that can befall men of overextended
ambitions in an underdeveloped economy. The eminent chairman of the committee of the whole died of a stroke at home
in Charlestown, Massachusetts, in 1796, the eminent warrior
for large-state nationalism of a stroke in a tavern in Edenton,
North Carolina, in 1798. Both men, sad to tell, were financial
wrecks. Gorham had contracted to purchase an immense
stretch of land in the Genesee country in certain depreciated
securities, and had come to grief when these securities, which
he was still assembling in 1790, suddenly quadrupled in value
in the warm air of Hamilton's funding system. Wilson had
gone on spreading himself too thinly across the landscape of
investment, and death found him in Edenton rather than
Philadelphia because some of his northern creditors saw
nothing improper in clapping a justice of the Supreme Court
of the United States into jail. One of Wilson's southern creditors had managed to catch up with him in Edenton, and only
the most abject pleading had gained his release. The creditor
was—so much for the fraternal spirit of the Framers—Pierce
Butler of South Carolina. The sum owed him—at least on
paper—was $197,000.

The manner and timing of the departure of George Washington on December 14, 1799, are too well known to bear
repeating in these pages. Suffice it to say that he had savored
his few remaining years at Mt. Vernon as a retired Cincinnatus, that he had been willing to leave the plow once again in
1798–1799 at his country's call (which did not, however, become too insistent), and that he might easily have lived on
another ten or fifteen years if his doctors had not been victims of the mania of the age for taking a pint of blood from
men with sore throats. Washington's death was the signal for
a vast outpouring of public grief, and most eulogists remembered to say a few admiring words about his services as president of the Convention of 1787. Within a year he was joined
in death—if not in every instance in heaven—by four more
Framers: John Rutledge, whose excited opposition to Jay's
Treaty had cost him the Chief Justiceship of the United
States in 1795, and who ended his magnificent life a poor and
unhinged man; John Blair, who had broken his silence of
Philadelphia and Richmond to say a few words as a justice of
the Supreme Court; Thomas Mifflin, who had lived too lavishly as three-time governor of Pennsylvania (1790–1799),
and who died, like many another man of his style and standing, on the run from a nagging creditor; and William Blount
—that "character strongly marked for integrity and honor"
—whose conspiratorial efforts to bring about a British and
Indian attack on Spanish Florida and Louisiana had earned

him expulsion from the Senate by a vote of 25–1 on July 8, 1797. Like many a later American politician who has been dealt with severely in the nation's capital, Blount found solace in the support of friends and neighbors at home. While under the shadow of an impeachment by the House of Representatives in 1798, he was elected to the state senate in Tennessee, then chosen by his fellow senators to be their presiding officer. There is no telling what the audacious Blount might have salvaged from his blighted political and financial fortunes if a stroke had not carried him off in March of 1800.

Four of the next six Framers to depart the world did so under circumstances so tragic that one wonders if some curse had been laid upon the Convention by the defeated gods of anarchy. The obstinate Yates and the stubborn Paterson went quietly enough—the former at home in Schenectady in 1801 after eight years of service as chief justice of New York (and an ill-advised attempt, with Hamilton's support, to win the governorship from Clinton in 1789), the latter at his daughter's home in Albany in 1806 after thirteen years of service as justice of the Supreme Court of the United States. To Spaight of North Carolina, Hamilton of New York, and Wythe of Virginia, however, death came in cruel guise. The eagerly Republican Spaight, who had been a governor, a Congressman, and a state senator during his last years, died in 1802 under the fire of a political enemy in a duel that he seems deliberately to have provoked. The zealously Federalist Hamilton, who spent his last years on a "darkling plain" between a public world that had lost its use for him and a private world that enlisted only a fraction of his enormous talents, died in 1804 under the fire of a political enemy, Aaron Burr, in a duel that he certainly had done nothing to avoid. The venerable Chancellor Wythe, who had removed to Richmond in 1790 to teach law privately to yet another generation of Virginians (including Henry Clay), fell an agonized victim in 1806 to a dose of arsenic that had been introduced —some say accidentally, others say by design—into his morning coffee (or evening strawberries) by a ne'er-do-well great-nephew. The poison is thought to have been intended for a servant for whom Wythe had made provision in his will, but somehow it also ended inside the master.[8]

Robert Morris, the last of this unhappy quartet, died a broken man in 1806 in a small house in Philadelphia owned by his wife and paid for by Gouverneur Morris. Ruined by speculations in land that one may describe as utterly fantastic, the sometime Superintendent of Continental Finance, Senator from Pennsylvania (1789–1795), and "richest man in the world" had spent three and a half miserable years in debtors' prison, had been released only after the providential passage of the Bankruptcy Act of 1800, and had found a friend in need in the fiercely loyal person of his old lieutenant, who opened wide his home, his purse, and his heart. No one will ever know for certain how many varieties of debt Morris left unpaid at the time of his death; the total is thought to have been more than three million dollars.

Three Framers died in 1807: Ellsworth of Connecticut, who had retired to his farm in Windsor in 1801 to dabble in snuff, theology, scientific agriculture, and disunionist mysteries after a decade of progressively less effective service as senator, Chief Justice, and special envoy to France; Alexander Martin of North Carolina, who had served erratic, undistinguished stints in the upper houses of both state and nation; and Baldwin of Georgia, who had earned a reputation as one of the steadiest of Jefferson's followers during ten years in the House and eight in the Senate. John Dickinson, like Martin and Baldwin an eminent patron of higher education, came to the end of his long ride in 1808, and two years later his colleague in the delegation from Delaware, Jacob Broom, exchanged obscurity for oblivion. Neither Dickinson nor Broom had served the new government in any important capacity, the former because he had had enough of the strains and pains of public life in the years between the Stamp Act Congress and the Convention, the latter because his ambition had never taken him, except for his one unaccountable sally to Phi'adelphia in 1787, beyond the boundaries of comforting Wilmington.

The demise of Broom marks the half-way point in this procession of the elite of 1787 to the grave—and beyond the grave to a collective immortality that has rescued even his name from oblivion. Fitzsimons in 1811, Bedford in 1812, Clymer and Randolph in 1813, Gilman and Gerry in 1814, Bassett in 1815, McHenry and Gouverneur Morris in 1816, Langdon, Williamson, Strong, and Johnson in 1819, Davie in 1820—so ran the roll call of death in the next decade. Most of these men lived generally happy lives: the exceptions were Thomas Fitzsimons, who was almost dragged under financially along with Robert Morris in 1805; James McHenry, whose tenure as Secretary of War under Adams was a classic instance of too small a man in too large a job under too many pressures; Edmund Randolph, whose tenure as successor to Jefferson as Washington's Secretary of State was so calamitous that he was shipped home to Richmond (there to earn even more lumps as senior counsel for Aaron Burr in the treason trial of 1807); and William Samuel Johnson, who gave up the presidency of Columbia because of failing health in 1800, and then survived for nineteen palsied years in Stratford.

Gunning Bedford had the best of both possible worlds by living at home in Delaware and serving as a federal judge, an undemanding post he relinquished only in death, while George Clymer, Richard Bassett, Hugh Williamson, and William R. Davie all retreated sooner or later into private worlds full of affection and achievement. Clymer retired voluntarily from public life in 1796 to devote himself to the charitable and cultural pursuits of the Philadelphia gentleman; Bassett retired under duress in 1801, having stood by helplessly while the victorious Republicans wiped out his position as one of the "midnight judges," and consoled himself with displays of piety and hospitality; and Williamson carried on one of the solid traditions of the Framers by marrying a wealthy lady. He moved to New York in 1793 to be near her family, and spent twenty-five delightful years in pursuit of his mistresses, the goddesses of astronomy, medicine, and history. Williamson's friend and colleague Davie also left North Carolina for a more polished part of the country. Finding himself an ever lonelier man in an ever more Republican state, this unabashed Federalist, whom President Adams had dispatched as special envoy to France in 1799 along with Chief Justice Ellsworth, moved to a plantation in South Carolina in 1805 and spent the last years cultivating his crops and his friends. He is not entirely forgotten even today in North Carolina, however, for he is celebrated in some circles as the "father" of the state university.

The last years of the men from New Hampshire were rather more productive than the hesitant weeks of service they had rendered in 1787. John Langdon put in two full terms as an independent Federalist senator (and, in 1789–1791 and 1792–1794, as president pro tempore of that "assembly of notables"), then went home to New Hampshire to enjoy life as first citizen of the state, a position in which he was left to grow old contentedly by the death of General Sullivan in 1795. Having already signaled his independence by voting more and more often with the rising Republicans in the Senate, he now proved it beyond a doubt by taking over leadership of the party in the state. Although President Jefferson offered him a post in his Cabinet, Langdon preferred the more easily manipulated ways of New Hampshire politics. At the time of his retirement in 1812 he had served yet another two years (1803–1805) as speaker of the legislature, yet another six (1805–1809, 1810–1812) as governor. Nicholas

Gilman, perhaps on Langdon's cue, also switched from Federalism to Republicanism after the victory of Jefferson, and spent his last years (1805–1814) as a senator in Washington. Always in just a bit over his head in the company of men like Langdon and Madison, and never quite aware of the fact, Gilman probably got more pure enjoyment out of his reputation as a Framer than any other of his fifty-four colleagues.

Those two remarkable sons of Massachusetts, Caleb Strong and Elbridge Gerry, spent most of their last years in the political ring pounding each other into insensibility. Strong, a staunch supporter of Washington and Hamilton in the Senate between 1789 and 1796, beat Gerry in the annual race for the governorship of the state four times in a row (1800–1803), went right on winning against other Republicans until felled by James Sullivan in 1807, beat Gerry once again in 1812, and retired in glory to Northampton in 1816. By refusing to surrender control of the state militia to the national government in the unpopular War of 1812, and by having more than a governor and Framer should have had to do with the ill-conceived Hartford Convention of 1814–1815, Strong had proved forcefully that New England, too, could play the states-rights game. Gerry, for his part, did an admirable stint as an independent Federalist in the House of Representatives (1789–1793), began to pass over into the Republican party sometime around 1796, made a dreadful hash of his one excursion into diplomacy (the infamous XYZ affair against Talleyrand in 1797–1798), and then ran and ran for the governorship of Massachusetts until finally elected in 1810. In 1812 the Republicans in Massachusetts made a brazen attempt to hold on to power by rearranging the election districts altogether grotesquely in their favor. The result of their labors was the beast still known as the "gerrymander," and the result of a stiff reaction on the part of several thousand voters was the defeat of Gerry by Strong. One of the few outspoken supporters in New England of "Mr. Madison's War," Gerry was placed on the ticket in Madison's bid for reelection in 1812. Although he could not carry Massachusetts, he earned his old rival's admiration through his efforts in the campaign. Gerry, like Madison's first Vice-President, the celebrated George Clinton, died in office twiddling his thumbs.

Of all the Framers who lived on for many years after 1787, none had a more exciting and satisfying life than that unique cross between beaver and butterfly, Gouverneur Morris. Shortly after the Convention he realized a dream of his youth by purchasing the manor in the Bronx that fate had denied him as an inheritance, then departed for ten years of business, travel, diplomacy, love-making, and adventure in Europe that left even his friend Hamilton gasping with envy. One had to admire a one-legged man who could win the affections of Adelaide de Flahaut; one had to respect a diplomat who could hang on in Paris throughout the Terror, especially when he had been the key figure in a plot to rescue Louis XVI from the Tuileries. The leading citizens of New York showed what they thought of his mind and presence by inviting him to be their orator upon the death of Washington (and also, thereafter, upon the deaths of Hamilton and George Clinton), and the Federalists in the state legislature showed what they thought by electing him to the Senate. Swept under in 1802 by the tide of Republicanism, Morris spent the last years of his life adding to his reputation as a man of parts by building a new and gracious mansion at Morrisania, offering the hand of kindness to Robert Morris, managing his large landholdings in upstate New York, marrying a hapless but attractive member of Virginia's first family (Anne Cary Randolph), and doing yeoman service as chairman of the commission charged with developing the Erie Canal. Like almost every other Federalist who lived on into the years of Thomas Jefferson, this nationalist of 1776 and 1787 lost much of his faith in the Union just when the Union needed him most. Still, he had served the cause magnificently in those earlier times, and his death in 1816 brought sorrow to the Framers who survived him.

By the time of the fortieth anniversary of the signing of the Constitution, September 17, 1827, only four Framers—the modest Few and Houstoun, the contrary Lansing, and the preeminent Madison—were left alive to look back in awe at the Great Happening. Of the nine to depart the world in the benign climate of the Era of Good Feelings or in the gathering storm that marked its appointed end, all but one or two had cause to think that their lives had been worthwhile.

John Francis Mercer, to the end a man with a style of his own, died in August, 1821, on a visit to Philadelphia in search of more sophisticated medical advice than was available in rural Maryland. A vociferous anti-Hamilton Congressman in 1791–1794 and an unpredictable Republican governor of Maryland in 1801–1803, Mercer had moved into the political wilderness in his last years by breaking with both Jefferson and Madison on issues of foreign policy. His truculent colleague Luther Martin went on for another five years, and it would have been better for him if he had died along with Mercer. At the time of his death he was a destitute, half-paralyzed alcoholic who had found an unusual place of refuge in the home of Aaron Burr in New York. Attorney general of Maryland from 1778 to 1805 and again from 1818 to 1822, Martin had been the passionate defender of such notable clients as Justice Samuel Chase (who, as a reward for his zeal in harrying Jeffersonian editors, was impeached by the Republican-dominated House of Representatives in 1804), Burr (in the treason trial of 1807), and the state of Maryland (in *McCulloch* v. *Maryland*, 1819), so passionate indeed in the second of these controversies that Jefferson described him irritably as "this unprincipled and impudent federal bull-dog." [4] Aaron Burr, pleasant to record, had not been the only person to come to the aid of this monumental yet somehow appealing misfit. Between 1821 and 1823 the members of the Maryland bar were taxed five dollars a head, in most instances willingly, for his support—an act of public charity without parallel in American legal history. Burr, uncharacteristically loyal even beyond the end to a man who had defended him and adored his Theodosia, did a last service to Martin by burying him in Trinity churchyard at the head of Wall Street, where he rests in dust not far from one of the two men whom neither of them could abide, Colonel Hamilton.

The three surviving members of the delegation from South Carolina all died in this period—Pierce Butler in 1822, Charles Pinckney in 1824, and C. C. Pinckney in 1825. Except for two independent stints in the Senate (1789–1796, 1803–1804) and several years as a director of the Bank of the United States, Butler had preferred to live the good life of the adopted southerner of impeccable lineage, excellent connections, large wealth, and unassailable prestige. Except for a disastrous experience in diplomacy (the XYZ affair) and a call to the colors as major general in the crisis of 1798–1800, the elder Pinckney, too, had given most of his time to business, planting, charity, and, whenever he felt up to it, a law practice both interesting and rewarding. In the years of Washington, public office sought him unsuccessfully, as he spurned, in succession, command of the army, a position on the Supreme Court, the Secretaryship of War, and the Secretaryship of State; while in the years of Jefferson and Madison the situation was exactly reversed, as he ran for Vice-President in 1800 and President in 1804 and 1808 in the increasingly hopeless cause of Federalism.

Charles Pinckney, on the other hand, could never get enough of the excitement of public life. A Federalist governor of South Carolina for several terms in the 1790's, he threw in his political fortunes with Jefferson in the aftermath of Jay's Treaty. He was senator in 1798–1801, minister to Spain in 1801–1805 (a sticky time, because of the festering problem of Florida), governor and legislator off and on in South Carolina in the decade that followed, and a loud opponent of the Missouri Compromise as a Congressman in 1819–1821. To the end of his life he was loved by the small farmers of South Carolina for his radically democratic views, despised by the Federalists of Charleston as "Blackguard Charlie" for his political apostasy or "Constitution Charlie" for his self-inflated opinion of his role in 1787, and scorned by Madison for continuing to falsify his age and for grossly exaggerating this role.

Three of the least important Framers also died in this period—Jared Ingersoll in 1822, James McClurg in 1823, and Jonathan Dayton in 1824. Ingersoll had divided his respected energies among service to his city as judge and councilor, service to his state as attorney general (1790–1799, 1811–1817), and practice as the kind of lawyer to whom a merchant as shrewd as Stephen Girard was happy to hand his business. Two of his major efforts were directed to notable losing causes: for the state of Georgia, and in direct combat with Randolph, in *Chisholm* v. *Georgia;* for an outraged group of Virginians, and in direct combat with Hamilton, in *Hylton* v. *United States.*[5] McClurg, who probably never did learn why he had been sent to Philadelphia, had continued his eminent practice of medicine almost to the day of his death, and had put at least one toe back into the murky water of public life by serving briefly as a member of the governor's council and a director of the Bank of the United States. Dayton, after periods of service as a leading Federalist in both the House (1791–1799) and Senate (1799–1805), had let his mutually sustaining urges for wealth and adventure run roughshod over his judgment in 1806, when only a providential illness kept him from journeying down the Ohio to infamy with Aaron Burr. Although he managed to escape the consequences of an indictment for treason, his career in Washington was blighted beyond saving. Dayton, like Blount before him, was still loved at home. He died, sad to relate, of a bad case of "hostmanship," the object of his hospitable exertions being his legendary friend the Marquis de Lafayette. Those who seek a monument to Dayton may gaze upon a fair city in Ohio, whose name reminds us that he once owned 250,000 acres of land in the state.

One of the brightest stars of the galaxy of 1787, Rufus King, rolled on happily and busily until 1827, and went to his grave in the knowledge that hardly anyone had ever wished him ill. Although he withdrew occasionally to his estate on Long Island to refresh his soul and tend his prize cattle, he outdid every other Framer except Madison in the length and variety of his public service: he was an intensely pro-Hamilton senator from New York from 1789 to 1796, a successful minister to Great Britain for Washington, Adams, and Jefferson (1796–1803), Federalist candidate for the Vice-Presidency in 1804 and 1808 and for the Presidency in 1816 (the electoral count: James Monroe, 183; Rufus King, 34), and senator once again between 1813–1825. This tenure was made notable by the fact that he was kept on the job by a Republican-dominated state legislature, and also by his opposition—for motives altogether different from those of Charles Pinckney—to the Missouri Compromise. Having served as a delegate to the New York constitutional convention of 1821, he went off once again as minister to Great Britain for John Quincy Adams. An affecting sign of the underlying continuity of American political history through all these years is the conversation of 1824 between Senators King of New York and Thomas Hart Benton of Missouri, who agreed, so Benton recorded thirty years later, that Alexander Hamilton had been indiscreet but not anti-republican in his dazzling performance of June 18, 1787.[6]

One of the dimmest stars, William Few of Georgia, followed King a year later. After four years as senator and three as federal judge, Few had moved to New York in 1799—to escape, according to his own testimony, from "the accumulating evils of fevers and Negro slavery, those enemies to human felicity"[7]—and had lived many worthy years as assemblyman, alderman, worker for prison reform, bank official, and pious Christian. He, in his turn, was followed by the last of the dissenting Framers, Lansing of New York, although the manner and exact timing of his going are still a spine-tingling mystery. Having served his state admirably for a quarter-century as justice (1790–1798), chief justice (1798–1801), chancellor (1801–1814), and regent of the state university—but his nation only offhandedly as presidential elector—Lansing returned to private practice in his native Albany. While on a trip to New York City in December, 1829, to attend to some legal business for Columbia College, he strolled over one evening to the dock at the foot of Cortland Street in order to post some letters on the Albany nightboat and was never seen again. To this day it is not known whether he was a victim of accident or foul play.

This left, according to "the Father of the Constitution," only the father himself.* To Jared Sparks, who pumped him

---

* In fairness to Madison, it ought to be stated clearly that even when all the other Framers had departed he brushed off every attempt to give him principal credit for the success of 1787.

unmercifully for information about the Convention, Madison wrote with wistful pride in 1831:

> It is quite certain that since the death of Col. Few I have been the only living signer of the Constitution of the United States. Of the members who were present and did not sign, and of those who were present part of the time but had left the Convention, it is equally certain that no one has remained since the death of Mr. Lansing who disappeared so mysteriously not very long ago. I happen also to be the sole survivor of those who were members of the Revolutionary Congress prior to the close of the war; as I had been for some years of the members of the convention of 1776 which formed the first constitution for Virginia. Have outlived so many of my contemporaries, I ought not to forget that I may be thought to have outlived myself.[8]

Madison was wrong, as a matter of fact, because Houstoun of Georgia still lived on in comfortable obscurity; but the Virginian's claim to the title of Last of the Framers was soon confirmed when Houstoun died in 1833. When Madison himself died at his home in Orange County on June 26, 1836, in the eighty-sixth year of a remarkable life, men of more than ordinary interest in the history of their country could tell each other solemnly that the Golden Age of American Statesmanship was at an end. Since his retirement in 1817 from the Presidency—an office in which he had known both good days and bad—Madison had busied himself entertaining distinguished visitors in company with the celebrated Dolley, proclaiming the virtues of the Union, chastising the nullifiers and secessionists of South Carolina (and denying that his Virginia Resolutions were a source of their ideas), explaining away some of his own zigs and zags as interpreter of the Constitution, sitting as a revered member of the Virginia constitutional convention of 1829, serving as Jefferson's successor in the rectorship of the University of Virginia, and reminiscing endlessly about the glorious days of 1787.

So long as he served in public office, Madison withstood all pressures and temptations to publish his precious notes (about which, indeed, not more than a few friends had any information),* and not until several years after his death did men learn most of the things we now know about the debates

---

* One type of pressure was applied in 1808 by the rascally Edmond Genêt, son-in-law of George Clinton, who published a distorted extract from the notes of Yates in which Madison was made to look like an advocate of total consolidation.[9]

and maneuvers in Philadelphia.[10] A few bits and pieces of trustworthy evidence, to be sure, did leak out in the early years. Franklin's closing remarks of September 17 appeared in several newspapers with his consent before the end of 1787; Luther Martin disclosed a number of secrets (although he was careful not to name names) during his savage campaign against ratification in 1787–1788; Hamilton's plan of June 18 was published in Pittsfield, Massachusetts, perhaps at the instigation of Yates or Lansing, in 1802; and at least two dozen Framers, including an irritated Washington and an other-minded Madison on one heated occasion in 1796, made public references to speeches or votes or understandings in the Convention.[11] To an extent that must seem astonishing in this age of instant and total publicity, however, the Framers continued to honor their formal and informal rules of secrecy.

In 1819, thanks to the history-minded Secretary of State John Quincy Adams, the journal kept so poorly by Major Jackson (and deposited by Washington in the State Department in 1796) appeared under official sponsorship,* and two years later the notes of Yates, which went no further than July 5, were published in Albany. Although Madison was now revealed to have been far more of a nationalist in the Convention than John Randolph and John Taylor had realized or Rufus King and the Pinckneys had remembered, he still refused to let go of his notes, and merely denied the accuracy of the inferences that unkind men insisted upon reading between the lines of Jackson and Yates. Not until 1836, when his will was opened and read, did his friends learn for certain that he desired publication of "the report as by me"; [13] and not until 1840, after Congress had paid his widow a handsome sum for his papers, did the notes finally see the light of day. It is, surely, one of the intriguing facts of American constitutional history that the people in whose name and by whose power the great charter of 1787 was proclaimed

---

* In this publication Charles Pinckney first went too far even for the patient Madison in claiming primacy, offhandedly but unmistakably, as the principal architect of the Constitution. Having read in the minutes of the Convention that Pinckney had presented a plan of government, and having found no such plan in the records, Adams wrote innocently to Pinckney asking for a copy. Pinckney answered by transmitting what he "believed" to be the plan submitted in 1787, which was in fact, as Madison suspected at once and historians were to prove in later years, a preliminary draft of the committee of detail. Adams, still much too innocent, inserted this fraudulent document at the correct place in the journal, and so began one of the enduring myths of American constitutional history. The kindest judgment that can be made about Pinckney is that his vanity was appalling and his memory even worse.[12]

should have had to wait more than half a century to learn
how it came to be written.

The framers of a constitution die; their constitution, if well
and truly framed, lives on to meet challenges of which they
could not have dreamed. The Constitution of 1787 lives on
today, and seems destined to live until the Republic is no
more, because it was as well and truly framed as any fundamental law of any people in history. The handiwork of an
elite uniquely trained to manipulate the levers of republican
power in behalf of an encompassing public good, the instrument of an elite strenuously concerned to build one nation
where as many as a dozen might have emerged to scramble
for survival or simply to stagnate, the monument of an elite
splendidly privileged to choose among political options and
thus to shape the course of history, the Constitution was designed far better than even Madison and Wilson must have
anticipated to serve the needs of a continental people and to
hold up under the pressures of a spectacular rate of economic
development and territorial expansion.

The history of the Constitution since the death of Madison
has not, to be sure, been uniformly happy. Between the successful beginnings of the Age of Washington and Jefferson
and the successful readjustments of the Age of Roosevelt and
Eisenhower there were at least three or four periods when the
Constitution was tortured almost out of shape and one in
which it was assaulted bloodily. Yet even the assault of
1861–1865, which John C. Calhoun touched off years before and Alexander H. Stephens finished off years after, was
launched not so much upon the Constitution itself—the Constitution of the Confederacy, after all, was a remarkably
faithful copy of it—as upon the "more perfect Union" with
which its fate is forever intertwined. Two of the three great
legacies of 1776, independence and republicanism, were clear
and simple, and the Framers had no trouble in confirming
them for all Americans to come. The third, however, was
undeniably ambiguous, and not until the ambiguities of "a
union partly federal, partly national" were erased from the
national consciousness in the aftermath of Antietam and Get-
tysburg could the labors of the nationalists of 1787 be
crowned with success. Yet crowned they were in the fullness
of time with a flourish and finality that would have pleased
Alexander Hamilton, and not even the most hot-blooded advocate of "states rights" now seems disposed to reopen this
awesome question.

Well and truly framed, the Constitution has also been, except for a few fearful or merely dull stages in the American
pilgrimage, well and imaginatively interpreted. It does more

than live through the crises of the twentieth century as a venerated fossil; it thrives upon them, and gives men both the will and nerve to face them, as a self-renewing instrument of ordered liberty. And it thrives because—with all due respect to the restrictive views of the anti-Federalists of 1788 (Clinton and Henry out of sorts) and those other anti-Federalists of 1798 (Madison and Jefferson out of power)—it is interpreted largely in the way Hamilton proposed and both Washington and Marshall agreed it would have to be interpreted if the Union were to endure and prosper: as the indulgent charter of a sovereign nation empowered to defend itself vigorously against all domestic problems.

There are those who still insist that the opinions of Hamilton about the powers of Congress, Washington about the responsibilities of the Presidency, and Marshall about the nature of the Union were something quite different from "the intent of the Framers." To them one can only rejoin that most talk about the intent of the Framers—whether in the orations of politicians, the opinions of judges, or the monographs of professors—is as irrelevant as it is unpersuasive, as stale as it is strained, as rhetorically absurd as it is historically unsound.[14] No one, surely, can read the records of the Grand Convention at Philadelphia (and also of the ratifying conventions at Boston, Poughkeepsie, and Richmond) and not come to this harsh yet honest conclusion. On some of the great issues of constitutional law that have agitated our times the Framers expressed no clear intent, or invited their descendants to generate an intent of their own; on others they divided into a dozen or a score or even fifty-five different camps (and more than one of these men was divided against himself); on still others they framed their intent in words whose meaning is now so different from what it was in 1787 that to quote a Framer at all is to quote him quite out of context.

The one clear intent of the Framers was that each generation of Americans should pursue its destiny as a community of free men. We honor them most faithfully, and do our best to make certain that other generations of free men will come after us, by cherishing the same spirit of constitutionalism that carried them through their history-making adventure. The spirit of the Framers was a blend of prudence and imagination, of caution and creativity, of principle and practicality, of idealism and realism about the governing and self-governing of men. In the constant regeneration of this spirit of 1787 in American public life rests the promise of a future in which our power is the servant of justice and our glory a reflection of moral grandeur.

# Acknowledgments

To write a book is to accept a sentence of solitary confinement, yet even in the loneliest stretches of creation one needs the encouragement and advice of trusted persons. I am more grateful than I could possibly express in words to the handful of such persons who helped me to see this book through to the end: Rosalie F. Slevin, Elaine F. Crane, Donald Robinson, Jane P. Weld, Walter LaFeber, and Mary Crane Rossiter.

CLINTON ROSSITER

*Ithaca, New York*
June, 1965

# APPENDIX A

## A Select Bibliography of

## Printed Materials Cited in the Notes and

## of Books and Articles Recommended

## for Further Reading

## I DOCUMENTS

*The Debates and Proceedings in the Congress of the United States* (Washington, 1834–), generally known by the short title *Annals of Congress.*

Edward S. Corwin, ed., *The Constitution of the United States of America: Analysis and Interpretation,* Sen. Doc. 170, 82nd Cong., 2nd sess. (1953).

*Documentary History of the Constitution of the United States of America,* 5 vols. (Washington, 1894–1905).

Jonathan Elliot, ed., *The Debates in the Several State Conventions on the Adoption of the Federal Constitution,* 2nd ed., 5 vols. (Philadelphia, 1876).*

\* All students of the Federal period look forward eagerly to the appearance of the promised twelve volumes of the Documentary History of the Ratification of the Constitution and the First Ten Amendments, a grand scheme upon which Robert E. Cushman has been working faithfully and imaginatively for many years. With the publication of "Cushman" the fragmentary and unreliable "Elliot" will be consigned to the oblivion it has long deserved.

Max Farrand, ed., *The Records of the Federal Convention of 1787,* 4 vols. (New Haven, 1911, 1937).

Peter Force, ed., *American Archives,* 9 vols. (Washington, 1837–1853).

W. C. Ford *et al.,* eds., *Journals of the Continental Congress 1774–1789,* 34 vols. (Washington, 1904–1937).

Saul K. Padover, *To Secure These Blessings* (New York, 1962).

Arthur T. Prescott, *Drafting the Federal Constitution* (University, La., 1941).

W. U. Solberg, ed., *The Federal Convention and the Formation of the Union of American States* (New York, 1958).

J. R. Strayer, ed., *The Delegate from New York, or Proceedings of the Federal Convention of 1787 from the Notes of John Lansing, jr.* (Princeton, 1939).

C. C. Tansill, ed., *Documents Illustrative of the Formation of the Union of the American States,* House Doc. 398, 69th Cong., 1st sess. (1927).

F. N. Thorpe, ed., *The Federal and State Constitutions,* 7 vols. (Washington, 1909).

## II LETTERS AND OTHER CONTEMPORARY WRITINGS

C. F. Adams, ed., *The Works of John Adams,* 10 vols. (Boston, 1851).

James T. Austin, *The Life of Elbridge Gerry,* 2 vols. (Boston, 1827–1829).

J. C. Ballagh, ed., *The Letters of Richard Henry Lee,* 2 vols. (New York, 1911–1914).

George Bancroft, *History of the Formation of the Constitution of the United States of America,* 2 vols. (New York, 1882).

Julian P. Boyd, ed., *The Papers of Thomas Jefferson,* 17 vols. to date (Princeton, 1950–).

E. C. Burnett, ed., *Letters of the Members of the Continental Congress,* 8 vols. (Washington, 1921–1936).

L. H. Butterfield, ed., *The Letters of Benjamin Rush,* 2 vols. (Princeton, 1951).

Lester Cappon, ed., *The Adams-Jefferson Letters,* 2 vols. (Chapel Hill, 1959).

H. A. Cushing, ed., *The Writings of Samuel Adams,* 4 vols. (New York, 1904–1908).

J. C. Fitzpatrick, ed., *The Diaries of George Washington,* 4 vols. (Boston, 1925).

———, *The Writings of George Washington,* 39 vols. (Washington, 1931–1944).

P. L. Ford, ed., *Essays on the Constitution of the United States* (Brooklyn, 1892).

———, *Pamphlets on the Constitution of the United States* (Brooklyn, 1888).

———, *The Writings of John Dickinson* (Philadelphia, 1895).

———, *The Writings of Thomas Jefferson,* 10 vols. (New York, 1892–1899).

S. M. Hamilton, ed., *The Writings of James Monroe,* 7 vols. (New York, 1898–1903).

W. W. Henry, *Patrick Henry: Life, Correspondence and Speeches,* 3 vols. (New York, 1891).

Gaillard Hunt, ed., *The Writings of James Madison,* 9 vols. (New York, 1910).

H. P. Johnston, ed., *The Correspondence and Public Papers of John Jay,* 4 vols. (New York, 1890–1893).

C. R. King, *The Life and Correspondence of Rufus King,* 6 vols. (New York, 1894–1900).

A. A. Lipscomb, ed., *The Writings of Thomas Jefferson,* 20 vols. (Washington, 1903).

H. C. Lodge, *Life and Letters of George Cabot* (Boston, 1878).

———, *The Works of Alexander Hamilton,* 12 vols. (New York, 1904).

*The Journal of William Maclay* (New York, 1927).

*Letters and Other Writings of James Madison,* 4 vols. (Philadelphia, 1867).

G. J. McRee, *Life and Correspondence of James Iredell*, 2 vols. (New York, 1858).

S. E. Morison, *The Life and Letters of Harrison Gray Otis*, 2 vols. (Boston, 1913).

Anne C. Morris, ed., *The Diary and Letters of Gouverneur Morris*, 2 vols. (New York, 1888).

W. T. Read, *The Life and Correspondence of George Read* (Philadelphia, 1870).

Clinton Rossiter, ed., *The Federalist Papers* (New York, 1961).

Kate Mason Rowland, *The Life of George Mason*, 2 vols. (New York, 1892).

A. H. Smyth, ed., *The Writings of Benjamin Franklin*, 10 vols. (New York, 1906).

Jared Sparks, ed., *Correspondence of the American Revolution*, 4 vols. (Boston, 1853).

———, *The Life of Gouverneur Morris*, 3 vols. (Boston, 1832).

B. C. Steiner, *The Life and Correspondence of James McHenry* (Cleveland, 1907).

Harold C. Syrett and Jacob E. Cooke, eds., *The Papers of Alexander Hamilton*, 7 vols. to date (New York, 1961–).

## III THE BACKGROUND OF 1787: GENERAL STUDIES

C. M. Andrews, *The Colonial Background of the American Revolution* (New Haven, 1924).

———, *The Colonial Period of American History*, 4 vols. (New Haven, 1934–1938).

Bernard Bailyn, *Education in the Forming of American Society* (Chapel Hill, 1960).

Whitfield Bell, jr., *Early American Science* (Chapel Hill, 1955).

P. W. Bidwell and J. I. Falconer, *History of Agriculture in the Northern United States, 1620–1860* (Washington, 1925).

B. E. Bond, jr., *The Civilization of the Old Northwest* (New York, 1934).

Carl Bridenbaugh, *Cities in the Wilderness* (New York, 1938).

———, *Myths and Realities: Societies of the Colonial South* (L.S.U., 1952).

———, and J. Bridenbaugh, *Rebels and Gentlemen: Philadelphia in the Age of Franklin* (New York, 1942).

H. J. Carman, *Social and Economic History of the United States* (Boston, 1930).

Victor S. Clark, *History of Manufactures in the United States, 1607–1860* (Washington, 1916).

S. H. Cobb, *The Rise of Religious Liberty in America* (New York, 1902).

E. P. Cubberley, *Public Education in the United States* (Boston, 1934).

J. H. Franklin, *From Slavery to Freedom* (New York, 1947).

L. H. Gipson, *The British Empire Before the American Revolution*, 10 vols. (Caldwell, Idaho, and New York, 1936–1961).

L. C. Gray, *History of Agriculture in the Southern United States to 1860*, 2 vols. (Washington, 1933).

E. B. Greene, *Religion and the State* (New York, 1941).

———, and Virginia Harrington, *American Population before the Federal Census of 1790* (New York, 1932).

L. M. Hacker, *The Triumph of American Capitalism* (New York, 1940).

M. L. Hansen, *The Atlantic Migration, 1607–1860* (Cambridge, 1940).

A. B. Hulbert, *Soil: Its Influence on the History of the United States* (New Haven, 1930).

E. F. Humphrey, *Nationalism and Religion in America 1774–1789* (Boston, 1924).

J. Franklin Jameson, *The American Revolution Considered as a Social Movement* (Princeton, 1926).

E. Johnson *et al.*, *History of Domestic and Foreign Commerce of the United States* (Washington, 1915).

E. C. Kirkland, *A History of American Economic Life* (New York, 1932).

E. W. Knight, *Education in the United States* (Boston, 1951).

Michael Kraus, *The Atlantic Civilization* (Ithaca, 1949).

———, *Intercolonial Aspects of American Culture on the Eve of the American Revolution* (New York, 1925).

L. W. Labaree, *Conservatism in Early American History* (New York, 1948).

R. G. Lillard, *The Great Forest* (New York, 1948).

M. S. Locke, *Anti-Slavery in America* (Boston, 1901).

John C. Miller, *Origins of the American Revolution* (Boston, 1943).

H. M. Morais, *Deism in Eighteenth Century America* (New York, 1934).

Edmund S. Morgan, *The Birth of the Republic, 1763–1789* (Chicago, 1956).

S. E. Morison, *Three Centuries of Harvard* (Cambridge, 1937).

R. B. Morris, *Government and Labor in Early America* (New York, 1946).

F. L. Mott, *American Journalism* (New York, 1941).

C. P. Nettels, *The Emergence of a National Economy, 1775–1815* (New York, 1962).

———, *The Roots of American Civilization* (New York, 1938).

H. L. Osgood, *The American Colonies in the Eighteenth Century*, 4 vols. (New York, 1924).

R. R. Palmer, *The Age of the Democratic Revolution*, 2 vols. (Princeton, 1959–1964).

C. O. Paullin, *Atlas of the Historical Geography of the United States* (Washington, 1932).

Clinton Rossiter, *Seedtime of the Republic* (New York, 1953).

Max Savelle, *Seeds of Liberty* (New York, 1948).

A. M. Schlesinger, *The Colonial Merchants and the American Revolution* (New York, 1917).

A. E. Smith, *Colonists in Bondage* (Chapel Hill, 1947).

A. P. Stokes, *Church and State in the United States*, 3 vols. (New York, 1950).

W. W. Sweet, *Religion in Colonial America* (New York, 1942).

C. S. Sydnor, *Gentlemen Freeholders* (Chapel Hill, 1952).

Dale Van Every, *Ark of Empire: The American Frontier, 1784–1803* (New York, 1963).

T. J. Wertenbaker, *Princeton, 1746–1896* (Princeton, 1946).

Carl Wittke, *We Who Built America* (New York, 1939).

Esmond Wright, *Fabric of Freedom, 1763–1800* (New York, 1961).

## IV THE BACKGROUND OF 1787: POLITICAL AND CONSTITUTIONAL PRACTICE

Carl Becker, *The History of Political Parties in the Province of New York, 1760–1776* (1909) (Madison, 1960).

Samuel F. Bemis, *The Diplomacy of the American Revolution* (New York, 1893).

C. F. Bishop, *History of Elections in the American Colonies* (New York, 1893).

Julian P. Boyd, ed., "The Articles of Confederation and Perpetual Union," *Old South Leaflets*, Nos. 228–229 (Boston, 1960).

E. C. Burnett, *The Continental Congress* (New York, 1941).

O. M. Dickerson, *American Colonial Government* (Cleveland, 1912).

Elisha P. Douglass, *Rebels and Democrats* (Chapel Hill, 1955).

E. B. Greene, *The Provincial Governor* (New York, 1898).

Merrill Jensen, *The Articles of Confederation* (Madison, 1940).

———, "Democracy and the American Revolution," *Huntington Library Quarterly*, XX (1957), 321.

———, "The Idea of a National Government During the Revolution," *Political Science Quarterly*, LVIII (1943), 356.

———, *The New Nation* (New York, 1950).

A. H. Kelly and W. A. Harbison, *The American Constitution* (New York, 1948).

L. W. Labaree, *Royal Government in America* (New Haven, 1930).

A. C. McLaughlin, *A Constitutional History of the United States* (New York, 1935).

———, *The Foundations of American Constitutionalism* (New York, 1932).

William C. Morey, "The First State Constitutions," *Annals*, IV (1893), 201.

———, "The Genesis of a Written Constitution," *Annals*, I (1891), 529.

Allan Nevins, *The American States During and After the Revolution* (New York, 1924).

John C. Ranney, "The Bases of American Federalism," *William and Mary Quarterly*, 3rd ser., III (1946), 1.

Jennings B. Sanders, *Evolution of Executive Departments of the Continental Congress, 1774–1789* (Chapel Hill, 1935).

———, *The Presidency of the Continental Congress, 1774–1789* (Chapel Hill, 1930).

J. Paul Selsam, *The Pennsylvania Constitution of 1776* (Philadelphia, 1936).

Carl B. Swisher, *American Constitutional Development* (Boston, 1943).

William C. Webster, "Comparative Study of the State Constitutions of the American Revolution," *Annals*, IX (1897), 380.

Benjamin F. Wright, "The Early History of Written Constitutions in America," in *Essays in History and Political Theory* (Cambridge, 1936).

———, "The Origins of the Separation of Powers in America," *Economica*, XIII (1933), 169.

# V THE BACKGROUND OF 1787 POLITICAL AND

## CONSTITUTIONAL THOUGHT

Douglass Adair, " 'That Politics May be Reduced to a Science': David Hume, James Madison and the Tenth Federalist," *Huntington Library Quarterly*, XX (1957), 343.

———, "The Tenth Federalist Revisited," *William and Mary Quarterly*, 3rd ser., VIII (1951), 48.

Randolph G. Adams, *Political Ideas of the American Revolution* (Durham, 1922).

Bernard Bailyn, "Political Experience and Enlightenment Ideas in Eighteenth Century America," *American Historical Review*, LXVII (1962), 339.

Alice M. Baldwin, *The New England Clergy and the American Revolution* (Durham, 1928).

Carl Becker, *The Declaration of Independence* (New York, 1922).

L. K. Caldwell, *The Administrative Theories of Hamilton and Jefferson* (Chicago, 1944).

Gilbert Chinard, "Polybius and the American Constitution," *Journal of the History of Ideas*, I (1940), 38.

Edward S. Corwin, *The "Higher Law" Background of American Constitutional Law* (Ithaca, 1955).

——, "The Progress of Constitutional Theory between the Declaration of Independence and the Meeting of the Philadelphia Convention," *American Historical Review*, XXX (1925), 511.

Merle Curti, *The Growth of American Thought* (New York, 1943).

Martin Diamond, "Democracy and the Federalist," *American Political Science Review*, LIII (1959), 52.

Joseph Dorfman, *The Economic Mind in American Civilization* (New York, 1946–1959), vol. I.

Edward Dumbauld, *The Constitution of the United States* (Norman, Okla., 1964).

Zera Fink, *The Classical Republicans* (Evanston, 1945).

Richard M. Gummere, *The American Colonial Mind and the Classical Tradition* (Cambridge, 1963).

Zoltan Haraszti, *John Adams and the Prophets of Progress* (Cambridge, 1952).

Louis Hartz, *The Liberal Tradition in America* (New York, 1955).

Norman Jacobson, "Political Realism and the Age of Reason," *Review of Politics*, XV (1953), 446.

Cecelia Kenyon, "Men of Little Faith: The Anti-Federalists on the Nature of Representative Government," *William and Mary Quarterly*, 3rd ser., XII (1955), 3.

Adrienne Koch, *Jefferson and Madison, the Great Collaboration* (New York, 1950).

——, *Power, Morals, and the Founding Fathers* (Ithaca, 1961).

Hans Kohn, *American Nationalism* (New York, 1957).

Cornelia LeBoutillier, *American Democracy and Natural Law* (New York, 1950).

A. T. Mason and R. H. Leach, *In Quest of Freedom* (Englewood Cliffs, N.J., 1959).

Charles H. McIlwain, *Constitutionalism: Ancient and Modern* (Ithaca, 1947).

Richard McKeon, "The Development of the Concept of Property in Political Philosophy: A Study of the Background of the Constitution," *Ethics*, XLVIII (1938), 297.

A. C. McLaughlin, *The Foundations of American Constitutionalism* (New York, 1932).

Paul C. Nagel, *One Nation Indivisible: The Union in American Thought, 1776–1861* (New York, 1964).

I. W. Riley, *American Philosophy. The Early Schools* (New York, 1907).

Caroline Robbins, *The Eighteenth-Century Commonwealthman* (Cambridge, 1959).

Clinton Rossiter, "The Legacy of John Adams," *Yale Review*, XLVI (1957), 528.

——, *The Political Thought of the American Revolution* (New York, 1963).

H. W. Schneider, *A History of American Philosophy* (New York, 1946).

David G. Smith, *The Convention and the Constitution: The Political Ideas of the Founding Fathers* (New York, 1965).

P. M. Spurlin, *Montesquieu in America* (University, La., 1940).

Benjamin F. Wright, *American Interpretations of Natural Law* (Cambridge, 1931).

# VI  THE CONVENTION: GENERAL STUDIES

Robert E. Brown, *Reinterpretation of the Formation of the American Constitution* (Boston, 1963).

George Ticknor Curtis, *History of the Origin, Formation, and Adoption of the Constitution,* 2 vols. (New York, 1854–1858).

Stanley Elkins and Eric McKitrick, "The Founding Fathers: Young Men of the Revolution," *Political Science Quarterly,* LXXVI (1961), 181.

Max Farrand, *The Framing of the Constitution of the United States* (New Haven, 1913).

Hastings Lyon. *The Constitution and the Men Who Made It* (Boston, 1936).

A. C. McLaughlin, *The Confederation and the Constitution* (New York, 1905).

John P. Roche, "The Founding Fathers: A Reform Caucus in Action," *American Political Science Review,* LV (1961), 799.

Robert L. Schuyler, *The Constitution of the United States* (New York, 1923).

Carl Van Doren, *The Great Rehearsal* (New York, 1948).

Charles Warren, *The Making of the Constitution* (Boston, 1928).

Benjamin F. Wright, *Consensus and Continuity, 1776–1787* (Boston, 1958).

# VII  THE CONVENTION: SPECIAL THEMES

Charles A. Beard, *An Economic Interpretation of the Constitution of the United States* (1913) (New York, 1935).

———, *The Enduring Federalist* (Garden City, 1948).

———, *The Supreme Court and the Constitution* (1912) (Englewood Cliffs, N.J., 1962).

Robert E. Brown, *Charles Beard and the Constitution* (Princeton, 1956).

Jane Butzner, *Constitutional Chaff* (New York, 1941).

Edward S. Corwin, *The Doctrine of Judicial Review* (Princeton, 1914).

———, "The Rise and Establishment of Judicial Review," *Michigan Law Review,* IX (1910–1911), 102, 283.

W. W. Crosskey, *Politics and the Constitution,* 2 vols. (Chicago, 1953).

Louise Dunbar, *A Study of "Monarchical" Tendencies in the United States from 1776 to 1801* (Urbana, 1922).

Charles G. Haines, *The American Doctrine of Judicial Supremacy,* 2nd ed., (New York, 1959).

Walton Hamilton and Douglass Adair, *The Power to Govern* (New York, 1937).

John F. Jameson, ed., *Essays in the Constitutional History of the United States in the Formative Period, 1775–1789* (Boston, 1889).

O. G. Libby, *The Geographical Distribution of the Vote of the Thirteen States on the Federal Constitution* (Madison, 1894).

Forrest McDonald, *We the People: The Economic Origins of the Constitution* (Chicago, 1963).

William M. Meigs, *The Growth of the Constitution* (Philadelphia, 1900).

Conyers Read, ed., *The Constitution Reconsidered* (New York, 1938).

Harvey Robinson, "The Original and Derived Features of the Constitution," *Annals,* I (1890), 203.

J. Allen Smith, *The Spirit of American Government* (New York, 1907).

Robert J. Steamer, "The Legal and Political Genesis of the Supreme Court," *Political Science Quarterly*, LXXVII (1962), 546.

C. C. Thach, jr., *The Creation of the Presidency, 1775–1789* (Baltimore, 1922).

Charles Warren, *Congress, the Constitution, and the Supreme Court* (Boston, 1925).

Chilton Williamson, *American Suffrage from Property to Democracy, 1760–1860* (Princeton, 1960).

Benjamin F. Wright, *The Contract Clause of the Constitution* (Cambridge, 1938).

## VIII  BIOGRAPHIES

The most useful guides to the lives of the Framers are the facts and bibliographical notes in the articles on these men (all except Jacob Broom and William Houstoun) ɪ the *Dictionary of American Biography*, as well as the materials collected by Forrest McDonald in *We the People*, pp. 38–92.

The number of first-rank Framers who have not been honored with a full-length, scholarly, modern biography—or in some instances with any biography at all—is remarkably large, and would include, at the very least, Gerry, Gorham, King, Livingston, the Morrises, Dickinson, Read, Luther Martin, Randolph, Williamson, Baldwin, and all four South Carolinians.

E. P. Alexander, *A Revolutionary Conservative: James Duane of New York* (New York, 1938).

H. S. Allan, *John Hancock* (New York, 1948).

Richard H. Barry, *Mr. Rutledge of South Carolina* (New York, 1942).

Albert J. Beveridge, *The Life of John Marshall*, 4 vols. (Boston, 1916–1919).

Roger S. Boardman, *Roger Sherman, Signer and Statesman* (Philadelphia, 1938).

Morton Borden, *The Federalism of James A. Bayard* (New York, 1955).

G. A. Boyd, *Elias Boudinot* (Princeton, 1952).

Irving Brant, *James Madison*, 6 vols. (Indianapolis, 1948–1956).

William G. Brown, *The Life of Oliver Ellsworth* (New York, 1905).

John A. Carroll and Mary W. Ashworth, *George Washington, First in Peace* (New York, 1957).

Varnum L. Collins, *President Witherspoon*, 2 vols. (Princeton, 1925).

Moncure D. Conway, *Omitted Chapters of History Disclosed in the Life and Papers of Edmund Randolph* (New York, 1888).

Marcus Cunliffe, *George Washington, Man and Monument* (New York, 1960).

George Dangerfield, *Chancellor Robert R. Livingston* (New York, 1960).

Dorothy R. Dillon, *The New York Triumvirate* (New York, 1949).

Douglas S. Freeman, *George Washington*, 6 vols. (New York, 1948–1954).

Sister Mary V. Geiger, *Daniel Carroll, A Framer of the Constitution* (Washington, 1943).

Henry P. Goddard, *Luther Martin* (Baltimore, 1887).

George C. Groce, *William Samuel Johnson* (New York, 1937).

Helen Hill, *George Mason, Constitutionalist* (Cambridge, 1938).

Milton M. Klein, ed., *The Independent Reflector* (Cambridge, 1963).

Dumas Malone, *Jefferson and His Time*, 3 vols. to date (Boston, 1948–).

William H. Masterson, *William Blount* (Baton Rouge, 1954).

Lawrence S. Mayo, *John Langdon of New Hampshire* (Concord, N.H., 1937).

David J. Mays, *Edmund Pendleton*, 2 vols. (Cambridge, 1952).

John C. Miller, *Alexander Hamilton* (New York, 1959).

————, *Sam Adams* (Stanford, 1960).

Broadus Mitchell, *Alexander Hamilton*, 2 vols. (New York, 1957–1962).

Frank Monaghan, *John Jay* (New York, 1935).

E. P. Oberholtzer, *Robert Morris* (New York, 1903).

Blackwell P. Robinson, *William R. Davie* (Chapel Hill, 1957).

George C. Rogers, *Evolution of a Federalist: William Loughton Smith of Charleston* (Columbia, S.C., 1962).

Clinton Rossiter, *Alexander Hamilton and the Constitution* (New York, 1964).

Nathan Schachner, *The Founding Fathers* (New York, 1954).

Ellen H. Smith, *Charles Carroll of Carrollton* (Cambridge, 1942).

Page Smith, *John Adams*, 2 vols. (Garden City, 1962).

————, *James Wilson* (Chapel Hill, 1956).

E. W. Spaulding, *His Excellency George Clinton* (New York, 1938).

C. J. Stille, *The Life and Times of John Dickinson* (Philadelphia, 1891).

Howard Swiggett, *The Extraordinary Mr. Morris* (Garden City, 1952).

Lynn W. Turner, *William Plumer of New Hampshire* (Chapel Hill, 1962).

Carl Van Doren, *Benjamin Franklin* (New York, 1938).

Clarence L. Ver Steeg, *Robert Morris: Revolutionary Financier* (Philadelphia, 1954).

David D. Wallace, *The Life of Henry Laurens* (New York, 1915).

Daniel Walther, *Gouverneur Morris: Témoin de Deux Revolutions* (Lausanne, 1932).

Henry C. White, *Abraham Baldwin* (Athens, Ga., 1926).

C. P. Whittemore, *A General of the Revolution, John Sullivan of New Hampshire* (New York, 1961).

Gertrude S. Wood, *William Paterson of New Jersey* (Fair Lawn, N.J., 1933).

Eleanor Young, *Forgotten Patriot, Robert Morris* (New York, 1950).

## IX THE STATES

W. W. Abbott, "The Structure of Politics in Georgia: 1782–1789," *William and Mary Quarterly*, 3rd ser., XIV (1957), 47.

J. T. Adams, *New England in the Republic, 1776–1850* (Boston, 1926).

Frank G. Bates, *Rhode Island and the Formation of the Union* (New York, 1898).

Hillman M. Bishop, "Why Rhode Island Opposed the Federal Constitution," *Rhode Island History*, VIII (1949), 1, 33, 85, 115.

Robert L. Brunhouse, *The Counter-Revolution in Pennsylvania, 1776–1790* (Harrisburg, 1942).

T. C. Cochran, *New York in the Confederation: An Economic Study* (Philadelphia, 1932).

Kenneth Coleman, *The American Revolution in Georgia, 1763-1789* (Athens, Ga., 1958).

Philip A. Crowl, *Maryland During and After the Revolution* (Baltimore, 1943).

————, "Anti-Federalism in Maryland 1787–1788," *William and Mary Quarterly*, 3rd ser., IV (1947), 446.

R. A. East, "The Massachusetts Conservatives in the Critical Period," in Richard B. Morris, ed., *The Era of the American Revolution* (1939).

H. B. Grigsby, *The History of the Virginia Federal Convention* (Richmond, 1890–1891).

Samuel B. Harding, *The Contest over the Ratification of the Federal Constitution in the State of Massachusetts* (New York, 1896).

F. H. Hart, *The Valley of Virginia in the American Revolution* (Chapel Hill, 1942).

Jackson T. Main, *The Antifederalists* (Chapel Hill, 1961).

Richard P. McCormick, *Experiment in Independence: New Jersey in the Critical Period, 1781–1789* (New Brunswick, 1950).

J. B. McMaster and F. D. Stone, *Pennsylvania and the Federal Constitution, 1787–1788* (Philadelphia, 1942).

C. E. Miner, *The Ratification of the Federal Constitution by the State of New York* (New York, 1921).

John A. Munroe, *Federalist Delaware, 1775–1815* (New Brunswick, 1954).

A. R. Newsome, "North Carolina's Ratification of the Federal Constitution," *North Carolina Historical Review*, XVII (1940), 287.

William C. Pool, "An Economic Interpretation of the Ratification of the Federal Constitution in North Carolina," *North Carolina Historical Review*, XXVII (1950), 119, 289, 437.

Charles G. Singer, *South Carolina in the Confederation* (Philadelphia, 1941).

E. Wilder Spaulding, *New York in the Critical Period, 1783–1789* (New York, 1932).

B. C. Steiner, "Connecticut's Ratification of the Federal Constitution," *Proceedings of the American Antiquarian Society*, XXV (1915), 70–127.

Louise Trenholme, *The Ratification of the Federal Constitution in North Carolina* (New York, 1932).

Richard F. Upton, *Revolutionary New Hampshire* (Hanover, 1936).

Joseph B. Walker, *A History of the New Hampshire Convention* (Boston, 1888).

## X THE BILL OF RIGHTS AND THE FIRST YEARS

Leland D. Baldwin, *Whiskey Rebels* (Pittsburgh, 1939).

Charles A. Beard, *Economic Origins of Jeffersonian Democracy* (New York, 1915).

Samuel F. Bemis, *Jay's Treaty*, rev. ed. (New Haven, 1962).

——, *Pinckney's Treaty*, rev. ed. (New Haven, 1960).

William N. Chambers, *Political Parties in a New Nation* (New York, 1963).

Joseph Charles, *The Origins of the American Party System* (Williamsburg, 1956).

Noble E. Cunningham, jr., *The Jeffersonian Republicans* (Chapel Hill, 1957).

Manning Dauer, *The Adams Federalists* (Baltimore, 1953).

Alexander De Conde, *Entangling Alliance: Politics and Diplomacy under George Washington* (Durham, 1958).

Edward Dumbauld, *The Bill of Rights* (Norman, Okla., 1957).

Bray Hammond, *Banks and Politics in America* (Princeton, 1957).

James Hart, *The American Presidency In Action: 1789* (New York, 1948).

Stephen G. Kurtz, *The Presidency of John Adams* (Philadelphia, 1957).

Leonard W. Levy, *Freedom of Speech and Press in Early American History* (Cambridge, 1960).

John C. Miller, *Crisis in Freedom: The Alien and Sedition Laws* (New York, 1951).

———, *The Federalist Era, 1789–1801* (New York, 1960).

Robert A. Rutland, *The Birth of the Bill of Rights* (Chapel Hill, 1955).

James M. Smith, *Freedom's Fetters* (Ithaca, 1956).

Charles Warren, *The Supreme Court in United States History* (Boston, 1947), vol. I.

Leonard D. White, *The Federalists* (New York, 1948).

———, *The Jeffersonians* (New York, 1951).

# APPENDIX B

# Documents

## THE ARTICLES OF CONFEDERATION

TO ALL to whom these Presents shall come, we the undersigned Delegates of the States affixed to our Names send greeting. Whereas the Delegates of the United States of America in Congress assembled did on the fifteenth day of November in the Year of our Lord One Thousand Seven Hundred and Seventy seven, and in the Second Year of the Independence of America agree to certain articles of Confederation and perpetual Union between the States of Newhampshire, Massachusetts-bay, Rhode-island and Providence Plantations, Connecticut, New York, New Jersey, Pennsylvania, Delaware, Maryland, Virginia, North-Carolina, South-Carolina and Georgia in the Words following, viz. "Articles of Confederation and perpetual Union between the states of Newhampshire, Massachusetts-bay, Rhodeisland and Providence Plantations, Connecticut, New-York, New-Jersey, Pennsylvania, Delaware, Maryland, Virginia, North-Carolina, South-Carolina, and Georgia."

Art. I. The Stile of this confederacy shall be "The United States of America."

Art. II. Each state retains its sovereignty, freedom and independence, and every Power, Jurisdiction and right, which is not by this confederation expressly delegated to the United States, in Congress assembled.

Art. III. The said states hereby severally enter into a firm league of friendship with each other, for their common defence, the security of their Liberties, and their mutual and general welfare, binding themselves to assist each other, against all force offered to, or attacks made upon them, or any of them, on account of religion, sovereignty, trade, or any other pretence whatever.

Art. IV. The better to secure and perpetuate mutual friendship and intercourse among the people of the different states in this union, the free inhabitants of each of these states, paupers, vagabonds and fugitives from Justice excepted, shall be entitled to all privileges and immunities of free citizens in the several states; and the people of each state shall have free ingress and regress to and from any other state, and shall enjoy therein all the privileges of trade and commerce, subject to the same duties, impositions and restrictions as the inhabitants thereof respectively, provided that such restriction shall not extend so far as to prevent the removal of property imported into any state, to any other state of which the Owner is an inhabitant; provided also that no imposition, duties or restriction shall be laid by any state, on the property of the united states, or either of them.

If any Person guilty of, or charged with treason, felony, or other high misdemeanor in any state, shall flee from Justice, and be found in any of the united states, he shall upon demand of the Governor or executive power, of the state from which he fled, be delivered up and removed to the state having jurisdiction of his offence.

Full faith and credit shall be given in each of these states to the records, acts and judicial proceedings of the courts and magistrates of every other state.

Art. V. For the more convenient management of the general interests of the united states, delegates shall be annually appointed in such manner as the legislature of each state shall direct, to meet in Congress on the first Monday in November, in every year, with a power reserved to each state, to recal its delegates, or any of them, at any time within the year, and to send others in their stead, for the remainder of the Year.

No state shall be represented in Congress by less than two, nor by more than seven Members; and no person shall be capable of being a delegate for more than three years in any term of six years; nor shall any person, being a delegate, be capable of holding any office under the united states, for which he, or another for his benefit receives any salary, fees or emolument of any kind.

Each state shall maintain its own delegates in a meeting of the states, and while they act as members of the committee of the states.

In determining questions in the united states, in Congress assembled, each state shall have one vote.

Freedom of speech and debate in Congress shall not be impeached or questioned in any Court, or place out of Congress, and the members of congress shall be protected in their persons from arrests and imprisonments, during the time of their going to and from, and attendance on congress, except for treason, felony, or breach of the peace.

Art. VI. No state without the Consent of the united states in congress assembled, shall send any embassy to, or receive any embassy from, or enter into any conference, agreement, or alliance or treaty with any King, prince or state; nor shall any person holding any office of profit or trust under the united states, or any of them, accept of any present, emolument, office or title of any kind whatever from any king, prince or foreign state; nor shall the united states in congress assembled, or any of them, grant any title of nobility.

No two or more states shall enter into any treaty, confederation or alliance whatever between them, without the consent of the united states in congress assembled, specifying accurately the purposes for which the same is to be entered into, and how long it shall continue.

No state shall lay any imposts or duties, which may interefere with any stipulations in treaties, entered into by the united states in congress assembled, with any king, prince or state, in pursuance of any treaties already proposed by congress, to the courts of France and Spain.

No vessels of war shall be kept up in time of peace by any state, except such number only, as shall be deemed necessary by the united states in congress assembled, for the defence of such state, or its trade; nor shall any body of forces be kept up by any state, in time of peace, except such number only, as in the judgment of the united states, in congress assembled, shall be deemed requisite to garrison the forts necessary for the defence of such state; but every state shall always keep up a well regulated and disciplined militia, sufficiently armed and accoutred, and shall provide and constantly have ready for use, in public stores, a due number of field pieces and tents, and a proper quantity of arms, ammunition and camp equipage.

No state shall engage in any war without the consent of the united states in congress assembled, unless such state be actually invaded by enemies, or shall have received certain advice of a resolution being formed by some nation of Indians to invade such state, and the danger is so imminent as not to admit of a delay, till the united states in congress assembled can be consulted: nor shall any state grant commissions to any ships or vessels of war, nor letters of marque or reprisal, except it be after a declaration of war by the united states in congress assembled, and then only against the kingdom or state and the subjects thereof, against which war has been so declared, and under such regulations as shall be established by the united states in congress assembled, unless such state be infested by pirates, in which case vessels of war may be fitted out for that occasion, and kept so long as the danger shall continue, or until the united states in congress assembled shall determine otherwise.

Art. VII. When land-forces are raised by any state for the common defence, all officers of or under the rank of colonel, shall be appointed by the legislature of each state respectively by whom such forces shall be raised, or in such manner as such state shall direct, and all vacancies shall be filled up by the state which first made the appointment.

Art. VIII. All charges of war, and all other expences that shall be incurred for the common defence or general welfare, and allowed by the united states in congress assembled, shall be defrayed out of a common treasury, which shall be supplied by the several states, in proportion to the value of all land within each state, granted to or surveyed for any Person, as such land and the buildings and improvements thereon shall be estimated according to such mode as the united states in congress assembled, shall from time to time direct and appoint. The taxes for paying that proportion shall be laid and levied by the authority and direction of the legislatures of the several states within the time agreed upon by the united states in congress assembled.

Art. IX. The united states in congress assembled, shall have the sole and exclusive right and power of determining on peace and war, except in the cases mentioned in the sixth article—of sending and receiving ambassadors—entering into treaties and alliances, provided that no treaty of commerce shall be made whereby the legislative power of the respective states shall be restrained from imposing such imposts and duties on foreigners, as their own people are subjected to, or from prohibiting the exportation or importation of any species of goods or commodities whatsoever—of establishing rules for deciding in all cases, what captures on land or water shall be legal, and in what manner prizes taken by land or naval forces in the service of the united states shall be divided or appropriated—of granting letters of marque and reprisal in times of peace—appointing courts for the trial of piracies and felonies committed on the high seas and establishing courts for receiving and determining finally appeals in all cases of captures, provided that no member of congress shall be appointed a judge of any of the said courts.

The united states in congress assembled shall also be the last resort on appeal in all disputes and differences now subsisting or that hereafter may arise between two or more states concerning boundary, jurisdiction or any other cause whatever; which authority shall always be exercised in the manner following. Whenever the legislative or executive authority or lawful agent of any state in controversy with another shall present a petition to congress, stating the matter in question and praying for a hearing, notice thereof shall be given by order of congress to the legislative or executive authority of the other state in controversy, and a day assigned for the appearance of the parties by their lawful agents, who shall then be directed to appoint by joint consent, commissioners or judges to constitute a court for hearing and determining the matter in question: but if they cannot agree, congress shall name three persons out of each of the united states, and from the list of such persons each party shall alternately strike out one, the petitioners beginning, until the number shall be reduced to thirteen; and from that number not less than seven, nor more than nine names as congress shall direct, shall in the presence of congress be drawn out by lot, and the persons whose names shall be so drawn or any five of them, shall be commissioners or judges, to hear and finally determine the controversy, so always as a major part of the judges who shall hear the cause shall agree in the determination: and if either party shall neglect to attend at the day appointed, without shewing reasons, which congress shall judge sufficient, or being present shall refuse to strike, the congress shall proceed to nominate three persons out of each state, and the secretary of congress shall strike in behalf of such party absent or refusing; and the judgment and sentence of the court to be appointed, in the manner before prescribed, shall be final and conclusive; and if any of the parties shall refuse to submit to the authority of such court, or to appear to defend their claim, or cause, the court shall nevertheless proceed to pronounce sentence, or judgment, which shall in like manner be final and decisive, the judgment or sentence and other proceedings being in either case transmitted to congress, and lodged among the acts of congress for the security of the parties concerned: provided that every commissioner, before he sits in judgment, shall take an oath to be administered by one of the judges of the supreme or superior court of the state, where the cause shall be tried, "well and truly to hear and determine the matter in question, according to the best of his judgment, without favour, affection or hope of reward:" provided also that no state shall be deprived of territory for the benefit of the united states.

All controversies concerning the private right of soil claimed under different grants of two or more states, whose jurisdictions as they may respect such lands, and the states which passed such grants are adjusted, the said grants or either of them being at the same time claimed to have originated antecedent to such settlement of jurisdiction, shall on the petition of either party to the congress of the united states, be finally determined as near as may be in the same manner as is before prescribed for deciding disputes respecting territorial jurisdiction between different states.

The united states in congress assembled shall also have the sole and exclusive right and power of regulating the alloy and value of coin struck by their own authority, or by that of the respective states—fixing the standard of weights and measures throughout the united states—regulating the trade and managing all affairs with the Indians, not members of any of the states, provided that the legislative right of any state within its own limits be not infringed or violated—establishing and regulating post-offices from one state to another, throughout all the united states, and exacting such postage on the papers passing thro' the same as may be requisite to defray the expences of the said office—appointing all officers of the land forces, in the service of the united states, excepting regimental officers—appointing all the officers of the naval forces, and commissioning all officers whatever in the service of the united states—making rules for the government and regulation of the said land and naval forces, and directing their operations.

The united states in congress assembled shall have authority to appoint a committee, to sit in the recess of congress, to be denominated "A Committee of the States," and to consist of one delegate from each state; and to appoint such other committees and civil officers as may be necessary for managing the general affairs of the united states under their direction—to appoint one of their number to preside, provided that no person be allowed to serve in the office of president more than one year in any term of three years; to ascertain the necessary sums of Money to be raised for the service of the united states, and to appropriate and apply the same for defraying the public expenses—to borrow money, or emit bills on the credit of the united states, transmitting every half year to the respective states an account of the sums of money so borrowed or emitted—to build and equip a navy—to agree upon the number of land forces, and to make requisitions from each state for its quota, in proportion to the number of white inhabitants in such state: which requisition shall be binding, and thereupon the legislature of each state shall appoint the regimental officers, raise the men and cloath, arm and equip them in a soldier like manner, at the expence of the united states, and the officers and men so cloathed, armed and equipped shall march to the place appointed, and within the time agreed on by the united states in congress assembled: But if the united states in congress assembled shall, on consideration of circumstances judge proper that any state should not raise men, or should raise a smaller number than its quota, and that any other state should raise a greater number of men than the quota thereof, such extra number shall be raised, officered, cloathed, armed and equipped in the same manner as the quota of such state, unless the legislature of such state shall judge that such extra number cannot be safely spared out of the same, in which case they shall raise, officer, cloath, arm and equip as many of such extra number as they judge can be safely spared. And the officers and men so cloathed, armed and equipped, shall march to the place appointed, and within the time agreed on by the united states in congress assembled.

The united states in congress assembled shall never engage in a war, not grant letters of marque and reprisal in time of peace, nor enter into any treaties or alliances, nor coin money, nor regulate the value thereof, nor ascertain the sums and expences necessary for the defence and welfare of the united states, or any of them, nor emit bills, nor borrow money on the credit of the united states, nor appropriate money, nor agree upon the number of vessels of war, to be built or purchased, or the number of land or sea forces to be raised, nor appoint a commander in chief of the army or navy, unless nine states assent to the same: nor shall a question on any other point, except for adjourning from day to day be determined, unless by the votes of a majority of the united states in congress assembled.

The congress of the united states shall have power to adjourn to any time within the year, and to any place within the united states, so that no period of adjournment be for a longer duration than the space of six Months, and shall publish the Journal of their proceedings monthly, except such parts thereof relating to treaties, alliances or military operations as in their judgment require secresy; and the yeas and nays of the delegates of each state on any question shall be entered on the Journal, when it is desired by any delegate; and the delegates of a state, or any of them, at his or their request shall be furnished with a transcript of the said Journal, except such parts as are above excepted, to lay before the legislatures of the several states.

Art. X. The committee of the states, or any nine of them, shall be authorised to execute, in the recess of congress, such of the powers of congress as the united states in congress assembled, by the consent of nine states, shall from time to time think expedient to vest them with; provided that no power be delegated to the said committee, for the exercise of which by the articles of confederation, the voice of nine states in the congress of the united states assembled is requisite.

Art. XI. Canada acceding to this confederation, and joining in the measures of the united states, shall be admitted into, and entitled to all the advantages of this union: but no other colony shall be admitted into the same, unless such admission be agreed to by nine states.

Art. XII. All bills of credit emitted, monies borrowed and debts contracted by, or under the authority of congress, before the assembling of the united states, in pursuance of the present confederation, shall be deemed and considered as a charge against the united states, for payment and satisfaction whereof the said united states, and the public faith are hereby solemnly pledged.

Art. XIII. Every state shall abide by the determinations of the united states in congress assembled, on all questions which by this confederation are submitted to them. And the Articles of this confederation shall be inviolably observed by every state, and the union shall be perpetual; nor shall any alteration at any time hereafter be made in any of them; unless such alteration be agreed to in a congress of the united states, and be afterwards confirmed by the legislatures of every state.

AND WHEREAS it hath pleased the Great Governor of the World to incline the hearts of the legislatures we respectively represent in congress, to approve of, and to authorize us to ratify the said articles of confederation and perpetual union. KNOW YE that we the undersigned delegates, by virtue of the power and authority to us given for that purpose, do by these presents, in the name and in behalf of our respective constituents, fully and entirely ratify and confirm each and every of the said articles of confederation and perpetual union, and all and singular the matters and things therein contained: And we do further solemnly plight and engage the faith of our respective constituents, that they shall abide by the determinations of the united states in congress assembled, on all questions, which by the said confederation are submitted to them. And that the articles thereof shall be inviolably observed by the states we respectively represent, and that the union shall be perpetual. In Witness thereof we have hereunto set our hands in Congress. Done at Philadelphia in the state of Pennsylvania the ninth Day of July in the Year of our Lord one Thousand seven Hundred and Seventy-eight, and in the third year of the independence of America.

JOSIAH BARTLETT
JOHN WENTWORTH Jun^r        } On the part and behalf of the
August 8^th 1778                State of New Hampshire

JOHN HANCOCK

SAMUEL ADAMS

ELDRIDGE GERRY             } On the part and behalf of
                               The State of Massachusetts
FRANCIS DANA                   Bay

JAMES LOVELL

SAMUEL HOLTEN

WILLIAM ELLERY             } On the part and behalf of the
HENRY MARCHANT                 State of Rhode-Island and
JOHN COLLINS                   Providence Plantations

ROGER SHERMAN

SAMUEL HUNTINGTON

OLIVER WOLCOTT             } On the part and behalf of the
                               State of Connecticut
TITUS HOSMER

ANDREW ADAMS

JA^S DUANE

FRA^S LEWIS                } On the part and behalf of the
W^M DUER                       State of New York

GOUV MORRIS

JNO WITHERSPOON            } On the part and behalf of the
NATH^L SCUDDER                 State of New Jersey.
                               Nov^r 26, 1778.—

ROB^T MORRIS

DANIEL ROBERDEAU

JON^A BAYARD SMITH         } On the part and behalf of the
                               State of Pennsylvania
WILLIAM CLINGAN

JOSEPH REED 22^d July
1778

THO M:KEAN Feby 12
1779

JOHN DICKINSON May 5th
1779

NICHOLAS VAN DYKE

} On the part and behalf of the
State of Delaware

JOHN HANSON March 1
1781

DANIEL CARROLL do

} On the part and behalf of the
State of Maryland

RICHARD HENRY LEE

JOHN BANISTER

THOMAS ADAMS

JNO HARVIE

FRANCIS LIGHTFOOT LEE

} On the part and behalf of the
State of Virginia

JOHN PENN July 21st 1778

CORNS HARNETT

JNO WILLIAMS

} On the part and behalf of the
State of No Carolina

HENRY LAURENS

WILLIAM HENRY DRAYTON

JNO MATHEWS

RICHD HUTSON

THOS HEYWARD Junr

} On the part and behalf of the
State of South-Carolina

JNO WALTON 24th July
1778

EDWD TELFAIR

EDWD LANGWORTHY

} On the part and behalf of the
State of Georgia

# THE VIRGINIA PLAN, MAY 29, 1787

1. RESOLVED, That the articles of Confederation ought to be so corrected and enlarged as to accomplish the objects proposed by their institution; namely, common defence, security of liberty and general welfare.

2. Resolved, therefore, That the rights of suffrage, in the National Legislature ought to be proportioned to the Quotas of contribution, or to the number of free inhabitants, as the one or the other rule may seem best in different cases.

3. Resolved, That the National Legislature ought to consist of two branches.

4. Resolved, That the members of the first branch of the National Legislature ought to be elected by the people of the several States every          for the term of          ; to be of the age of          years at least; to receive liberal stipends by which they may be compensated for the devotion of their time to public service; to be ineligible to any office established by a particular State, or under the authority of the United States, except those peculiarly belonging to the functions of the first branch, during the term of service, and for the space of          after its expiration; to be incapable of re-election for the space of          after the expiration of their term of service; and to be subject to recall.

5. Resolved, That the members of the second branch of the National Legislature ought to be elected by those of the first, out of a proper number of persons nominated by the individual Legislatures; to be of the age of          years, at least; to hold their offices for a term sufficient to ensure their independency; to receive liberal stipends, by which they may be compensated for the devotion of their time to public service; and to be ineligible to any office established by a particular State, or under the authority of the United States, except those peculiarly belonging to the functions of the second branch, during the term of service, and for the space of          after the expiration thereof.

6. Resolved, That each branch ought to possess the right of originating Acts; that the National Legislature ought to be impowered to enjoy the Legislative Rights vested in Congress by the Confederation, and moreover to legislate in all cases to which the separate States are incompetent, or in which the harmony of the United States may be interrupted by the exercise of individual Legislation; to negative all laws passed by the several States, contravening in the opinion of the National Legislature the articles of Union; and to call forth the force of the Union against any member of the Union failing to fulfil its duty under the articles thereof.

7. Resolved, That a national executive be instituted; to be chosen by the National Legislature for the term of        years; to receive punctually at stated times, a fixed compensation for the services rendered, in which no increase or diminution shall be made so as to affect the Magistracy existing at the time of increase or diminution; and to be ineligible a second time; and that besides a general authority to execute the National laws, it ought to enjoy the Executive rights vested in Congress by the Confederation.

8. Resolved, That the executive and a convenient number of the National Judiciary, ought to compose a council of revision with authority to examine every act of the National Legislature before it shall operate, and every act of a particular Legislature before a Negative thereon shall be final; and that the dissent of the said Council shall amount to a rejection, unless the act of the National Legislature be again passed, or that of a particular Legislature be again negatived by        of the members of each branch.

9. Resolved, That a national judiciary be established to consist of one or more supreme tribunals, and of inferior tribunals to be chosen by the National Legislature, to hold their offices during good behaviour; and to receive punctually at stated times fixed compensations for their services, in which no increase or diminution shall be made so as to affect the person actually in office at the time of such increase or diminution. That the jurisdiction of the inferior tribunals shall be to hear and determine in the first instance, and of the supreme tribunal to hear and determine, in the dernier resort, all piracies and felonies on the high seas; captures from an enemy; cases in which foreigners or citizens of other States applying to such jurisdictions may be interested, or which respect the collection of the National revenue; impeachments of any National officer; and questions which involve the national peace or harmony.

10. Resolved, That provision ought to be made for the admission of States lawfully arising within the limits of the United States, whether from a voluntary junction of Government and Territory, or otherwise, with the consent of a number of voices in the National Legislature less than the whole.

11. Resolved, That a Republican Government and the territory of each State, except in the instance of a voluntary junction of Government and territory, ought to be guaranteed by the United States to each State.

12. Resolved, That provision ought to be made for the continuance of Congress and their authorities and privileges, until a given day after the reform of the articles of Union shall be adopted, and for the completion of all their engagements.

13. Resolved, That provision ought to be made for the amendment of the articles of Union whensoever it shall seem necessary; and that the assent of the National Legislature ought not to be required thereto.

14. Resolved, That the legislative, executive, and judiciary powers within the several States, ought to be bound by oath to support the articles of union.

15. Resolved, That the amendments which shall be offered to the Confederation, by the Convention ought at a proper time, or times, after the approbation of Congress, to be submitted to an assembly or assemblies of Representatives, recommended by the several Legislatures to be expressly chosen by the people, to consider and decide thereon.

# THE REPORT OF THE COMMITTEE
# OF THE WHOLE, JUNE 13, 1787

1. RESOLVED, That it is the opinion of this Committee, that a national government ought to be established, consisting of a Supreme Legislative, Judiciary, and Executive.

2. Resolved, That the National Legislature ought to consist of Two Branches.

3. Resolved, That the members of the first branch of the national Legislature ought to be elected by the People of the several States, for the term of Three years; to receive fixed stipends, by which they may be compensated for the devotion of their time to public service, to be paid out of the National Treasury; to be ineligible to any Office established by a particular State, or under the authority of the United States (except those peculiarly belonging to the functions of the first branch) during the term of service, and under the national government for the space of one year after its expiration.

4. Resolved, That the Members of the second Branch of the national Legislature ought to be chosen by the individual Legislatures; to be of the age of thirty years at least; to hold their offices for a term sufficient to ensure their independency, namely, seven years; to receive fixed stipends, by which they may be compensated for the devotion of their time to public service, to be paid out of the National Treasury; to be ineligible to any Office established by a particular State, or under the authority of the United States (except those peculiarly belonging to the functions of the second branch) during the term of service, and under the national government, for the space of one Year after its expiration.

5. Resolved, That each branch ought to possess the right of originating acts.

6. Resolved, That the national Legislature ought to be empowered to enjoy the legislative rights vested in Congress by the confederation; and moreover to legislate in all cases to which the separate States are incompetent, or in which the harmony of the United States may be interrupted by the exercise of individual legislation; to negative all laws passed by the several States contravening, in the opinion of the national legislature, the articles of union, or any treaties subsisting under the authority of the union.

7. Resolved, That the right of suffrage in the first branch of the national Legislature ought not to be according to the rule established in the articles of confederation, but according to some equitable ratio of representation; namely, in proportion to the whole number of white and other free citizens and inhabitants, of every age, sex, and condition, including those bound to servi-

tude for a term of years, and three fifths of all other persons not comprehended in the foregoing description, except Indians not paying taxes in each State.

8. Resolved, That the right of suffrage in the second branch of the national Legislature ought to be according to the rule established for the first.

9. Resolved, That a national Executive be instituted to consist of a Single Person; to be chosen by the National Legislature, for the term of Seven years; with power to carry into execution the National Laws; to appoint to Offices in cases not otherwise provided for; to be ineligible the second time; and to be removable on impeachment and conviction of malpractice, or neglect of duty; to receive a fixed stipend, by which he may be compensated for the devotion of his time to public service, to be paid out of the national Treasury.

10. Resolved, That the national executive shall have a right to negative any legislative act, which shall not be afterwards passed unless by two third parts of each branch of the national Legislature.

11. Resolved, That a national Judiciary be established to consist of One supreme Tribunal; the Judges of which to be appointed by the second Branch of the National Legislature; to hold their offices during good behaviour; to receive punctually, at stated times, a fixed compensation for their services, in which no encrease or diminution shall be made, so as to affect the persons actually in office at the time of each encrease or diminution.

12. Resolved, That the national Legislature be empowered to appoint inferior Tribunals.

13. Resolved, That the jurisdiction of the national Judiciary shall extend to cases which respect the collection of the national revenue; impeachments of any National officers; and questions which involve the national peace and harmony.

14. Resolved, That provision ought to be made for the admission of States, lawfully arising within the limits of the United States, whether from a voluntary junction of government and territory, or otherwise, with the consent of a number of voices in the National legislature less than the whole.

15. Resolved, That provision ought to be made for the continuance of Congress and their authorities until a given day after the reform of the articles of Union shall be adopted; and for the completion of all their engagements.

16. Resolved, That a republican Constitution, and its existing laws, ought to be guaranteed to each State by the United States.

17. Resolved, That provision ought to be made for the amendment of the articles of Union, whensoever it shall seem necessary.

18. Resolved, That the Legislative, Executive, and Judiciary powers within the several States ought to be bound by oath to support the articles of Union.

19. Resolved, That the amendments which shall be offered to the confederation by the Convention, ought at a proper time or times, after the approbation of Congress, to be submitted to

an assembly or assemblies of representatives, recommended by the several Legislatures, to be submitted to an assembly or assemblies of representatives, recommended by the several Legislatures, to be expressly chosen by the People to consider and decide thereon.

# THE NEW JERSEY PLAN, JUNE 15, 1787

1. RESOLVED, That the articles of Confederation ought to be so revised, corrected and enlarged, as to render the federal Constitution adequate to the exigencies of Government, and the preservation of the Union.

2. Resolved, That in addition to the powers vested in the United States in Congress, by the present existing articles of Confederation, they be authorized to pass acts for raising a revenue, by levying a duty or duties on all goods and merchandizes of foreign growth or manufacture, imported into any part of the United States, by Stamps on paper, vellum, or parchment, and by a postage on all letters and packages passing through the general post-office, to be applied to such federal purposes as they shall deem proper and expedient; to make rules and regulations for the collection thereof; and the same from time to time, to alter and amend in such manner as they shall think proper; to pass Acts for the regulation of trade and commerce, as well with foreign nations as with each other: provided that all punishments, fines, forfeitures, and penalties to be incurred for contravening such rules and regulations shall be adjudged by the Common law Judicarys of the State in which any offence contrary to the true intent and meaning of such Acts, rules and regulations shall have been committed or perpetrated, with liberty of commencing in the first instance all suits or prosecutions for that purpose, in the superior Common law Judiciary of such State; subject nevertheless, for the correction of all errors, both in law and fact in rendering judgment, to an appeal to the Judiciary of the United States.

3. Resolved, That whenever requisitions shall be necessary, instead of the rule for making requisitions mentioned in the articles of Confederation the United States in Congress be authorized to make such requisitions in proportion to the whole number of white and other free citizens and inhabitants of every age, sex, and condition, including those bound to servitude for a term of years, and three fifths of all other persons not comprehended in the foregoing description, except Indians not paying taxes; that if such requisitions be not complied with, in the time specified therein, to direct the collection thereof in the non-complying States, and for that purpose to devise and pass acts directing and authorizing the same; provided that none of the powers hereby vested in the United States in Congress shall be exercised without the consent of at least          States; and in that proportion, if the number of confederated States should hereafter be increased or diminished.

4. Resolved, That the United States in Congress be authorized to elect a federal Executive to consist of          persons, to continue in office for the term of          years; to receive punctually at stated times a fixed compensation for their services in which no

increase or diminution shall be made so as to affect the persons composing the Executive at the time of such increase or diminution, to be paid out of the federal treasury; to be incapable of holding any other office or appointment during their term of service, and for        years thereafter; to be ineligible a second time, and removable by Congress on application by a majority of the Executives of the several States. That the executive, besides their general authority to execute the federal acts ought to appoint all federal officers not otherwise provided for, and to direct all military operations; provided, that none of the persons composing the federal executive shall on any occasion take command of any troops, so as personally to conduct any military enterprise as General, or in any other capacity.

5. Resolved, That a federal Judiciary be established, to consist of a supreme Tribunal the Judges of which to be appointed by the Executive, and to hold their offices during good behaviour; to receive punctually at stated times a fixed compensation for their services, in which no increase or diminution shall be made, so as to affect the persons actually in office at the time of such increase or diminution. That the Judiciary so established shall have authority to hear and determine in the first instance on all impeachments of federal officers, and by way of appeal in the dernier resort in all cases touching the rights and privileges of Ambassadors; in all cases of captures from an enemy; in all cases of piracies and felonies on the high seas; in all cases in which foreigners may be interested, in the construction of any treaty or treaties, or which may arise on any of the acts for regulation of trade, or the collection of the federal Revenue. That none of the Judiciary shall during the time they remain in Office be capable of receiving or holding any other office or appointment during their term of service, or for        thereafter.

6. Resolved, That all acts of the United States in Congress, made by virtue and in pursuance of the powers hereby and by the articles of confederation vested in them, and all treaties made and ratified under the authority of the United States, shall be the supreme law of the respective States as far forth as those Acts or Treaties shall relate to the said States or their Citizens; and that the judiciary of the several States shall be bound thereby in their decisions, any thing in the respective laws of the Individual States to the contrary notwithstanding; and if any State, or any body of men in any State, shall oppose or prevent the carrying into execution such acts or treaties, the federal Executive shall be authorized to call forth the powers of the Confederated States, or so much thereof as may be necessary, to enforce and compel an obedience to such Acts, or an Observance of such Treaties.

7. Resolved, That provision be made for the admission of new States into the Union.

8. Resolved, That the rule for naturalization ought to be the same in every State.

9. Resolved, That a citizen of one State committing an offence in another state of the Union shall be deemed guilty of the same offence as if it had been committed by a citizen of the State in which the offence was committed.

# RESOLUTIONS REFERRED TO THE
# COMMITTEE OF DETAIL, JULY 26, 1787

RESOLVED:

That the Government of the United States ought to consist of a Supreme Legislative, Judiciary and Executive.

That the Legislature of the United States ought to consist of two Branches.

That the Members of the first Branch of the Legislature of the United States ought to be elected by the People of the several States—for the Term of Two Years—to be of the Age of twenty five Years at least—to be ineligible to and incapable of holding any Office under the Authority of the United States (except those peculiarly belonging to the Functions of the first Branch) during the Time of Service of the first Branch.

That the Members of the second Branch of the Legislature of the United States ought to be chosen by the Individual Legislatures—to be of the Age of thirty Years at least—to hold their Offices for the Term of six Years; one third to go out biennially —to receive a Compensation for the Devotion of their Time to the public service—to be ineligible to and incapable of holding any Office under the Authority of the United States (except those peculiarly belonging to the Functions of the second Branch) during the Term for which they are elected, and for one Year thereafter.

That each Branch ought to possess the Right of originating Acts.

That the Right of Suffrage in the first Branch of the Legislature of the United States ought not to be according to the Rules established in the Articles of Confederation but according to some equitable Ratio of Representation.

That in the original Formation of the Legislature of the United States the first Branch thereof shall consist of sixty five Members of which Number New Hampshire shall send *three*—Massachusetts *eight*—Rhode Island *one*—Connecticut *five*—New York *six* —New Jersey *four*—Pennsylvania *eight*—Delaware *one*—Maryland *six*—Virginia *ten*—North Carolina *five*—South Carolina *five*—Georgia *three*.

But as the present Situation of the States may probably alter in the Number of their Inhabitants, the Legislature of the United States shall be authorized from Time to Time to apportion the Number of Representatives; and in Case any of the states shall hereafter be divided, or enlarged by Addition of Territory, or any two or more States united, or any new States created within the Limits of the United States, the Legislature of the United States shall possess Authority to regulate the Number of Representatives in any of the foregoing Cases, upon the Principle of the Number of their Inhabitants, according to the Provisions herein after mentioned namely—Provided always that Representation ought to be proportioned according to direct Taxation: And in order to ascertain the Alteration in the direct Taxation, which may be required from Time to Time, by the Changes in the relative Circumstances of the States—

Resolved that a Census be taken, within six years from the first Meeting of the Legislature of the United States, and once within the Term of every ten Years afterwards, of all the Inhabitants of the United States in the Manner and according to the Ratio recommended by Congress in their Resolution of April 18th, 1783—And that the Legislature of the United States shall proportion the direct Taxation accordingly.

Resolved that all Bills for raising or Appropriating Money, and for fixing the Salaries of Officers of the Government of the United States shall originate in the first Branch of the Legislature of the United States, and shall not be altered or amended by the second Branch; and that no money shall be drawn from the public Treasury but in Pursuance of Appropriations to be originated by the first Branch.

That from the first Meeting of the Legislature of the United States until a Census shall be taken, all Monies for supplying the public Treasury by direct Taxation shall be raised from the several States according to the Number of their Representatives respectively in the first Branch.

That in the second Branch of the Legislature of the United States each State shall have an equal vote.

That the Legislature of the United States ought to possess the legislative Rights vested in Congress by the Confederation; and moreover to legislate in all Cases for the general Interests of the Union, and also in those Cases to which the States are separately incompetent, or in which the Harmony of the United States may be interrupted by the Exercise of Individual Legislation.

That the legislative Acts of the United States made by Virtue and in Pursuance of the Articles of Union, and all Treaties made and ratified under the Authority of the United States shall be the supreme Law of the respective States so far as those Acts or Treaties shall relate to the said States, or their Citizens and Inhabitants; and that the Judicatures of the several States shall be bound thereby in their Decisions, any thing in the respective Laws of the individual States to the contrary notwithstanding.

That a national Executive be instituted to consist of a single Person—to be chosen for the Term of six Years—with Power to carry into Execution the national laws—to appoint to Offices in Cases not otherwise provided for—to be removable on Impeachment and Conviction of mal Practice or Neglect of Duty—to receive a fixed Compensation for the Devotion of his Time to public Service—to be paid out of the public Treasury.

That the national Executive shall have a Right to negative any legislative Act, which shall not be afterwards passed, unless by two third Parts of each Branch of the national Legislature.

That a national Judiciary be established to consist of one Supreme Tribunal—the Judges of which shall be appointed by the second Branch of the national Legislature—to hold their Offices during good behaviour—to receive punctually at stated Times a fixed Compensation for their Services, in which no Diminution shall be made so as to affect the Persons actually in Office at the Time of such Diminution.

That the Jurisdiction of the national Judiciary shall extend to Cases arising under the Laws passed by the general Legislature, and to such other Questions as involve the national Peace and Harmony.

That the national Legislature be empowered to appoint inferior Tribunals.

That Provision ought to be made for the Admission of States lawfully arising within the Limits of the United States, whether from a voluntary Junction of Government and Territory, or otherwise, with the Consent of a number of Voices in the national Legislature        less than the whole.

That a Republican Form of Government shall be guaranteed to each State; and that each State shall be protected against foreign and domestic Violence.

That Provision ought to be made for the Amendment of the Articles of Union, whensoever it shall seem necessary.

That the legislative, executive, and judiciary Powers, within the several States, and of the national Government, ought to be bound by Oath to support the Articles of Union.

That the Amendments which shall be offered to the Confederation by the Convention ought at a proper Time or Times, after the Approbation of Congress, to be submitted to an Assembly or Assemblies of Representatives, recommended by the several Legislatures, to be expressly chosen by the People to consider and decide thereon.

That the Representation in the second Branch of the Legislature of the United States consist of two Members of each State, who shall vote *per capita*.

That a National Executive be instituted—to consist of a Single Person—to be chosen by the National Legislature—for a Term of Seven Years—to be ineligible a second time; with power to carry into execution the national Laws; to appoint to Offices in cases not otherwise provided for; to be removable on impeachment and conviction of malpractice or neglect of duty; to receive a fixed compensation for the devotion of his time to public service; to be paid out of the public Treasury.

That it be an instruction of the Committee to whom are referred the proceedings of the Convention for the establishment of a national government, to receive a clause or clauses, requiring certain qualifications of property and citizenship in the United States for the Executive, the Judiciary, and the Members of both branches of the Legislature of the United States.

# THE CONSTITUTION AS REPORTED BY THE COMMITTEE OF DETAIL, AUGUST 6, 1787

WE THE PEOPLE of the States of New Hampshire, Massachusetts, Rhode-Island and Providence Plantations, Connecticut, New-York, New-Jersey, Pennsylvania, Delaware, Maryland, Virginia, North-Carolina, South-Carolina, and Georgia, do ordain, declare, and establish the following Constitution for the Government of Ourselves and our Posterity.

### ARTICLE I

The stile of this government shall be, "The United States of America."

### ARTICLE II

The Government shall consist of supreme legislative, executive, and judicial powers.

### ARTICLE III

The legislative power shall be vested in a Congress, to consist of two separate and distinct bodies of men, a House of Representatives and a Senate; each of which shall, in all cases, have a negative on the other. The legislature shall meet on the first Monday in December in every year.

### ARTICLE IV

Sect. 1. The members of the House of Representatives shall be chosen every second year, by the people of the several States comprehended within this Union. The qualifications of the electors shall be the same, from time to time, as those of the electors in the several States, of the most numerous branch of their own legislatures.

Sect. 2. Every member of the House of Representatives shall be of the age of twenty five years at least; shall have been a citizen in the United States for at least three years before his election; and shall be, at the time of his election, a resident of the State in which he shall be chosen.

Sect. 3. The House of Representatives shall, at its first formation, and until the number of citizens and inhabitants shall be taken in the manner herein after described, consist of sixty five Members, of whom three shall be chosen in New Hampshire, eight in Massachusetts, one in Rhode-Island and Providence Plantations, five in Connecticut, six in New-York, four in New-Jersey, eight in Pennsylvania, one in Delaware, six in Maryland, ten in Virginia, five in North-Carolina, five in South-Carolina, and three in Georgia.

Sect. 4. As the proportions of numbers in the different States will alter from time to time; as some of the States may hereafter be divided; as others may be enlarged by addition of territory; as two or more States may be united; as new States will be erected within the limits of the United States, the legislature shall, in each of these cases, regulate the number of representatives by the number of inhabitants, according to the provisions hereinafter made, at the rate of one for every forty thousand.

Sect. 5. All bills for raising or appropriating money, and for fixing the salaries of the officers of the government, shall originate in the House of Representatives, and shall not be altered or amended by the Senate. No money shall be drawn from the public Treasury, but in pursuance of appropriations that shall originate in the House of Representatives.

Sect. 6. The House of Representatives shall have the sole power of impeachment. It shall choose its Speaker and other officers.

Sect. 7. Vacancies in the House of Representatives shall be supplied by writs of election from the executive authority of the State, in the representation from which they shall happen.

ARTICLE V

Sect. 1. The Senate of the United States shall be chosen by the Legislatures of the several States. Each Legislature shall choose two members. Vacancies may be supplied by the Executive until the next meeting of the Legislature. Each member shall have one vote.

Sect. 2. The Senators shall be chosen for six years; but immediately after the first election they shall be divided, by lot, into three classes, as nearly as may be, numbered one, two, and three. The seats of the members of the first class shall be vacated at the expiration of the second year, of the second class, at the expiration of the fourth year, of the third class at the expiration of the sixth year, so that a third part of the members may be chosen every second year.

Sect. 3. Every member of the Senate shall be of the age of thirty years at least; shall have been a citizen in the United States for at least four years before his election; and shall be, at the time of his election, a resident of the State from which he shall be chosen.

Sect. 4. The Senate shall chuse its own President and other officers.

ARTICLE VI

Sect. 1. The times and places, and the manner of holding the elections of the members of each House shall be prescribed by the Legislature of each State; but their provisions concerning them may, at any time, be altered by the Legislature of the United States.

Sect. 2. The Legislature of the United States shall have authority to establish such uniform qualifications of the members of each House, with regard to property, as to the said legislature shall seem expedient.

Sect. 3. In each House a majority of the members shall constitute a quorum to do business; but a smaller number may adjourn from day to day.

Sect. 4. Each House shall be the judge of the elections, returns and qualifications of its own members.

Sect. 5. Freedom of speech and debate in the Legislature shall not be impeached or questioned in any Court or place out of the Legislature; and the members of each House shall, in all cases, except treason, felony, and breach of the peace, be privileged from arrest during their attendance at Congress, and in going to and returning from it.

Sect. 6. Each House may determine the rules of its proceedings; may punish its members for disorderly behaviour; and may expel a member.

Sect. 7. The House of Representatives, and the Senate, when it shall be acting in a legislative capacity, shall keep a journal of their proceedings, and shall, from time to time, publish them: and the yeas and nays of the members of each House, on any question, shall, at the desire of one fifth part of the members present, be entered on the journal.

Sect. 8. Neither House, without the consent of the other, shall adjourn for more than three days, nor to any other place than that at which the two Houses are sitting. But this regulation shall not extend to the Senate, when it shall exercise the powers mentioned in the article.

Sect. 9. The members of each House shall be ineligible to, and incapable of holding any office under the authority of the United States, during the time for which they shall respectively be elected: and the members of the Senate shall be ineligible to, and incapable of holding any such office for one year afterwards.

Sect. 10. The members of each House shall receive a compensation for their services, to be ascertained and paid by the State, in which they shall be chosen.

Sect. 11. The enacting stile of the laws of the United States shall be, "Be it enacted by the Senate and Representatives in Congress assembled."

Sect. 12. Each House shall possess the right of originating bills, except in the cases before mentioned.

Sect. 13. Every bill, which shall have passed the House of Representatives and the Senate, shall, before it becomes law, be presented to the President of the United States, for his revision: if, upon such revision, he approve of it, he shall signify his approbation by signing it: But if, upon such revision, it shall appear to him improper for being passed into a law, he shall return it, together with his objections against it, to that House in which it shall have originated, who shall enter the objections at large on their journal, and proceed to reconsider the bill. But if after such reconsideration, two thirds of that House shall, notwithstanding the objections of the President, agree to pass it, it shall together with his objections, be sent to the other house, by which it shall likewise be reconsidered, and if approved by two thirds of the other House also, it shall become law. But in all such cases, the votes of both Houses shall be determined by yeas and nays; and the names of the persons voting for or against the bill shall be entered in the journal of each House respectively. If any bill shall not be returned by the president within seven days after it shall have been presented to him, it shall be a law, unless the legislature by their adjournment, prevent its return; in which case, it shall not be a law.

### ARTICLE VII

Sect. 1. The Legislature of the United States shall have the power to lay and collect taxes, duties, imposts, and excises;

To regulate commerce with foreign nations, and among the several States;

To establish a uniform rule of naturalization throughout the United States;

To coin money;

To regulate the value of foreign coin;

To fix the standard of weights and measures;

To establish Post-offices;

To borrow money, and emit bills on the credit of the United States;

To appoint a Treasurer by ballot;

To constitute tribunals inferior to the Supreme Court;

To make rules concerning captures on land and water;

To declare the law and punishment of piracies and felonies committed on the high seas, and the punishment of counterfeiting the coin of the United States, and of offences against the law of nations;

To subdue a rebellion in any State, on the application of its legislature;

To make war;

To raise armies;

To build and equip fleets;

To call forth the aid of the militia, in order to execute the laws of the Union; enforce treaties, suppress insurrections, and repel invasions;

And to make all laws that shall be necessary and proper for carrying into execution the foregoing powers, and all other powers vested, by this constitution, in the government of the United States, or in any department or officer thereof.

Sect. 2. Treason against the United States shall consist only in levying war against the United States, or any of them; and in adhering to the enemies of the United States, or any of them. The Legislature of the United States shall have power to declare the punishment of treason. No person shall be convicted of treason, unless on the testimony of two witnesses. No attainder of treason shall work corruption of blood, nor forfeiture, except during the life of the person attainted.

Sect. 3. The proportions of direct taxation shall be regulated by the whole number of white and other free citizens and inhabitants of every age, sex, and condition, including those bound to servitude for a term of years, and three fifths of all other persons not comprehended in the foregoing description, (except Indians not paying taxes); which number shall, within six years after the first meeting of the Legislature, and within the term of every ten years afterwards, be taken in such manner as the said Legislature shall direct.

Sect. 4. No tax or duty shall be laid by the Legislature on articles exported from any State; nor on the migration or importation of such persons as the several States shall think proper to admit; nor shall such migration or importation be prohibited.

Sect. 5. No capitation tax shall be laid, unless in proportion to the census hereinbefore directed to be taken.

Sect. 6. No navigation act shall be passed without the assent of two thirds of the members present in each House.

Sect. 7. The United States shall not grant any title of nobility.

## ARTICLE VIII

The acts of the Legislature of the United States made in pursuance of this Constitution, and all treaties made under the authority of the United States shall be the supreme law of the several States, and of their citizens and inhabitants; and the judges in the several States shall be bound thereby in their decisions; any thing in the Constitution or laws of the several States to the contrary notwithstanding.

## ARTICLE IX

Sect. 1. The Senate of the United States shall have power to make treaties, and to appoint Ambassadors, and Judges of the Supreme Court.

Sect. 2. In all disputes and controversies now subsisting, or that may hereafter subsist between two or more States, respecting jurisdiction or territory, the Senate shall possess the following powers. Whenever the Legislature, or the Executive authority, or the lawful Agent of any State, in controversy with another, shall by memorial to the Senate, state the matter in question, and apply for a hearing; notice of such memorial and application shall be given by order of the Senate, to the Legislature or the Executive authority of the other State in controversy. The Senate shall also assign a day for the appearance of the parties, by their agents, before that House. The Agents shall be directed to appoint, by joint consent, commissioners or judges to constitute a Court for hearing and determining the matter in question. But, if the Agents cannot agree, the Senate shall name three persons out of each of the several States; and from the list of such persons each party shall alternately strike out one, until the number shall be reduced to thirteen; and from that number not less than seven, nor more than nine names, as the Senate shall direct, shall in their presence, be drawn out by lot; and the persons whose names shall be so drawn, or any five of them shall be commissioners or Judges to hear and finally determine the controversy; provided a majority of the Judges, who shall hear the cause, agree in the determination. If either party shall neglect to attend at any day assigned, without showing sufficient reasons for not attending, or being present shall refuse to strike, the Senate shall proceed to nominate three persons out of each State, and the clerk of the Senate shall strike in behalf of the party absent or refusing. If any of the parties shall refuse to submit to the authority of such Court, or shall not appear to prosecute or defend their claim or cause, the Court shall nevertheless proceed to pronounce judgment. The judgment shall be final and conclusive. The proceedings shall be transmitted to the President of the Senate, and shall be lodged among the public records for the security of the parties concerned. Every Commissioner shall, before he sit in judgment, take an oath, to be administered by one of the judges of the Supreme or Superior Court of the State where the cause shall be tried, "well and truly to hear and determine the matter in question according to the best of his judgment, without favor, affection, or hope of reward."

Sect. 3. All controversies concerning lands claimed under different grants of two or more States, whose jurisdictions as they respect such lands shall have been decided or adjusted subsequent to such grants, or any of them, shall, on application to the Senate, be finally determined, as near as may be, in the same manner as is before prescribed for deciding controversies between different States.

ARTICLE X

Sect. 1. The Executive Power of the United States shall be vested in a single person. His stile shall be, "The President of the United States of America"; and his title shall be, "His Excellency." He shall be elected by ballot by the Legislature. He shall hold his office during the term of seven years; but shall not be elected a second time.

Sect. 2. He shall, from time to time, give information to the Legislature, of the state of the Union: he may recommend to their consideration such measures as he shall judge necessary and expedient: he may convene them on extraordinary occasions. In case of disagreement between the two Houses, with regard to the time of adjournment, he may adjourn them to such time as he thinks proper: he shall take care that the laws of the United States be duly and faithfully executed: he shall commission all the officers of the United States; and shall appoint officers in all cases not otherwise provided for by this Constitution. He shall receive Ambassadors, and may correspond with the supreme Executives of the several States. He shall have power to grant reprieves and pardons; but his pardon shall not be pleadable in bar of an impeachment. He shall be commander in chief of the Army and navy of the United States, and of the Militia of the several States. He shall, at stated times, receive for his services a compensation, which shall neither be increased nor diminished during his continuance in office. Before he shall enter on the duties of his department, he shall take the following oath or affirmation: "I —— —— solemnly swear (or affirm), that I will faithfully execute the office of President of the United States of America." He shall be removed from his office on impeachment by the House of Representatives, and conviction in the Supreme Court, of treason, bribery, or corruption. In case of his removal as aforesaid, death, resignation, or disability to discharge the powers and duties of his office, the President of the Senate shall exercise those powers and duties until another President of the United States be chosen, or until the disability of the President be removed.

### ARTICLE XI

Sect. 1. The Judicial Power of the United States shall be vested in one Supreme Court, and in such inferior Courts as shall, when necessary, from time to time, be constituted by the Legislature of the United States.

Sect. 2. The Judges of the Supreme Court, and of the Inferior Courts, shall hold their offices during good behaviour. They shall, at stated times, receive for their services a compensation, which shall not be diminished during their continuance in office.

Sect. 3. The Jurisdiction of the Supreme Court shall extend to all cases arising under laws passed by the Legislature of the United States; to all cases affecting Ambassadors, other Public Ministers, and Consuls; to the trial of impeachments of Officers of the United States; to all cases of Admiralty and maritime jurisdiction; to controversies between two or more States (except such as shall regard Territory or Jurisdiction), between a State and citizens of another State, between Citizens of different States, and between a State or the citizens thereof and foreign states, citizens, or subjects. In cases of impeachment, cases affecting Ambassadors, other Public Ministers, and Consuls, and those in which a State shall be a party, this jurisdiction shall be original. In all the other cases before mentioned, it shall be appellate, with such exceptions and under such regulations as the Legislature shall make. The Legislature may assign any part of the jurisdiction above mentioned (except the trial of the President of the United States) in the manner and under the limitations which it shall think proper, to such Inferior Courts as it shall constitute from time to time.

Sect. 4. The trial of all criminal offences (except in cases of impeachments) shall be in the State where they shall be committed; and shall be by jury.

Sect. 5. Judgment, in cases of Impeachment, shall not extend farther than to removal from Office, and disqualification to hold and enjoy any office of honor, trust, or profit under the United States. But the party convicted shall, nevertheless, be liable and subject to indictment, trial, judgment, and punishment according to law.

### ARTICLE XII

No State shall coin money; nor grant letters of marque and reprisal; nor enter into any treaty, alliance, or confederation; nor grant any title of Nobility.

### ARTICLE XIII

No State, without the consent of the Legislature of the United States, shall emit bills of credit, or make any thing but specie a tender in payment of debts; nor lay imposts or duties on imports; nor keep troops or ships of war in time of peace; nor enter into any agreement or compact with another State, or with any foreign power; nor engage in any war, unless it shall be actually invaded by enemies, or the danger of invasion be so imminent, as not to admit of a delay, until the Legislature of the United States can be consulted.

### ARTICLE XIV

The Citizens of each State shall be entitled to all privileges and immunities of citizens in the several States.

### ARTICLE XV

Any person charged with treason, felony, or high misdemeanor, in any State, who shall flee from justice, and shall be found in any other State, shall, on demand of the Executive power of the State from which he fled, be delivered up and removed to the State having jurisdiction of the offence.

### ARTICLE XVI

Full faith shall be given in each State to the acts of the Legislatures, and to the records and judicial proceedings of the Courts and Magistrates of every other State.

### ARTICLE XVII

New States lawfully constituted or established within the limits of the United States may be admitted, by the Legislature, into this government; but to such admission the consent of two thirds of the members present in each House shall be necessary. If a new State shall arise within the limits of any of the present States, the consent of the Legislatures of such States shall be also necessary to its admission. If the admission be consented to, the new States shall be admitted on the same terms with the original States. But the legislature may make conditions with the new States concerning the public debt which shall be then subsisting.

### ARTICLE XVIII

The United States shall guaranty to each State a Republican form of Government; and shall protect each State against foreign invasions; and, on the application of its Legislature, against domestic violence.

### ARTICLE XIX

On the application of the Legislatures of two thirds of the States in the Union for an amendment of this Constitution, the Legislature of the United States shall call a Convention for that purpose.

### ARTICLE XX

The members of the Legislatures, and the Executive and Judicial officers of the United States, and of the several States, shall be bound by oath to support this constitution.

### ARTICLE XXI

The ratification of the Conventions of          States shall be sufficient for organizing this Constitution.

### ARTICLE XXII

This Constitution shall be laid before the United States in Congress assembled, for their approbation; and it is the opinion of this Convention, that it should be afterwards submitted to a Convention chosen in each State, under the recommendation of its legislature, in order to receive the ratification of such Convention.

### ARTICLE XXIII

To introduce this government, it is the opinion of this convention, that each assenting Convention should notify its assent and ratification to the United States in Congress assembled; that Congress, after receiving the assent and ratifications of the Conventions of          States, should appoint and publish a day, as early as may be, and appoint a place for commencing proceedings under this Constitution; that after such publication, the Legislatures of the several States should elect members of the Senate, and direct the election of members of the House of Representatives; and that the members of the Legislature should meet at the time and place assigned by Congress, and should, as soon as maybe, after their meeting, choose the President of the United States, and proceed to execute this Constitution.

# THE CONSTITUTION OF THE UNITED STATES

WE THE PEOPLE of the United States, in Order to form a more perfect Union, establish Justice, insure domestic Tranquility, provide for the common defence, promote the general Welfare, and secure the Blessings of Liberty to ourselves and our Posterity, do ordain and establish this CONSTITUTION for the United States of America.

SECTION 1. All legislative Powers herein granted shall be vested in a Congress of the United States, which shall consist of a Senate and House of Representatives.

SECTION 2. The House of Representatives shall be composed of Members chosen every second Year by the People of the several States, and the Electors in each State shall have the Qualifications requisite for Electors of the most numerous Branch of the State Legislature.

No Person shall be a Representative who shall not have attained to the Age of twenty five Years, and been seven Years a Citizen of the United States, and who shall not, when elected, be an Inhabitant of that State in which he shall be chosen.

Representatives and direct Taxes shall be apportioned among the several States which may be included within this Union, according to their respective Numbers, which shall be determined by adding to the whole Number of free Persons, including those bound to Service for a Term of Years, and excluding Indians not taxed, three fifths of all other Persons. The actual Enumeration shall be made within three Years after the first Meeting of the Congress of the United States, and within every subsequent Term of ten Years, in such Manner as they shall by Law direct. The Number of Representatives shall not exceed one for every thirty Thousand, but each State shall have at least one Representative; and until such enumeration shall be made, the State of New Hampshire shall be entitled to chuse three, Massachusetts eight, Rhode-Island and Providence Plantations one, Connecticut five, New-York six, New Jersey four, Pennsylvania eight, Delaware one, Maryland six, Virginia ten, North Carolina five, South Carolina five, and Georgia three.

When vacancies happen in the Representation from any State, the Executive Authority thereof shall issue Writs of Election to fill such Vacancies.

The House of Representatives shall chuse their Speaker and other Officers; and shall have the sole Power of Impeachment.

SECTION 3. The Senate of the United States shall be composed of
two Senators from each State, chosen by the Legislature thereof,
for six years; and each Senator shall have one Vote.

Immediately after they shall be assembled in Consequence of
the first Election, they shall be divided as equally as may be into
three Classes. The Seats of the Senators of the first Class shall
be vacated at the Expiration of the second Year, of the second
Class at the Expiration of the fourth Year, and of the third
Class at the Expiration of the sixth Year, so that one third may
be chosen every second Year; and If Vacancies happen by Resignation, or otherwise, during the Recess of the Legislature of any
State, the Executive thereof may make temporary Appointments
until the next Meeting of the Legislature, which shall then fill
such Vacancies.

No Person shall be a Senator who shall not have attained to
the Age of thirty Years, and been nine Years a Citizen of the
United States, and who shall not, when elected, be an Inhabitant
of that State for which he shall be chosen.

The Vice President of the United States shall be President of
the Senate, but shall have no Vote, unless they be equally divided.

The Senate shall chuse their other Officers, and also a President
pro tempore, in the Absence of the Vice President, or when he
shall exercise the Office of President of the United States.

The Senate shall have the sole Power to try all Impeachments.
When sitting for that Purpose, they shall be on Oath or Affirmation. When the President of the United States is tried, the Chief
Justice shall preside: And no Person shall be convicted without
the Concurrence of two thirds of the Members present.

Judgment in Cases of Impeachment shall not extend further
than to removal from Office, and disqualification to hold and
enjoy any Office of honor, Trust or Profit under the United
States: but the Party convicted shall nevertheless be liable and
subject to Indictment, Trial, Judgment and Punishment, according
to Law.

SECTION 4. The Times, Places and Manner of holding Elections
for Senators and Representatives, shall be prescribed in each
State by the Legislature thereof; but the Congress may at any
time by Law make or alter such Regulations, except as to the
Places of chusing Senators.

The Congress shall assemble at least once in every Year, and
such Meeting shall be on the first Monday in December, unless
they shall by Law appoint a different Day.

SECTION 5. Each House shall be the Judge of the Elections, Returns and Qualifications of its own Members, and a Majority of
each shall constitute a Quorum to do Business; but a smaller
Number may adjourn from day to day, and may be authorized
to compel the Attendance of absent Members, in such Manner,
and under such Penalties as each House may provide.

Each House may determine the Rules of its Proceedings, punish
its Members for disorderly Behaviour, and, with the Concurrence
of two thirds, expel a Member.

Each House shall keep a Journal of its Proceedings, and from time to time publish the same, excepting such Parts as may in their Judgment require Secrecy; and the Yeas and Nays of the Members of either House on any question shall, at the desire of one fifth of those Present, be entered on the Journal.

Neither House, during the Session of Congress, shall, without the Consent of the other, adjourn for more than three days, nor to any other Place than that in which the two Houses shall be sitting.

SECTION 6. The Senators and Representatives shall receive a Compensation for their Services, to be ascertained by Law, and paid out of the Treasury of the United States. They shall in all Cases, except Treason, Felony and Breach of the Peace, be privileged from Arrest during their Attendance at the Session of their respective Houses, and in going to and returning from the same; and for any Speech or Debate in either House, they shall not be questioned in any other Place.

No Senator or Representative shall, during the Time for which he was elected, be appointed to any civil Office under the Authority of the United States, which shall have been created, or the Emoluments whereof shall have been encreased during such time; and no Person holding any Office under the United States, shall be a Member of either House during his Continuance in Office.

SECTION 7. All Bills for raising Revenue shall originate in the House of Representatives; but the Senate may propose or concur with Amendments as on other Bills.

Every Bill which shall have passed the House of Representatives and the Senate, shall, before it becomes a Law, be presented to the President of the United States; If he approves he shall sign it, but if not he shall return it, with his Objections to that House in which it shall have originated, who shall enter the Objections at large on their Journal, and proceed to reconsider it. If after such Reconsideration two thirds of that House shall agree to pass the Bill, it shall be sent, together with the Objections, to the other House, by which it shall likewise be reconsidered, and if approved by two thirds of that House, it shall become a Law. But in all such Cases the Votes of both Houses shall be determined by yeas and Nays, and the Names of the Persons voting for and against the Bill shall be entered on the Journal of each House respectively. If any Bill shall not be returned by the President within ten Days (Sundays excepted) after it shall have been presented to him, the Same shall be a Law, in like Manner as if he had signed it, unless the Congress by their Adjournment prevent its Return, in which Case it shall not be a Law.

Every Order, Resolution, or Vote to which the Concurrence of the Senate and House of Representatives may be necessary (except on a question of Adjournment) shall be presented to the President of the United States; and before the Same shall take Effect, shall be approved by him, or being disapproved by him, shall be repassed by two thirds of the Senate and House of Representatives, according to the Rules and Limitations prescribed in the Case of a Bill.

SECTION 8. The Congress shall have Power To lay and collect Taxes, Duties, Imposts and Excises, to pay the Debts and provide for the common Defence and general Welfare of the United States; but all Duties, Imposts and Excises shall be uniform throughout the United States;

To borrow Money on the credit of the United States;

To regulate Commerce with foreign Nations, and among the several States, and with the Indian Tribes;

To establish an uniform Rule of Naturalization, and uniform Laws on the subject of Bankruptcies throughout the United States;

To coin Money, regulate the Value thereof, and of foreign Coin, and fix the Standard of Weights and Measures;

To provide for the Punishment of counterfeiting the Securities and current Coin of the United States;

To establish Post Offices and post Roads;

To promote the Progress of Science and useful Arts, by securing for limited Times to Authors and Inventors the exclusive Right to their respective Writings and Discoveries;

To constitute Tribunals inferior to the supreme Court;

To define and punish Piracies and Felonies committed on the high Seas, and Offences against the Law of Nations;

To declare War, grant Letters of Marque and Reprisal, and make Rules concerning Captures on Land and Water;

To raise and support Armies, but no Appropriation of Money to that Use shall be for a longer Term than two Years;

To provide and maintain a Navy;

To make Rules for the Government and Regulation of the land and naval Forces;

To provide for calling forth the Militia to execute the Laws of the Union, suppress Insurrections and repel Invasions;

To provide for organizing, and disciplining, the Militia, and for governing such Part of them as may be employed in the Service of the United States, reserving to the States respectively, the Appointment of the Officers, and the Authority of training the Militia according to the discipline prescribed by Congress;

To exercise exclusive Legislation in all Cases whatsoever, over such District (not exceeding ten Miles square) as may, by Cession of particular States, and the Acceptance of Congress, become the Seat of the Government of the United States, and to exercise like Authority over all Places purchased by the Consent of the Legislature of the State in which the Same shall be, for the Erection of Forts, Magazines, Arsenals, dock-Yards, and other needful Buildings;—And

To make all Laws which shall be necessary and proper for carrying into Execution the foregoing Powers, and all other Powers vested by this Constitution in the Government of the United States, or in any Department or Officer thereof.

SECTION 9. The Migration or Importation of such Persons as any of the States now existing shall think proper to admit, shall not be prohibited by the Congress prior to the Year one thousand eight hundred and eight, but a Tax or duty may be imposed on such Importation, not exceeding ten dollars for each Person.

The Privilege of the Writ of Habeas Corpus shall not be suspended, unless when in Cases of Rebellion or Invasion the public Safety may require it.

No Bill of Attainder or ex post facto Law shall be passed.

No Capitation, or other direct, Tax shall be laid, unless in Proportion to the Census or Enumeration herein before directed to be taken.

No Tax or Duty shall be laid on Articles exported from any State.

No Preference shall be given by any Regulation of Commerce or Revenue to the Ports of one State over those of another: nor shall Vessels bound to, or from, one State, be obliged to enter, clear, or pay Duties in another.

No Money shall be drawn from the Treasury, but in Consequence of Appropriations made by Law; and a regular Statement and Account of the Receipts and Expenditures of all public Money shall be published from time to time.

No Title of Nobility shall be granted by the United States: And no Person holding any Office of Profit or Trust under them, shall, without the Consent of the Congress, accept of any present, Emolument, Office, or Title, of any kind whatever, from any King, Prince, or foreign State.

SECTION 10. No State shall enter into any Treaty, Alliance, or Confederation; grant Letters of Marque and Reprisal; coin Money; emit Bills of Credit; make any Thing but gold and silver Coin a Tender in Payment of Debts; pass any Bill of Attainder, ex post facto Law, or Law impairing the Obligation of Contracts, or grant any Title of Nobility.

No State shall, without the Consent of the Congress, lay any Imposts or Duties on Imports or Exports, except what may be absolutely necessary for executing its inspection Laws: and the net Produce of all Duties and Imposts, laid by any State on Imports or Exports, shall be for the Use of the Treasury of the United States; and all such Laws shall be subject to the Revision and Controul of the Congress.

No State shall, without the Consent of Congress, lay any Duty on Tonnage, Keep Troops, or Ships of War in time of Peace, enter into any Agreement or Compact with another State, or with a foreign Power, or engage in War, unless actually invaded, or in such imminent Danger as will not admit of delay.

## ARTICLE II

SECTION 1. The executive Power shall be vested in a President of the United States of America. He shall hold his Office during the Term of four Years, and, together with the Vice President, chosen for the same Term, be elected, as follows

Each State shall appoint, in such Manner as the Legislature thereof may direct, a Number of Electors, equal to the whole Number of Senators and Representatives to which the State may be entitled in the Congress: but no Senator or Representative, or Person holding an Office of Trust or Profit under the United States, shall be appointed an Elector.

The electors shall meet in their respective States, and vote by Ballot for two Persons, of whom one at least shall not be an Inhabitant of the same State with themselves. And they shall make a List of all the Persons voted for, and of the Number of Votes for each; which List they shall sign and certify, and transmit sealed to the Seat of the Government of the United States, directed to the President of the Senate. The President of the Senate shall, in the Presence of the Senate and House of Representatives, open all the Certificates, and the Votes shall then be counted. The Person having the greatest Number of Votes shall be the President, if such Number be a Majority of the whole Number of Electors appointed; and if there be more than one who have such Majority, and have an equal Number of Votes, then the House of Representatives shall immediately chuse by Ballot one of them for President; and if no Person have a Majority, then from the five highest on the List the said House shall in like Manner chuse the President. But in chusing the President, the Votes shall be taken by States, the Representation from each State having one Vote; A quorum for this Purpose shall consist of a Member or Members from two thirds of the States, and a Majority of all the States shall be necessary to a Choice. In every Case, after the Choice of the President, the Person having the greatest Number of Votes of the Electors shall be the Vice President. But if there should remain two or more who have equal Votes, the Senate shall chuse from them by Ballot the Vice President.

The Congress may determine the Time of chusing the Electors, and the Day on which they shall give their Votes; which Day shall be the same throughout the United States.

No Person except a natural born Citizen, or a Citizen of the United States, at the time of the Adoption of this Constitution, shall be eligible to the office of President; neither shall any Person be eligible to that Office who shall not have attained to the Age of thirty five Years, and been fourteen Years a Resident within the United States.

In Case of the Removal of the President from Office, or of his Death, Resignation, or Inability to discharge the Powers and Duties of the said Office, the Same shall devolve on the Vice President, and the Congress may by Law provide for the Case of Removal, Death, Resignation or Inability, both of the President and Vice President, declaring what Officer shall then act as President, and such Officer shall act accordingly, until the Disability be removed, or a President shall be elected.

The President shall, at stated Times, receive for his Services a Compensation, which shall neither be encreased nor diminished during the Period for which he shall have been elected, and he shall not receive within that Period any other Emolument from the United States, or any of them.

Before he enter on the Execution of his Office, he shall take the following Oath or Affirmation:—"I do solemnly swear (or affirm) that I will faithfully execute the Office of the President of the United States, and will to the best of my Ability, preserve, protect and defend the Constitution of the United States."

SECTION 2. The President shall be Commander in Chief of the Army and Navy of the United States, and of the Militia of the several States, when called into the actual Service of the United States; he may require the Opinion, in writing, of the principal Officer in each of the executive Departments, upon any Subject relating to the Duties of their respective Offices, and he shall have Power to grant Reprieves and Pardons for Offences against the United States, except in Cases of Impeachment.

He shall have Power, by and with the Advice and Consent of the Senate, to make Treaties, provided two thirds of the Senators present concur; and he shall nominate, and by and with the Advice and Consent of the Senate, shall appoint Ambassadors, other public Ministers and Consuls, Judges of the supreme Court, and all other Officers of the United States, whose Appointments are not herein otherwise provided for, and which shall be established by Law; but the Congress may by Law vest the Appointment of such inferior Officers, as they think proper, in the President alone, in the Courts of Law, or in the Heads of Departments.

The President shall have Power to fill up all Vacancies that may happen during the Recess of the Senate, by granting Commissions which shall expire at the End of their next Session.

SECTION 3. He shall from time to time give to the Congress Information of the State of the Union, and recommend to their Consideration such Measures as he shall judge necessary and expedient; he may, on extraordinary Occasions, convene both Houses, or either of them, and in Case of Disagreement between them, with Respect to the Time of Adjournment, he may adjourn them to such Time as he shall think proper; he shall receive Ambassadors and other public Ministers; he shall take Care that the Laws be faithfully executed, and shall Commission all the Officers of the United States.

SECTION 4. The President, Vice President and all civil Officers of the United States, shall be removed from Office on Impeachment for, and Conviction of, Treason, Bribery, or other high crimes and Misdemeanors.

## ARTICLE III

SECTION 1. The judicial Power of the United States, shall be vested in one supreme Court, and in such inferior Courts as the Congress may from time to time ordain and establish. The Judges, both of the supreme and inferior Courts, shall hold their Offices during good Behaviour, and shall, at stated Times, receive for their Services, Compensation, which shall not be diminished during their continuance in Office.

SECTION 2. The judicial Power shall extend to all Cases, in Law and Equity, arising under this Constitution, the Laws of the United States, and Treaties made, or which shall be made, under their Authority;—to all Cases affecting Ambassadors, other public Ministers and Consuls;—to all Cases of admiralty and maritime Jurisdiction;—to Controversies to which the United States shall be a Party;—to Controversies between two or more States;

—between a State and Citizens of another State;—between Citizens of different States,—between Citizens of the same State claiming Lands under Grants of different States, and between a State, or the Citizens thereof, and foreign States, Citizens or Subjects.

In all Cases affecting Ambassadors, other public Ministers and Consuls, and those in which a State shall be Party, the supreme Court shall have original Jurisdiction. In all the other Cases before mentioned, the supreme Court shall have appellate Jurisdiction, both as to Law and Fact, with such Exception, and under such regulations as the Congress shall make.

The Trial of all Crimes, except in Cases of Impeachment, shall be by Jury; and such Trial shall be held in the State where the said Crimes shall have been committed; but when not committed within any State, the Trial shall be at such Place or Places as the Congress may by Law have directed.

SECTION 3. Treason against the United States, shall consist only in levying War against them, or in adhering to their Enemies, giving them Aid and Comfort. No person shall be convicted of Treason unless on the Testimony of two Witnesses to the same overt Act, or on Confession in open Court.

The Congress shall have Power to declare the Punishment of Treason, but no Attainder of Treason shall work Corruption of Blood, or Forfeiture except during the Life of the Person attainted.

### ARTICLE IV

SECTION 1. Full Faith and Credit shall be given in each State to the public Acts, Records, and judicial Proceedings of every other State. And the Congress may by general Laws prescribe the Manner in which such Acts, Records and Proceedings shall be proved, and the Effect thereof.

SECTION 2. The Citizens of each State shall be entitled to all Privileges and Immunities of Citizens in the several States.

A Person charged in any State with Treason, Felony, or other Crime, who shall flee from Justice, and be found in another State, shall on demand of the executive Authority of the State from which he fled, be delivered up, to be removed to the State having Jurisdiction of the Crime.

No Person held to Service or Labour in one State, under the Laws or Regulation therein, be discharged from such Service or Labour, but shall be delivered up on Claim of the Party to whom such Service or Labour may be due.

SECTION 3. New States may be admitted by the Congress into this Union; but no new State shall be formed or erected within the Jurisdiction of any other State; nor any State be formed by the Junction of two or more States, or Parts of States, without the Consent of the Legislatures of the States concerned as well as of the Congress.

The Congress shall have Power to dispose of and make all needful Rules and Regulations respecting the Territory or other Property belonging to the United States; and nothing in this

Constitution shall be so construed as to Prejudice any Claims of the United States, or of any particular State.

Section 4. The United States shall guarantee to every State in this Union a Republican Form of Government, and shall protect each of them against Invasion; and on Application of the Legislature, or of the Executive (when the Legislature cannot be convened) against domestic Violence.

## ARTICLE V

The Congress, whenever two thirds of both Houses shall deem it necessary, shall propose Amendments to this Constitution, or, on the Application of the Legislatures of two thirds of the several States, shall call a Convention for proposing Amendments, which, in either Case, shall be valid to all Intents and Purposes, as Part of this Constitution, when ratified by the Legislatures of three fourths of the several States, or by Conventions in three fourths of the several States, or by Conventions in three fourths thereof, as the one or the other Mode of Ratification may be proposed by the Congress; Provided that no Amendment which may be made prior to the Year One thousand eight hundred and eight shall in any Manner affect the first and fourth Clauses in the Ninth Section of the first Article; and that no State, without its Consent, shall be deprived of its equal Suffrage in the Senate.

## ARTICLE VI

All Debts contracted and Engagements entered into, before the Adoption of this Constitution, shall be valid against the United States under this Constitution, as under the Confederation.

This Constitution, and the Laws of the United States which shall be made in Pursuance thereof; and all Treaties made, or which shall be made, under the Authority of the United States, shall be the supreme Law of the Land; and the Judges in every State shall be bound thereby, any Thing in the Constitution or Laws of any State to the Contrary notwithstanding.

The Senators and Representatives before mentioned, and the Members of the several State Legislatures, and all executive and judicial Officers, both of the United States and of the several States, shall be bound by Oath or Affirmation, to support this Constitution; but not religious Test shall ever be required as a Qualification to any Office or public Trust under the United States.

## ARTICLE VII

The Ratification of the Conventions of nine States, shall be sufficient for the Establishment of this Constitution between the States so ratifying the Same.

Done in Convention by the Unanimous Consent of the States present the Seventeenth Day of September in the Year of our Lord one thousand seven hundred and eighty seven and of the

Independence of the United States of America the Twelfth In Witness whereof We have hereunto subscribed our Names,

George Washington—President and deputy from Virginia Attest WILLIAM JACKSON *Secretary*

| New Hampshire | JOHN LANGDON |
| | NICHOLAS GILMAN |

| Massachusetts | NATHANIEL GORHAM |
| | RUFUS KING |

| Connecticut | WM: SAML. JOHNSON |
| | ROGER SHERMAN |

| New York | ALEXANDER HAMILTON |

| New Jersey | WIL: LIVINGSTON |
| | DAVID BREARLEY |
| | WM. PATERSON |
| | JONA: DAYTON |

| Pennsylvania | B. FRANKLIN |
| | THOMAS MIFFLIN |
| | ROBT. MORRIS |
| | GEO. CLYMER |
| | THOS. FITZ SIMONS |
| | JARED INGERSOLL |
| | JAMES WILSON |
| | GOUV MORRIS |

| Delaware | GEO: READ |
| | GUNNING BEDFORD jun |
| | JOHN DICKINSON |
| | RICHARD BASSETT |
| | JACO: BROOM |

| Maryland | JAMES MCHENRY |
| | DAN OF ST THOS. JENIFER |
| | DANL CARROLL |

| Virginia | JOHN BLAIR |
| | JAMES MADISON JR. |

| North Carolina | { | WM: BLOUNT |
| | | RICHD. DOBBS SPAIGHT |
| | | HU WILLIAMSON |

| South Carolina | { | J. RUTLEDGE |
| | | CHARLES COTESWORTH PINCKNEY |
| | | CHARLES PINCKNEY |
| | | PIERCE BUTLER |

| Georgia | { | WILLIAM FEW |
| | | ABR BALDWIN |

# RESOLUTIONS OF THE CONVENTION, SEPTEMBER 17, 1787

PRESENT, The States of New-Hampshire, Massachusetts, Connecticut, Mr. Hamilton from New-York, New Jersey, Pennsylvania, Delaware, Maryland, Virginia, North Carolina, South Carolina, and Georgia.

*Resolved,* That the preceding Constitution be laid before the United States in Congress assembled, and that it is the opinion of this convention, that it should afterwards be submitted to a convention of delegates, chosen in each State by the people thereof, under the recommendation of its legislature, for their assent and ratification; and that each convention assenting to, and ratifying the same should give notice thereof to the United States in Congress assembled.

*Resolved,* That it is the opinion of this convention, that as soon as the conventions of nine States shall have ratified this Constitution, the United States in Congress assembled should fix a day on which electors should be appointed by the States which shall have ratified the same, and a day on which the electors should assemble to vote for the President, and the time and place for commencing proceedings under this Constitution; that after such publication the electors should be appointed, and the senators and representatives elected; that the electors should meet on the day fixed for the election of the President, and should transmit their votes certified, signed, sealed, and directed, as the Constitution requires, to the secretary of the United States in Congress assembled; that the senators and representatives should convene at the time and place assigned; that the senators should appoint a president of the Senate, for the sole purpose of receiving, opening and counting the votes for President; and that after he shall be chosen, the Congress, together with the President, should without delay proceed to execute this Constitution.

*By the unanimous order of the convention.*

GEORGE WASHINGTON, President.

WILLIAM JACKSON, Secretary.

# LETTER OF THE CONVENTION TO CONGRESS,
## SEPTEMBER 17, 1787

SIR, we have now the honor to submit to the consideration of the United States in Congress assembled, that Constitution which has appeared to us the most advisable.

The friends of our country have long seen and desired, that the power of making war, peace, and treaties, of levying money and regulating commerce, and the correspondent executive and judicial authorities should be fully and effectually vested in the general government of the Union: but the impropriety of delegating such extensive trust to one body of men is evident—Hence results the necessity of a different organization.

It is obviously impracticable in the federal government of these States, to secure all rights of independent sovereignty to each, and yet provide for the interest and safety of all—individuals entering into society, must give up a share of liberty to preserve the rest. The magnitude of the sacrifice must depend as well on situation and circumstances as on the object to be obtained. It is at all times difficult to draw with precision the line between those rights which must be surrendered, and those which may be reserved; and on the present occasion this difficulty was increased by a difference among the several States as to their situation, extent, habits, and particular interests.

In all our deliberations on this subject we kept steadily in our view, that which appears to us the greatest interest of every true American, the consolidation of our Union, in which is involved our prosperity, felicity, safety, perhaps our national existence. This important consideration, seriously and deeply impressed on our minds, led each State in the Convention to be less rigid on points of inferior magnitude, than might have been otherwise expected; and thus the Constitution, which we now present, is the result of a spirit of amity, and of that mutual deference and concession which the peculiarity of our political situation rendered indispensable.

That it will meet the full and entire approbation of every State is not perhaps to be expected; but each will doubtless consider, that had her interest alone been consulted, the consequences might have been particularly disagreeable or injurious to others; that it is liable to as few exceptions as could reasonably have been expected; we hope and believe; that it may promote the lasting welfare of that country so dear to us all, and secure her freedom and happiness, is our most ardent wish.

With great respect,

We have the honor to be

SIR,

Your Excellency's most

Obedient and Humble Servants,

GEORGE WASHINGTON, President

By Unanimous Order of the Convention

HIS EXCELLENCY
THE PRESIDENT OF CONGRESS

# THE BILL OF RIGHTS

[December 15, 1791]

### ARTICLE I

Congress shall make no law respecting an establishment of religion, or prohibiting the free exercise thereof; or abridging the freedom of speech, or of the press; or the right of the people peaceably to assemble, and to petition the Government for a redress of grievances.

### ARTICLE II

A well regulated Militia, being necessary to the security of a free State, the right of the people to keep and bear Arms, shall not be infringed.

### ARTICLE III

No Soldier shall, in time of peace be quartered in any house, without the consent of the Owner, nor in time of war, but in a manner to be prescribed by law.

### ARTICLE IV

The right of the people to be secure in their persons, houses, papers, and effects, against unreasonable searches and seizures, shall not be violated, and no Warrants shall issue, but upon probable cause, supported by Oath or affirmation, and particularly describing the place to be searched, and the person or things to be seized.

### ARTICLE V

No person shall be held to answer for a capital, or otherwise infamous crime, unless on a presentment or indictment of a Grand Jury, except in cases arising in the land or naval forces, or in the Militia, when in actual service in time of War or public danger; nor shall any person be subject for the same offence to be twice put in jeopardy of life or limb; nor shall be compelled in any Criminal Case to be a witness against himself, nor be deprived of life, liberty, or property, without due process of law; nor shall private property be taken for public use, without just compensation.

### ARTICLE VI

In all criminal prosecutions, the accused shall enjoy the right to a speedy and public trial, by an impartial jury of the State and district wherein the crime shall have been committed, which district shall have been previously ascertained by law, and to be informed of the nature and cause of the accusation; to be confronted with the witnesses against him; to have compulsory process for obtaining witnesses in his favor, and to have the Assistance of Counsel for his defence.

### ARTICLE VII

In Suits at common law, where the value in controversy shall exceed twenty dollars, the right of trial by jury shall be preserved, and no fact tried by a jury, shall be otherwise re-examined in any Court of the United States, than according to the rules of the common law.

### ARTICLE VIII

Excessive bail shall not be required, nor excessive fines imposed, nor cruel and unusual punishments inflicted.

### ARTICLE IX

The enumeration in the Constitution, of certain rights, shall not be construed to deny or disparage others retained by the people.

### ARTICLE X

The powers not delegated to the United States by the Constitution, nor prohibited by it to the States, are reserved to the States respectively, or to the people.

# AMENDMENTS XI-XXIV

[Janary 8, 1798]

The Judicial power of the United States shall not be construed to extend to any suit in law or equity, commenced or prosecuted against one of the United States by Citizens of another State, or by Citizens or Subjects of any Foreign State.

[September 25, 1804]

The Electors shall meet in their respective states, and vote by ballot for President and Vice-President, one of whom, at least, shall not be an inhabitant of the same state with themselves; they shall name in their ballots the person voted for as President, and in distinct ballots the person voted for as Vice-President, and they shall make distinct lists of all persons voted for as President, and of all persons voted for as Vice-President, and of the number of votes for each, which lists they shall sign and certify, and transmit sealed to the seat of the government of the United States, directed to the President of the Senate;—The President of the Senate shall, in presence of the Senate and House of Representatives, open all the certificates and the votes shall then be counted;—The person having the greatest number of votes for President, shall be the President, if such number be a majority of the whole number of Electors appointed; and if no person have such majority, then from the persons having the highest numbers not exceeding three on the list of those voted for as President, the House of Representatives shall choose immediately, by ballot, the President. But in choosing the President, the votes shall be taken by states, the representation from each state having one vote; a quorum for this purpose shall consist of a member or members from two-thirds of the states, and a majority of all the states shall be necessary to a choice. And if the House of Representatives shall not choose a President whenever the right of choice shall devolve upon them, before the fourth day of March next following, then the Vice-President shall act as President, as in the case of the death or other constitutional disability of the President. The person having the greatest number of votes as Vice-President, shall be the Vice-President, if such number be a majority of the whole number of Electors appointed, and if no person have a majority, then from the two highest numbers on the list, the Senate shall choose the Vice-President; a quorum for the purpose shall consist of two-thirds of the whole number of Senators, and a majority of the whole number shall be necessary to a choice. But no person constitutionally ineligible to the office of President shall be eligible to that of Vice-President of the United States.

## ARTICLE XIII

### [December 18, 1865]

Section 1. Neither slavery nor involuntary servitude, except as a punishment for crime whereof the party shall have been duly convicted, shall exist within the United States, or any place subject to their jurisdiction.

Section 2. Congress shall have power to enforce this article by appropriate legislation.

## ARTICLE XIV

### [July 21, 1868]

Section 1. All persons born or naturalized in the United States, and subject to the jurisdiction thereof, are citizens of the United States and of the State wherein they reside. No State shall make or enforce any law which shall abridge the privileges or immunities of citizens of the United States; nor shall any State deprive any person of life, liberty, or property, without due process of law; nor deny to any person within its jurisdiction the equal protection of the laws.

Section 2. Representatives shall be apportioned among the several States according to their respective numbers, counting the whole number of persons in each State, excluding Indians not taxed. But when the right to vote at any election for the choice of electors for President and Vice President of the United States, Representatives in Congress, the Executive and Judicial officers of a State, or the members of the Legislature thereof, is denied to any of the male inhabitants of such State, being twenty-one years of age, and citizens of the United States, or in any way abridged, except for participation in rebellion, or other crime, the basis of representation therein shall be reduced in the proportion which the number of such male citizens shall bear to the whole number of male citizens twenty-one years of age in such State.

Section 3. No person shall be a Senator or Representative in Congress, or elector of President and Vice President, or hold any office, civil or military, under the United States, or under any State, who, having previously taken an oath, as a member of Congress, or as an officer of the United States, or as a member of any State legislature, or as an executive or judicial officer of any State, to support the Constitution of the United States, shall have engaged in insurrection or rebellion against the same, or given aid or comfort to the enemies thereof. But Congress may by a vote of two-thirds of each House, remove such disability.

SECTION 4. The validity of the public debt of the United States, authorized by law, including debts incurred for payment of pensions and bounties for services in suppressing insurrection or rebellion, shall not be questioned. But neither the United States nor any State shall assume or pay any debt or obligation incurred in aid of insurrection or rebellion against the United States, or any claim for the loss or emancipation of any slave; but all such debts, obligations and claims shall be held illegal and void.

SECTION 5. The Congress shall have power to enforce, by appropriate legislation, the provisions of this article.

## ARTICLE XV

### [March 30, 1870]

SECTION 1. The right of citizens of the United States to vote shall not be denied or abridged by the United States or by any State on account of race, color, or previous condition of servitude.

SECTION 2. The Congress shall have power to enforce this article by appropriate legislation.

## ARTICLE XVI

### [February 25, 1913]

The Congress shall have the power to lay and collect taxes on incomes, from whatever source derived, without apportionment among the several States, and without regard to any census or enumeration.

## ARTICLE XVII

### [May 31, 1913]

SECTION 1. The Senate of the United States shall be composed of two Senators from each State, elected by the people thereof, for six years; and each Senator shall have one vote. The electors in each State shall have the qualifications requisite for electors of the most numerous branch of the State Legislature.

SECTION 2. When vacancies happen in the representation of any State in the Senate, the executive authority of such State shall issue writs of election to fill such vacancies; Provided, That the Legislature of any State may empower the executive thereof to make temporary appointment until the people fill the vacancies by election as the Legislature may direct.

SECTION 3. This amendment shall not be so construed as to affect the election or term of any Senator chosen before it becomes valid as part of the Constitution.

### ARTICLE XVIII

[January 29, 1919]

SECTION 1. After one year from the ratification of this article, the manufacture, sale, or transportation of intoxicating liquors within, the importation thereof into, or the exportation thereof from the United States and all territory subject to the jurisdiction thereof, for beverage purposes, is hereby prohibited.

SECTION 2. The Congress and the several States shall have concurrent power to enforce this article by appropriate legislation.

SECTION 3. This article shall be inoperative unless it shall have been ratified as an amendment to the Constitution by the legislatures of the several States, as provided in the Constitution, within seven years from the date of the submission hereof to the States by the Congress.

### ARTICLE XIX

[August 26, 1920]

SECTION 1. The rights of citizens of the United States to vote, shall not be denied or abridged by the United States or by any State on account of sex.

SECTION 2. Congress shall have power to enforce this article by appropriate legislation.

### ARTICLE XX

[February 6, 1933]

SECTION 1. The terms of the President and Vice President shall end at noon on the twentieth day of January, and the terms of Senators and Representatives at noon on the third day of January, of the years in which such terms would have ended if this article had not been ratified; and the terms of their successors shall then begin.

SECTION 2. The Congress shall assemble at least once in every year, and such meeting shall begin at noon on the third day of January, unless they shall by law appoint a different day.

SECTION 3. If, as the time fixed for the beginning of the term of the President, the President elect shall have died, the Vice President elect shall become President. If a President shall not have been chosen before the time fixed for the beginning of his term, or if the President elect shall have failed to qualify, then the Vice President elect shall act as President until a President shall have qualified; and the Congress may by law provide for the case wherein neither a President elect nor a Vice President elect shall have qualified, declaring who shall then act as President, or the manner in which one who is to act shall be selected, and such person shall act accordingly until a President or Vice President shall have qualified.

SECTION 4. The Congress may by law provide for the case of the death of any of the persons from whom the House of Representatives may choose a President whenever the right of choice shall have devolved upon them, and for the case of the death of any of the persons from whom the Senate may choose a Vice President whenever the right of choice shall have devolved upon them.

SECTION 5. Sections 1 and 2 shall take effect on the fifteenth day of October following the ratification of this article.

SECTION 6. This article shall be inoperative unless it shall have been ratified as an amendment to the Constitution by the legislatures of three-fourths of the several States within seven years from the date of its submission.

## ARTICLE XXI

### [December 5, 1933]

SECTION 1. The eighteenth article of amendment to the Constitution of the United States is hereby repealed.

SECTION 2. The transportation or importation into any State, Territory, or possession of the United States for delivery or use therein of intoxicating liquors, in violation of the laws thereof, is hereby prohibited.

SECTION 3. This article shall be inoperative unless it shall have been ratified as an amendment to the Constitution by conventions in the several States, as provided in the Constitution, within seven years from the date of the submission hereof to the States by the Congress.

## ARTICLE XXII

### [February 26, 1951]

SECTION 1. No person shall be elected to the office of the President more than twice, and no person who has held the office of President, or acted as President for more than two years of a term to which some other person was elected President shall be elected to the office of the President more than once. But this Article shall not apply to any person holding the office of President when this Article was proposed by the Congress, and shall not prevent any person who may be holding the office of President, or acting as President, during the term within which this Article becomes operative from holding the office of President or acting as President during the remainder of such term.

SECTION 2. This Article shall be inoperative unless it shall be ratified as an amendment to the Constitution by the Legislatures of three-fourths of the several States within seven years from the date of its submission to the States by the Congress.

## ARTICLE XXIII

## [April 3, 1961]

SECTION 1. The District constituting the seat of Government of the United States shall appoint in such number as the Congress may direct:

A number of electors of President and Vice President equal to the whole number of Senators and Representatives in Congress to which the District would be entitled if it were a State, but in no event more than the least populous State; they shall be in addition to those appointed by the States but they shall be considered, for the purposes of election of President and Vice President, to be electors appointed by a State; and they shall meet in the District and perform such duties as provided by the twelfth article of amendment.

SECTION 2. The Congress shall have power to enforce this article by appropriate legislation.

## ARTICLE XXIV

## [January 23, 1964]

SECTION 1. The right of citizens of the United States to vote in any primary or other election for President or Vice President, or for Senator or Representative in Congress, shall not be denied or abridged by the United States or any State by reason of failure to pay any poll tax or other tax.

# NOTES

## 1. THE PRIMACY OF 1787

[1] Quoted in a letter of Rufus King to Theophilus Parsons, Feb. 20, 1788; *Life of King*, I, 320–321.

[2] For my understanding of this aspect of the Convention I am especially indebted to my student, friend, and colleague John P. Roche. See his "The Founding Fathers: A Reform Caucus in Action," *American Political Science Review*, LV (1961), 799.

## 2. THE UNITED STATES IN 1787

[1] Richard Price, *Observations on the Importance of the American Revolution, and the Means of Making It a Benefit to the World* (London, 1785), 102, 123.

[2] Hector St. John de Crèvecoeur, *Letters from an American Farmer* (1782) (London, 1912), 41.

[3] Crèvecoeur, *Letters*, 58.

[4] C. F. Volney, *A View of the Soil and Climate of the United States of America* (Philadelphia, 1804), 7.

[5] U.S. Bureau of the Census, *Historical Statistics of the United States* (Washington, 1960), 7–14.

[6] Francisco de Miranda (1783), in John S. Ezell, ed., *The New Democracy in America* (Norman, Okla., 1963), 41–42.

[7] Miranda, *New Democracy*, 57.

[8] Edward Young, *Special Report on Immigration* . . . (Washington, 1871), xi.

[9] John Jay to William Bingham, May 31, 1785; *Correspondence of Jay*, III, 154.

[10] Gray, *History of Agriculture in the Southern United States*, II, 614; Greene and Harrington, *American Population Before the Federal Census* of 1790, *passim*.

[11] Crèvecoeur, *Letters*, 40; Miranda, *New Democracy*, 73.

[12] Louis Otto to the Comte de Vergennes, October 10, 1786; Bancroft, II, 399–400. Otto, who saw America through French eyes, was perhaps more impressed than he should have been by signs of envy and distrust on the part of "the common people."

[13] Madison to Jefferson, Dec. 9, 1787; *Writings of Madison*, V. 66.

[14] Crèvecoeur, *Letters*, 24–25.

[15] McDonald, *We the People*, 45–47, 58, 89.

[16] Jedidiah Morse, *An American Geography* (Elizabeth, N.J., 1789), 64.

[17] Crèvecoeur, *Letters*, 48–51.

[18] *Writings of Washington*, XXX, 291–96.

## 3. ILLS AND REMEDIES

1 *Writings of Washington,* XXIX, 51.
2 Ezra Stiles, *The United States Elevated to Glory and Honor* (New Haven, 1783).
3 To George Mason, jr., June 1, 1787; Farrand, III, 32.
4 To R. H. Lee, July 7, 1785; *Writings of Madison* (1867 ed.), I, 158.
5 McLaughlin, *Confederation and Constitution,* 107.
6 The Continentalist; *Papers of Hamilton,* III, 106.
7 *Writings of Madison,* II, 361–69.
8 To Edmund Randolph, Feb. 15, 1783; *Papers of Jefferson,* VI, 248.
9 To Rufus King, July 15, 1787; *Life of King,* I, 228.
10 To James Madison, sr., April 1, 1787; *Writings of Madison,* II, 335.
11 May 29, 1787; Farrand, I, 18.
12 Nettels, *National Economy,* 94.
13 June 16, 27, 1787; Farrand, I, 252, 437.
14 *Sketches of American Policy* (Hartford, 1785), 32.
15 *Federalist* (No. 15), 108.
16 September 3, 1780; *Papers of Hamilton,* II, 400–418.
17 To John Adams, Jan. 14, 1784; Burnett, *Letters,* VII, 414. Osgood, under the lash of experience, had changed his mind by 1786, as witness a letter to Rev. William Gordon, Jan. 19, 1786; Osgood Papers, New-York Historical Society.
18 *Journals of Continental Congress,* XXXI, 494–98.
19 Jan. 21, 1786; Tansill, 38.
20 Sept. 14, 1786; Tansill, 39–43.
21 To the Comte de Vergennes, Oct. 10, 1786; Bancroft, II, 400.
22 *Journals of Continental Congress,* XXXII, 71–74; XXXIII, 723–24.
23 To Henry Knox, Dec. 26, 1786; *Writings of Washington,* XXIX, 122.
24 To David Humphreys, Oct. 22, 1786; to Madison, Nov. 5, 1786; *Writings of Washington,* XXIX, 27, 51.
25 To Henry Lee, October 31, 1786; *Writings of Washington,* XXIX, 34.
26 (Trenton) *New-Jersey Gazette,* Nov. 6, 1786.

## 4. MATERIALS AND CHOICES

1 *Annals of Congress,* V. 2630–31.
2 *The Jubilee of the Constitution* (New York, 1839), 40–41.
3 John Adams, *Thoughts on Government* (1776), in *Works of Adams,* IV, 200.
4 In this discussion of the political and constitutional thought of eighteenth-century America I have drawn on my *Seedtime of the Republic* (New York, 1953) especially pp. 139–46, 326–449.
5 *American Archives,* VI, 748–54; F. Chase, *History of Dartmouth College* (Brattleboro, Vt., 1928), 654–63.
6 *Works of Adams,* IV, 193–200.
7 Thorpe, III, 1888*ff.*
8 Madison, in *Federalist* (No. 10), 79.
9 Hamilton, in *Federalist* (No. 73), 443.
10 Aug. 13, 1787; Farrand, II, 273.
11 *Notes on the State of Virginia* (1785) (Chapel Hill, 1955), 120, quoted by Madison, in *Federalist* (No. 48), 310–11.
12 *Works of Adams,* IV, 186.
13 *Works of Madison,* II, 316–61.
14 Feb. 24, 1787; *Works of Madison,* II, 319. For numerous ex-

amples of men toying with this idea (for a variety of reasons both sincere and subtle), see Main, *Antifederalists*, app. A.

15 Washington to Jefferson, May 30, 1787; *Writings of Washington*, XXIX, 224.

16 Especially by William Paterson, as on June 9, 16, 1787; Farrand, I, 178, 251.

17 Knox to King, July 15, 1787; *Life of King*, I, 228.

18 Thorpe, I, 77.

19 Adams, *Jubilee of the Constitution*, 17–40.

## 5. THE MEN OF THE NORTH

1 Farrand, II, 450.

2 Farrand, I, 3–5, 17–18, 23.

3 Washington to Arthur Lee, May 20, 1787; *Writings of Washington*, XXIX, 213.

4 *New York Journal*, May 17, 1787. For guides to the primary and secondary sources of information on the life of each Framer, see the references in the bibliography, especially pages 297–98.

5 Farrand, III, 87–97, 232–38.

6 Farrand, III, 88.

7 Sept. 3, 1785; Burnett, *Letters*, VIII, 206–10.

8 Feb. 11, 1787; *Life of King*, I, 201–202.

9 Farrand, I, 9; III, 18–20.

10 June 18, 1787; Farrand, III, 47–48.

11 (Boston) *Massachusetts Centinel*, May 19, 1787.

12 *Life of King*, I, 221.

13 Farrand, III, 88–89.

## 6. THE MEN OF THE MIDDLE STATES

1 *Writings of Franklin*, IX, 551.

2 Pierce, in Farrand, III, 90.

3 Farrand, II, 91–92; 236.

4 (Philadelphia) *Pennsylvania Packet*, Feb. 7, 1782.

5 June 10, 1784; *Life of Morris*, I, 266–67.

6 Miranda, *New Democracy*, 46.

7 Too relaxed, it would seem, even for the French chargé d'affaires. Farrand, III, 236.

8 Farrand, III, 92.

9 Farrand, III, 92.

10 Farrand, III, 93.

11 Farrand, III, 93.

## 7. THE MEN OF THE SOUTH

1 *The Works of Edmund Burke* (Boston, 1839), II, 35–36.

2 June 3, 1776; *Works of Adams*, IX, 387.

3 *New-York Journal*, May 17, 1787.

4 Adams to Benjamin Rush, April 4, 1790; *Old Family Letters* (Philadelphia, 1892), I, 55.

5 March 31, 1787; Fitzpatrick, *Writings of Washington*, XXIX, 191–92.

6 To George Mason, jr., June 1, 1787; Farrand, III, 32.

7 Farrand, III, 94.

8 April 19, 1782; Conway, *Randolph*, 45.

9 April 16, 1787; Hunt, *Writings of Madison*, II, 344–49.

10 Farrand, III, 237.

11 To Madison, June 2, 1788; *Documentary History of the Constitution*, IV, 678–79.

12 Farrand, III, 95.

13 Farrand, III, 96, 238.

14 *Journals of the Continental Congress*, XXXI, 494–98.

15 Farrand, III, 96.

16 Farrand, III, 97.

17 Farrand, III, 97.

18 Farrand, III, 97.

## 8.  THE MEN OF PHILADELPHIA

1 Farrand, III, 15.

2 Aug. 30, 1787; *Adams-Jefferson Letters*, I, 196.

3 (New York) *Daily Advertiser*, May 21, 1787; (Philadelphia) *Pennsylvania Herald*, June 13, 1787; *New-York Journal*, May 3, 1787; (Philadelphia) *Independent Gazetteer*, June 23, 1787; (Boston) *Massachusetts Centinel*, June 20, 1787.

4 Franklin to Thomas Jordan, May 18, 1787; Madison to William Short, June 6, 1787; Mason to George Mason, jr., June 1, 1787; Farrand, III, 21, 32, 37.

5 July 27, 1787; Warren, *Making of the Constitution*, 370.

6 McDonald, *We the People*, 37.

7 See the mass of data, much of which I have been able to check independently (and with slightly different conclusions), assembled by McDonald, *We the People*, 38–92.

8 *An Address to the People of the State of New-York* (1788), in Ford, *Pamphlets*, 115.

9 Tansill, 43.

10 Tansill, 46.

11 Tansill, 55–84.

12 Tansill, 58.

13 Tansill, 67.

14 To John Dickinson, Jan. 17, 1787, in *Life of Read*, 438–40; Munroe, *Federalist Delaware*, 106–107.

## 9.  THE CONVENTION, MAY 14–JUNE 20

1 Farrand, I, 255–56.

2 *Washington Diaries*, III, 216; (Philadelphia) *Pennsylvania Packet*, May 14, 1787; (Philadelphia) *Independent Gazetteer*, May 14, 1787; (Philadelphia) *Pennsylvania Gazette*, May 14, 1787.

3 *Washington Diaries*, III, 217.

4 To George Mason, jr., May 20, 27, 1787; Farrand, III, 23, 28.

5 To Noah Webster, Oct. 12, 1804; to John Tyler, 1833 (?); Farrand, III, 409, 525.

6 Farrand, I, 1–6.

7 Farrand, III, 550.

8 Farrand, III, 586–90.

9 Davie to James Iredell, Aug. 6, 1787; Farrand, III, 67–68.

10 Carroll to Michael O'Brien, May 25, 1787; Farrand, IV, 62–63.

11 Tansill, 931.

12 To Jeremiah Wadsworth, May 24, 1787; Farrand, III, 26.

13 Farrand, I, 7–17.

14 Farrand, I, 10–11.

15 Farrand, III, 15.

16 To George Mason, jr., May 27, June 1, 1787; Farrand, III, 28, 33; entry of April 19, 1830, in H. B. Adams, ed., *Life and Writings of Jared Sparks* (Boston, 1893), I, 561.

17 See generally, Farrand, III, 28, 33, 35, 48, 51, 59, 71–73, 86, and IV 65; Freeman, *Washington*, VI, 94n.; Warren, *Making of the Constitution*, 179, 183, 184, 193, 204–205, 225, 230, 233, 266, 301, 304, 343, 353, 354, 369–75, 399, 432, 434, 436, 464, 492, 605, 703.

18 *Washington Diaries*, III, 220; Rev. James Madison to Madison, Aug. 1, 1787; *Writings of Madison*, IV, 90–91n.

19 Blount to Caswell, July 19, 1787; Alice B. Keith, ed., *The John Gray Blount Papers* (Raleigh, 1952–1959), I, 322–23; Farrand, III, 29, 46–47, 70–75, 83–84.

20 *New-York Journal*, June 7, 1787; *Boston Gazette*, June 11, 1787; *New York Packet*, June 15, 1787; (Hartford) *Connecticut Courant*, July 2, 1787; Aug. 30, 1787; *Adams-Jefferson Letters*, I, 196.

21 Farrand, III, 61, 78, 361.

22 July 19, 1787; *Writings of Madison*, IV, 152n.

23 See generally Brant, *Madison*, III, 27–29; Warren, *Making of the Constitution*, 142–43; Farrand, III, 427, 445, 479, 504*ff.*, 534, 595*ff.*, esp. 604–609.

24 Farrand, I, 30, 33, 38–39.

25 *Life of King*, VI, 697–700.

26 Farrand, I, 200, 202.

27 Farrand, I, 179, 183, 201.

28 Farrand, I, 180.

29 Farrand, I, 48–50.

30 Farrand, I, 240.

31 Farrand, I, 242–45; III, 611–15.

32 Farrand, I, 242.

33 Farrand, I, 249–52, 257–60, 263–68, 270–76.

34 Farrand, I, 282–311; Tansill, 979–88.

35 Farrand, I, 314–22, 325–27.

36 Farrand, I, 334, 335, 344.

37 Farrand, I, 334–39.

38 North Carolina delegates to Caswell, June 14, 1787; Madison to Jefferson, July 18, 1787; Farrand, III, 46, 60.

39 Gouverneur Morris, July 5, 1787; Farrand, I, 529. For other expressions of the sense of mission "for all mankind," see Farrand, I, 405, 423, 424, 515, 519; II, 249; III, 37, 449; Elliot, II, 529; and for prophecies of greatness for the United States, see Farrand, I, 405, II, 452; Warren, *Making of the Constitution*, 181, 740. Lansing's remarks were made June 20, 1787; Farrand, I, 336.

40 April 19, 1787; *Writings of Franklin*, IX, 574.

41 (Philadelphia) *Pennsylvania Herald*, June 13, 20, 1787; (Philadelphia) *Independent Gazetteer*, Aug. 7, 1787; (Philadelphia) *Pennsylvania Gazette*, Aug. 29, Sept. 5, 1787.

42 Benjamin Rush to Richard Price, June 2, 1787; Farrand, III, 33.

## 10.   THE CONVENTION, JUNE 21–AUGUST 5

1 Farrand, I, 468–69.

2 Farrand, I, 466.

3 July 5, 1787; Farrand, I, 529.

4 Farrand, I, 353–435.

5 Farrand, I, 436.

6 Farrand, I, 437–45, 453–55, 459.

7 (Baltimore) *Maryland Journal*, Feb. 29, 1788; Ford, *Essays*, 183.

8 Farrand, I, 450–52.

9 July 2, 1787; Farrand, I, 512–13.

10 Farrand, I, 480, 481, 494.

11 Farrand, I, 229–30, 236.

12 Farrand, II, 13–16.

[13] Farrand, I, 460–61, 468.
[14] Farrand, I, 509–10.
[15] Farrand, I, 509–20.
[16] Brant, *Madison*, III, 90–91.
[17] Farrand, I, 522–23, 526.
[18] Farrand, I, 524–26.
[19] Farrand, I, 538, 540, 542.
[20] Farrand, I, 557–59.
[21] Farrand, I, 563–70.
[22] Farrand, I, 575–88.
[23] Farrand, I, 589–97.
[24] Farrand, II, 1–11.
[25] Farrand, I, 489–93, 500–502, 514, 519, 531–32.
[26] June 29, 1787; Farrand, I, 464.
[27] Farrand, I, 177, 178, 180, 202, 251, 321.
[28] Farrand, I, 87, 196, 342–43, 461–62, 468–69.
[29] Farrand, I, 527.
[30] Gouverneur Morris, July 5, 1787; Farrand, I, 530.
[31] June 29, July 14, 1787; Farrand, I, 461–62, 470; II, 5.
[32] June 29, 1787; Farrand, I, 461–62. And see Mason's speech of June 7, in Farrand, I, 155–57.
[33] Especially in *Federalist*, No. 39, first published in the (New York) *Independent Journal* and (New York) *Daily Advertiser*, Jan. 16, 1788.
[34] Farrand, II, 17–19.
[35] Farrand, II, 19–20.
[36] Bancroft, II, 88; May 13, 1828, in Farrand, III, 477.
[37] Farrand, II, 26–29, 46, 47–49, 94–95.
[38] Farrand, II, 41–44, 83.
[39] Farrand, II, 88–93.
[40] Farrand, II, 64–69.
[41] Farrand, II, 73–80.
[42] Farrand, I, 533–34, 542; II, 2–3, 46.
[43] Roche, "Founding Fathers," 810.
[44] Farrand, II, 29–32, 51–58, 99–106, 108–115, 118–20.
[45] *Washington Diaries*, III, 230.
[46] July 16, 20, 1787; II, 17, 70.
[47] July 23, 1787; Farrand, II, 95.
[48] For the critical documents, see Farrand, II, 129–75.
[49] Farrand, II, 137; IV, 37–38.
[50] Farrand, II, 115.
[51] (Philadelphia) *Pennsylvania Packet*, July 7, 1787; (Philadelphia) *Pennsylvania Gazette*, July 18, 1787; (New York) *Daily Advertiser*, July 23, 1787; (Hartford) *Connecticut Courant*, July 30, 1787; (Boston) *American Herald*, July 30, 1787.
[52] To F. L. Lee, July 14, 1787; *Letters of Lee*, II, 424.
[53] Mary Norris to ?, July 4, 1787; Farrand, IV, 67.
[54] July 5, 1787; Farrand, I, 529.

## 11.   THE CONVENTION, AUGUST 6–SEPTEMBER 11

[1] Brearly to Dayton, July 27, 1787; Farrand, IV, 72.
[2] Farrand, II, 177–89.
[3] Aug. 15, 18, 24, 1787; Farrand, II, 301, 328, 406. See also Brearly to Paterson, Aug. 21, 1787; Farrand, III, 73.
[4] Aug. 7, 8; Farrand, II, 205, 212, 215. For Mercer's own explanation of his tardiness, which rings altogether falsely, see his letter to Governor Smallwood, June 29, 1787; Farrand, IV, 66–67.
[5] Aug. 8; Farrand, II, 221.

6 Aug. 8, 11, 13; Farrand, II, 223–25, 262–63, 273–80.

7 Aug. 8, 9, 10, 13; Farrand, II, 216–19, 235–39, 248–51, 267–72.

8 Aug. 14; Farrand, II, 290–92.

9 Aug. 15; Farrand, II, 298–302.

10 Aug. 28; Farrand, II, 439–40.

11 Aug. 29, 30; Farrand, II, 454–56, 461–64.

12 Aug. 30, 31; Farrand, II, 468–69, 475–79.

13 Aug. 23, 24; Farrand, II, 389, 400–401.

14 Aug. 15, 23; Farrand, II, 298, 390–91.

15 Farrand, II, 440, 589.

16 Aug. 16*ff.*; Farrand, II, 305*ff*.

17 Farrand, II, 497, 499; Madison to Andrew Stevenson, Nov. 17, 1830; Farrand, III, 483–94.

18 Aug. 8; Farrand, II, 220–23.

19 Aug. 21, 22; Farrand, II, 357–75.

20 Farrand, II, 400.

21 Farrand, II, 414–17, 449–54.

22 Farrand, II, 481.

23 Sept. 4; Farrand, II, 496–99.

24 Sept. 5–6; Farrand, II, 511–29.

25 Farrand, II, 521.

26 *Federalist*, 424.

27 Farrand, I, 103.

28 To Weedon Butler, May 5, 1788; Farrand, III, 302.

29 Sept. 7, 1787; Farrand, II, 537.

30 Sept. 7; Farrand, II, 541.

31 (Philadelphia) *Pennsylvania Herald*, Aug. 18, 1787; (Philadelphia) *Pennsylvania Journal*, Aug. 22, 1787; *Boston Gazette*, Aug. 27, 1787; *Salem Mercury*, Aug. 28, 1787. On this whole question, see Dunbar, *A Study of "Monarchical Tendencies" in the United States from 1776 to 1801*, chap. 5.

32 Sept. 7, 8; Farrand, II, 538–39; 540, 447–48.

33 Farrand, II, 314–15.

34 Farrand, II, 535–64.

35 Farrand, II, 553–54.

36 Sept. 6; Farrand, II, 524.

37 F. B. Dexter, ed., *The Literary Diary of Ezra Stiles* (New York, 1901), 293–95.

38 Dec. 22, 1814; *Life of Morris*, III, 322–23.

39 To Jared Sparks, Apr. 8, 1831; Farrand, III, 499.

40 *Diary of Stiles*, III, 295; Warren, *Making of the Constitution*, 687–88.

41 Farrand, III, 499. The materials with which the committee of style worked are gathered in Farrand, II, 565–80.

42 Farrand, II, 585–87.

43 Farrand, II, 587–88.

## 12.   THE CONVENTION, SEPTEMBER 12–17

1 Tansill, 1003–1004; Farrand, II, 667. The draft of this letter of transmission is in the handwriting of Gouverneur Morris, although one scholar (Brant, *Madison*, III, 147) thinks that Madison should get the credit.

2 See the speech of Albert Gallatin in the House of Representatives, June 19, 1798, in which he accused Morris of trying to "throw" the words about "the common defense and general welfare" into a "distinct paragraph" (with the aid of a sly but short-lived semicolon). *Annals of Congress*, V, 1976, Farrand, III, 379. See also Morris to H. W. Livingston, Dec. 4, 1803; Morris to Timothy Pickering, Dec.

22, 1814; *Life of Morris*, III, 192, 329. The report of the committee of style is in Farrand, II, 590–603.

3 Tansill, 471, 989.

4 Elliot, III, 22. See also the speech of William Findley in the Pennsylvania ratifying convention reported in the (Philadelphia) *Pennsylvania Packet*, Dec. 6, 1787.

5 Farrand, II, 439–40, 597, 619.

6 Farrand, II, 604–631.

7 Farrand, II, 631.

8 Farrand, II, 631–33.

9 Farrand, II, 563–64.

10 William Lewis (?) to Thomas Lee Shippen (?), Oct. 11, 1787; Madison to Jefferson, Oct. 24, 1787; Farrand, III, 104, 135. The Lewis-Shippen letter is preserved in the handwriting of Jefferson. See *Papers of Jefferson*, XII, 228–34.

11 For Mason's detailed objections, see Farrand, II, 636–40; Rowland, *Life of Mason*, II, 382–90.

12 Lewis (?) to Shippen (?), Oct. 11, 1787; Farrand, III, 104.

13 *Washington Diaries*, III, 236.

14 Farrand, II, 641–49.

15 Dickinson to Read, Sept. 15, 1787; *Life of Read*, 456–57.

16 Farrand, II, 649. I have used the version of this speech written down by Madison. Franklin liked it so much that he made several copies, one of which, a gift to Charles Carroll, I have also consulted in the Cornell University Library.

17 See also the observation of McHenry, which he may or may not have spoken on the floor, in Farrand, II, 649–50.

18 *Washington Diaries*, III, 237; Madison to Jefferson, Sept. 6, 1787, *Writings of Madison*, IV, 389–91.

19 Farrand, I, 423–24.

20 Aug. 18, 22, 25, 29, 31, 1787; Farrand, II, 328, 375, 418, 448, 481.

21 To George Hay, Aug. 23, 1823; *Writings of Madison*, IX, 147.

22 Farrand, I, 250, 253, 255.

23 Farrand, I, 125, 185–86, 215, 249–54, 372, 500–501; II, 215–16, 309–10, 329, 332, 356, 386, 391, 509.

24 Farrand, I, 186.

25 Farrand, I, 366.

26 Farrand, I, 372.

27 Dec. 31, 1799; Farrand, III, 381–82.

28 The British Constitution continued to be an object of fascination to these men, as witness the representative remarks recorded in Farrand, I, 66, 86, 99–101, 139, 150, 233, 234, 238, 253–54, 288, 376, 381, 398–99, 425, 484, 545; II, 75–76, 77, 203, 250, 278–79; III, 102, 301.

29 Farrand, II, 100, 248, 298, 329–30, 427, 550; IV, 19.

30 Brant, *Madison*, III, 154. Madison's own disclaimer is in a letter to William Cogswell, March 10, 1834; Farrand, III, 533. See Jackson's testimony of 1819, as reported to John Quincy Adams, in Farrand, III, 426.

31 *Washington Diaries*, III, 215–37.

32 Farrand, II, 238, 415, 537; Madison to Jared Sparks, April 8, 1831; *Life of Morris*, I, 286. See also Morris's recollection of the vigor of his efforts, in a letter to Thomas Pickering, Dec. 22, 1814; *Life of Morris*, III, 322.

33 Sept. 20, 1787; Farrand, III, 98.

34 McClurg's unhappy day was July 17. Farrand, II, 33, 36.

35 Farrand, III, 83.

## 13.  THE FINISHED WORK

1 *Papers of Jefferson*, XIV, 678. For other, less enthusiastic comments of Jefferson on the new Constitution, see *Papers*, XII, 350–51, 439–42, 571; XIII, 208–209.

2 *Pennsylvania Packet*, Sept. 18, 1787; *Pennsylvania Herald*, Sept. 20, 1787.

3 *Pennsylvania Packet*, *Pennsylvania Journal*, (Philadelphia) *Independent Gazetteer*, *Pennsylvania Gazette*, all Sept. 19, 1787; *Pennsylvania Herald*, Sept. 20, 1787; *Pennsylvania Mercury*, Sept. 21, 1787; *New-York Packet*, Sept. 21, 1787; (New York) *Independent Journal*, Sept. 22, 1787; (Boston) *Massachusetts Centinel*, Sept. 21, 1787; (Boston) *Independent Chronicle*, Sept. 27, 1787; *Boston Gazette*, Oct. 1, 1787; (Charleston) *Columbian Herald*, Oct. 2, 1787; (Poughkeepsie) *Country Journal*, Sept. 26, Oct. 3, 1787; *New-Haven Gazette*, Sept. 27, 1787; (Hartford) *Connecticut Courant*, Oct. 1, 1787; *Salem Mercury*, Oct. 2, 1787; (Lexington) *Kentucky Gazette*, Oct. 27, 1787; (Providence) *United States Chronicle*, Sept. 27, 1787; *Providence Gazette*, Sept. 29, 1787; *Newport Mercury*, Oct. 8, 1787; (Bennington) *Vermont Gazette*, Oct. 1, 8, 1787; *Gemeinnutzige Philadelphische Correspondenz*, Sept. 25, 1787; *Lancaster Zeitung*, Sept. 26, 1787.

4 Farrand, II, 137.

5 Wait to George Thatcher, Jan. 8, 1788; *Historical Magazine*, XVI (1869), 262.

6 Jan. 16, 1788; Elliot, II, 25.

7 Farrand, II, 350, 427.

8 March 14, 1796; *Annals of Congress*, IV, 537.

9 Charles A. and Mary R. Beard, *The Rise of American Civilization* (New York, 1927), I, 317.

10 Nov. 24, 1803; *Annals of Congress*, VIII, 100–101.

11 Gouverneur Morris, July 23, 1787; Farrand, II, 92.

12 Thorpe, VII, 3812.

13 Aug. 30, 1787; Farrand, II, 469.

14 Aug. 31, 1787; Farrand, II, 476.

15 *Federalist*, 108–120.

16 Salmon P. Chase, in *Texas* v. *White*, 7 Wallace 700, 725 (1869).

17 July 26, Aug. 13, 1787; Farrand, II, 122, 268.

18 Aug. 25, 1787; Farrand, II, 412–14.

19 Aug. 7–8, 1787; Farrand, II, 201–208, 215–16.

20 On the still controversial question of the attitude of the Framers toward judicial review, see the comments and notes of Alan F. Westin in his introduction to the Spectrum edition of Charles A. Beard, *The Supreme Court and the Constitution* (1912), 1–34, as well as the evidence amassed, not all of it entirely relevant, in Beard's own chapter 2. For expressions of this doctrine in the Convention itself, see Farrand, I, 97–98, 109; II, 25–28, 73–80, 299, 376, 430; and for doubts and denials see Farrand, I, 100; II, 298–99.

21 See the remarks of Luther Martin, Aug. 21, 1787; Farrand, II, 364.

22 Aug. 22, 1787; Farrand, II, 371. For some critical exchanges on the subject of slavery, see Farrand, II, 220–23, 364–65, 369–74, 415–17.

23 Aug. 8, 1787; Farrand, II, 221.

24 See the remarks of Baldwin and Dayton in the House of Representatives, June 16, 1797; *Annals of Congress*, V, 1968ff.

25 Aug. 22, 1787; Farrand, II, 364, 371–72. See the evidence recorded in Farrand, III, 135, 149, 161, 253–54, 324–25, as well as Baldwin's remarks in the House of Representatives, Feb. 12, 1790; *Annals of Congress*, I, 1200–1201.

26 *Works* (Lipscomb ed.), I, 72–73.

27 In the Virginia ratifying convention, June 24, 1788; Elliot, III, 591.

28 Staughton Lynd, "The Compromise of 1787," an unpublished paper of considerable ingenuity that Prof. Lynd kindly permitted me to read.

29 For a bouquet of Gerry's pungent comments on democracy and the people, see Tansill, 125, 127, 137, 156, 159, 172, 413, 435, 454, 744.

30 *Works* (Boston, 1903), I, 299.

## 14. THE STRUGGLE FOR RATIFICATION

1 *Writings of Washington*, XXIX, 507–508.

2 *Journals of the Continental Congress*, XXXII, 334–43.

3 Tansill, 1007; *Journals of the Continental Congress*, XXXIII, 487–503, 540–44, 548–49; Burnett, *Continental Congress*, 693–700.

4 *Journals of the Continental Congress*, XXXIII, 716.

5 Burnett, *Continental Congress*, 690–91.

6 Farrand, II, 506, 510–511; *Journals of the Continental Congress*, XXXII, 228; XXXIII, 488.

7 (Philadelphia) *Independent Gazetteer*, Oct. 5, 1787; (Boston) *American Herald*, Jan. 14, 1788.

8 McHenry in the Maryland House of Delegates, Nov. 29, 1787; Farrand, III, 150. And see similar comments of other Framers in Farrand, III, 82 (Gilman), 100–101 (Pierce), 102, 140 (Wilson), 242 (Washington), 243 (Robert Morris), 301 (Charles Pinckney), 303–304 (Butler), 333 (Hamilton), 335 (Madison), 423 (Few), as well as *Federalist*, 225–26, 234, 255–56, 326, 364, 377, 401, 523.

9 To Edmund Pendleton, Feb. 21, 1788; *Writings of Madison*, V, 108.

10 To Joseph Gilman, Sept. 18, 1787; Farrand, III, 82. See also Washington to Patrick Henry, Sept. 24, 1787; *Writings of Washington*, XXIX, 278.

11 To Archibald Stuart, Oct. 30, 1787; *Writings of Madison*, V, 47.

12 June 9, July 23, 1787; Farrand, I, 176; II, 89.

13 Rev. Lemuel Burkitt, in W. C. Watson, ed., *Men and Times of the Revolution; or, Memoirs of Elkanah Watson* (New York, 1856), 263.

14 Van Doren, *Great Rehearsal*, 194–95.

15 Elliot, III, 23. For a full (and fully documented) review of the anti-Federalist objections to the Constitution, see Main, *Antifederalists*, chap. 6–8.

16 Oct. 16, 1787; *Letters of Lee*, II, 450.

17 (Philadelphia) *Independent Gazetteer*, Oct. 3, Nov. 6, 1787; (Boston) *Massachusetts Centinel*, Jan. 2, 1788. For the Federalist rebuttal of the charge of illegality, see *Federalist* (No. 40), 247–55, an effective piece of special pleading by Madison, as well as Spaight's speech to the first North Carolina ratifying convention, July 30, 1788; Elliot, IV, 206–207.

18 Elliot, III, 50.

19 Nov. 10, 1787; *Adams-Jefferson Letters*, I, 210.

20 Nov. 13, 1787; *Adams-Jefferson Letters*, I, 212.

21 *New-York Journal*, Dec. 16, 1787; Ford, *Essays*, 273.

22 (Boston) *American Herald*, Nov. 9, 1787.

23 Elliot, III, 22, 29.

24 Notes of James Wilson, in McMaster and Stone, *Pennsylvania and the Constitution*, 767ff.

25 To George Thatcher, Nov. 22, 1787; *Historical Magazine*, XVI (1869), 258.

26 Elliot, II, 34; III, 384*ff*.

27 Elliot, II, 34.

28 Cecelia Kenyon, "Men of Little Faith," *William and Mary Quarterly*, 3rd ser., XII (1955), 3.

29 Tansill, 1009; Munroe, *Federalist Delaware*, 107–109; McDonald, *We the People*, 116–23.

30 Tansill, 1011–14; McCormick, *Experiment in Independence*, 261–79; McDonald, *We the People*, 123–29.

31 Tansill, 1014–15; Coleman, *American Revolution in Georgia*, chap. 17; McDonald, *We the People*, 129–36.

32 Tansill, 1016–17; Groce, *William Samuel Johnson*, 152–57; B. C. Steiner, "Connecticut's Ratification of the Federal Constitution," *Proceedings of the American Antiquarian Society*, XXV (1915), 70–127; McDonald, *We the People*, 136–48; Elliot, II, 185–202.

33 Tansill, 1010; McMaster and Stone, *Pennsylvania and the Constitution*; Brunhouse, *Counter-Revolution in Pennsylvania*, 202–211; McDonald, *We the People*, 163–82; Elliot, II, 415–546; Smith, *James Wilson*, chap. 18.

34 To Washington, Oct. 30, 1787; *Documentary History of the Constitution*, IV, 357.

35 Tansill, 1018–20; Harding, *Constitution in Massachusetts*, esp. chap. 3–5; McDonald, *We the People*, 182–202; Elliot, II, 1–183.

36 Elliot, II, 182–83.

37 Tansill, 1024–27; Walker, *New Hampshire Convention;* McDonald, *We the People*, 235–51.

38 See especially his famous *Genuine Information*, which is printed in Farrand, II, 172–232.

39 Tansill, 1021–22; Crowl, *Maryland*, 117*ff*.; McDonald, *We the People*, 148–61; Elliot, II, 547–56.

40 Tansill, 1022–24; McDonald, *We the People*, 202–35; Elliot, IV, 318–41.

41 Elliot, IV, 286.

42 Tansill, 1027–34; Grigsby, *Virginia Convention*, esp. vol. I; Brant, *Madison*, III, chap. 15–17; McDonald, *We the People*, 255–83; Elliot, III.

43 Elliot, III, 652.

44 July 12, 1788; *Writings of Monroe*, I, 198.

45 Tansill, 1034–44; Miner, *Ratification in New York*, esp. chap. 3–5; Spaulding, *New York in the Critical Period*, chap. 11–14; Main, *Antifederalists*, 233–242; Mitchell, *Hamilton*, I, chap. 26–27; Rossiter, *Hamilton and the Constitution*, 50–70; McDonald, *We the People*, 283–310; Elliot, II, 205–414.

46 Elliot, IV, 249–51.

47 See in particular McDonald, *We the People*, esp. 161–62, 252–54, 283, 310, 358*ff*.; J. T. Main's review of this book (and McDonald's rebuttal) in *William and Mary Quarterly*, 3rd ser., XVII (1960), 86–110; Main, *Antifederalists*, esp. 249*ff*.; Brown, *Charles Beard and the Constitution*, esp. 196–200; and, of course, the famous book that touched off the controversy, Charles A. Beard, *An Economic Interpretation of the Constitution of the United States* (1913) (New York, 1948).

## 15.   THE FIRST YEARS OF THE CONSTITUTION

1 *Writings of Franklin*, X, 41.

2 *Journals of the Continental Congress*, XXXIV, 281–82, 315n., 317–18, 358–360, 367–68, 383–88, 392–404, 415–19, 455–57, 481–88, 495–97, 515–23.

3 *New-York Journal*, July 24, 1788; (New York) *Daily Advertiser*,

July 26, 1788; Whitfield J. Bell, jr., ed., "The Federal Procession of 1788," *New-York Historical Society Quarterly*, XLVI (1962), 5; "Francis Hopkinson's 'Account of the Grand Federal Procession,'" Philadelphia, 1788," *Old South Leaflets*, no. 230–31 (Boston, 1962).

4 *Journals of the Continental Congress*, XXXIV, 599–605.

5 July 24, 1789 is another reasonable candidate for the honor of "the last day of the Confederation." See Burnett, *Continental Congress*, 726.

6 Freeman, *Washington*, VI, 178–84; (New York) *Daily Advertiser*, April 24, 1789; *New-York Daily Gazette*, April 25, 1789.

7 I *Stat.* 73–98.

8 *Annals of Congress*, I, 383–99, 473–608.

9 For anticipations of Amendment X (and also IX), see Tansill, 1018 (Massachusetts), 1023 (South Carolina), 1025 (New Hampshire), 1031 (Virginia), and 1035 (New York), as well as 1047 (North Carolina) and 1052 (Rhode Island).

10 *Federalist*, 510–15; Farrand, III, 143–44.

11 To Jefferson, Oct. 17, Dec. 8, 1788; to George Eve, Jan. 2, 1789; *Writings of Madison*, V, 271–75, 311, 319–20.

12 Rutland, *Bill of Rights*, chap. 9; Levy, *Freedom of Speech and Press*, 214–33; Dumbauld, *Bill of Rights*, pt. 1, and pp. 206–22.

13 Tansill, 1044–51; Trenholme, *Ratification in North Carolina*, chap. 5–6; McDonald, *We the People*, 310–21.

14 Tansill, 1052–59; Bates, *Rhode Island and the Union*, chap. 5–6; Bishop, in *Rhode Island History*, VIII (1949), 1, 33, 85, 115; McDonald, *We the People*, 321–46.

15 June 4, 1790; *Writings of Washington*, XXXI, 47–48.

16 Hamilton to Tobias Lear, Jan. 2, 1800; *Works of Hamilton*, X, 357.

17 *Annals of Congress*, I, 1951–52. The act is in I *Stat.* 191–96.

18 *Works of Hamilton*, III, 445–93.

19 To Madison, June 23, 1793; *Writings of Jefferson* (Ford ed.), VI, 315.

20 *Works of Hamilton*, IV, 435–44.

21 *Works of Hamilton*, VII, 339.

22 April 19, 1793; *Writings of Jefferson* (Ford ed.), VI, 217.

23 *Writings of Washington*, XXXI, 430–31.

24 (Philadelphia) *Gazette of the United States*, June 29, July 3, 6, 10, 13, 17, 20, 1793; *Works of Hamilton*, IV, 432–89.

25 (Philadelphia) *Gazette of the United States*, Aug. 24, 28, Sept. 7, 11, 14, 18, 1793; *Writings of Madison*, VI, 138–88.

26 *Works of Hamilton*, IV, 70–198.

27 I *Stat.* 566–69, 570–72, 596–97; Elliot, IV, 528–45.

28 *Writings of Washington*, XXXV, 226–28.

29 *Writings of Jefferson* (Lipscomb ed.), III, 319.

30 Brant, *Madison*, VI, 403; *Annals of Congress*, XIV, 684–88.

31 9 Wheaton 1 (1824); 4 Wheaton 316 (1819); 6 Cranch 87 (1810).

32 1 Cranch 137 (1803).

## 16.  THE LAST YEARS OF THE FRAMERS

1 Farrand, III, 551; Brant, *Madison*, VI, 515.

2 *Life of Mason*, II, 364.

3 Julian Boyd, "The Murder of George Wythe," *William and Mary Quarterly*, 3rd ser., XII (1955), 513.

4 To George Hay, June 19, 1807; *Writings of Jefferson* (Ford ed.), IX, 58.

5 2 Dallas 419 (1793); 3 Dallas 171 (1796).

6 Benton, *Thirty Years' View* (New York, 1866), I, 58.

7 "Autobiography of Col. William Few of Georgia," *Magazine of American History*, VII (1881), 341, 355.

8 June 1, 1831; *Writings of Madison*, IX, 460.

9 *A Letter to the Electors of President and Vice-President of the United States*, by "A Citizen of New York" (New York, 1808).

10 See generally H. C. Hockett, *The Constitutional History of the United States, 1826–1876* (New York, 1939), chap. 4; Farrand, I, xii-xxv.

11 Farrand, III, 371-74; *Annals of Congress*, IV, 761, 774-80.

12 *Journal, Acts, and Proceedings of the Convention . . . which Formed the Constitution of the United States* (Boston, 1819), 71 81; Farrand, III, 427, 431, 501–15, 531, 534–37, 595–604; Brant, *Madison*, III, 27–29, 478. For the other side of the story, see C. C. Nott, *The Mystery of the Pinckney Draught* (New York, 1908).

13 April 19, 1835; *Writings of Madison*, IX, 549.

14 From these strictures I would exempt the admirable study of Leonard Levy, *Freedom of Speech and Press in Early American History*, one of the lessons of which is that those men of power who know least about "the intent of the Framers" are most likely to appeal to it for support of their views. For a classic instance of the way in which each side in a controversial issue tries to read the minds of the Framers to its own advantage, see the majority and minority opinions in *Wesberry* v. *Sanders* 376 U.S. 1 (1964).

# Index